CONFLICT AND COHESION IN
SOCIALIST YUGOSLAVIA

CONFLICT AND COHESION IN SOCIALIST YUGOSLAVIA

Political Decision Making
Since 1966

STEVEN L. BURG

JN
9663
1983

PRINCETON UNIVERSITY PRESS
PRINCETON, NEW JERSEY

FOR JUDITH

ACKNOWLEDGMENTS

In preparing this volume I have incurred a large number of debts. By acknowledging them here I do not seek to earn credit against them. Nor do I seek to avoid responsibility for any of the shortcomings of this work, for they surely are the product of my own weaknesses alone. Rather, I hope to encourage opportunities for the repayment of as many of these debts as possible.

This volume never could have been written without the generous support of the International Research and Exchanges Board (IREX). An IREX Preparatory Fellowship in 1974-1975 allowed me to branch out from Soviet politics to the study of Yugoslavia, and an IREX Exchange Fellowship in 1975-1976 helped finance the dissertation research that produced a large part of the present volume. I am, however, indebted to IREX for far more than mere financial support. The service IREX has performed for me and, in fact, for the entire community of American scholars engaged in the study of Eastern Europe and the Soviet Union and all those who make use of the knowledge they gather is immeasurable.

My ten months in Yugoslavia during 1975-1976 were also financed by a Fulbright-Hays Dissertation Research Abroad Grant. The dissertation itself was written in the Department of Political Science of the University of Chicago. The members of that department provided training and guidance that I appreciate now even more than I did then. Aristide R. Zolberg and Philippe C. Schmitter were stimulating teachers and served me well as members of my dissertation committee. Lloyd I. Rudolph is another member of that department whose intellectual influence I continue to feel even as I pursue my own work today. I am grateful to each of them.

I have also been fortunate in moving to another institution that, like Chicago, encourages and supports scholarly research by conceding to the demands such research places on its faculty. I have profited immensely from being in the Department of Politics at Brandeis University. More than any other factor, the protection from bureaucratic and other responsibilities extended to me by the senior members of the department during my first year at Brandeis made it possible for me to adjust to the new demands of teaching without having to sacrifice my research or writing. My colleague, Roy C. Macridis, has provided the wise and honest criticism and advice to which I had become accustomed at Chicago, and has helped to make my stay at Brandeis a continuing learning experience. Robert Art, Seyom Brown, and Thomas Ilgen have also contributed, each in his own way, to that experience. Our chairman,

ACKNOWLEDGMENTS

Donald Hindley, helped me formulate a title for this volume that I hope conveys its contents immediately.

I have also benefited enormously from the comments and suggestions of Professor Paul Shoup of the University of Virginia. Professor Shoup read two earlier versions of this work. His detailed and insightful critiques led me to introduce several revisions and additions that significantly improved the quality and coherence of this volume. He unselfishly shared his intimate knowledge of Yugoslavia in a manner consistent with the highest standards of intellectual collegiality. I am deeply grateful to him for this.

My own understanding of Yugoslavia has also been enhanced by countless hours of open and honest discussion with many, many Yugoslavs, both in the United States and in Yugoslavia. I am indebted to party, state, and government officials at the federal and regional levels in Yugoslavia who discussed the issues and events covered in this volume and sometimes argued with me over my views; to scholars and students at several universities and institutes who shared their views of Yugoslav politics with me, including some of their own misgivings and doubts; and to my many personal friends in Yugoslavia who helped familiarize me with Yugoslav society and its cultures. I hope this volume will justify the trust in my honesty as a scholar all of them showed by sharing their thoughts with me, even if they may not agree with the views I express in it.

No one has influenced my thinking and my work more, or provided as much support over so long a period, as my former advisor and dissertation chairman, Jeremy R. Azrael. As Professor of Political Science and Chairman of the Committee on Slavic Area Studies at the University of Chicago, Jeremy Azrael provided every possible form of protection and support for my studies there. And even now, as I work at Brandeis and he serves as Senior Advisor on Soviet Affairs at the State Department, he continues as teacher, colleague, and friend. My debt to him is unlikely ever to be fully repaid. I can only hope that he knows how much his many efforts are appreciated, and that he will be pleased by what they have helped make possible.

Above all others, however, stands my debt to my wife Judith. Her contribution to this work has quite simply been incalculable. She has not only done much to make this volume possible, she has also foregone much. It is in order to acknowledge that she bore more than her share of the burdens associated with this work, and therefore deserves much of the credit for it, that I have dedicated it to her.

S.L.B.
Needham, Massachusetts
January 1982

CONTENTS

CONTENTS

LIST OF TABLES

LIST OF TABLES

CONFLICT AND COHESION IN
SOCIALIST YUGOSLAVIA

INTRODUCTION

The lands known today as Yugoslavia have long been divided by more than
the mountain ranges, river valleys, and forests that separate them into distinct
geographic regions. Through the centuries these divisions have been reinforced by others based on national, cultural, religious, linguisitic, economic,
and political differences arising out of both the distinct historical traditions
of the peoples native to these lands and the distinct cultural and political
legacies of those who have conquered them. In comparison to the centuries-
long history of these lands as the disputed territories of first one principality,
kingdom, or empire and then another, the contentious sixty-three-year history
of the Yugoslav state represents but an historical moment. In this study I
focus on a still shorter moment: the period since 1966. For during it, the
rulers of Yugoslavia have been attempting to ensure that country's continuing
survival as a unified state by developing a formula for the regulation of the
age-old conflicts that divide it.

Efforts undertaken by the communist leadership of Yugoslavia to control
conflict in the period 1966 to 1974 were in many respects similar to efforts
of leaders in other countries divided by similar conflicts. In the late 1960s,
the Yugoslav leadership carried out a series of changes by which they altered
the fundamental characteristics of the political decision-making process in
both the state and the party in an effort to resolve policy conflicts among
themselves and control rising levels of inter-nationality hostility and conflict
among the masses. In the early 1970s, they drafted a series of constitutional
amendments and then adopted an entirely new constitution in an effort to
establish institutional mechanisms for the regulation of conflict. During almost
precisely the same period, the political leadership of Belgium, for example,
attempted by a remarkably similar strategy to control conflict between the
French and Flemish linguistic communities into which that country is divided.

Attempts by the political leaders of Western countries such as Belgium to
control conflict between distinct and sometimes hostile cultural communities
has given rise to a substantial literature on elite strategies for the regulation
of such conflict. However, no detailed study of the efforts of the Yugoslav
leadership to control conflict comparable to existing case studies of conflict
regulation, decision making, and institutional change in Western countries
has been carried out; and almost no attempt has been made to incorporate
Yugoslav experience into the comparative study of elite strategies for the
regulation of the conflict between cultural communities. Paul Shoup's *Com-*

munism and the Yugoslav National Question remains the single most comprehensive study of the development of party policies and practices with respect to nationality conflict.[1] Although published before the emergence of the specialized literature on conflict regulation in divided societies, Shoup's work anticipates much of the analytical focus developed in it and provides a wealth of material for the analyst approaching the subject from this perspective. Unfortunately, no more recent work has followed this lead. Bogdan Denitch's attempt to demonstrate that the communist leadership has carried out a revolutionary transformation of Yugoslav society does include a brief treatment of the "institutionalization of multinationalism,"[2] but it does not provide the kind of detailed study of the development or actual operation of current institutions or decision-making practices that lends itself to comparison with other cases in the literature on divided societies. Despite the general conviction among scholars, diplomats, journalists, and others interested in Yugoslav affairs that the fate of that country hinges on the ability of its leadership to control the nationality and other conflicts that divide it, no study of Yugoslavia provides a basis for assessing the effectiveness of the mechanisms they have developed to do so.

The literature on conflict regulation in divided societies identifies a wide variety of factors as contributing to the successful regulation of political conflict between cultural communities. These may be grouped into four broad and overlapping categories: (1) political culture or tradition; (2) political structures; (3) political processes; and (4) factors and conditions external to these systems. It is the fundamental proposition of the literature that, even in a state characterized by deep, politically salient cleavages that divide the population into stable, conflicting 'blocs,' purposeful overarching cooperation among the leaders of the blocs will tend to regulate the effects of interbloc conflict and thereby increase political stability.[3] However, not all of the relevant factors are subject to manipulation even by a determined political elite. Political culture or tradition, for example, is not susceptible to short-term alteration in any state. Where it has been cited as contributing to the regulation of conflict, it is the product of long-standing, even centuries-long, accommodationist practices. This has led some scholars to question whether elite action can in fact succeed in the absence of such a cultural base.[4] Nor

[1] New York: Columbia University Press, 1968.

[2] *The Legitimation of a Revolution* (New Haven: Yale University Press, 1976), pp. 105-48.

[3] Arend Lijphart, "Consociational Democracy," in Kenneth McRae, ed., *Consociational Democracy* (Toronto: McClelland and Stewart, 1974), pp. 70-74; Hans Daalder, "The Consociational Democracy Theme," *World Politics* 26 (July 1974), pp. 604-21; and Arend Lijphart, *The Politics of Accommodation*, 2nd ed., rev. (Berkeley and Los Angeles: University of California Press, 1975), chap. 1.

[4] Hans Daalder, "On Building Consociational Nations: The Cases of the Netherlands and Switzerland," in McRae, *Consociational Democracy*, pp. 107-24; and Brian Barry, "Review

can certain political structures be altered even in the long term. The significance attached by the leadership of Belgium to the preservation of a unitary political order in the face of distinct regional divisions, for example, compelled them to devise a solution that has been characterized as "federalization without federalism."[5] It is also difficult for any political leadership to control external factors and conditions. Consequently, it is not surprising that the leaders of countries divided by conflicts between cultural communities have focused their efforts to regulate those conflicts on factors subject to conscious, short-term manipulation: the organizational and procedural characteristics of the political decision-making process.

The dramatic changes that took place in the state and party in Yugoslavia during the period 1966-1974 suggest that the Yugoslav leadership, like those in Belgium and elsewhere, understood that organizational and procedural characteristics of the decision-making process might be manipulated in order to regulate conflict. The "rules of the game" established in Yugoslavia in this period—sometimes explicitly articulated—demonstrate that that leadership has identified and encouraged forms of elite behavior that tended to regulate conflict, and has identified and discouraged behavior that exacerbated it. The successful regulation of conflicts in Yugoslavia since 1974 suggests, therefore, that a case study of the development of organizational and procedural provisions for decision making in Yugoslavia since 1966, informed by the analytical insights of the literature on divided societies, can provide valuable evidence concerning the ability of determined elites to regulate interbloc conflict and increase political stability through purposeful political action even in the absence of any long-standing historical tradition of accommodationist practices among the elite or political culture of cooperation among the masses. For no such tradition or culture has yet been established in Yugoslavia.

Such a study can also provide a clear basis for assessing, through comparison with experiences elsewhere, the costs and benefits for Yugoslavia of the regulatory process developed by its leadership and the prospects for its continued success. It can provide a basis for answering the question "will Yugoslavia long survive the death of Tito?" Even more important, however, such a study can provide a basis for moving beyond the question of survival itself to the more speculative realm of future development. For in identifying the conditions essential to the continued successful operation of the Yugoslav system we also identify the limits on changes consistent with the preservation

Article: Political Accommodation and Consociational Democracy," *British Journal of Political Science* 5 (October 1975), pp. 486-88, 500.

[5] Aristide R. Zolberg, "Splitting the Difference: Federalization without Federalism in Belgium," in Milton J. Esman, ed., *Ethnic Conflict in the Western World* (Ithaca: Cornell University Press, 1977), pp. 103-42.

of that system. And on this basis we can offer speculative answers to the question ''whither Yugoslavia?''

The present study, therefore, is an attempt to view Yugoslav politics since 1966 in terms of the communist leadership's search for organizational and procedural formulas—both formal and informal—for the maintenance of political cohesion in the face of interbloc conflict. It outlines the historical bases of conflict in the Yugoslav lands, the suppression of conflict with the onset of communist power, and its forceful reemergence in the late 1960s and early 1970s. It examines the dimensions of conflict and its divisive impact on Yugoslav society, and traces in detail the leadership's efforts to control it. Yugoslav politics in this period was dominated by the direct challenge to communist political power posed by the conflict between forceful, mutually hostile nationalisms, and it remains today haunted by the specter of their return, fueled by the formidable economic problems confronting the post-Tito leadership. Any study of the leadership's efforts to ensure cohesion, therefore, must at the same time be a study of its struggle to retain power.

The party underwent profound change as the result of this struggle. Some Western treatments of the impact of ethnic diversity on political stability would predict that such changes would move the party in the direction of greater authoritarianism.[6] Instead, however, they reinforced movement in the direction of wider decentralization of power in the party. Although the crisis of 1971 revealed to the Yugoslav leadership some of the limits that would have to be imposed on such movement if the party was to retain power, and in this way confirmed some of this Western analysis, it rapidly became clear that the changes undertaken up to then could not be completely reversed. For, in its effort to preserve party authority and defend its political power, the communist leadership had transformed the very character of the party itself.

This study of conflict regulation in Yugoslavia, therefore, is also a study of the impact of organizational and procedural changes on the party itself. Changes adopted in the late 1960s and early 1970s transferred substantial power and authority from central organs of the party to the regional organizations. On the one hand, these were an essential element in the development of a strategy for preserving the integrity of the Yugoslav state. But, at the same time, they reinforced the division of Yugoslav society into distinct 'blocs' by reproducing those divisions in the party itself, thereby perpetuating interbloc conflict—the very basis of the threat to Yugoslavia's survival—as a central feature of Yugoslav politics. These changes left the party with an additional and difficult task, now made even more difficult by the death of

---

[6] See, for example, Alvin Rabushka and Kenneth A. Shepsle, *Politics in Plural Societies: A Theory of Democratic Instability* (Columbus, Ohio: Merrill, 1972).

Tito: maintaining its own cohesiveness in the face of divergent and frequently conflicting bloc interests.

The party leadership must succeed in this task if the complex decision-making institutions and processes of the Yugoslav state are not once again to fall subject to paralyzing deadlock. While many of the factors likely to affect their success are beyond the control of the Yugoslav leadership, the analyses of political decision making presented in this study demonstrate that other, important factors remain very much under their control. This study concludes, therefore, by suggesting that the success or failure of the post-Tito system will in large part be the product of the communist political leadership's own choosing; and that their choices will be shaped by their experience of the events described and analyzed in the next six chapters.

I. SOCIAL CLEAVAGES AND
POLITICAL CONFLICT IN
THE YUGOSLAV LANDS TO 1966

Yugoslavia is divided by language, religion, culture, territory, and nationality. None of these divisions, however, completely coincides with or cross-cuts another. Nationality divides the society into mutually exclusive and mutually antagonistic groups. But each national group shares at least one primordial characteristic with one or more others. For some groups that characteristic is simply ancestral territory. For others it is a common religion or language. At the same time, however, no single primordial characteristic is shared by all the nationalities. Yugoslavia is similarly divided by wide disparities in levels of regional development. These disparities neither completely coincide with nor cross-cut the primordial divisions. They divide the country into a highly developed North and West and an underdeveloped South and East, and most national territories fall wholly into one or the other category. Some national territories, however, are themselves further divided into subregions with widely disparate levels of development. This mosaic-like distribution of social cleavages is hierarchically ordered with respect to their salience for the political life of the country. Nationality and the relative levels of development of the national territories have been the two dominant cleavages since before the creation of the Yugoslav state. In the period up to the establishment of communist power, nationality alone dominated South Slavic and, later, Yugoslav politics. With the suppression by the communist leadership of the national question during the 1940s and 1950s, the relative levels of development of the national territories became the dominant cleavage in Yugoslavia. However, the close correspondence between developmental and national divisions led to a revival of the latter in the early 1960s, and the fusion of the two during the late 1960s and early 1970s.

Primordial, Political, and Economic Divisions
in the Yugoslav Lands to 1918[1]

The Kingdom of Serbs, Croats, and Slovenes created in 1918 by the union of the independent kingdom of Serbia, the Croat and Slovene provinces of

---

[1] This section is based on secondary materials. The most useful of these were Robert Lee

the Austro-Hungarian Empire, and the independent kingdom of Montenegro was a patchwork of territories and peoples who were at the same time both united and divided by language, religion, culture, history, and political tradition. The northwestern region of the new state—Slovenia—encompassed most of the territory historically inhabited by the Slovenes, a Slavic people who speak a South Slavic language distinct from the languages of the other South Slavs and written in a Latin alphabet. Centuries of Frankish and Austrian political and cultural domination imparted a highly Germanic and central European character to Slovenian culture. As a result of this assimilation to European culture and the Roman Catholic heritage common to both Slovenia and the Imperial center, the Slovenes had lived under the Hapsburgs, in the words of one Western historian, "with apparent contentment."[2]

Slovenia had been one of the economically more backward territories in the Austro-Hungarian Empire. But in comparison to the rest of the new Yugoslav state Slovenia was, like Croatia to its south, an economically well-developed region. Croatia comprised the territories just to the south and east of Slovenia, including most of both the Slavonian plain and the Dalmatian littoral. Like the Slovenes, the Croats are a Slavic people who speak a South Slavic language written in a Latin alphabet reflecting their Roman Catholic cultural heritage. Also like the Slovenes, centuries of Frankish, Hungarian, and Austrian political and cultural domination imparted a Germanic and central European character to Croatian culture. Unlike Slovenia, however, the relationship between Croatia and those who ruled her—both Magyars and Austrians—had been characterized by continuing political conflict over the formal status of the Croatian state.

Within the Austro-Hungarian Empire, Croatia, like Slovenia, had been economically backward. In the new Yugoslav kingdom, however, it was one of the economically most advanced regions. Zagreb, its capital, became a major financial and industrial center of the new state. But just as the status of the Croatian lands had been an issue of contention between Croatia and its former rulers, so it became one between Croatian political leaders and the Serbian political elite that ruled the new state.

Serbia comprised the eastern and southern territories of the new state. The Serbs, although also a South Slavic people, are distinguished from both the Slovenes and Croats by having accepted Christianity from the East, in its

---

Wolff, *The Balkans in Our Time* (New York: Norton and Co., 1967); Leftan S. Stavrianos, *The Balkans Since 1453* (New York: Holt, Rinehart and Winston, 1950); Charles Jelavich and Barbara Jelavich, *The Balkans* (Englewood Cliffs: Prentice-Hall, 1965); William Miller, *The Ottoman Empire and Its Successors* (Cambridge: University Press, 1936); C. A. Macartney, *Hungary and Her Successors* (London: Oxford University Press, 1937); Robert J. Kerner, ed., *Yugoslavia* (Berkeley: University of California Press, 1949); and Jozo Tomasevich, *Peasants, Politics and Economic Change in Yugoslavia* (Stanford: Stanford University Press, 1955).

[2] Wolff, *The Balkans in Our Time*, p. 67.

Orthodox variant. The Montenegrins, an ethnically Serb people concentrated in the mountainous southwest corner of the new state, were similarly distinguished. The historical mutual antagonism of the Eastern and Western Churches was imparted to the peasants and reinforced the cultural and linguistic differences between the Serbs and Montenegrins on the one hand and the Croats and Slovenes on the other. The Eastern religious heritage of the Serbs and Montenegrins led to the adoption of a modified Cyrillic alphabet for the Serbian literary language they shared, just as the Western religious heritage of the Croats and Slovenes led to the adoption of Latin alphabets for both the Slovenian and the Croatian literary languages. Despite their religious and cultural differences, however, the Serbs and Croats were united by their common Slavic origins and the mutual comprehensibility of their languages.

To an outsider, the Croatian and Serbian *spoken* languages even today— after more than a century of separate literary development—appear to be dialects of a single language. The differences between them may be compared to those between American and British English. They are different, but mutually comprehensible to native speakers without any difficulty. In fact, local variations in style, vocabulary and pronunciation within each regional language often make it difficult for the non-native to distinguish in conversation between speakers of one and those of the other. The modern *literary* languages of the South Slavs were created artificially during the nineteenth century by intellectuals intent on promoting the unity and political independence of the South Slavic peoples. They succeeded in establishing exactly corresponding Latin and (modified) Cyrillic alphabets for the Croatian and Serbian dialects, respectively. But the establishment of written languages using different alphabets seemed over time to emphasize the *differences* rather than the commonalities between them, and served as a constant reminder of the broader cultural and historical gulf between East and West.

Religious and linguistic differences between the Croats and Serbs united in 1918 in the new Yugoslav state had been reinforced by differences between the cultural and political development of the former Austro-Hungarian and Ottoman lands. The territories that had been part of the Austro-Hungarian Empire—Slovenia, Croatia, and the Vojvodina (the northeastern corner of the country)—experienced a tremendous cultural awakening during the nineteenth century that resulted in the advancement of Slovene and Croat cultural activities and organizations. That awakening was shared by the Serbs of the Vojvodina.

Attempts to create a unified literary language for all the South Slavs were both a manifestation of and an impetus to this awakening. But at the same time each of the South Slavic groups in the Austro-Hungarian lands began to develop its own distinctive linguistic and cultural heritage. During the latter half of the century, Croatian culture in particular underwent a strong revival.

In response to the challenge of rising nationalism among the Magyars who ruled them, the Croats demanded and achieved the restoration of Croatian as the official language of Croatia. This was followed by the establishment, expansion, and improvement of Croatian educational and cultural institutions and the institutions of the Catholic Church in Croatia. This revival of Croatian culture was accompanied by the revival of Croatian nationalism in both its pan-South Slavic and exclusivist variants. The pan-South Slavic—or "Yugoslav"—variant of Croatian nationalism remained dominant until the end of the century.

The Serbs of the Vojvodina and Croatia experienced a similar pattern of cultural and intellectual revival during this period. The nationalism of these Serbs also was dominated by a pan-South Slavic orientation, focusing on cooperation with the Croats of the Empire in an effort to win South Slavic autonomy. Thus the Croats and Serbs—and, to a lesser degree, the Slovenes— of the Austro-Hungarian territories shared a growing cultural awareness and political consciousness. But their tentative cooperative efforts failed to achieve the goal of a unified South Slavic state. The Serbs of the Ottoman Empire experienced their own cultural revival in the nineteenth century, paralleling the one taking place in the Austro-Hungarian lands, and became the first of the South Slavs to regain independence.[3]

Ottoman rule was extended over the lands that later would become the Serbian state and still later the central, eastern, and southern regions of Yugoslavia through a series of military conquests during the fourteenth, fifteenth, and sixteenth centuries. It was exercised through the elimination of native central political institutions and the native feudal aristocracy and their replacement by Turkish representatives of the sultan. Native local government and society was left relatively undisturbed. The result was the development of a Serbian peasant society and culture strongly influenced by, but not assimilated to, Turkish culture. The gulf between the Muslim culture of the Ottomans and the Orthodox culture of the Serbs, Montenegrins, and Macedonians under their occupation perpetuated the usual tensions between rulers and ruled associated with military conquest and incorporation. Indeed, much of the folk culture of the Serbs focused on tales of military heroism and resistance to foreign rule. Thus, the relationship between the Serbs and Ottomans was vastly different from that between the Croats and their rulers and provided an historical impetus to violent resistance.

Resistance to Ottoman rule began early in the nineteenth century in the form of a local revolt against representatives of the sultan—themselves in revolt against the Empire. Victory over the renegades led the Serbs, who had

---

[3] We exclude here, of course, the tributary city-state of Dubrovnik and the tributary kingdom of Montenegro, which maintained quasi-independent existences throughout the period.

in effect been fighting on behalf of the sultan, to seek from him concessions to Serbian autonomy. These were refused. The sultan's refusal to grant such concessions transformed the Serbian movement into a national revolt. By 1830 Serbia had achieved the status of an autonomous principality, or tributary state of the Ottoman Empire. By 1867 it had achieved functional independence with the withdrawal of Turkish troops from its territories. At the Congress of Berlin in 1878 Serbian independence was formally ratified by the European powers.

Progress toward independence, however, was not accompanied by further development of pan-South Slavic sentiments corresponding to that taking place at the same time among the Serbs and other South Slavs in the Austro-Hungarian lands just to the north and west. Despite certain limited contacts between Croatian exponents of pan-South Slav or "Yugoslav" nationalism and the Serbian political leadership, and a brief period of coincidence between the goals of Croatian and Serbian nationalisms during the mid-nineteenth century, the growing political and military force of the Serbian state was placed in the service of a more restricted vision of Serbian nationalism. That Serbian nationalism was fueled by the cultural isolation of the Serbs during four centuries of Ottoman rule, by the immediate requirements of establishing the security of the Serbian state against the return of the Ottomans, by the encroachment of Austrian power, and, by the competing national claims of neighboring states and peoples to lands viewed by the Serbs as historically Serbian.

The 1878 Congress of Berlin also transferred the territories of Bosnia and Hercegovina from Turkish to Austrian control. This added still further to the complex set of factors dividing and uniting the Yugoslav lands. The Bosnian lands had come under Turkish control in the late fifteenth century. At the time of conquest, the territories were inhabited by Catholic Croats, Orthodox Serbs, and a local Slavic feudal nobility that adhered to the Manichean Bogomil Church. This local nobility converted to Islam and provided the basis for the development of an indigenous, Slavic, Moslem community in these and neighboring Balkan territories of the Empire. By the nineteenth century this Moslem community represented a substantial proportion of the population and had become the object of competition between exclusivist Croatian and Serbian nationalists, each of whom claimed it as part of their own nation. The transfer of the Bosnian lands from Turkish to Austrian rule frustrated hopes among Serbs in both Serbia and Bosnia itself for the incorporation of those lands into the Serbian state. These lands once had been part of a medieval Serbian Empire stretching from the Adriatic to the Aegean and still contained a very substantial population of Orthodox Serbs. At the same time, the transfer impelled the Moslem community there to organize itself socially, culturally, and politically. For now it had been subjected to culturally alien rule.

The period between 1878 and the outbreak of World War I was marked by increasing Serbian and Croatian nationalisms and growing Moslem political consciousness. The growth of Serbian nationalism was stimulated by increasing conflict between the Serbian state and Austrian Empire, between Serbs and Croats in the Austro-Hungarian lands, between Serbia and Bulgaria over Macedonia, and by territorial expansion achieved through military victories in the Balkan Wars of 1912-1913. The latter whetted Serbian appetites for further expansion. Increasingly, Serbian nationalism found expression in policies of the Serbian state and the actions of Serbs organized into secret nationalist territorist organizations in Serbia, the Austro-Hungarian lands, and Bosnia aimed at the unification of all Serbs under the protection of a single, enlarged Serbian state. In the Austro-Hungarian lands, Hungarian seizure of Croatian territory and exploitation of Serb-Croat antagonisms by the Hungarian and Austrian authorities provided renewed impetus to the development of Croatian nationalism. In 1905, Stjepan Radić founded the strongly nationalist Croatian Peasant Party. The outbreak of World War I, however, compelled proponents of Serbian, Croatian, and pan-South Slav nationalisms to overcome their differences and agree to the establishment of a unified South Slav state.

World War I and the Creation of a Unified South Slavic State[4]

The political leadership of Serbia viewed the outbreak of war with Austria-Hungary as an opportunity to add additional South Slavic lands to their recently expanded state. In contrast, the war led the South Slavs of the Hapsburg lands to organize in support of the creation of a new state comprising all the South Slavic territories, including independent Serbia. In April 1915 representatives of the South Slavs of the Hapsburg Empire established a Yugoslav Committee in exile to influence the Allied powers on behalf of the idea of such a state. This same goal was supported by the political opposition in Serbia itself. Clearly, the preferences of the government of the Serbian state—an Allied power and a theater of early fighting—carried greater weight with the Allied powers than those of either the opposition in that country or the Yugoslav Committee—an organization of private citizens from an enemy state. But even the preferences of the Serbian political leadership were outweighed in the judgment of the Allied powers by other considerations.

Allied policy toward the Balkans was the product of a veritable witch's

[4] In addition to the materials cited in note 1, above, this section is based on Robert W. Seton-Watson, *The South-Slav Question and the Hapsburg Monarchy* (London: Constable, 1911); Robert A. Kann, *The Multinational Empire* (New York: Columbia University Press, 1950); and Ivo J. Lederer, *Yugoslavia at the Paris Peace Conference* (New Haven: Yale University Press, 1963).

brew of secret treaties and agreements among the Great Powers. In order to gain the participation of Italy in the Allied war effort, the British, French, and Russians agreed in 1915 to a secret treaty awarding Italy territories along the Dalmatian coast then part of the Austro-Hungarian Empire. With this treaty the Allies in effect committed themselves to opposing the creation of a South Slavic state along the lines proposed by the Yugoslav Committee. In negotiations with Bulgaria and Rumania they also committed themselves to positions contradictory to Serbian interests and aspirations.

Allied disregard for the expressed interests of Serbia and the Yugoslav Committee led both of them to realize that they would have to cooperate with each other if any South Slavic state was to be created. The first Russian Revolution in March and the American entry into the war in April 1917 led the Serbian government in particular to realize the necessity of such cooperation. The Russian Revolution eliminated from Allied political councils the strongest and perhaps only supporter of Serbian territorial aspirations, and the entry of the Americans lent considerable weight to the idea of granting the right of self-determination to the peoples of the Austro-Hungarian Empire, a principle that corresponded more closely to the position of the Committee than to the concept of a "Greater Serbia." Consequently, despite unsuccessful tentative contacts, the political leaders of Serbia and representatives of the Committee met on Corfu in July 1917 and reached agreement in principle on the creation of a unified South Slavic state to take the form of a constitutional monarchy under the Serbian dynasty and to be called the Kingdom of Serbs, Croats, and Slovenes. The Corfu Declaration affirmed the equality of the South Slavic nations and of their languages, alphabets, and religions, but left the precise organization of the state to be determined in the future by the adoption of a constitution.

Although the Corfu Declaration itself had little impact on the course of events, it did provide the general framework for a later act of union establishing a South Slavic state. The establishment of that state was prompted by the precipitous collapse of the Austro-Hungarian Empire in 1918 and the threat of Italian occupation of its South Slavic territories. In October of that year, with the fall of the Empire imminent, a National Council of Slovenes, Croats, and Serbs was established in the Empire to facilitate the transfer of sovereignty from the Empire to a South Slavic state. Although not intended by its founders to serve as such, the National Council began almost immediately to function as the government of a de facto South Slavic state composed of the South Slavic provinces of the Austro-Hungarian Empire. The National Council quickly established contact with the Yugoslav Committee and empowered it to serve as the diplomatic representative of the incipient state. In November the Council, the Committee and the Serbian premier met in Geneva in an abortive attempt to establish a union of all the South Slavic lands in a single state. However, the failure of that attempt delayed union for only a short time.

The landing of Italian troops in Dalmatia and the movement of Italian troops into Slovenia in an attempt to enforce the secret provisions of the 1915 treaty threatened to subject the former Austro-Hungarian lands to military occupation and probable annexation. In response to this threat, representatives of the National Council met with the Serbian government in Belgrade and agreed to a hastily-drawn act of union creating a Kingdom of Serbs, Croats and Slovenes composed of the Serbian kingdom, the Montenegrin kingdom and the former Hapsburg lands. This act brought the Kingdom of Serbs, Croats and Slovenes into existence on December 1, 1918. But, like the Corfu Declaration before it, the act of union left most details concerning the organization of the new state to the future.

Inter-Nationality Hostility and Political Conflict in the Interwar Kingdom[5]

Establishing the boundaries of the new kingdom involved its leadership in long and difficult conflicts with the Western Allies, the Italians, the Austrians, the Hungarians, the Romanians, the Bulgarians, and the Albanians. The borders were not finally established until mid-1926. But these external conflicts did not prevent that leadership from becoming at the same time hopelessly divided within itself over the internal organization of the new state. The Serb political leadership of the prewar Serbian state now argued for the establishment of a centralized state by extending the bureaucratic organizations of prewar Serbia to the other areas of the new kingdom. Some of the proponents of this view were motivated by purely Serbian nationalist sentiments, while others saw a centralized state as the most effective means to forge national unity. In the latter view, the expanded bureaucratic structures were to be distinguished from their Serbian predecessors. But it was unlikely that they could be, or that their effective control by the Serbian political leadership could be avoided. Hence, they inevitably would be perceived by non-Serbs as evidence of the establishment of a "Greater Serbia." Consequently, the political leaders of the other regions and nationalities each proposed their own formula for a more decentralized state organization. Each of those proposals, however, conflicted in some respect with the others.

The Serbian government, after adding to its ranks ministers drawn from the leaders of the former Hapsburg lands, acted as the provisional government

---

[5] This section is based primarily on Wolff, *The Balkans in Our Time*; Stavrianos, *The Balkans Since 1453*; Fritz W. Hondius, *The Yugoslav Community of Nations* (The Hague: Mouton and Co., 1968); and Bruce E. Bigelow, "The Yugoslav Radical Union: A Failing Attempt at National Integration in Yugoslavia, 1935-1941" (Ph.D. Dissertation, University of Chicago, 1972).

of the new state. Organization of the new state was left up to a Constituent Assembly composed of representatives elected in November 1919. Each of the political parties represented in the Assembly was based on a constituency defined by a particular set of regional, ethnic, social, and economic factors. None drew its support across all—or even several—of the regions, nationalities, or broad social and economic groups in the country. Consequently, the Assembly comprised a mosaic of narrowly defined political interests organized into fifteen parties, each represented by between one and ninety-two delegates. The conflict arising out of the pursuit of narrowly defined self-interests by these groups plagued the Assembly from the outset.

The adoption of rules of procedure for the Constituent Assembly immediately engendered divisive conflict over the basis for decision making. Schemes based on simple majorities, various forms of qualified majorities, and even concurrent majorities all were proposed and debated. Much of the debate focused on a futile effort to define the rules implied by the purposely imprecise provisions of the Corfu Declaration. Finally, the Serbian-dominated provisional government pushed through a simple majority rule. Additional conflicts arose out of attempts to define the internal administrative units of the new state, the relationships among those units, and the relationship between them and the central government. Each of the plans proposed by the various parties reflected the particular national, cultural, linguistic, and religious bases of its own support and the particular politico-historical traditions of the region in which that support was concentrated. Even the name of the new country itself was subject to debate.

Stjepan Radić and the nationalist Croatian Peasant Party (now renamed the Croatian Republican Peasant Party) had received the third largest popular vote in the November 1919 elections and had the fourth largest number of seats in the Constituent Assembly. Consequently, it could have played a highly influential and, given the situation, perhaps decisive role in the deliberations of the Assembly. But Radić and his party refused to participate in the debates or to negotiate with representatives of other parties. Instead, he simply insisted on the creation of a loose confederation between otherwise autonomous Slovenian, Croatian, Serbian, and Montenegrin states.

Not surprisingly, in 1921 the Constituent Assembly produced a constitution—the so-called Vidovdan Constitution—that was supported only by the Serbian government parties. It represented a more centralistic version of the Serbian constitutional arrangements of 1903. Under its provisions, the kingdom became a unitary, centralized state divided into twenty-two "regions." These "regions" subdivided the larger, historical national regions into smaller administrative units linked directly to the central government. The period of the Vidovdan Constitution (1921-1928) was characterized by continuing conflict between the ethnically, religiously, and regionally based parties, reflected in a series of political alliances whose rapid formation, dissolution, and re-formation resembled a game of political musical chairs. The result was a political deadlock for which no compromise could be developed and during which the state continued to function as a centralized organization under the effective control of the Serbs. The mounting political tensions arising out of this deadlock culminated in June 1928, when Stjepan Radić was shot and mortally wounded on the floor of the parliament by a Montenegrin delegate of the governing party. Radić's successor, Vlatko Maček, demanded immediate and complete federalization of the state on the basis of the historical national-territorial divisions. Within six months, in January 1929, the king dissolved the parliament, suspended the constitution, and declared a royal dictatorship.

During the period of the royal dictatorship the name of the country officially was changed to Yugoslavia. A new constitution decreed by the king in 1931 changed the internal political-territorial division of the country. The twenty-two "regions" of the earlier period were consolidated into nine "provinces" determined by a combination of physical and historical factors. These were named for the prominent physical features that distinguished them (primarily river valleys) rather than for the nations to whose homelands they roughly corresponded. Regional and ethnic political parties were banned. These efforts to de-emphasize the national divisions plaguing the country were, however, futile. No national (ethnic) figure of any stature would participate in a government appointed by the king. An alliance composed of the Croats under Maček, who continued to agitate for Croatian autonomy, and the Slovenes, Bosnian Moslems (who were advancing the notion of a distinct "Muslim" nationality), and Serbs of Croatia and Vojvodina was formed to oppose the continuing domination of the country by the political leadership of the prewar Serbian state. Although this alliance represented most of the country and its population, it could not break that domination.

The assassination of the king during a visit to Marseilles in October 1934 brought both further unrest and an opportunity to resolve the problems surrounding the organization of the state. The dictatorship was continued by Prince Paul, regent for the eleven-year-old heir to the assassinated king. But the assassination had generated a mood of reconciliation in the country. In 1935 a new political party called the Yugoslav Radical Union was formed. An alliance of that faction of the Serbian political leadership now in control of the government and the former Muslim and Slovene clerical parties, the Yugoslav Radical Union represented a genuine attempt at national integration.[6] But the attempt foundered on the difficulty of reaching agreement with Maček over the organization of the state and the status of Croatia, the de-

---

[6] The finest account of this attempt is to be found in Bigelow, "The Yugoslav Radical Union."

termined resistance of the Orthodox Church to an attempt by the government to regulate relations between the state and the Roman Catholic Church through a concordat with the Vatican, and the growing pressures of the international political environment in Europe.

The continuation of the royal dictatorship and the failure of the government appointed by the regent to resolve the domestic turmoil led to the formation of an alliance between Maček and the Serbian opposition parties. This Serb-Croat alliance demanded an end to the dictatorship and called for the adoption of a new constitution. More important, the alliance and its program—rejected by the regent—generated enormous popular support in both Serbia and Croatia. Both this popular support for a settlement of the "Croatian question" and the potential danger inherent in allowing Croatian national discontent to go unsatisfied in the face of increasing pressure from fascists at home (especially in Croatia) and abroad led the regent to direct his government to come to agreement with Maček on a formula for the autonomy of Croatia within the framework of Yugoslavia.

The resulting Agreement of August 1939 created an autonomous Croatia composed of two of the nine provinces that had been created in 1931 and parts of a third. In terms of the historical-national territories, it was composed of Croatia (including both Dalmatia and Slavonia) and parts of the Vojvodina and Bosnia. Consequently, the new autonomous Croatian province included large Serb and Muslim minority populations. The Agreement assigned to the province autonomous control over its internal economic, social, and cultural affairs and local administration, but maintained central control over security and public order, major economic endeavors, interprovincial trade and transport, and other areas commensurate with the maintenance of a uniform economic system. The Croatian province remained an integral part of the Yugoslav state, but its actual status remained unclear. It has been suggested that the Agreement of 1939 created a relationship "reminiscent of the relationship between medieval Croatia and Hungary" that had been the cause of so much Croatian discontent for so long.[7]

Indeed, the Agreement of 1939 did not satisfy the more extreme Croatian nationalist elements and especially not the Croatian fascists, who saw it as a half-measure, far short of the independence they demanded. The presence of an extreme nationalist fascist alternative led Maček to take increasingly anti-Serb, extreme Croatian nationalist positions. The Agreement also generated increasing resentment among Serbs in Serbia, who viewed it as a grant of privileged status to the Croatians, and especially among Serbs in Croatia, who saw themselves cut off from Serbia and subjected to Croatian rule. Serbian opposition leaders were particularly embittered by Maček's aban-

[7] Hondius, *Yugoslav Community*, p. 111.

donment of their alliance in order to strike a separate agreement with the dictatorship, and they began to advance Serbian nationalism as a mobilizing theme. Consequently, both national frustrations and the level of inter-nationality hostility in Yugoslavia were on the rise as World War II began.

The interwar Yugoslav kingdom foundered on the inability of its political leaders to come to agreement on either the organization of the new state or the rules by which it was to be governed. Political parties and their leaders represented narrow ethnic, territorial, and ideological constituencies and were unwilling or unable to accept compromise arrangements for the sharing of power. The formulation of such arrangements is always difficult among multiple actors with many competing and conflicting interests and few common ones, and it is especially difficult among actors with divergent past political experiences and traditions. In Yugoslavia these difficulties were further exacerbated by the reluctance of Serbian political leaders to agree to any significant diminution of their power through decentralization, and the refusal of Croatian leaders to accept any arrangement short of full ethno-territorial autonomy, in large part for fear that it would jeopardize their own power in Croatia by opening them to political attack from extreme nationalist forces. Thus, by prolonging conflict, the political elites of the interwar period in fact preserved their respective power bases from encroachment.

As a result, the Agreement of 1939, like the agreement to establish the state little more than twenty years earlier, did not reflect genuine agreement among the elites who were party to it. It represented yet another experiment in structural change to solve the conflict over the organization of the state, motivated in large part by an increasingly threatening international environment. It did not represent agreement on substantive policy issues. Moreover, it treated the Croats and the other nations of Yugoslavia unequally, and this lack of reciprocity did not bode well for future relations between those who struck the Agreement and those who felt betrayed by it.

War, Resistance, and Revolution in Yugoslavia[8]

The German invasion of Yugoslavia in April 1941 culminated in the dismemberment of the Yugoslav state. Portions of the country were occupied by the Axis powers, other portions were annexed by them, and still others were placed under the control of native collaborationist forces. The Yugoslav army disintegrated in the face of the invasion, and the king and most of the government fled the country. As a result, the claim to national leadership, if not the legitimacy, of both the dynasty itself and the government parties was

---

[8] The literature on World War II in Yugoslavia is voluminous. The single best account for the study of national conflict, and the one relied on most heavily here, is Shoup, *Communism and the Yugoslav National Question.*

seriously weakened. At the same time, the invasion and occupation put an end to the domestic activity of most of the oppositional regional and national political parties that had been active in the interwar period. These conditions presented the communist party with an historic opportunity to unite the peoples and territories of Yugoslavia.

The Communist Party of Yugoslavia had been divided over policy with respect to the national question for most of the period before World War II.[9] The official position of the party had changed over time as the result of both changes in the views of its leaders (or of the leaders themselves) and changes in the policy of the Comintern, to which the Yugoslav party generally subordinated itself. At times the party was pro-Yugoslav in its orientation; at times it—or at least its Serb-dominated leadership—seemed to lean toward a "Greater Serbia" view; at still other times it attempted, at the urging of the Comintern, to exploit the national discontent of the non-Serbs as a means to foment revolution, even going so far as to support the secessionist demands of extremists among each of them. But the abandonment by the Comintern in 1935 of its militant revolutionary policy of the 1920s allowed the Yugoslav communist party to return once again to policies based on Yugoslav patriotism. The communist party of the late 1930s, however, was significantly different from that of earlier periods.

After a relatively short but distinguished career as a party organizer in Croatia and a Comintern functionary in Moscow, Josip Broz (Tito) was appointed by the Comintern in September 1936 to the position of organizational secretary of the Yugoslav party's Central Committee—a position second in importance only to that of general secretary.[10] The Yugoslav leadership then was based in Vienna in order to avoid arrest—the party had been illegal inside Yugoslavia and hunted by the police since 1920-1921—but at the urging of Tito the Comintern permitted the transfer of a part of that leadership to Yugoslavia itself. In October 1936 Tito left his Comintern post in Moscow and joined the Yugoslav Central Committee in Vienna where he was given responsibility for reconstructing the party organization inside Yugoslavia. In July 1937 the general secretary of the Yugoslav party departed for Moscow, never to be heard from again, and Tito became in all but name the general secretary; a position that would be officially conferred on him by the Comintern only in 1939, after he had won a factional struggle for it.

Tito spent much of 1937 and early 1938 inside the country, building a new, disciplined, and secret party organization. During this period an organizational change with long-lasting consequences for the party was carried out: Regional organizations were established for Croatia and for Slovenia, setting a precedent

[9] Ibid., chapter 1.
[10] Phyllis Auty, *Tito: A Biography* (New York: McGraw-Hill, 1970), pp. 77-144.

for the creation during the war of communist party organizations for each of the major national regions in the country. Tito built these organizations and the party as a whole by entrusting authority and responsibilities only to proven communist activists and, in another change that would have long-lasting consequences for the party, by elevating a new generation of dedicated younger communists not yet known to the police to positions of responsibility in leadership organs. These younger communists were fiercely dedicated not only to the party but to Tito personally. Even more important than their dedication and loyalty, however, was the fact that they were drawn from among all the major regions and nationalities. Only the Macedonians were not represented among them. Together, they would provide the leadership that would prove essential in the years ahead.

The German invasion in April 1941 ushered in an extremely violent period in Yugoslav history. Much of the killing resulted from military conflicts between resistance and occupation forces. But a large proportion of it resulted from the fratricidal warfare that erupted among the nations and nationalities of Yugoslavia (primarily between Serbs and Croats) and from the ethnically motivated slaughter of Yugoslav nationalities (primarily of Serbs and Slovenes) by the occupying powers. Two native collaborationist regimes became involved in the killing, as well. The Germans installed a "Government of National Salvation" under the former minister of war of the royal government, General Milan Nedić, in the territory that corresponded approximately to nineteenth-century Serbia. This government was empowered to handle only local affairs, and the military forces under its control were used by the Germans primarily to combat resistance. This Serbian Quisling regime was not permitted the status of an "independent" state. The Germans placed the territories of Croatia (including the portions of Dalmatia not claimed by Italy and the portions of Slavonia and Vojvodina not claimed by Hungary) and Bosnia and Hercegovina under the control of a fascist puppet state called "The Independent State of Croatia." This state was ruled by a group of extreme nationalist Croatian fascists—the *Ustaša*—whose leader, Ante Pavelić, had enjoyed the prewar sponsorship and support of the Italians. Although "independent Croatia" was granted the status of an independent state and entered into treaty alliances with the Axis powers, it remained a Quisling state under the control of the Germans.

Under the guise of nationalism, the Croatian fascists pursued a set of brutal policies of discrimination and persecution against non-Croats throughout the territories under their control. With the support of some members of the Croatian Catholic clergy and hierarchy, they pursued a policy of forced conversion of Orthodox Serbs to Catholicism. The military forces under their control conducted genocidal war against Serbs and Moslems, participated directly in Nazi efforts to exterminate Yugoslav Jews, and engaged in military

21

actions against resistance forces. The impact of these events on the image of Croatian nationalism and Croatian nationalists, and especially on relations between Serbs and Croats who lived through the war, remains an important factor in Yugoslav politics and society even today.

The German invasion and subsequent internal warfare increased the popular appeal of the communist party and its program. Following the German invasion of the Soviet Union in June, the party quickly organized an armed resistance movement. The details of that Partisan movement have been reported elsewhere.[11] It is important to note here only that, throughout the war, the communists pursued with considerable success—but not without difficulties and setbacks—a policy of encouraging mutual tolerance and cooperation among the nationalities within the ranks of its military Partisan units and in the territories that came under their control, under the slogan "brotherhood and unity." As Paul Shoup has suggested in his study of the nationality policy of the Partisans, "Party propaganda never really attempted to persuade the Partisan that he was a Yugoslav rather than a Serb, Croat, or Macedonian, but sought rather to get him to tolerate persons of other national origins."[12] In this way the communist-led Partisan resistance movement provided a haven for those looking to escape the physical terror of the occupation and collaborationist forces.

At the same time, the Partisan movement offered the only organized opportunity for Yugoslav peasants—even those whose lives were not directly threatened by the occupation—to escape foreign rule. The Partisans were the only major resistance movement engaged in active opposition to the occupation and collaborationist forces. The only other major guerrilla force consisted of the remnants of the Royal Yugoslav Army under the command of a Serbian army colonel, Draža Mihailović. These forces were composed almost entirely of Serbs, took the traditional Serbian name for guerrilla bands— Chetniks (Četnici)—and limited their activity to Serbian territory. Out of fear of provoking German reprisals against the civilian populace—a fear motivated by the demonstrated brutality of such reprisals (in one such incident in October 1941 the Germans had massacred more than 7,000 Serbs in the town of Kragujevac)—the Chetniks engaged in no direct resistance to the occupation forces. Mihailović hoped instead to reserve his forces for a link-up with the Allies when they reached Yugoslav soil and thereby reclaim state power in the name of the royal government in exile. Out of loyalty to the royal government and concern for the growing strength of the communists, Mihailović collaborated with the Germans in actions against the Partisans. This left the Partisans the only major fighting force untainted by collaboration.

[11] Shoup, *Communism and the Yugoslav National Question*, chapter 2.
[12] Ibid., p. 98.

The flight of the royal government and the absence of activity inside the country by representatives of the prewar ethnic and regional parties left the political organization of the resistance movement, as well, to the communists. Throughout the war, the communists were careful not to emphasize the revolutionary goals of their movement, although these were not hidden. While political indoctrination was carried out among the Partisan soldiers, the leadership focused their efforts on assuring "brotherhood and unity" and commitment to a unified Yugoslavia in the ranks. But, at the same time, as the Partisans liberated territory from occupation they established People's Liberation Committees composed of local citizens to replace prewar governmental bodies and take over the tasks of local administration. These committees would later constitute the backbone of the postwar communist government.

No central governmental or administrative body separate from the Partisan command was established until the end of 1942. In November of that year the first meeting of the Anti-Fascist Council of People's Liberation (*Antifašističko Veće Narodnog Oslobodjenja Jugoslavije*, or AVNOJ) was convened in the Bosnian town of Bihać. The AVNOJ was composed of delegates from all the Partisan organizations in the country. It elected an Executive Committee headed by Tito and charged it with direction of the People's Liberation Movement—the name now given to the resistance movement—and the administration of liberated territories. The Executive Committee thus was to function as the de facto government of the country. This meeting was followed by the establishment of regional councils for Slovenia, Croatia, and Bosnia and Hercegovina.

This duplication in the regions of the structure of the central AVNOJ reflected the territorially decentralized character of the Partisan movement itself. Although centrally directed by the Supreme Command under Tito, the Partisan movement was divided into regional organizations under the immediate command and control of regional leaders. These regional commanders kept in constant contact, and met periodically, with Tito and the Supreme Command to discuss, develop, and coordinate policy. But they enjoyed considerable autonomy of action in order to adapt the movement to the particular conditions in their regions. The leaders of these regional organizations—together with the members of the Supreme Command—would provide the top political leadership of the country following the war. It is not surprising, therefore, that the incipient state structure of the People's Liberation Movement embodied in the AVNOJ was organized on a similarly territorially and administratively decentralized, but politically centralized, basis. This organizational arrangement proved to be a precursor of the federal formula for the organization of the state adopted the following year at the second meeting of the AVNOJ, held in Jajce in November 1943.

At its second meeting, the AVNOJ—that is, the communist Partisan leadership—declared itself the legal government of Yugoslavia for the duration of the war, forbade the return of the king until the people of Yugoslavia had decided whether to continue the dynasty, adopted a federal principle for the postwar organization of the state, and guaranteed the legal equality and national rights of the nations and nationalities. By the end of war, the Communist Party of Yugoslavia under the leadership of Tito had achieved what no other political or military force had been able to achieve in the past: It had forged a political movement with a multinational leadership and significant popular support among all the nations and nationalities and in all the regions of the Yugoslav lands that was identified with, and had reconciled, the heretofore conflicting goals of satisfying the national grievances of the South Slavic peoples and, at the same time, maintaining the territorial integrity of the Yugoslav state.

National, Regional-Economic, and Political Conflict in Socialist Yugoslavia, 1945-1965[13]

Adoption of a federal formula based on the Soviet model for the organization of the state was both the party leadership's response to the manifest national conflicts of the interwar period and a reflection of the pattern of organization in the party and Partisan movement itself. The postwar federation consisted of six socialist republics: Slovenia, Croatia, Serbia, Bosnia and Hercegovina, Montenegro, and Macedonia. The Serbian republic was further divided into Serbia proper and two autonomous provinces—Vojvodina and Kosovo-Metohija (henceforth to be called simply Kosovo). The internal boundaries of the postwar federation corresponded more closely to the historical boundaries between political regions of the pre-1918 period than to ethnographic boundaries between the nations and nationalities. But locating boundaries on the basis of historical rather than ethnic considerations did not entirely eliminate conflict over them. Indeed, even the number of units to be created was the object of some controversy.

There were large numbers of Serbs within the boundaries of both Croatia and Macedonia. The republic of Bosnia and Hercegovina was itself a multinational state composed of Serbs, Croats, and Muslims. The province of Vojvodina contained a majority Serb population with a large Hungarian mi-

---

[13] This section is based on the accounts contained in Shoup, *Communism and the Yugoslav National Question*; Hondius, *Yugoslav Community*; George W. Hoffman and Fred W. Neal, *Yugoslavia and the New Communism* (New York: Twentieth Century Fund, 1962); Paul Lendvai, *Eagles in Cobwebs* (Garden City: Anchor Books, 1969); and Dennison Rusinow, *The Yugoslav Experiment* (Berkeley and Los Angeles: University of California Press, 1977). The text follows closely that presented in Burg, "Ethnic Conflict and the Federalization of Socialist Yugoslavia: The Serbo-Croat Conflict," *Publius* 7, 4 (1977): 119-43.

nority, in addition to less numerous minorities. The province of Kosovo contained a majority Albanian population with a large Serb minority. Only Slovenia and Montenegro approached ethnic homogeneity. Nonetheless, the republics substantially corresponded to, and quickly came to be considered, the historical national-territorial "homelands" of their titular nationalities. The autonomous provinces of Vojvodina and Kosovo came to be considered the national territories of the Hungarians and Albanians, respectively. This claim was disputed, however, by more nationalistic Serbs who were inclined to consider them simply part of Serbia.

Territorial and structural federalization of the state did not mean, however, federalization of political power within that state. Despite the decentralized character of the Partisan war, the party elite remained a tightly knit and strongly Stalinist group whose shared ideology and vision of the future outweighed regional loyalties or responsibilities. Political power remained highly centralized and concentrated in the highest organs of the party. As Paul Shoup has pointed out, the "primary purpose" of the federal system in the immediate postwar period "was to serve as a lightning rod for national emotions, without limiting the power of the Party."[14]

Although political power remained centralized, the decision to adopt a federal structure for the state and to establish individual party organizations for each of the regions did have other important consequences. Shoup suggests that federalization of the state "helped satisfy important psychological needs of the Yugoslav peoples for recognition of their national individuality, and . . . it gave each nationality the assurance, for the first time, of enjoying a truly equal status with the other national groups."[15] Even more important than this for the long-term development of the political system, however, was the fact that each of the regions was endowed from the outset with its own political institutions in both the state and party sectors, and developed native political cadres to staff them.

The 1948 break with Stalin compelled the Yugoslav political leadership to reexamine the ideological bases of the political system and to construct a genuinely Yugoslav ideology.[16] As an indigenous Yugoslav formula for the construction of a socialist state began to develop, the role of the republics began to increase significantly, and political influence, if not coercive power, began to be federalized. The Sixth Party Congress in 1952 adopted a new ideological formulation that defined the role of the party in a decidedly less authoritarian manner, suggesting that it would lead society through the power of persuasion and example, rather than coercion. This change was reflected

[14] Shoup, *Communism and the Yugoslav National Question*, p. 113.

[15] Ibid., p. 119.

[16] The best study of this change is A. Ross Johnson. *The Transformation of Communist Ideology: The Yugoslav Case, 1945-1953* (Cambridge: M.I.T. Press, 1972).

in the re-naming of the party as the League of Communists of Yugoslavia (LCY). In 1953, the Stalinist constitution that had been adopted in 1946 was revised to increase the role of the republican governments in federal decision making. Each of them was now represented on the newly created executive organ of the federal government, the Federal Executive Council. The Council rapidly became the focal point of increasingly important federal legislative politics. With the increased role of the republics in political life came an increase in expressions of national consciousness within the republics.

The still-centralized party responded to rising national consciousness in the regions by encouraging contacts, exchanges, and cooperation between national groups on the assumption that this would lead to the development of a shared sentiment of "Yugoslavness" or *Jugoslovenstvo*. Their efforts departed sharply from wartime policies, which had been based on a strategy of isolating hostile communities and groups from one another, or at least of limiting contact, and encouraging no more than mutual toleration. One result of the new policy was an agreement concluded in Novi Sad in 1954 between representatives of Serbian and Croatian cultural organizations, and intellectuals and cultural figures from both communities. The Novi Sad agreement represented a "truce" imposed on the two cultural communities by the communist party-political leadership of the country. It asserted that Serbs, Croats, and Montenegrins shared a single language with two alphabets and a single culture, albeit with local differences. The signatories committed themselves to undertake joint work on the development of a single dictionary of their common language as well as other forms of cultural cooperation. The agreement clearly implied that these groups constituted a single "people," but this remained unstated. The policy of encouraging contact and cooperation between the republics and national communities was incorporated in the Program adopted at the Seventh Party Congress in 1958. While the leadership disclaimed any intention to create a "Yugoslav nation" through the cultural merger of the distinct nations and nationalities, the 1958 party program did call for the development of a Yugoslav socialist consciousness.

During the next few years, however, the policy of encouraging interregional contact and cooperation was abandoned in the face of growing tensions within the leadership itself arising out of increasing economic and political conflicts. At the Eighth Party Congress in 1964, the leadership renounced the concept of *Jugoslovenstvo*.

Despite the abandonment of *Jugoslovenstvo*, the party itself remained a highly centralized organization during the 1950s and early 1960s. Power resided in a central Executive Committee that varied in size from thirteen to nineteen members during this period. The Committee was not composed according to any explicit formula or principle of representation. Rather, its membership consisted of the most powerful or personally authoritative individuals in the party regardless of their official positions. It included both leaders of regional party organizations and individuals who made their careers primarily in the central institutions of the party or the state, and it was dominated by members of the prewar and wartime leadership. Individuals were added to its membership through a process of cooptation.

Certain members of the Committee served simultaneously as secretaries of the party. These secretaries controlled organizational and personnel policies throughout the party, including its regional organizations. This gave them personally, and the Committee in whose name they served, enormous power. That power, and the power of the party as a whole, was reinforced by the simultaneous control over internal security affairs and the coercive powers of the secret police exercised by one of those secretaries, Aleksandar Ranković.

With the exception of the expulsion of Milovan Djilas in 1954 and the deaths and replacement of several of its members, the membership of the Executive Committee remained stable throughout the 1950s and early 1960s, and the Committee maintained a high degree of unity despite the policy shifts of the period. By the late 1950s, however, the leadership began to divide over questions of economic policy and their implications for the development of the political system. During the late 1950s and early 1960s a series of reforms partially decentralized the organization and operation of the economy and partially democratized the political system. These changes increased dramatically both the ability of regional leaderships in the party and state to represent the economic interests of their respective regions in decision making at the center and the necessity that they do so. These changes were adopted with the support of only a majority of the Committee's members, including Tito, rather than unanimously. Economic and political decentralization was opposed by those members who adhered to a more centralized vision of the system, and by their supporters and clients in the party and state apparatuses. This minority, led by Ranković, used their control over party personnel policies and the security police apparatus to obstruct implementation of the reforms.

The ensuing conflict ostensibly concerned the extent to which the state, or federal government, would participate directly in the economy. The institutional locus of the conflict shifted at times from the higher party councils to the federal government and back again, and the focus of the conflict shifted between the formulation of ideology and the choice of substantive policies. But regional conflict was never entirely absent from the deliberations of either the party or the federal government. For the underlying condition that drove the conflict remained constant: the coincidence of political cleavages based on the internal divisions of the federal state and the party, and social cleavages based on nationality and levels of economic development.

Burks has suggested that, in terms of levels of development, there are two

Yugoslavias: a developed North composed of Slovenia, Vojvodina, Croatia north of the Sava river, and Belgrade and its environs, and an underdeveloped South composed of Serbia proper, Bosnia and Hercegovina, Montenegro, Kosovo, Macedonia, and the regions of Croatia south of the Sava river.[17] The developed North corresponds roughly to the areas that had been part of the Austro-Hungarian Empire, and the underdeveloped South corresponds roughly to the areas that had been part of the Ottoman Empire, including the provinces of Bosnia and Hercegovina. The growing economic and political autonomy of the republics and provinces and the central leadership's willingness to concede the vitality of the ethno-national differences that divided them did not diminish its commitment to reduce, if not eliminate, the vast differences in levels of economic development among them. The seeming incompatibility of these commitments, however, led inevitably to interregional conflict in the central organs of the state and the party over the allocation of scarce resources for investment.

Debate over the economic reforms of the early 1960s and over the major reform of 1965 revealed clearly the political division between the regional leaderships.[18] The decision to establish a modified market economy linked the conflict between regional economic interests to an even more divisive ideological conflict between "liberals" and "conservatives." The latter viewed centralized allocation as the most appropriate means of achieving the redistribution and equalization of wealth to which the party was committed. "Liberals," on the other hand, argued that while the operation of a market system would at first encourage greater investment in the already developed regions, it would lead later to investment in, and the development of, the underdeveloped regions. This conflict, in turn, was linked to a broader conflict between two visions of the role of the party in society. Those in favor of centralized allocation tended also to favor the direct party control characteristic of the pre-1952 period, while those in favor of reliance on the market tended to favor the less coercive vision of the party embodied in the decisions of the Sixth Congress. Not surprisingly, the leaders of the lesser-developed regions mostly were numbered among the "conservatives," while the "liberals" came primarily from the more developed regions. The fact that the republics and provinces were generally viewed as national homelands and that the ethno-nationalisms of their populations historically had been mutually antagonistic only made the apparent contradiction between the commitments to redistribution and economic reform even more difficult to resolve.

The central leadership was divided between "liberal" and "conservative"

[17] R. V. Burks, *The National Problem and the Future of Yugoslavia*, Rand Report No. P-4761 (Santa Monica: The Rand Corporation, 1971), p. iv.

[18] Rusinow, *The Yugoslav Experiment*, chapters 4 and 5; and Deborah D. Milenkovitch, *Plan and Market in Yugoslav Economic Thought* (New Haven: Yale University Press, 1971).

elements for the entire period from the Seventh Congress in 1958 to the Eighth Congress in 1964. During this time Tito played a central role in determining party policy. Although he supported measures aimed at decentralization of the economy and reduction of the role of the state in the emergent self-managing economy, he continued to support the more authoritative and centralistic vision of the party held by opponents of those reforms. With his support, the "liberal" majority in the leadership was powerful enough to win the adoption of specific reform measures and even a new, liberal constitution that emphasized the direct participation of representatives of the self-managing economy in the decision-making processes of the state. But they could not effectively implement those measures or transfer real power from the party to the institutions of the state as long as their opponents retained control over party personnel policies and the instruments of coercion and continued to enjoy Tito's support for their exercise of those powers. Following the 1964 Party Congress, the "liberal" majority won progressively greater power until, in 1966, it won Tito's support for the ouster of Ranković from the leadership and the removal of his supporters in the party and state apparatuses.

Ranković had been strongly opposed to the liberal direction of the political and economic reforms adopted in the early 1960s, and led the conservative opposition to them. As organizational secretary of the party in charge of cadres, de facto head of the state security apparatus, vice-president of the Republic, and heir-apparent to Tito, Ranković used his formal and informal powers of appointment, control, and coercion to place his supporters into key positions in party and state organs. Together, they acted to obstruct implementation of the reforms. By 1966, the conflict between Ranković and his supporters and the majority of the political leadership who supported the reforms had assumed the dimensions of what Tito himself called "a struggle for power" within the party.[19]

In the mid-60s it was not unreasonable for conservative opponents of the reforms to expect that a majority in the party leadership might soon support a return to more "orthodox," and therefore more acceptable, policies. That had happened several times during the previous decade when reforms had proved difficult to implement or had had undesirable unintended consequences. In 1966, however, the liberal majority in the party leadership, with the support of President Tito, responded not by retreating, but by identifying and moving against the source of resistance to its policies. A conjunction of favorable circumstances brought the resources of the military counterintelligence organization into the service of the majority coalition, and through it they were able to collect evidence suggesting that Ranković had misused the

[19] Savez komunista Jugoslavije (SKJ), Centralni komitet (CK), *Četvrti Plenum Centralnog komiteta Saveza komunista Jugoslavije* (Beograd: Komunist, 1966), p. 9.

secret police apparatus under his control not only to enhance his personal power and oppose party policies but also to conduct operations against the privacy and personal security of other members of the leadership, including even Tito. With this information in hand, the liberal majority forced Ranković and his closest supporters to resign their positions in the state and party leaderships at the Fourth Plenum of the Central Committee in July 1966. Their ouster marked the beginning of a series of changes in the organization and operation of the party and the government that altered the character of political decision making in Yugoslavia.

II. INTERREGIONAL CONFLICT
AND THE FEDERALIZATION OF
YUGOSLAV POLITICS, 1966-1969

In the period following the ouster of Ranković, the liberal majority in the party leadership carried out changes that dramatically restructured Yugoslav politics. In reaction to the abuses of the conservative opposition, the post-Ranković leadership restricted the activities of the secret police apparatus and subordinated it to closer, regional supervision, thereby reducing the coercive powers of the central party organs and permitting the rise of autonomous, nonparty social groups, organizations, and institutions. The latter process was stimulated even further by implementation during this period of the economic reforms that had been adopted earlier, but opposed by Ranković. Other changes in the organization and operation of the party itself, state institutions, and the federal government devolved increasing power and authority onto the regional political leaderships and impelled them to become more responsive to the particularistic interests of their respective republics and provinces. As a result, the very different consequences of economic reform for each of the regions intensified conflicts between their leaderships. At the same time, interregional conflicts became intertwined with, and reinforced by the reemergence at the mass level of mutually antagonistic nationalisms. The Yugoslav political system thus was transformed during this period from one that was highly centralized into one characterized by multiple regional centers of political and economic power divided by conflicting interests and rising popular hostilities.

Post-Ranković Changes in the Party

Because of the "tremendous trust" the other members of the central party leadership had in him—a legacy of their shared experiences during the war, revolution, and postwar break with Stalin—Aleksandar Ranković's activities as the party's secretary for cadres and de facto head of the secret police apparatus had not been subjected to supervision or review.[1] As a result, he was able to forge the security police into "a strongly centralized organization"

[1] This and the following material on Ranković and the secret police are taken from SKJ, CK, *Četvrti Plenum*, pp. 8, 9, 15, 21-23.

dominated by individuals appointed by and loyal to him personally, rather than to the party, its Central Committee, or the Executive Committee. He preserved that organization against decentralization and used it as a weapon to oppose implementation of the reforms supported by the liberal coalition then in the majority in the party leadership.

The conservative opposition led by Ranković was based largely in Serbia and consisted primarily of Serbs. His closest supporters included a secretary of the Serbian party and the secretaries in charge of the Yugoslav secret police and the secret police of the Serbian republic. They used their influence over the cadres they had appointed and the coercive powers of the secret police to maintain a rigidly centralized informal command structure within the Serbian party, in opposition to formal party authorities. They effectively stripped the Serbian Central Committee of its supervisory and control functions by denying information to its members and by preventing them from meeting in full session. When the Executive Committee of the Serbian Central Committee attempted to take action to implement the reforms, Ranković himself effectively sidetracked it.[2] Ranković used his control over the secret police apparatus to operate against the central party leadership in the same way. "State security became a kind of political-information or political-intelligence service within the country," used by Ranković to supply the other members of the party leadership with information and analyses. As a result, the central party leadership "neglected in large measure its own work on political assessment and surveying" and became vulnerable to purposive "disinformation" and "disorientation" efforts aimed at undermining its commitment to, and neutralizing its efforts to implement the reform. Indeed, Tito lamented at the Fourth Plenum that, because of the conservative opposition,

> we were not able to carry out the decisions that we adopted at [party] plenums and congresses, especially at the Eighth Congress [1964]. After that [time] there occurred a certain stagnation, nothing happened. Decisions were wonderful, the people embraced them, [and] were happy, our working people were glad. They said: 'Eh, finally we will move ahead.' But nevertheless, it did not come to pass.

The July 1966 removal of Ranković and his collaborators from their official positions thus constituted a dramatic victory for the majority in the party leadership committed to the continuation of economic and political reform in Yugoslavia. At the same time that they removed Ranković, the reformers undertook an internal reorganization of the party. They appointed a forty-one member "Commission for the reorganization and further development of the

[2] Savez komunista Srbije (SKS), CK, *Aktivnost Saveza komunista Srbije posle četvrte sednice CK SK Jugoslavije* (Beograd: Sedma Sila, 1966) pp. 122-23, 137-38, 246, 275ff.

LCY'' from among the ranks of the Central Committee and charged it with developing plans for further changes in the party. They also charged it with developing suggestions "as soon as possible, [and] without waiting for the final results of its own work," for the reorganization of the Central Committee of the LCY and the central committees of the republican party organizations.[3]

The Commission presented its proposals for reorganization of the regional central committees at the next (fifth) session of the Yugoslav Central Committee in October 1966.[4] As a symbolic change, the position of general secretary was abolished and replaced by the position of president of the League of Communists of Yugoslavia. Tito was, of course, elected president. The nineteen-member Executive Committee was replaced by two new bodies: a Presidium of thirty-five members including the president of the party and a new Executive Committee of eleven members including one secretary. The new Executive Committee was intended to function in a primarily administrative/executive capacity, while the Presidium was intended to be more of an authoritative policy-making organ. By creating two bodies with a relatively large membership (forty-six persons constituted more than one-fourth of the 155-member Central Committee) and by organizationally separating the policy-making and administrative functions, the Commission hoped "to put an end to, or at least to reduce to a minimum the danger of monopoly and concentration of competencies" which had existed in the old Executive Committee in the person of Aleksandar Ranković.

The Commission for reorganization also created five new permanent commissions to be attached to the Central Committee: for international relations and the international workers' movement; for socio-political relations; for socio-economic relations; for social and ideo-political questions of education, science, and culture; and for inter-nationality and interrepublican relations. These commissions were intended to provide institutional frameworks for the "active participation" of greater numbers of Central Committee members in "the analyses, [and] development and preparation of proposals and decisions of the Central Committee"—the formal functions of the old party secretaries. In order to provide formal channels of communication between the Central Committee and party members, membership on these commissions was opened to individuals outside the Central Committee.

Another important consideration in the Commission's work was the need "to adapt the organizational structure and method of work of the League of Communists to the new relations and to the development of the federative organization" of the country. During the course of the debate over economic

---

[3] SKJ, CK, *Četvrti Plenum*, pp. 96, 100.

[4] The following description of the Commission's proposals is taken from SKJ, CK, *Peta Sednica Centralnog komiteta Saveza komunista Jugoslavije i izlaganja na sednicama CK SK u republikama* (Beograd: Komunist, 1966), pp. 24, 26.

reform, the leaders of the republican party organizations had become out-spoken in representing the particularistic and often conflicting interests of their respective regions. The Commission members therefore anticipated that because of "the ever greater decentralization of social and state functions, the Leagues of Communists of the republics will come to have greater in-dependence in the formulation of ideological and political positions and es-pecially in operational functions within the League of Communists of Yu-goslavia." Consequently, the Commission proposed to apportion membership in the central party organs according to a centrally devised formula that would secure "appropriate national and republican representation."[5] Specific indi-viduals were to be selected from among lists submitted by the republican party leaderships.[6]

Membership in the Presidium and Executive Committee was distributed according to the following formula:

Republic	No. of Members
Serbia	11
Croatia	9
Slovenia	7
Bosnia	7
Macedonia	6
Montenegro	6

This formula maintained substantially the same proportional distribution of positions to each republic as existed before. One position specifically allocated to each of the two autonomous provinces, Kosovo and Vojvodina, was in-cluded among the eleven positions assigned to Serbia.[7] This allocation of positions in the central party organs to the autonomous provinces reflected the growing importance of the nationality factor in both Yugoslav society as a whole and party decision making in particular. It constituted an attempt to recognize and accommodate the grievances of the Albanian and Hungarian minorities in Kosovo and Vojvodina, respectively, and to establish the native party leaderships in these regions as their political representatives at the center.

The investigations of secret police activities that accompanied the removal of Ranković revealed publicly the widespread abuses against the Albanian and Hungarian minorities carried out by the police. Within the security serv-ices themselves, there had been a systematic policy of discrimination against them. Not a single Albanian or Hungarian was employed by the republican secretariat of Serbia for security affairs. Not a single Hungarian was employed in the secretariat for Vojvodina, and only one Albanian was to be found in

[5] Ibid., pp. 19, 53.
[6] SKS, CK, *Sedma Sednica CK SK Srbije* (Beograd: Sedma Sila, 1966), pp. 21-35.
[7] SKJ, CK, *Peta Sednica*, p. 54.

the secretariat for Kosovo. "A relationship of distrust toward the national minorities was always present, even concerning the most responsible political and party functionaries, respected and honored persons from the ranks of the national minorities."[8]

As a consequence of this distrust, the secret police in Kosovo had carried out extensive surveillance of and had compiled detailed—but often inaccurate—dossiers about the political activities of people at all levels, "from the village to members of the Provincial [party] committee, Central Committee of Serbia and Central Committee of Yugoslavia, and even all types of [parliamentary] representatives, from provincial to federal." All persons "who in any way were engaged in political work and who were of significance for life in the area" were subject to suspicion. "Special measures were taken against the intelligentsia from the ranks of the Albanian people." In Vojvodina, the police kept an especially close watch for "autonomist tendencies."[9]

Provincial secret police functionaries in Kosovo had opposed the advancement of Albanians to the position of secretary of the provincial party committee or to membership in either the Serbian or provincial Executive Committees. As Albanian participation in the political life of both Kosovo and Yugoslavia increased, "the organs of security filled up more notebooks, expanded lists, and proclaimed all these peoples enemies of Yugoslavia and enemies of socialism." It is not surprising, therefore, that members of the central party leadership from Kosovo and Vojvodina were the most vigorous in their denunciations of Ranković and the secret police. In Vojvodina, the removal of Ranković was the occasion for a spontaneous and lively mass celebration among Hungarian members of the party.[10]

The Ranković dismissal prompted an emotional reaction among Croats as well. One Western observer in Zagreb during the summer of 1966 described the Croatian reaction as "euphoria" and noted an "almost universal tendency to interpret it primarily as a victory for Croatian interests."[11] In Serbia and among Serbs outside of Serbia, however, the affair was viewed as an attack on the Serb nation and its position in Yugoslavia. Complaints were raised to the effect that "Serbia no longer has its own representatives who will represent her interests" and that this was "an organized action of Croats and Slovenes against Serbs."[12] Consequently, the granting of separate representation in the central party organs to Vojvodina and Kosovo (despite the purposeful formulaic inclusion of these positions in the allocation to Serbia) was likely to be viewed by large numbers of Serbs as a first step toward the dismemberment

[8] SKS, CK, *Aktivnost SKS posle četvrte sednice*, pp. 279-80.
[9] Ibid., pp. 59, 287.
[10] Ibid., pp. 69-70, 177, 240.
[11] Rusinow, *The Yugoslav Experiment*, p. 194.
[12] SKS, CK, *Aktivnost SKS posle četvrte sednice*, pp. 25, 50, 51.

of Serbia through recognition of these provinces as separate units in the political system.

Perhaps it was as a consequence of these reactions that the leadership carefully avoided reducing the relative participation of Serbs in the central organs of the party. Ranković was replaced as party secretary by Mijalko Todorović; as member of the (old) Executive Committee by Milentije Popović; and as vice-president of the Republic by Koča Popović—each of them a Serb from Serbia. Serbs removed as a result of the cadre changes that followed were also replaced by other Serbs. In the new party Presidium and new Executive Committee, Serbia retained its relative share of positions, including the position of secretary of the new Executive Committee (Todorović).[13]

Of the forty-five positions in the new Presidium and Executive Committee other than president of the party, fourteen went to members of the Commission for reorganization. Consequently, these new bodies could have been expected to be heavily committed to implementation of that Commission's future recommendations for reorganization. Nonetheless, some party members freely expressed their doubts about the degree to which power had in fact been decentralized in the party. The chairman of the Commission for reorganization reported that

> the greatest number of questions, reservations and comments [expressed to the Commission] were with respect to the establishment of a presidium of the Central Committee and the greatest part of those [arose] from the fear that the existence of a presidium in addition to the Executive Committee . . . will reduce the remaining members of the Central Committee to passivity, . . . that the presidium will [simply] take the place of the old Executive Committee, and so on.[14]

These fears probably were reinforced by the careful preservation of Serbian representation in the central party organs, by the election to the new Presidium of all but one of the eighteen remaining members of the old Executive Committee, and by the election to the new Executive Committee of generally younger persons with little personal prestige and negligible personal authority within the party. These fears would prove to be unfounded, however, as other changes taking place in the party were weakening both the authority and cohesiveness of the central party leadership as a whole.

Up to the time of his ouster, Ranković had controlled the appointment of middle-level political functionaries from the party center. After the Fourth Plenum, "that right was transferred entirely to the [party] organs of the republics, which first strengthened the power of republican organs and second

---

[13] SKJ, CK, *Četvrti Plenum*, p. 107; and idem, *Peta Sednica*, p. 18.
[14] Ibid., p. 25.

re-oriented functionaries of the federation toward the republics.''[15] At the same time, the relative importance of this control was decreasing. A process of election from the base upward was established within the party. Members of the *opština* (commune, or county) party conferences henceforth were to be elected directly by the members of basic party organizations in the commune, and delegates to both republican and Yugoslav party congresses were to be elected by the commune conferences. "In many organizations it went even further than that, so that basic organizations proposed candidates for membership in the executive organs of the commune conference and commune conferences put forward candidates for membership in republican leadership organs and [central] organs of the LCY." At the same time, the principle of rotation, which before the Fourth Plenum was applied "primarily on the occasion of elections of commune leaderships," was now being applied vigorously to the whole party.[16] As a result, party leaderships at all levels increasingly were becoming subject to pressures from the memberships that elected them.

The effects of these organizational and procedural changes were reinforced by other changes in party membership. New members were being enrolled from among the ranks of workers and managers with experience in self-management. Older members with more conservative orientations were being expelled and were resigning. Democratization of party elections, therefore, made possible the election of lower and middle-level party functionaries who had little, if any, prior experience in party work. Both these new functionaries and the new general membership would be unlikely to accept restraints on free discussion within the party that were absent outside of it.

In the aftermath of the ouster of Ranković, Mihailo Švabić, a member of the Serbian Central Committee, noted the contrast between discussions in the party and those in other organizations and institutions. "When certain issues are raised" outside the party, he observed, "discussion is extensive, the conflict of opinions is extensive." But, "when those same issues are raised in a party committee, here there are monologues, speeches prepared in advance are read, here then there is no real discussion."[17] In large part, this was the result of concerted efforts by the conservative opposition to prevent such discussion.

Even prior to the Fourth Plenum, the activity of an informal group within the party opposed to the reform had been the focus of some public concern. Six months before the ouster of Ranković, one Yugoslav critic noted that informal groups opposed to "the democratic essence of self-management"

[15] Dušan Bilandžić, *Ideje i Praksa Društvenog Razvoja Jugoslavije 1945-1973* (Beograd: Komunist, 1973), pp. 270-71.

[16] SKJ, CK, *Nacrti dokumenata za Deveti Kongres SKJ* (Beograd: Komunist, 1969), p. 32.

[17] SKS, CK, *Aktivnost SKS posle četvrte sednice*, pp. 124-25.

were using their control over basic party organizations to restrict their independent activity.[18] At the Fourth Plenum, it was revealed that Ranković and his collaborators had supported these "informal groups" of conservative opponents to the reforms by using the secret police apparatus to carry out "wire-tapping, surveillance, and the gathering of reports from staff members engaged in work with functionaries," and to create "an extended net of their own collaborators."[19] This surveillance encompassed even the highest party leaders, including Tito and Edvard Kardelj, the main architect of the liberal reforms and Ranković's chief competitor for succession to leadership of the party.[20] The effect of these activities on party life was unmistakable. In Tito's words, "people began to whisper, distrust between one another was created, from top to bottom. *And doesn't that remind you a little,*" he poignantly asked the members of the Central Committee assembled for the Fourth Plenum, *"of what it was like at one time under Stalin?"*[21]

With the sharp curtailment of secret police activities and the lifting of the clouds of mutual suspicion that followed the Fourth Plenum, the nature of party life inevitably changed. An empirical investigation of the socio-political views of party members in Slovenia, carried out in April 1966, had revealed that, even before the removal of Ranković, party members were subject to the same forces that were generating conflicts in other organizations. Increasingly, *"the network of personal and social interests* in which individual groups of communists are found exercises an important influence on the formation of their socio-political views," and, of these, *"the work place represents the most important source."* As a result of the wide range of personal and social interests among communists, as well as of differences in individual "interests and knowledge of the issues," "all categories of members of the LC are as a rule classified along the whole list of answers [to opinion questions], which means that communists with positive and negative signs are found in all groups."[22]

The renewed emphasis on democratization of party life that followed the removal of Ranković compelled the republican and central leaderships to involve greater numbers of cadres in the formal decision-making process. In the absence of coercion, not only new party members and newly elected middle- and lower-level party functionaries, but even current members of

---

[18] Dragomir Drašković, "Neformalno grupisanje u osnovnoj organizaciji Saveza komunista," *Gledišta* 7 (January 1966): 49-51.

[19] SKJ, CK, *Četvrti Plenum*, pp. 16-17, 18.

[20] Paul Lendvai, *Eagles in Cobwebs*, pp. 195-200, but esp. 198.

[21] SKJ, CK, *Četvrti Plenum*, pp. 10-11 (emphasis added).

[22] Vinko Trček, "Društveno-politička stajališta komunista u većim privrednim organizacijama SR Slovenije," in Ante Fiamengo, ed., *Komunisti i Samoupravljanje* (Zagreb: Fakultet Političkih Nauka u Zagrebu, 1967), pp. 370-71.

leading party organs would be unlikely to refrain from open discussion of party policies. Indeed, the party decision-making process quickly became characterized by debate and disagreement—even within the central and regional leaderships themselves.

The leadership of the Serbian party, for example, almost immediately was subject to divisive pressures from middle- and lower-level cadres as it attempted to carry out the first stage of the post-Ranković reform—reorganization of its own central organs and the election of a new leadership—and was forced to drop even the pretense of unanimity. At its first session following the Fourth Plenum, the Serbian party leadership created its own twenty-one-member "Commission for the reorganization of the Central Committee of the League of Communists of Serbia and the nomination of candidates for election to its organs." The Commission included strong representation of the regions and nationalities in the republic. It was charged with the task of drafting specific proposals for reorganizing the party organs of the republic in accordance with the general proposals to be prepared by the central party's Commission.[23]

Prior to the Fourth Plenum, the Executive Committee of the Serbian Central Committee had "to a great extent acted as the political leadership in the Republic." "It often made decisions in place of the Central Committee."[24] In the post-Ranković period, such control by the party leadership was viewed as a negative phenomenon to be combatted. Consequently, the decision-making authority of the Serbian Commission was carefully restricted. First, the Commission was required to present to the Serbian Central Committee several alternatives rather than a single proposal for the reorganization of each party organ. Second, the Commission was required to consult not only with the members of leading party organs of the republic and its two autonomous provinces but with the members of middle- and lower-level party organizations as well. And third, the alternative proposals prepared by the Commission would be submitted to the Serbian Central Committee for adoption by secret ballot.[25]

During September and October 1966, therefore, the members of the Serbian reorganization commission conducted thirty-four consultative meetings attended by over 1,100 participants. They met with the members of the Yugoslav Central Committee from Serbia, the members of the Serbian Central Committee, the provincial committees of Vojvodina and Kosovo, the city committee of Belgrade, and even with the political secretaries of district and commune committees. The Commission itself reported that these meetings

[23] SKS, CK, *Aktivnost SKS posle četvrte sednice*, p. 319.
[24] SKS, *Šesti Kongres Saveza komunista Srbije* (Beograd: Komunist, 1968), p. 253.
[25] SKS, CK, *Aktivnost SKS posle četvrte sednice*, p. 319.

generally were characterized by "the diverse and discordant proposals, opinions, and demands of individuals and groups." Indeed, opinions were both so numerous and so discordant that "at a number of the consultative meetings wide discussion of individual proposals, stated opinions, and arguments was not conducted, so that mainly individual proposals and criticisms were submitted to the Commission."[26] A later report on the work of the Serbian Central Committee would describe this period as one characterized by "a new atmosphere of free expression of opinions, suggestions and proposals."[27]

In formulating its proposals for reorganization, the members of the Serbian Commission "adopted in principle the organizational structure of the CC [Central Committee] LCY." There were no conflicting opinions concerning the role of the Executive Committee either within the Commission itself or at the consultative meetings. However, there were "various opinions" about "the functions, number [of members] and composition of the Presidium." Proposals "ranged from not introducing a presidium [at all] to a presidium with a great number of members, composed more or less of the most respected and experienced members of the Central Committee." As was the case in discussions concerning the Yugoslav Presidium, a central concern in these discussions was the "danger of establishing this body [the Serbian Presidium] as a supraorgan in relation to the Executive Committee and Commissions [of the Serbian Central Committee] . . . and [therefore] to sketch its functions, composition, and size so that objectively it does not reduce the independence or damage the maintenance of equality of the other [party] organs [in Serbia]."[28]

The "new atmosphere of free discussion" in the party permitted the expression not only of views more liberal but also of views more conservative than or in direct opposition to those of the then-dominant leadership coalition. Individual members of the party opposed to liberalization apparently used the consultative meetings organized by the Commission to put forth suggestions for reorganization that undermined the purpose for which it had been undertaken in the first place. The new atmosphere even made possible the nomination by individual party members of several candidates for the positions of president of the Central Committee and secretary of the Executive Committee, and of numerous candidates for positions on the Presidium and Executive Committee. In fact, almost every member of the Central Committee was nominated for membership in the Presidium, and one-half were nominated for membership in the Executive Committee. At the eleventh hour, there even

[26] SKS, CK, *Reorganizacija i izbor organa Centralnog komiteta Saveza komunista Srbije (sedma sednica CK SK Srbije)* (Beograd: Sedma Sila, 1966), pp. 23-24, 32.

[27] SKS, *Šesti Kongres*, p. 246.

[28] SKS, CK, *Reorganizacija i izbor*, pp. 28-29.

was an unsuccessful attempt to reverse the leadership's commitment to election by secret ballot.[29]

Sixteen members, or almost twelve percent of the Central Committee membership voted against Dobrivoje Radosavljević, the Commission's candidate for president of the Central Committee and a supporter of the liberal coalition in the central Yugoslav party leadership. Twenty-one members, or almost sixteen percent of the Central Committee voted against Stevan Doronjski, the Commission's candidate for secretary. Several of the Commission's nominees for membership on the Presidium and Executive Committee were rejected by the Central Committee as a whole. Such results at this level of the political system were unprecedented in Yugoslav politics and quite rare in communist political systems generally. The total number of places on the Presidium and on the Executive Committee had to be increased in order to accommodate numerous demands for representation by regional, ethnic, occupational, and ideological groups within the Serbian party.[30] In the end, the Serbian leadership retained only tenuous control over the party.[31]

Democratization of party life was paralleled by democratization of political life in general. Prior to the Fourth Plenum, the party had usurped much of the authority and responsibility of parliamentary bodies and other social institutions. After the Fourth Plenum, the leadership began to withdraw the party from direct involvement in the day-to-day operations of state and governmental institutions. Party functionaries no longer were permitted simultaneously to hold positions in the state or governmental administrations, and the professional staffs of these bodies no longer were permitted to perform party functions. These were assumed by the specialized services of the central party organs. Paradoxically, this resulted in an increase in the number of cadres working in the central party apparatus at a time when the independent power and authority of the central party organs was on the decline.[32]

The withdrawal of direct party supervision over the operation of state institutions permitted these institutions increasing autonomy. Already rooted in local territorial and functional constituencies, the federal and republican parliaments quickly became arenas for the expression of conflicting local interests. Rather than providing an institutional "transmission belt" for the implementation of party policies, the parliamentary system rapidly was trans-

[29] Ibid., pp. 32, 36-41, 78-82.

[30] Ibid., pp. 33-34.

[31] The vigorous character of the political debate at the highest level of the Serbian party organization was duplicated at all levels. For an extensive retrospective report on the debates and discussions in local party organizations—and a sense of the weakness of central leadership control in the Serbian party—see SKS, CK, *Reorganizacija i razvoj Saveza komunista Srbije: 10 Sednica CK SK Srbije* (Beograd: Biblioteka SKS, 1967), passim.

[32] Savo Martinović, ed., *Deveti Kongres Saveza komunista Jugoslavije: Stenografske beleške*, 6 vols. (Beograd: Komunist, 1970), 1: 239-40.

formed into a channel for the expression of local and popular demands on the government and the party.

The post-Ranković period was characterized by the general organizational expansion of Yugoslav society. The provisions of the 1963 constitution guaranteeing individual liberties gained new life. Small groups of citizens undertook organized social and economic activities free from close party or police supervision. The communications media expanded dramatically with the establishment or expansion of regional newspapers and periodicals and radio and television stations; especially in the languages of the national minorities. All these institutions and organizations—as well as self-managing economic enterprises—enjoyed greater autonomy from direct police and party supervision than ever before. With this autonomy came greater freedom of expression. The public media soon became the site of political debates even more wide-ranging and unrestricted than those taking place at the same time in the party itself.

Having renounced simple repression as a tool for the regulation of political conflict and having permitted the rise of relatively autonomous social forces, the communist political leadership now faced the task of reconciling conflicting social forces not fully under their control. This was made more difficult by the fact that all but the very highest party leaders were becoming increasingly dependent on the support of the broader party membership in their respective republics and provinces, and especially on the middle- and lower-level party cadres who staffed major social and political institutions and were key actors in party elections. Without their support it would be impossible for any regional party leader to implement policy, and difficult for him to retain his position. The party masses in each of the regions, in turn, were now even more strongly under the influence of social forces and institutions outside the party. This influence was difficult to break even through the manipulation of party personnel policies, and it made members more difficult to mobilize on behalf of party policy.

Mass Constraints on Elite Action:
Yugoslav Public Opinion, 1965-1967

The growing dependence of political leaders on popular support, and especially on support from within the ranks of the politically active populations in their home republics put a premium on the collection of information about popular attitudes and beliefs. It is not surprising, therefore, that the mid-1960s saw an increase in both the number and scope of social research projects conducted in the country by both Yugoslav and foreign scholars. Many such projects received support from, or were commissioned by, state institutions and socio-political organizations, including the party, at a time when the direct involvement of the state and party in other areas of social life was being cut back dramatically.

The studies conducted by Yugoslav scholars during this period are a rich source of information about the state of public perceptions. But it must not be forgotten that a major weakness of the party prior to the ouster of Ranković had been its lack of sources of information about Yugoslav society independent of the secret police. These studies, therefore, also are important as indicators of the perceptions of the political leadership that in many cases sponsored them; they suggest the issues and problems that required the collection of "objective" information for the purpose of policy formulation. In effect, they are a partial reflection of the leadership's issue agenda.

Two broad issues dominated the public opinion surveys of this period: inter-nationality relations and economic relations between the republics and provinces. Survey questions focused on identifying the causes and intensity of inter-nationality frictions; popular perceptions of the effects of the economic reform; the policy preferences of the population with respect to economic relations between the republics and provinces; and on the degree of satisfaction of the population with the state of inter-nationality relations, with their standard of living, and with their prospects for the future. The published findings of these studies must be used with care. The researchers themselves approached their work with a great deal of caution. Indeed, in most of these studies the *numbers* of responses to individual questions were not published. Only *percentage distributions* of responses were presented. Certain types of questions apparently were not asked, and detailed analyses of the responses to known questions—if carried out—were not published, probably because of their obvious political sensitivity. Moreover, the rate of refusals to answer policy-relevant questions not only is consistently very high but is much higher than the rates for other questions asked at the same time. This is indicative more of the sensitivity of the issues than of the uncertainty of respondents concerning the interview experience itself, and raises doubts about both the candor of the responses that were collected and the meaning of small differences between the frequencies of different responses. Nonetheless, the patterns of responses in the published data are clear enough to suggest several important findings.

In June 1965 the Center for Public Opinion Research of the Institute of Social Sciences in Belgrade surveyed public perceptions of "the main cause of the phenomenon of chauvinism and nationalism" as part of a general survey of public opinions on a variety of social and political issues.[33] More than

[33] Ljiljana Baćević, "Mišljenja o glavnim uzrocima pojava šovinizma i nacionalizma," in Ljiljana Baćević et al., *Jugoslovensko javno mnenje o aktuelnim političkim i društvenim pitanjima 1965* (Beograd: Institut Društvenih Nauka, Centar za istraživanje javnog mnenja, 1965), pp. 97-109.

fifty-five percent of those surveyed refused to answer the open-ended question on this topic. Among those who did respond, however, there were important differences in the pattern of responses between republics and between nationality groups. These differences strongly reflect the character of the social divisions that distinguish these groups from one another.

In every region except Slovenia a large proportion of respondents identified "backwardness, primitivism, ignorance, [or] the influence of older generations" as the main cause of chauvinist and nationalist phenomena, suggesting that they believed such phenomena would be eliminated with continued social development. This proportion was highest in Kosovo, the least developed and in many ways most "backward" area. In Montenegro and Macedonia—two underdeveloped republics whose leaderships were then deeply involved in the political struggle over regional development policies—significant proportions of respondents also cited "unequal economic development" as the main cause of chauvinism and nationalism. "Unequal economic development" also was identified as the main cause by significant proportions of respondents in Slovenia and Croatia, the two most highly developed republics. But in Slovenia a higher proportion of respondents cited "historical, cultural, traditional, and linguistic differences" as the main cause—a clear reflection of the salience for Slovenian perceptions of the factors that distinguish that republic from its neighbors. Similarly, in both Croatia and Bosnia significant proportions of respondents identified "differences in religion and the activity of religious organizations" as the main cause of nationalist and chauvinist phenomena— a clear reflection of the fact that religion differentiates Croats and Serbs in Croatia and Croats, Serbs, and Muslims in Bosnia.[34]

The salience of these economic, religious, and cultural divisions is suggested by the relative frequency of responses based on them among respondents grouped by nationality rather than republic. Significant proportions of Serb, Croat, and Muslim respondents identified religious differences as the main cause of nationalist and chauvinist phenomena. But much larger proportions of these nationalities and of the nationalities concentrated in underdeveloped areas of Yugoslavia—Macedonians, Montenegrins, and Albanians—cited "unequal economic development" or "backwardness" as the main cause. Among Slovenes, however, more respondents identified "cultural differences" than cited "backwardness."[35]

For the country as a whole, education had a strong impact on the respondents' perceptions of ethnic factors as the cause of nationalistic and chauvinistic events. The proportion of respondents who identified economic causes of such events increased as the level of education increased. At the same time, the

[34] Ibid., p. 103.
[35] Ibid., p. 105. The responses of Hungarians are not reported.

proportion of respondents who identified ethnic factors decreased.[36] The relationship between socio-political activity and perceptions of nationalistic and chauvinistic events, however, was less clear. The proportion of respondents who identified economic factors did increase as the level of activity increased, and the proportion who identified religious factors did decrease. However, the proportion of those at the highest level of socio-political activity who identified "historical cultural differences" was as great as the proportion among the inactive population.[37]

Thus, nationalism and chauvinism generally were perceived at this time to be caused more by objective economic and developmental differences than by primordial differences and, by implication, to be subject to elimination through development. This was especially true among the more highly educated. In Slovenia and among Slovenes, however, primordial factors—"historical, cultural, traditional and linguistic differences"—were cited more frequently as causes of nationalism and chauvinism than either economic or developmental factors. And, even more important from the perspective of the political leadership, individuals with a high level of participation in officially sanctioned, regime-supportive activities remained no more convinced of the susceptibility of inter-nationality enmity to amelioration through economic development alone than those who remained uninvolved.

The relatively greater salience of ethnic factors for Slovenes than for other nationality groups also was suggested by the results of a study of "ethnic distance" carried out by the Center for Public Opinion Research in 1966.[38] Respondents in this study were asked about their probable reactions to six types of relationships with "an average, neither the best nor the worst," person of each of the major Yugoslav nationalities—Serb, Croat, Slovene, Macedonian, Montenegrin, Albanian, Hungarian, and Muslim. For each of these groups other than their own, respondents were asked the following six questions:

(1) Would you be in favor of this person living permanently in your republic? (2) Would you be in favor of this person being employed in the same enterprise where you work? (3) Would you agree to become friends with this person and for this person to be your friend? (4) Would you agree to marry this person? (5) Would you be in favor of this person being your superior at work? (6) Would you be in favor of this person having a leading position in your republic?

[36] Ibid., p. 106.
[37] Ibid., p. 108.
[38] Dragomir Pantić, *Etnička Distanca u SFRJ*, Izveštaj i studije, sveska 2 (Beograd: Institut Društvenih Nauka, Centar za istraživanje javnog mnenja, 1967).

"Ethnic distance" was measured simply in terms of the number of negative responses. Significantly higher proportions of respondents in Slovenia and of Slovene respondents gave a higher number of negative responses to these questions, indicating strong feelings of "ethnic distance."[39]

For respondents in Slovenia, as for respondents in every other republic, ethnicity was relatively unimportant with respect to questions of employment and friendship but very important for the selection of a marriage partner. Unlike elsewhere, however, for large proportions of respondents in Slovenia ethnicity also was very important for the definition of territorial community and for the allocation of economic and political authority. Moreover, the frequency of negative responses in Slovenia to each question was fairly uniform for all nationality groups.[40] These results suggest the existence at this time of a pervasive, far stronger, and more exclusive feeling of ethno-political community among Slovenians than among any other group in Yugoslavia.

The results of this survey also revealed strong feelings of ethnic distance among the most highly educated respondents. A much larger proportion of those with higher education than of those with lower levels of education gave relatively high numbers of negative responses to these questions. To some extent, this finding may be a reflection of the greater feelings of ethnic distance among Slovenes—a generally more highly educated population. But even in that republic it appeared that enmity toward other nationalities increased rather than decreased with socio-economic status. Indeed, one Slovene sociologist found in a later survey of public opinion in Slovenia that "the majority of problems and negativity [with respect to inter-nationality relations] is in great measure present in the consciousness of social groups with a higher level of qualifications." "Social categories with lower qualifications," he found, "feel certain problems in inter-nationality relations less or are affected only by those which momentarily receive the greatest publicity."[41]

While the salience of social divisions in the population for particular issues may have varied among the republics and nationalities at this time, perceptions of the relative importance of the issues themselves were identical. Moreover, the issues perceived by the population as important corresponded precisely to the issues then dividing the political leadership. At the same time that it surveyed "ethnic distance" in Yugoslavia, the Center for Public Opinion Research asked its respondents to identify "the most important problem before which Yugoslavia finds itself today." In every republic and province, respondents who answered cited "the carrying out of the economic reform"

[39] Ibid., pp. 16, 21.

[40] Ibid., p. 24.

[41] Peter Klinar, "Federacija kao društvena zajednica," in Ljubiša Stankov, ed., *Karakter i funkcije federacije u procesu konstituisanja samoupravnog društva* (Beograd: Institut za Političke Studije, 1968), pp. 142-43.

most frequently as the most important problem. After "the preservation of peace in the world," the next most frequently cited problems were "improvement of the standard of living" and "economic development." The nationality problem ("equality of the peoples of Yugoslavia"/"Brotherhood-Unity") ranked seventh in frequency and was cited by only two percent or less of the respondents in each republic and province.[42]

The divisive nature of these economic issues can be seen in the patterns of responses to questions about the effects of the 1965 economic reform and in the policy preferences expressed by the respondents. In response to the question "Have you noticed that after the economic reform the material position of certain republics (provinces) has changed in relation to the others?" respondents generally answered "I don't know." Only in Slovenia did a substantial proportion of respondents answer differently, and that was to suggest that there had been no change.[43] However, when responses were classified on the basis of the socio-economic status of respondents, a distinctly different picture emerged. Fewer respondents among the higher socio-economic groupings answered "I don't know" than among the lower groupings. Substantially larger proportions of them answered that "some republics have a better position."[44] When they were asked to identify the republics that "have a better position" as a result of the reform, large proportions of respondents in every republic except Slovenia named Slovenia. In Slovenia, on the other hand, a large proportion of respondents identified Croatia. Indeed, as can be seen from Table 2.1, relatively small proportions of respondents in each republic and province identified their own region as having a better position. When asked directly to evaluate the effects of the reform on the position of their own region, much larger proportions of respondents in every region except Serbia answered that that position had "worsened" than answered that it had "improved."[45] In sharp contrast to the pattern of responses to questions about inter-nationality relations, few respondents failed to express an opinion on these economic issues.

This willingness to express an opinion extended even to the question "How should economic relations between the economically developed republics (provinces) and the less developed be [organized]?" As can be seen from Table 2.2, the dominant preference among respondents in all regions except Slovenia was for the developed republics to help the less developed. In both the developed and the underdeveloped regions, these preferences were motivated primarily by belief in either "the idea of solidarity" or "the idea of

---

[42] Firdus Džinić (Editor), *Jugoslovensko javno mnenje 1966* (Beograd: Institut Društvenih Nauka, Centar za istraživanje javnog mnenja, 1967), p. 15.

[43] Ibid., p. 34.

[44] Ibid., p. 39.

[45] Ibid., p. 37.

TABLE 2.1
Republics Perceived to Have Improved Position as Result
of Economic Reform by Region, 1966 (percentages)

	Developed Republics	Under-developed Republics	Slovenia	Croatia	Vojvodina	Serbia	Bosnia	Montenegro	Macedonia	Kosovo	No Change	No Answer	Total
Slovenia	10.2	10.5	5.2	31.0	—	7.2	2.6	2.4	8.6	—	0.8	21.4	100.0
Croatia	18.1	5.3	55.4	0.6	—	12.1	2.1	—	2.3	—	—	4.2	100.0
Vojvodina	21.7	16.6	14.3	0.8	2.5	36.5	1.7	0.8	5.0	—	—	—	100.0
Serbia	19.7	1.4	50.2	—	0.7	12.8	6.9	6.3	0.7	—	—	1.3	100.0
Bosnia	17.2	5.4	44.1	20.6	—	4.6	2.6	1.0	0.2	—	—	4.4	100.0
Montenegro	33.7	4.5	39.7	—	—	—	—	22.1	—	—	—	—	100.0
Macedonia	13.6	8.9	38.9	1.5	—	2.5	—	—	1.0	0.5	—	8.0	100.0
Kosovo	22.4	13.2	20.4	—	—	11.7	—	—	2.4	13.1	—	16.0	100.0
Yugoslavia	21.2	7.7	39.5	4.6	—	12.5	2.7	2.2	1.9	1.7	0.1	5.2	100.0

SOURCE: Džinić, *Jugoslovensko javno mnenje 1966*, p. 36.

TABLE 2.2

Policy Preferences Concerning Economic Relations Between
the Republics and Provinces by Region, 1966 (percentages)

	Developed Should Help Less-Devel.	Developed & Less-Devel. Should Devel. Equally	Less-Devel. Should Devel. Themselves On Their Own	Undecided	No Answer	Total
Slovenia	29.7	21.2	21.3	27.8	—	100.0
Croatia	44.4	18.8	4.9	31.7	0.2	100.0
Vojvodina	55.1	12.8	0.6	31.5	—	100.0
Serbia	49.5	14.1	4.0	32.4	—	100.0
Bosnia	48.6	11.2	3.9	36.0	0.2	100.0
Montenegro	53.5	14.4	2.6	29.4	—	100.0
Macedonia	40.4	13.4	3.7	42.0	0.4	100.0
Kosovo	55.3	8.6	2.0	33.3	0.8	100.0
Yugoslavia	46.9	15.1	5.4	32.4	0.2	100.0

SOURCE: Džinić, *Jugoslovensko javno mnenje 1966*, p. 41.

unity'' among the republics, rather than by consideration of the economic benefits that might accrue to the individual regions and republics as the result of such help.[46] The policy preferences of respondents in Slovenia were distributed almost evenly across all the responses. Among those in Slovenia who answered that "the less developed republics should develop themselves on their own," more than half explained that they preferred this policy because "the developed republics have been victimized enough."[47] There were relatively few differences between the response patterns of socio-economic groupings, except that a somewhat higher proportion (ten percent) of those in the highest group thought that "the less developed republics should develop themselves on their own."[48]

Despite this evidence of dissatisfaction with the effects of past policies, the populace in every republic and province was not discouraged about prospects for the future. In spring 1967 the Center for Public Opinion Research asked respondents "In general, would you say that you are very satisfied, mainly satisfied, or unsatisfied with your family's prospects for the future?" Seventy-seven percent or more of the respondents in every republic and

[46] Ibid., p. 42.
[47] Ibid.
[48] Ibid., p. 45.

province except Slovenia answered that they were "satisfied." Sixty-one percent of the respondents in Slovenia answered that they were satisfied.[49]

Thus, popular views on the central political issues of the mid-1960s in Yugoslavia corresponded quite closely to the general orientation of the liberal, reformist leadership then consolidating its control of the party. Inter-nationality relations ranked very low among the concerns of the population, especially in comparison to economic issues, and popular preferences on the issue of economic relations between the republics and provinces generally coincided with the current political platform of the central party. Moreover, the inter-nationality tensions that did exist were perceived primarily as consequences of economic problems, and the population appeared to be generally satisfied with its economic prospects for the future. To a political leadership intent on continuing the economic reform, reducing the disparities between the levels of economic development of the regions, and controlling the level of inter-nationality tensions, these findings must have offered great hope of success. But they also revealed certain potentially important constraints on the kinds of action they might undertake to achieve these goals.

First among these was the strongly negative view of the impact of the economic reform. Respondents perceived the effects of the reform on their own republic to be negative. At the same time, they perceived its effects on one or more other republics as positive. This represented a potentially explosive basis for political dissatisfaction because of the close correspondence between republican divisions and nationality differences, and because of the continuing salience of ethnic factors for perceptions of non-ethnic issues. It was, however, one that the leadership might defuse through its own actions. But to do so would require the members of that leadership to respond to, and successfully defend the economic interests of their respective regions in policy debates at the center. This would be difficult for them to do without exacerbating inter-nationality hostilities.

Despite the low importance assigned by the population to inter-nationality relations in comparison to economic issues at this time, inter-nationality relations continued to be a topic of great sensitivity. Indeed, when the Center for Public Opinion Research asked respondents in 1967 to identify "the basic causes of the problems and difficulties in inter-nationality relations," the rate of refusals to respond was substantially higher than it had been for the equivalent question in 1965, and very much higher than the rate for other questions asked at the same time.[50] The Center did not include in its published analyses

[49] Dragomir Pantić, *Barometar zadovoljstva gradjana (drugi ispitivanje)* Izveštaji i studije, Sveska 39 (Beograd: Institut Društvenih Nauka, Centar za istraživanje javnog mnenja, 1970), pp. 39, 55.

[50] The 1967 results are reported in Dragomir Pantić, *Jugoslovensko javno mnenje o nekim aspektima medjunacionalnih odnosa*, Izveštaji i studije, Sveska 7 (Beograd: Institut Društvenih

of the 1967 survey a breakdown of the responses to this question by nationality. This sensitivity would make it difficult for any regional leadership to improve the economic position of its own republic or province if that improvement would be achieved, or even appear to be achieved at the cost of one of the others. An even more worrisome problem was indicated by the strength of ethnic distance among respondents in upper-level socio-economic groupings: These data suggested that, as socio-economic development proceeded, the points of contention between the nationalities in Yugoslavia were shifting from cultural to economic issues, but that inter-nationality relations did not appear to be improving. This, in turn, should have suggested to the leadership that conflicts over even "purely economic" issues would have to be approached with caution if they were not to activate and themselves become intensified by inter-nationality hostilities.

The Political Economy of Elite Conflict, 1966-1971

In the years following the ouster of Ranković, the central party leadership accelerated the implementation of the economic reforms adopted in the early 1960s. The reforms increased existing disparities between the levels of development of the republics and provinces; magnified the role of large, self-managing enterprises in the economic and, therefore, political system; and embroiled the regional political leaderships in conflicts over a whole range of economic issues. These conflicts, in turn, drew them into conflict over the organization and operation of central political institutions. The relative share of each of the regions in the total social product and national income of Yugoslavia, shown in Table 2.3, remained relatively constant during the period 1966-1971. However, if we compare figures for per capita social product and national income in the regions for the census years 1961 and 1971, as shown in Table 2.4, it becomes evident that the economic gap between the developed and the underdeveloped regions actually widened during this period. While the per capita social product and national income of the most developed region (Slovenia) were only about five times those of the least developed region (Kosovo) in 1961, they had grown to almost nine times the size by 1971. The index shown in Table 2.4 indicates that the per capita social products and national incomes of the underdeveloped regions of Bosnia, Montenegro, and Kosovo actually declined in relation to the all-Yugoslav figure. Among the underdeveloped regions, only Macedonia im-

Nauka, Centar za istraživanje javnog mnenja, 1967), p. 10. This survey included questions on language instruction in the schools and the activity of the Church among young people. The latter results are reported in Dragomir Pantić, *Neki aspekti religijskog fenomena u našoj zemlji*, Izveštaji i studije, Sveska 10 (Beograd: Institut Društvenih Nauka, Centar za istraživanje javnog mnenja, 1967), p. 7.

TABLE 2.3

Distribution of Social Product and National Income
by Region, 1961, 1966, 1971
(1966 Prices, in percentages)

	Social Product			National Income		
	1961	1966	1971	1961	1966	1971
Slovenia	15.1	14.5	15.5	15.0	14.5	15.6
Croatia	27.1	26.3	26.5	27.1	26.2	26.5
Vojvodina	11.1	12.1	11.5	11.2	12.2	11.5
Serbia	25.3	25.4	25.2	25.5	25.7	25.3
Bosnia	12.9	12.4	11.7	12.7	12.2	11.6
Montenegro	1.9	1.8	1.8	1.8	1.7	1.7
Macedonia	4.8	5.4	5.8	4.9	5.4	5.8
Kosovo	1.9	2.1	2.0	1.9	2.1	2.0
Yugoslavia	100.0	100.0	100.0	100.0	100.0	100.0

SOURCE: Savezni Savod za Statistiku [henceforth: SZS], *Statistički godišnjak Jugoslavije* [henceforth: *SGJ*] *1975* (Beograd: SZS, 1976), pp. 132-33.

proved its relative position. The most dramatic gains in per capita production and income were registered in the province of Vojvodina, which by 1971 had overtaken even Slovenia.

The declining relative positions of the underdeveloped regions resulted in large part from rapid population growth there. As can be seen in Table 2.5, the economies of the underdeveloped republics and provinces expanded at impressive rates during the period 1961-1971. The population growth recorded in these regions during the same period, however, negated whatever effect that expansion might have had, for it sharply increased the size of the dependent, nonworking, and therefore nonproductive population. As indicated in Table 2.6, the gap between the productivity of the employed population in the underdeveloped republics and provinces and the developed ones was substantially narrower than that for simple per capita production. The problem for the political leaderships of the underdeveloped regions, therefore, was to secure the expansion of the economies of their regions at rates commensurate with population growth.

Up to 1963, the federal and republican governments had controlled relatively large proportions of the total domestic capital available for investment and had used that control to subsidize development of the underdeveloped regions. However, as can be seen from the data presented in Tables 2.7 and 2.8, changes adopted in 1963 as part of the economic reform reduced sharply the proportion of investment capital under the control of the federal govern-

TABLE 2.4

Per Capita Social Product and National Income by Region, 1961, 1971
(in 1966 Dinars)

	Social Product				National Income			
	1961	Index	1971	Index	1961	Index	1971	Index
Slovenia	6,530	176	12,051	184	6,038	175	11,196	185
Croatia	4,478	121	8,062	123	4,162	121	7,417	123
Vojvodina	4,111	111	12,406	189	3,872	112	11,482	190
Serbia	3,611	97	6,462	98	3,384	98	5,982	99
Bosnia	2,699	73	4,204	64	2,474	72	3,808	63
Montenegro	2,718	73	4,651	71	2,437	71	4,063	67
Macedonia	2,371	64	4,754	72	2,209	64	4,371	72
Kosovo	1,333	36	1,404	21	1,232	36	1,248	21
Yugoslavia	3,710	100	6,561	100	3,449	100	6,041	100

SOURCE: SZS, *Statistički Bilten 727* ["Nacionalni sastav stanovništva po opštinama"] (Beograd: SZS, 1972), passim; SZS, *Aneks uz Statistički Bilten 727* (Beograd: SZS, 1972), p. 4; SZS, *SGJ 1971*, pp. 363, 365; and SZS, *SGJ 1975*, pp. 398, 400.

TABLE 2.5

Economic and Demographic Expansion by Region, 1961-1971

	Social Product[a]			Population		
	1961	1971	Percent Change	1961	1971	Percent Change
Slovenia	10,393	19,421	86.9	1,591,523	1,727,137	8.5
Croatia	18,626	32,920	76.7	4,159,696	4,426,221	6.4
Vojvodina	7,627	13,565	77.9	1,854,965	1,952,533	5.3
Serbia	17,419	31,471	80.7	4,823,274	5,250,365	8.9
Bosnia	8,849	14,535	64.3	3,277,948	3,746,111	14.3
Montenegro	1,283	2,358	83.8	471,894	529,604	12.2
Macedonia	3,334	6,879	106.3	1,406,003	1,647,308	17.2
Kosovo	1,285	2,576	100.5	963,988	1,243,693	29.0
Yugoslavia	68,814	123,726	79.8	18,549,291	20,522,972	10.6

SOURCE: Same as Table 2.4.
[a] Millions of 1966 dinars.

ment and increased dramatically the proportion under the control of banks. As a result of the growing emphasis on the autonomy of self-managing enterprises in the post-1966 period, the investment decisions of these banks now were becoming increasingly independent of governmental control. At the same

TABLE 2.6
Social Product per Employed Person by Region,
1961, 1966, 1971 (1966 Dinars)

	Social Product per Employed Person			Indexes		
	1961	1966	1971	1961	1966	1971
Slovenia	22,311	28,452	36,337	109	103	109
Croatia	20,872	28,116	35,570	102	102	107
Vojvodina	18,013	29,607	36,432	88	107	109
Serbia	22,618	29,449	33,202	111	106	99
Bosnia	19,451	24,851	28,823	95	90	86
Montenegro	18,562	25,435	29,079	91	92	87
Macedonia	15,617	22,662	28,594	77	82	86
Kosovo	15,610	23,592	25,569	76	85	77
Yugoslavia	20,410	27,676	33,380	100	100	100

SOURCE: SZS, *SGJ 1971*, pp. 363, 365; SZS, *SGJ 1975*, pp. 398, 400; SZS, *SGJ 1962*, p. 337; SZS, *SGJ 1967*, p. 337; SZS, *SGJ 1972*, p. 353.

time, accelerated implementation of economic reforms increased the autonomous control of self-management workers' councils over the wage, price, and investment policies of their enterprises. Consequently, during 1966-1971 the vast proportion of investment capital from domestic sources in Yugoslavia was under the control not of state or governmental agencies, but of relatively autonomous banks and economic enterprises.

Table 2.9 shows the regional distribution of capital invested by self-managing enterprises, banks, the federation, and other governments in Yugoslavia, and special investment funds during 1963-1971. The proportion of capital controlled by banks that was invested in Bosnia, Macedonia, and Kosovo generally declined in the period 1966-1971, while the proportion invested in Croatia and, to a lesser degree, Slovenia increased. At the same time, the proportion of capital controlled by self-managing enterprises that was invested in Bosnia, Montenegro, Serbia, and Kosovo declined, while the proportion invested in Slovenia gradually increased. In large part, these shifts were the result of the fact that capital could be invested more efficiently in the developed regions. That is, its investment there would result in greater output and, therefore, greater income for those who invested it.[51] More parochial considerations, however, cannot be discounted completely.

[51] See the analysis of regional incremental capital-output ratios for the 1960s presented in The World Bank, *Yugoslavia: Development with Decentralization* (Baltimore: Johns Hopkins University Press, 1975), pp. 189ff, but esp. 196-201.

TABLE 2.7
Sources of Expenditures for Capital Investment,
1963-1971 (Current Prices, in percentages)

| Year | Self-Mngng. Economic Orgs. | Banks | The State | | | Total |
			Govts.	Special Funds & Budgets	Sub-Total (State Exp.)	
1963	34.6	9.1	42.5	13.9	56.4	100.0
1964	32.2	31.4	25.4	11.0	36.4	100.0
1965	36.7	36.6	17.7	9.0	26.7	100.0
1966	45.8	41.3	3.5	9.5	13.0	100.0
1967	37.5	44.9	9.0	8.6	17.6	100.0
1968	37.0	50.0	9.5	6.6	16.1	100.0
1969	34.9	49.4	9.8	5.9	15.7	100.0
1970	33.4	51.1	9.3	6.2	15.5	100.0
1971	33.9	50.9	8.8	6.3	15.1	100.0

SOURCE: SZS, *SGJ 1965*, pp. 487-92; SZS, *SGJ 1966*, pp. 468-74; SZS, *SGJ 1967*, pp. 453, 456-60; SZS, *SGJ 1968*, pp. 457, 460-63; SZS, *SGJ 1969*, pp. 455, 458-61; SZS, *SGJ* 1970, pp. 451-54; SZS, *SGJ 1971*, pp. 464-67; SZS, *SGJ 1972*, pp. 473-76; and SZS, *SGJ 1973*, pp. 477-81.

The federation and other governments generally continued to direct almost all of the capital under their control to the underdeveloped regions. But the amount of this capital was relatively small. Because the proportion of total domestic investment capital under the autonomous control of banks and self-managing enterprises—and especially of banks—increased steadily during this period, these patterns reflect a significant redirection of capital away from the underdeveloped regions and toward the more developed ones.

As a consequence of these trends, the economies of the more developed regions—Slovenia, Croatia, and Vojvodina—became increasingly dependent on banks for investment capital. As the data displayed in Table 2.10 show, this was also true of the economy of Serbia proper. The economies of the underdeveloped regions of Macedonia, Montenegro, and especially Kosovo, on the other hand, while also receiving substantial proportions of their capital from banks, grew increasingly dependent on the redistributive powers of the state—and especially of the federation. Only the Bosnian economy developed more evenly balanced sources of capital for investment. These differences had important consequences for the behavior of regional political leaderships in Yugoslavia in the post-1966 period.

Compelled to represent and defend the interests of their respective republics

TABLE 2.8
Sources of Expenditures for Capital Investment,
1962-1971 (Current Prices, in percentages)

Year	Self-Mngng. Economic Orgs.	Banks	The Federation	Republics & Communes	Total
1962	37.4	2.9	30.5	29.2	100.0
1963	—	—	—	—	—
1964	32.2	31.4	6.5	29.9	100.0
1965	36.7	36.6	3.2	23.8	100.0
1966	45.8	38.9	5.9	9.4	100.0
1967	37.3	44.9	9.2	8.6	100.0
1968	—	—	—	—	—
1969	34.8	49.4	9.3	6.5	100.0
1970	—	—	—	—	—
1971	33.9	50.9	7.7	7.5	100.0

SOURCE: SZS, *Jugoslavija između VIII i IX Kongresa SKJ* (Beograd: SZS, 1969), p. 63; SZS, *Samoupravljanje i društveno-ekonomski razvitak Jugoslavije 1950-1970* (Beograd: SZS, 1971), p. 153; SZS, *Materijalni i društveni razvoj SFR Jugoslavije 1947-1972* (Beograd: SZS, 1973), p. 69.

and provinces, the political leaderships became embroiled in conflicts over domestic economic development strategies, foreign trade and foreign currency regulations, the scope of self-management authority in banks and large enterprises, and other issues affecting regional access to investment capital. As the economies of the more developed republics grew increasingly dependent on the Belgrade-based banks as sources of capital, for example, their political leaderships—primarily the Croatian leadership—demanded increased republican control over the capital generated by such investment. Conversely, as the amount of capital received from these banks by the underdeveloped regions declined, the leaderships of these regions demanded increased control over their investment decisions by central political institutions. For their political power in those institutions far exceeded the economic power of their regions in the Yugoslav market. In effect, the political leaderships of the underdeveloped republics and provinces became advocates of central political institutions capable of forcing the redistribution of resources among the regions.

Political leaders also were drawn into conflict in response to the actions of the large, powerful industrial and agricultural enterprises and foreign trade companies that enjoyed increased freedom of action in the post-Ranković period. These ostensibly economic organizations were not perceived as politically neutral by either the leaderships of the republics and provinces or the general population. Most foreign trade organizations, for example, were based

TABLE 2.9

Regional Distribution of Expenditures for Capital Investment
by Source, 1963-1971 (Current Prices, in percentages)

	Year	Slovenia	Croatia	Bosnia	Montenegro	Macedonia	Serbia	Vojvodina	Kosovo
Self-mngng. Economic Orgs.	1963	17.0	27.0	12.9	1.6	3.8	—	—	—
	1964	16.0	27.2	12.7	2.1	4.1	—	—	—
	1965	14.8	27.9	12.7	2.6	3.9	—	—	—
	1966	13.4	27.4	12.4	2.1	3.9	—	—	—
	1967	15.1	26.7	11.7	1.6	4.0	29.8	9.8	1.3
	1968	15.2	23.6	12.3	1.6	5.5	30.0	10.0	1.9
	1969	15.8	24.3	11.9	1.2	6.0	29.5	9.7	1.5
	1970	17.4	25.6	11.6	1.1	5.8	27.5	9.5	1.4
	1971	20.8	27.2	11.7	1.2	5.2	23.3	9.6	1.1
Banks	1963	23.3	30.0	7.9	0.7	3.0	—	—	—
	1964	17.8	26.4	13.1	2.1	10.4	—	—	—
	1965	12.7	17.7	12.9	3.8	15.0	—	—	—
	1966	13.3	19.2	13.8	2.7	12.7	—	—	—
	1967	15.3	24.1	7.8	1.9	10.9	29.5	7.4	3.1
	1968	14.2	23.6	8.0	2.2	9.9	30.2	8.4	3.5
	1969	15.0	26.7	6.9	3.1	8.1	31.2	7.0	2.1
	1970	15.9	30.3	9.3	3.3	6.3	25.3	7.9	1.6
	1971	16.6	27.7	9.0	3.4	6.3	25.9	9.7	1.4
Federation & Other Socio-Pol. Comms.	1963	12.1	21.8	12.9	5.4	14.7	—	—	—
	1964	8.4	18.0	13.1	7.8	20.3	—	—	—
	1965	13.2	24.9	14.6	3.1	11.6	—	—	—
	1966	0.9	6.3	22.3	8.7	29.8	—	—	—
	1967	0.5	5.5	24.5	12.7	23.9	6.3	6.1	20.5
	1968	1.8	3.0	27.5	8.7	15.8	10.6	7.5	25.0
	1969	0.2	1.5	21.1	13.3	22.0	12.7	7.6	21.7
	1970	0.2	1.2	21.4	14.1	21.6	15.6	5.5	20.4
	1971	0.1	0.6	18.5	19.7	22.8	14.5	2.8	20.9
Funds & Budgets	1963	13.5	15.2	7.1	1.7	35.0	—	—	—
	1964	13.9	19.8	8.7	1.2	24.9	—	—	—
	1965	13.6	24.0	10.6	1.8	17.9	—	—	—
	1966	9.3	19.7	9.6	0.7	15.9	—	—	—
	1967	9.7	18.5	12.4	1.0	20.7	25.0	8.2	2.9
	1968	9.2	20.2	17.9	1.9	15.2	25.7	7.5	2.3
	1969	11.2	20.9	22.3	0.7	12.6	23.2	6.8	2.3
	1970	17.8	17.1	26.8	0.8	17.1	18.2	5.1	2.6
	1971	20.4	17.1	26.3	0.5	17.1	20.7	5.2	1.7

SOURCE: Same as Table 2.7.

TABLE 2.10
Sources of Expenditures for Capital Investment by Region,
1963-1971 (Current Prices, in percentages)

	Year	Sources of Capital			
		Economic Organizations	Banks	Federation & Other Socio-Pol. Communities	State Funds & Budgets
Slovenia	1963	39.4	14.1	33.9	12.6
	1964	35.8	38.8	14.8	10.7
	1965	39.8	34.1	17.2	8.9
	1966	48.9	43.7	0.3	7.1
	1967	42.2	51.2	0.3	6.2
	1968	42.9	51.1	1.3	4.7
	1969	40.6	54.4	0.1	4.9
	1970	38.5	54.0	0.1	7.3
	1971	41.9	50.3	.05	7.7
Croatia	1963	40.1	11.7	39.2	9.1
	1964	36.7	34.8	19.3	9.2
	1965	43.9	27.8	19.0	9.3
	1966	55.6	35.2	1.0	8.3
	1967	43.7	47.2	2.1	6.9
	1968	40.6	51.8	1.3	6.2
	1969	36.8	57.2	0.6	5.4
	1970	33.9	61.5	0.4	4.2
	1971	37.7	57.7	0.2	4.4
Bosnia	1963	38.6	6.2	46.7	8.5
	1964	32.6	33.0	26.7	7.7
	1965	36.0	36.6	20.0	7.4
	1966	43.5	43.5	6.0	7.0
	1967	39.3	31.3	19.8	9.6
	1968	37.5	31.2	21.5	9.8
	1969	37.9	31.0	19.0	12.1
	1970	31.6	38.7	16.2	13.5
	1971	33.5	38.6	13.8	14.1
Montenegro	1963	18.1	2.1	72.2	7.6
	1964	19.9	18.9	57.4	3.9
	1965	31.2	45.4	18.1	5.2
	1966	39.1	45.8	12.5	2.6
	1967	22.8	32.0	42.2	3.1
	1968	23.0	39.7	32.5	4.9
	1969	12.4	46.4	39.9	1.3
	1970	10.7	49.6	38.3	1.4
	1971	10.0	44.6	44.6	0.8

TABLE 2.10 (*cont.*)

	Year	Sources of Capital			
		Economic Organi- zations	Banks	Federation & Other Socio-Pol. Communities	State Funds & Budgets
Macedonia	1963	10.5	2.1	48.8	38.6
	1964	10.6	26.1	41.3	22.0
	1965	13.4	51.8	19.5	15.2
	1966	18.5	54.8	10.9	15.8
	1967	14.5	47.3	20.8	17.3
	1968	22.0	50.8	16.3	10.9
	1969	23.3	44.3	24.0	8.3
	1970	24.4	40.8	25.6	9.2
	1971	23.6	42.7	26.8	6.9
Serbia	1963	—	—	—	—
	1964	—	—	—	—
	1965	—	—	—	—
	1966	—	—	—	—
	1967	41.2	48.8	2.1	7.9
	1968	39.7	50.7	3.6	6.1
	1969	36.3	54.4	4.4	4.9
	1970	37.2	52.4	5.9	4.6
	1971	33.3	55.7	5.4	5.5
Vojvodina	1963	—	—	—	—
	1964	—	—	—	—
	1965	—	—	—	—
	1966	—	—	—	—
	1967	44.5	40.2	6.6	8.6
	1968	41.8	44.5	8.1	5.6
	1969	42.5	43.1	9.4	5.0
	1970	39.4	50.2	6.4	3.9
	1971	37.2	56.2	2.8	3.7
Kosovo	1963	—	—	—	—
	1964	—	—	—	—
	1965	—	—	—	—
	1966	—	—	—	—
	1967	12.1	35.4	46.1	6.4
	1968	14.6	33.9	48.3	3.1
	1969	13.7	27.3	55.4	3.6
	1970	14.1	24.3	56.7	4.8
	1971	12.3	23.5	60.7	3.5

SOURCE: Same as Table 2.7.

in Belgrade. As formerly state-run enterprises, they were controlled by former government bureaucrats and politicians. These individuals were closely connected to the central rather than the regional political elites and were able to use their political connections to secure substantial advantages for their organizations, including a near-monopolistic control over the foreign currency market in Yugoslavia. Because convertible foreign currency was required to import goods and raw materials, control over its exchange—coupled with the compulsory limits established by the federal government on the retention of such currency by the firms that earned it—gave those foreign trade organizations enormous economic and political power. Because large proportions of the foreign currency earned in Yugoslavia was earned by enterprises catering to the tourist trade on the Dalmatian coastline in the Slovenian and Croatian republics, the role of these companies became a particularly sore point for the leaderships of these republics, who demanded changes in federal policy that would increase their control over the investments and earnings of these companies. The foreign trade companies became a symbol for the political leaderships and masses alike of alleged exploitation of their regions by a small ''Belgrade elite.''

Large industrial and agricultural enterprises were, of course, also formerly state-run. In some cases, such enterprises had been allocated by the central political leadership to the various regions during the postwar period of central planning as symbols of their commitment to the equality of the nationalities and equalization of the regional economies. Such enterprises often duplicated capacity already established elsewhere, and production in them frequently was inefficient. During the period of economic centralization, such duplication and inefficiency were subsidized through interregional transfers of resources to cover operating losses. Even as the period of economic reforms began in the early 1960s, the central government still controlled sufficient independent financial resources to subsidize inefficient operations.[52] After 1966, however, nonprofitable enterprises established on the basis of political rather than economic criteria came to be perceived even more clearly by wide segments of the public and by important members of the elite as anomalous. Many such factories were located in, and formed a large and important share of, the economies of the less-developed regions. Consequently, the continuation of support for such ''political factories'' became a bone of contention between members of the leadership from the republics.

At the same time, such large economic organizations were becoming better able to protect themselves politically as a result of economic and political

[52] For an examination of regional duplication and inefficiencies in the Yugoslav economy during the pre-1966 period, see Jack C. Fisher, *Yugoslavia: A Multinational State* (San Francisco: Chandler, 1968), passim.

reforms. The managers of large enterprises commanded substantial organizational resources for independent political action: their control over access to jobs in a period of increasing unemployment, their communications facilities and distribution networks, and their ready audiences of employees and their families. Moreover, the growing independence of basic party organizations in such enterprises and their increasing identification with the particular interests of the enterprise of which they were a part substantially reduced the degree to which managers of large enterprises were subject to party supervision and control from above.[53] Consequently, the managers of such enterprises wielded increasing independent political influence over local politico-administrative elites, the leaderships of their respective regions, and central decision makers in the federal parliament and federal administrative bodies. Managers of inefficient enterprises did not hesitate to use their political resources in an effort to secure financial ones.

The more efficient and profitable enterprises also frequently pursued economic policies and took economic actions that directly affected interregional and inter-nationality relations. Some of them controlled relatively large capital resources for investment and used them to penetrate lucrative markets in other republics. We have already noted that the Belgrade-based foreign trade organizations invested heavily in the development of tourist facilities on the Adriatic coast, which led inevitably to protests of "exploitation" from Slovenia and Croatia. Other enterprises sought to establish profitable cooperative relationships with foreign suppliers of products or technology also available from domestic producers in other regions of Yugoslavia. Such action usually prompted vigorous demands by these domestic producers for the reversal of such actions, directed at regional and central political institutions. The conflicts that ensued in such situations usually took on interrepublican characteristics.[54]

Regional political leaders could be drawn into controversy and conflict not only by the actions of relatively autonomous economic enterprises pursuing their self-interest but also by local governments defending the interests of their territories. Local commune politics had been dominated by elite cartels composed of local party secretaries, elected officials, and economic elites even before 1966. Although policies in the commune were determined largely by bargaining among these elites, their influence on the broader political system prior to 1966 was limited.[55] But the political reforms which followed

[53] Trček, "Društveno-politička stajališta komunista," p. 370; and *Borba* (Belgrade), 2-25 July 1970.

[54] See, for example, the development of the conflict between Radio-Television Skopje and Radio-industry Zagreb over the former's purchase of a transmitter manufactured in Switzerland, reported in *Politika* (Belgrade), 27 May, 27-30 June, and 1 July 1969; and *NIN* 13 July 1969.

[55] Stojan Tomić, "Savez komunista u komuni i centri usmjeravanja i centri političke vlasti,"

the ouster of Ranković increased the role of local organizations in the selection of higher political functionaries and thereby enhanced the ability of strongly entrenched local political elites to influence their republican political leaderships. Increasingly, a republican political leadership might be led to oppose federal policies, not on their own, but as the result of local opposition to such policies mobilized by local elites motivated by local interests.

The ability of economic elites, local political leaders, and others to bring pressure on the regional leaderships, and the increasing difficulty of resisting that pressure, made it difficult for republican and provincial leaders to compromise the interests of their respective regions in order to resolve conflicts over federal policies. Unable to come to agreement on substantive solutions, the leaderships appear to have attempted to circumvent these conflicts by altering the organization and process by which federal policies were formulated. The leaders of the developed regions sought to enhance their power over the formulation of central policies in order to restrict the autonomy of central bodies and thereby limit, if not reduce, the transfer of resources out of their regions. The leaders of the underdeveloped regions also sought to enhance their role in central decision making. But they did so in order to preserve, if not enlarge, those transfers. These conflicting motivations made it difficult for them to agree on the areas that would remain subject to joint decision making and the rules by which decisions in those areas would be made. Consequently, they continued the devolution of power and authority from the center to the regions begun with the ouster of Ranković, but without any agreed conception of the ultimate scope and character of the changes they were undertaking.

Federalization of the Party, State, and Government, 1967-1969

The 1966 reorganization of the Yugoslav and republican central committees carried out following the removal of Ranković was only the first in a series of organizational and procedural changes within the party. In a major break with past practice, the central party leadership agreed in November 1967 that, in keeping with the statute adopted at the Eighth Congress in 1964, the Ninth Yugoslav Party Congress would be convened *after* meetings of republican party congresses.[56] This alone devolved enormous influence to the republican party organizations. But the decision went even further. Heretofore, the Yugoslav congress had imposed a compulsory party line determined by the central leadership on both the republican organizations and the general membership. Even the party statute adopted in 1964 preserved the primacy of the all-

---

in Fiamengo, *Komunisti i Samoupravljanje*, pp. 373-86; and Radivoje Marinković, *Ko odlučuje u komuni* (Beograd: Institut Društvenih Nauka, 1971), chaps. 3 and 4.

[56] SKJ, CK, *Osma Sednica Centralnog komiteta SKJ* (Beograd: Komunist, 1967), p. 140.

Yugoslav congress. Now, however, the leadership agreed that the Yugoslav congress was to develop "a synthesis of the results of the congresses of the Leagues of Communists of the republics" and establish this synthesis as a guideline for the central leadership.[57] This decision, despite numerous disclaimers by party leaders both at the center and in the republics, was both a clear reflection of and a strong impetus to "federalization" of the Yugoslav party.[58]

Further changes recommended by the Commission for Reorganization sustained the process of federalization. In July 1968 the Yugoslav Central Committee accepted the Commission's proposal that the thirty-five-member Presidium established in 1966 be expanded to "about fifty members" and that it replace the Central Committee; that the new Presidium be given a smaller, nonpolitical secretariat; and that a new, larger central party organ—the party Conference—be created as the "highest forum" of the party between congresses. The Conference would convene "as needed, but at least once a year."[59] In effect, the Commission was simply expanding the size of the existing central organs, changing their names, and requiring that they meet less frequently. Such changes could only weaken the effectiveness of these organs as arenas for the resolution of ongoing interrepublican and provincial conflicts. The existing Presidium of thirty-five members and Executive Committee of eleven members already had proven too large to be effective; leading to the formation of an informal, smaller leadership group composed of an unspecified but small number of the members of these two bodies and known only as the "coordinative group."[60]

The independent power and authority of the newly established central organs were weakened by the party's Commission for Cadres Policy. The cadres commission had been created by the Yugoslav Central Committee in November 1967 to develop explicit principles by which membership in central party organs would be determined. In its July 1968 report to the Central Committee,[61] the Commission justified the principles it was about to propose by referring obliquely to the highly politicized atmosphere in which it had to carry out its work. "Besides other things," the Commission reported, "it is necessary to take into account the present political situation, disposition and expectations in the party and wider social public." In other words, the Commission had to accommodate increasing demands by republican and provincial leaderships for stronger control over the central party organs. It recommended, therefore, that "with the election of the *Presidium of the LCY* it is necessary

---

[57] SKJ, CK, *Pripreme 9. Kongresa* (Beograd: Sedma Sila, 1967), p. 13.

[58] Bilandžić, *Ideje i Praksa*, pp. 272-73.

[59] SKJ, CK, *Deveta Sednica Centralnog komiteta* (Beograd: Komunist, 1968), pp. 103ff.

[60] A passing reference to the existence of this group can be found in ibid., p. 12.

[61] Ibid., pp. 116-18.

to ensure *equal representation of the republics* and to this number would be added a certain equal number for each autonomous province." In effect, the Commission was recommending replacement of the 1966 formula for proportional representation of the republics and provinces by a formula based on equal representation of the republics and equivalent representation of the provinces. This change received strong support from the smaller party organizations, and particularly from the Macedonian leadership.

The Commission also observed that "it is natural that the deciding role in the nomination of members for the Presidium of the LCY belongs to the republican organizations of the League of Communists." It suggested, therefore, that "affirmation of the list of candidates for membership in the [central] organs of the LCY from the republics should be performed by an expanded session of the central committee of the republic, and *election* [performed by] the *republican congress*. The federal Congress will perform [only] *verification* of that election." These changes meant that the members of central party organs—with a few important exceptions—would owe their allegiance to the republican and provincial organizations that had placed them there, and not to their colleagues at the center. In a sense, they no longer could be described as "members of the leadership from a republic." They now had become "*representatives* of a republic in the central leadership."

This dramatically altered the nature of the decision-making process within the leadership. It very rapidly came to be the case that "important decisions no longer were made at the federal summit but rather [by] direct contacts among representatives of the republics—in the form of bilateral and multilateral interpersonal visits and discussions of republican state and party delegations." By the time of the Ninth (Yugoslav) Party Congress in March 1969, there no longer would be an independent "party center" other than President Tito—"who all the more frequently received delegations of the republics for political discussions and in this way created a platform for political decisions."[62]

Federalization of the leading party organs was accompanied by a simultaneous increase in the influence of republican and provincial representatives in the government (the Federal Executive Council, or FEC) and in state institutions (the Federal Assembly, or parliament, and federal secretariats and other administrative bureaucracies). However, while changes in the party had been initiated by members of the leadership from the developed regions intent on pursuing economic reform, those in the state were initiated largely by representatives of the underdeveloped regions intent on ensuring continued support for the development of their regions.

Up to 1967, the influence in parliament of the republics and provinces,

[62] Bilandžić, *Ideje i Praksa*, p. 271.

represented directly in the Federal Assembly's Chamber of Nationalities, had been limited. The Chamber of Nationalities had been one of two houses of parliament in the immediate postwar period, when the institution as a whole was a powerless symbol in a fundamentally Stalinist system. After the break with Stalin and the abandonment of Stalinism, the constitutional reform of 1953 reduced the chamber to a component part of the Federal Chamber, which retained general legislative competence. It remained a subunit of the Federal Chamber under the provisions of the new, more liberal constitution adopted in 1963. That constitution established four functionally based chambers in addition to the Federal Chamber: an Economic Chamber, an Educational-Cultural Chamber, a Social-Health Chamber, and an Organizational-Political Chamber.[63] The seventy members of the Chamber of Nationalities—ten delegates elected by each of the six republican assemblies (parliaments) and five elected by each of the assemblies of the two autonomous provinces—were obligated under the 1963 constitution to meet in separate session only to consider a motion to amend the constitution, or when requested to do so by a majority of delegates from one republic, by ten of its own members, or by the president of the Federal Assembly. They were empowered to convene to consider any matter "affecting the equality of the peoples and Republics, or pertaining to the constitutional rights of the Republics."[64] In practice, however, the Chamber of Nationalities convened in separate session only to perform symbolic functions.

Up to 1967, real discussion of these issues had taken place in the central party leadership. Edvard Kardelj observed in 1967 that, because of "fear of carrying a conflict into an organ such as the chamber," conflict between the regional leaderships or conflicts with nationality implications were resolved by "discussion and direct negotiation [among] interested parties, outside of the Chamber of Nationalities." This was, he acknowledged, a conscious policy of the leadership:

> Precisely in the last four years we have had several such situations. With respect to these conflicts, we thought it was better not to discuss them at sessions of the Chamber of Nationalities but to resolve them by political means and by internal discussions.[65]

[63] For a survey of the organizational history of the Federal Assembly, see Lenard J. Cohen, "Conflict Management and Political Institutionalization in Socialist Yugoslavia: A Case Study of the Parliamentary System," in Albert F. Eldridge, ed., *Legislatures in Plural Societies: The Search for Cohesion in National Development* (Durham, N.C.: Duke University Press, 1977), pp. 122-65.

[64] Federal Assembly Information Service, *The Constitution of the Socialist Federal Republic of Yugoslavia* (Belgrade: Prosveta, 1969), articles 165, 166, 190 [henceforth: *1963 Constitution*].

[65] Firdus Džinić, ed., *Izborni sistem u uslovima samoupravljanja* (Beograd: Institut Društvenih Nauka, 1967), p. 334.

The restriction of the Chamber of Nationalities to a symbolic role thus appears to have been a result of the leadership's effort to limit the consequences of interregional conflicts by restricting their public discussion. This period in Yugoslav political history is sometimes viewed as one in which interregional and inter-nationality conflict was less intense. It would appear, however, that such conflicts did exist but were maintained at a low level of intensity as a result of concerted, cooperative efforts by the leadership.

By 1967, the party leadership no longer could provide the institutional setting for the resolution of such conflicts. It had become preoccupied with its own internal reorganization. Meetings of the Central Committee, Presidium, and Executive Committee held during the period from July 1966 to the Ninth Party Congress in March 1969 were devoted almost exclusively to issues related to the reorganization and to foreign policy (especially the Czechoslovak crisis of 1968), or to preparation of the Ninth Congress. With the exception of an oft-mentioned but remarkably vague "directive" issued in June 1968, there is very little evidence in the documents from these meetings or in the newspaper accounts of them to suggest that the central party leadership was providing specific policy guidance to government and state bodies. Consequently, when in December 1966 representatives of the republic of Bosnia and Hercegovina on the Managing Board of the special federal fund for the accelerated development of the underdeveloped regions were dissatisfied with that Board's decision concerning the allocation of resources for the period 1967-1970, they turned to state and governmental institutions for redress.

That republic, through its representatives in the Federal Chamber of the Federal Assembly, called for a meeting of the Chamber of Nationalities to discuss the decision of the Board. Such a step was unprecedented and the potential consequences were weighed carefully. Indeed, one Bosnian representative noted that he and his colleagues "had carefully considered in which place and in which form to submit these problems which are, in our opinion, very significant, fundamental, and politically delicate," and had decided to place the question before the Chamber "only after long hesitation."[66] The evidence suggests that this action was not taken without the support and even encouragement of the party leadership of the republic.[67]

Because both Bosnia itself and the Bosnian political leadership were multiethnic, the call by that republic for a meeting of the Chamber of Nationalities was unlikely to be interpreted by the central party leadership, the leaders of the other regional party organizations, or the masses as a politically threatening

[66] Cited in Cohen, "Conflict Management," p. 156.

[67] See the retrospective comments of the republican party leadership in *Republičko savjetovanje Saveza komunista o nekim obilježjima političke situacije u Bosni i Hercegovini* (Sarajevo: Oslobodjenje, 1968), p. 314.

manifestation of nationalism. Rather, it could be accepted as a legitimate exercise of the constitutional right of a republic to protect its own interests.

The Chamber met in January 1967.[68] Although all the underdeveloped regions did not act as a bloc, the Chamber as a whole did agree that the decision of the Managing Board should be investigated. At the same time, it created a working group to determine whether changes in the constitution were required to bring the organization of state institutions into line with the increasing political importance of the republics. Significantly, the working group that investigated the decision of the Managing Board concluded that the Board had, in fact, applied the existing rules for decision making correctly. It was the rules themselves that required revision. This conclusion gave further impetus to the move to amend the constitution.

The Bosnian initiative itself, by breathing political life into a previously symbolic institution, significantly enhanced the power of the republics in the process of federal decision making. The constitutional amendments that were adopted only a few months later reinforced and institutionalized these gains. Under the 1967 amendments, the Chamber of Nationalities now also met separately, and mandatorily, "to consider . . . drafts of the Social Plans of Yugoslavia, bills regarding the determination of the sources and kinds of revenue of socio-political communities, and drafts of basic or general laws." "Acting on terms of equality with the Federal Chamber," the Chamber of Nationalities also was to meet separately to consider "all affairs which under the Constitution fall within the independent jurisdiction of the Federal Chamber." Thus, the jurisdiction of the Chamber was extended to include all issues affecting the interests of the republics, making it in all but formal organization a separate chamber of the Assembly. The number of delegates required to call the Chamber into session was lowered from ten to five, thereby raising the status of the autonomous provinces as units of the federation. The task of the Chamber, remained, however, to consider issues from the perspective of both interrepublican (or provincial) and inter-nationality relations.[69]

In reaction to the revelations accompanying the ouster of Ranković only a year earlier, the amendments subjected matters of state security to the joint responsibility of the federation and the republics. This constituted formal recognition of the fact that a major instrument of coercive force that up to 1966 had been under the exclusive control of the party center—even if during that entire period it had been monopolized by one man—was now divided among the republics and provinces and under the effective control of their respective party leaderships. This left the military as the only all-Yugoslav instrument of force still under the control of the center. The amendments also

[68] The following account is adapted from Burg, "Ethnic Conflict and the Federalization of Socialist Yugoslavia," pp. 125ff.

[69] *1963 Constitution*, amend. I.

eliminated the office of vice-president of the Republic, and transferred the functions of the vice-president to the president of the Federal Assembly, thereby enhancing the status of the Assembly. This change was a return to the arrangement that had existed prior to the creation of the vice-presidency in 1963.

The 1967 amendment process suggests the potential importance of even purely formal constitutional provisions for decision making in the politics of a federal system in which there exist objective bases for conflicts of interest between the constituent units. The invocation of constitutional provisions for change by a constituent unit confronts the central political leadership of such a state with a choice between allowing a potentially successful attempt to disperse power—however marginally—to take place, and displaying an incongruous and perhaps self-defeating predominance of power. In the Yugoslav context, of course, the change initiated by the Bosnian political leadership was acceptable to the central leadership because it conformed to the direction of changes which they themselves were carrying out in their own organization and which they already were considering for application to the institutions of the state. The Bosnian initiative therefore, only accelerated the schedule of change. The danger of such acceleration, however, lay in the fact that the implementation of constitutional change takes place in the public realm. Hence, any difficulty that might arise in implementing these changes would be subject to public scrutiny. This holds untold consequences for a multinational system in which conflicts between the units are difficult to distinguish from conflicts between the national groups that populate them. In effect, once the amendment process has been initiated it opens the door to further debate not only over relationships between the constituent units but also over relationships between the nations that inhabit them. The boundaries that the leadership would be likely to set for itself on the latter debate would be difficult to enforce on the public at large.

In fact, while the 1967 amendments were being formulated, an event of extreme importance to the development of directly ethnic relations did take place. On March 17th, seventeen Croatian cultural organizations, led by the *Matica Hrvatska*, published a "Declaration on the name and position of the Croatian literary language" and thereby broke the tenuous "truce" on the question of Serb-Croat relations. The Declaration denounced the 1954 Novi Sad agreement and asserted the distinctiveness of the Croatian literary language. It included the accusation that the Serbian language was being employed as a de facto official state language and demanded that the literary language of Croatia be elevated to the status of an official language along with and equal to Serbian and the other languages of the Yugoslav peoples.[70]

[70] Originally published in *Telegram* (Zagreb), 17 March 1967. This account is based on the text that appeared in *Vjesnik* (Zagreb [Dalmatian edition]), 19 March 1967.

While the party reacted to the Bosnian initiative with tolerant and perhaps even "embarrassed silence,"[71] its response to the publication of the Declaration was swift and uncompromising. It was received by the party leadership not as a cultural or intellectual event, but as a political statement with clearly nationalistic overtones. The party organizations of Zagreb and of Croatia, local Croatian party organizations, and Tito himself all denounced the Declaration as an unacceptable nationalistic manifestation; "a return to the past," the substance of which was contradicted by the facts of contemporary Yugoslav language policies. The Serbian party leadership also criticized the Declaration but balanced its statement with criticism of the reaction to it of Serbian writers.[72]

The Declaration had prompted a group of Serbian writers—including nineteen members of the party and one member of the Serbian Central Committee—immediately to draft a counterresolution for submission to the next regular meeting of the Assembly of the Literary Association of Serbia, scheduled for the next day. The Executive Committee of the Serbian party learned of this action the same day and sent representatives to a meeting of the Association's leadership to dissuade them from accepting the resolution. The resolution was in fact defeated at the Assembly meeting but soon appeared in the press under the title "A Proposal for Consideration." The Serbian party leadership simultaneously condemned both the Proposal and the Declaration as nationalistic and chauvinistic and forced the resignation of the Serbian Central Committee member involved in preparing the Proposal.[73]

The contrasting responses of the party to the Bosnian initiative and to the Declaration/Proposal episode highlight the dilemma that would continue to confront the political leadership of Yugoslavia for years to come: The party's commitment to economic and political reform arising out of the ideology of self-management legitimized efforts to reduce the powers of the federation and to increase those of the republics. Given general agreement among representatives of the republics and of the federation in the party and state leaderships, the federal framework provided a means for implementing those reforms. But in order to carry out such change without undermining the stability of the larger state, the regional leaderships would have to ensure against the radicalization of demands. The post-1966 party reforms, however, accelerated the withdrawal of the party from close supervision of society and reduced its peremptory coercive power. This meant that political debate, as the publication of the Declaration and the Proposal foreshadowed, increasingly

[71] Hondius, *Yugoslav Community*, p. 325.

[72] See "Politika a ne lingvistika," *Vjesnik* (Zagreb [Dalmatian edition]), 19 March 1967; Miloš Žanko, "O različitim putevima i metodama rješavanja nacionalnog pitanja i medjunacionalnih odnosa," *Vjesnik* (Zagreb [Dalmatian edition]), 20-22, 26 March 1967.

[73] SKS, CK, *Aktuelna pitanja i zadaci komunista u borbi za reformu (9. Sednica CK SK Srbije)* (Beograd: Biblioteka SKS, 1967), pp. 19-20, 128-31.

would become open to demands from organized groups in society not subject to close control by either the central or republican party leaderships. If conflicts between the republics over largely economic issues reached some as yet unknown level they might become linked with nationality issues such as those raised by the Declaration. Such linkage might create the conditions for an ethnic upheaval that could destroy the larger state. In effect, the onset of genuine federalization and the democratization of political debate potentially had created the conditions for the destruction of the federation itself.

Inter-nationality hostility between Serbs and Croats was not the only basis for such linkage. Bosnian relations with both Croatia and Serbia were subject to aggravation by the hostility between Muslims on the one hand and Croats and Serbs on the other. The question of Muslim national identity had long been a point of contention between Serbian and Croatian nationalists. The former were inclined to define Muslims as "Serbs of the Islamic faith," while the latter defined them as "Croats of the Islamic faith." In the post-1966 period, Croatian and Serbian cultural organizations based in Croatia and Serbia, respectively, began to penetrate areas of the Bosnian republic inhabited by Catholic Croats and Orthodox Serbs.[74] The Catholic Church, an organizational bastion of Croatian nationalism, became particularly active in Bosnia. This, in turn, prompted Orthodox and Islamic organizations to become more active. It was not long before local party officials were reporting "serious problems" arising out of a general upsurge in religious instruction, construction of religious institutions, and organized social activity sponsored by the religious communities—the latter often designed to reinforce adherence to the faith.[75]

The Bosnian political leadership was particularly concerned about the general increase in the number and frequency of "incidents of chauvinism and nationalism" that accompanied the increased activity of religious organizations. These included incidents of verbal assault; the singing of nationalistic songs; verbal attacks on the political system, on individual nations and nationalities, and on outstanding social and political personalities; the sending of ethnically provocative letters to individuals; the spreading of rumors about the preparation by Muslims of a list of Serbs and Croats who were to be liquidated; the spreading of rumors about the unwillingness of Muslim authorities to protect Serbs or Croats against physical assault; and even murder.[76] At the same time, Muslim intellectuals in Yugoslavia were actively asserting the existence of a separate Muslim national identity distinct even from ad-

[74] *Republičko savetovanje o nekim obilježjima*, p. 310.
[75] See, for example, the testimony of the party secretary of Zepča. Ibid., pp. 53-55.
[76] Ibid., passim, but esp. pp. 331-40 and 383ff.

herence to the precepts of Islam.[77] In May 1968, this position was endorsed by the Bosnian Central Committee.[78]

The heightened sense of separateness among Muslims directly conflicted with intensifying Croat and Serb nationalisms. Moreover, recognition of a Muslim nation would add yet another element to formulas for the construction of representative institutions and decision-making bodies on the federal level in both the state and the party.[79]

Political relations between Serbia proper and the autonomous province of Kosovo, too, were complicated by interethnic hostilities. Tensions in Kosovo arising out of Albanian resentment over Serbian political domination of that province and out of conflicting Albanian and Serbian reactions to the post-Ranković reforms have been described above. Those tensions did not subside in the period following the ouster of Ranković. On the contrary, they increased. The Albanian leadership of the Kosovo party organization reported in 1968 that the province continued to be plagued by both "nihilistic" Albanian nationalists and "great-state, unitaristic" Serb nationalists. The former were "not satisfied with anything and negated everything which had been achieved, and blamed the League of Communists, the system and the socialist order, and especially the leadership" not only for a failure to fulfill nationalist aspirations but "even for objective difficulties." The latter attacked concessions to Albanian nationalist aspirations as "endangerment of the position and rights of the Serb and Montenegrin peoples."[80]

The increasing power and status of provincial representatives in central party organs and state institutions in relation to representatives of the republics raised corollary questions concerning the position of the autonomous provinces of Kosovo and Vojvodina within the Serbian republic. The Albanian leadership of Kosovo pressed for increasing autonomy for both the party organization and the state and government institutions of the province, and for increased Albanian control over them. They did so within the framework of continued symbolic subordination of the province within the Serbian republic.[81] But rising Albanian nationalism made it difficult to defend even symbolic

---

[77] Atif Purivatra, *Nacionalni i politički razvitak Muslimana* (Sarajevo: Svjetlost, 1969), pp. 30-39. For a review of this literature as a whole see Steven L. Burg, "The Muslim Community of Yugoslavia," paper presented at Conference on Islamic Communities under Communist Rule, University of Chicago, Center for Middle Eastern Studies, October 27, 1978.

[78] Purivatra, *Nacionalni i politički razvitak*, p. 30.

[79] See the speech by the president of the Bosnian party, in *Borba* (Belgrade), 21 November 1969.

[80] SKS, Pokrajinski komitet za Kosovo i Metohiju (PK Kosovo), *Deseta Konferencija Saveza komunista Srbije za Kosovo i Metohiju* (Priština: Rilindja, 1969), p. 32.

[81] Veli Deva, "Medjunacionalni odnosi i politička situacija na Kosovu," in Ljubiša Stankov, ed., *Politička situacija: Medjunacionalni odnosi u savremenoj fazi socijalističkog razvitka i zadaci Saveza komunista Srbije* (Beograd: Institut za političke studije FPN, 1969), p. 146.

subordination, and rising Serb nationalism made it difficult to push too strongly for de facto autonomy.

Albanian and Serbian nationalisms also affected relations between the Macedonian republic and both Serbia and Kosovo. Large numbers of Albanians live in the northwest section of Macedonia, and large numbers of Serbs live in northern Macedonia. The growth of Serb and Albanian nationalism was accompanied by demands from nationalistic Serb elements for political subordination of the Macedonian leadership to Serbian tutelage, and from Albanian nationalistic elements for the separation of northwestern Macedonia and its incorporation in a "greater Albania."

In assessing the situation in its own republic, the Bosnian party leadership suggested a means for controlling the level of such hostilities everywhere. In some places in Bosnia, it noted, local party organizations had responded to nationalistic incidents by organizing meetings of citizens at which ethnically provocative materials were read and discussed, and their "unfriendly character" was explained. In this way these local party organizations sensitized the population in their areas to "the practical techniques" of ethnic agitation, and thereby reduced their effectiveness. Consequently, nationality tensions in these areas were substantially reduced. This could be done, of course, only where the party membership itself remained uninfected by nationalist sentiments. This was not always the case even in Bosnia.[82] And, as was demonstrated during the Declaration/Proposal episode, it certainly was not the case in Croatia and Serbia.

The increasing power of representatives of the republics and provinces in the highest decision-making bodies of the party and the state was paralleled by their increasing power in the federal government. A later Yugoslav analysis of the period suggests that "a qualitatively new political situation was created in Yugoslavia" by this time.

> The legality of the struggle of the republics and provinces for their current and long-term interests was definitively recognized in political life. The authoritative position of the federal state and of the political structure was undermined and weakened. Members of the federal administration began to listen to the political leaderships of the republics and provinces which they represented more than they took into account the interests of all.[83]

The 1967 constitutional amendments eliminated ex-officio membership on the Federal Executive Council (FEC) for the presidents of the republican executive councils because recent experience had demonstrated the incom-

[82] *Republičko savetovanje o nekim obilježjima*, pp. 127-30, 341.
[83] Bilandžić, *Ideje i Praksa*, p. 274.

patibility of dual membership in both federal and republican governments.[84] But, at the same time, the Council introduced the practice of holding "consultative meetings" with representatives of the executive councils of the republics and provinces to determine the position to be taken by the federal government on the "more important socio-economic questions." As the Chamber of Nationalities expanded its domain of competence, and regional control over its decisions increased, the need for the government to achieve inter-republican agreement on federal policy prior to its submission to the parliament also increased. Consequently, consultative meetings quickly assumed such importance that "not a single more significant issue could be presented to the Council before it had been discussed at a consultative meeting." This practice became institutionalized after 1969 with the establishment of a Co-ordinating Commission within the FEC, composed of representatives of the federal, republican, and provincial executive councils.[85]

The increased control of the republics over federal policy making sharply reduced the ability of the government to make decisions. During 1967 and 1968 enormous problems began to build up in the Yugoslav economy as the federal government, which still retained important monetary, fiscal, and taxing powers required to implement policy, was prevented from acting because of continuing disagreement between the republics over the substance of the policy to be pursued in each area. The increasingly important role of banks in the economy in general, the investment policies of banks and governments, the foreign currency exchange system, and tax policies all became the subjects of interrepublican bargaining and conflict. At the same time, growing economic problems were generating increasing dissatisfaction in the population.

In June 1968 Belgrade University students staged a week-long strike. The strike focused on the problems of growing unemployment, increasing economic inequality and materialism, and on the frustrations of the younger generation over the log-jam in career advancement caused by the near-monopoly over executive and professional positions enjoyed by the still only middle-aged, and sometimes poorly qualified cadres of the revolution. The strike received support from the provincial campuses of that university, and from the students of other universities, including Zagreb University. The student demonstrators' clearly socialist orientation toward these problems was little consolation to the political leadership faced with the task of solving them.[86]

The outside threat posed by the Soviet invasion of Czechoslovakia in August

---

[84] Hondius, *Yugoslav Community*, p. 324.

[85] Nikola Stjepanović, *Upravno Pravo SFRJ* (Beograd: Privredni Pregled, 1973), p. 166.

[86] The strike is best described in the reports of Dennison Rusinow, "Anatomy of a Student Revolt," I, II, *American Universities Fieldstaff Report*, Southeast Europe Series 15, 4 and 5 (1968).

1968 served to calm internal Yugoslav quarreling—but did not completely eliminate it. Throughout 1967 and 1968 and into 1969, the Croatian language issue simmered. Nationalists on both sides of the issue continued to exploit the freedom of action that came with the post-Ranković democratization of Yugoslav society. The same issues raised by the Declaration continued to be raised by Croat writers at conferences and meetings, and they continued to be answered by their Serb counterparts. These exchanges simply remained off the front pages of the major newspapers.[87] In the fall of 1968, large-scale riots broke out among the Albanian populations of several cities in Kosovo and northwestern Macedonia. The riots were characterized by extreme hostility between Albanians on the one hand and Serbs, Montenegrins, and Macedonians on the other. The demonstrators raised several ethnically motivated political demands, including even a demand for the right of self-determination, separation from Yugoslavia, and attachment of the Albanian-inhabited regions of Yugoslavia to Albania. One of the more moderate demands was for elevation of Kosovo's status within the Yugoslav federation to that of a Socialist Republic.[88]

The latter demand was at least partially accommodated in another series of constitutional amendments adopted in December 1968. The appellation "Socialist" was added to that of "Autonomous Province" for both Vojvodina and Kosovo, and the basic legal order of each of these regions was now to be established by a constitution separate from that for the republic of Serbia. In addition, ethnic groups with the official status of "national minorities" (Albanians and Hungarians among them) were granted the same rights—including the use of their native languages in public institutions—as the "nations" of Yugoslavia. Both Socialist Autonomous Provinces, however, remained constituent units of the Serbian republic.[89]

The 1968 amendments were undertaken largely in order to fulfill the intent of the 1967 amendments, that is, to strengthen the control of the republics and provinces over federal decision making. Even after 1967, representatives of the republics and provinces in the Chamber of Nationalities did not enjoy "sufficient influence on the formulation of federal policy." Moreover,

> the status itself of the Chamber . . . , which operated within the Federal Chamber, was rather intricate and hindered the functioning of the Assembly as a whole. The Chamber of Nationalities was not able to exercise any major influence on decision making in the Assembly, nor could it

[87] Christopher Spalatin, "Language and Politics in Yugoslavia in the Light of the Events Which Happened from March 17, 1967, to March 14, 1969," *Journal of Croatian Studies* 11-12 (1970-1971): 83-104.

[88] Peter R. Prifti, *Kosovo in Ferment* Report No. C/69-15 (Cambridge: M.I.T. Center for International Studies, June 1969), passim, but esp. p. 13.

[89] *1963 Constitution*, amends. VII, XVIII, XIX.

by itself influence the federal executive and administrative agencies in the implementation of Assembly decisions.[90]

Consequently, the regional leaderships amended the constitution to elevate the Chamber to a fully independent body and to make it the chamber of general competence instead of the Federal Chamber. All federal legislation now had to be approved by the Chamber of Nationalities.[91] The number of representatives in it was doubled, but the ratio of republican to provincial representation remained the same.

These changes led to public discussion in Yugoslavia of whether the country could be considered a "confederation."[92] Officially, this view was rejected because the amendments had not altered the rules for decision making within the Chamber. Article 181 of the 1963 constitution stipulated that "each Chamber shall take valid decisions by a majority vote at sessions attended by the majority of its members." It was argued officially, therefore, that:

> This method of decision making will prevent any possibility of the institutionalization of the delegations elected by republican and provincial assemblies, make impossible any misuse of a veto on the part of delegates from a particular republic or province, and preclude the use of a so-called imperative mandate.[93]

A more realistic Yugoslav analyst, however, viewed the operation of the Federal Assembly quite differently. The author of an empirical study of the operation of the Assembly acknowledged in 1969 that

> the fact can not be overlooked that this kind of resolution of the position and role of the Chamber of Nationalities represents, as has already been noted in the public, the introduction of certain elements of confederalism in our contemporary federal structure. Although these elements of confederalism, connected to the dominant role of the Chamber of Nationalities . . . would be more obvious if voting by delegations and the right of veto of delegations were introduced, they nevertheless cannot be completely ignored . . . because it seems hardly likely that delegates . . . will act and vote completely independently, and independently of each other, that is, [independently] of the remaining members of the delegation. The nature of the election of the delegates . . . and their attachment to the republican or provincial parliament, among other [things], points to this.[94]

[90] "Constitutional Changes in Yugoslavia," *Yugoslav Survey* 10 (August, 1969), p. 10.
[91] *1963 Constitution*, amends. VIII, IX.
[92] *Politika* (Belgrade), 24 June 1969.
[93] "Constitutional Changes in Yugoslavia," p. 10.
[94] Pavle S. Nikolić, *Savezna Skupština u Ustavnom i Političkom Sistemu Jugoslavije* (Beograd: Savez Udruženja Pravnika Jugoslavije, 1969), p. 40.

The inability of the party and government to forge interrepublican agreements on specific policy issues led by default to increased activity on the part of the reorganized federal parliament. Following the 1967 elections, debates and discussions both in the committees of the Assembly and on the floor of the chambers themselves became increasingly lively. In early 1969 a conference of assembly functionaries and legal scholars, organized in conjunction with the preparation of new internal rules of procedure for the Assembly, presented a detailed picture of the increased activity of the intervening two years. One participant suggested that, as a result of this increase,

> the committees of the chambers, in relation to the situation of only a few years ago, have become bodies which remind us in name only of their not too distant predecessors. The number and intensity of the sessions of the committees, the number and variety of questions with which they deal, and especially the lively, indeed even polemical struggle of opinions of representatives at these sessions undoubtedly speak [of the fact] that new and qualitative changes really have begun in the work of these bodies.[95]

A highly placed assembly functionary reported that representatives of federal administrative organs, the federal and republican executive councils, socio-political organizations, and self-managing enterprises interested in legislation before the Assembly, as well as representatives of scientific institutes and individual experts in fields related to legislation before the committees, were participating with increasing frequency in the work of the committees.[96] There was general agreement among all participants that not only the volume but also the scope of assembly work had increased.

While the increased activity of the Chamber of Nationalities suggested to some foreign observers at that time that Yugoslavia was moving in the direction of parliamentarism, the luxury of hindsight allows us to suggest that it would have been more accurate to suggest that the Yugoslav state was moving toward *immobilisme*. The 1967 and 1968 amendments rendered the parliament—through the Chamber of Nationalities—susceptible to the same stalemating forces that were affecting the party and government. As one Yugoslav analyst was quick to point out, "it is entirely natural and, what's more, necessary that the republican delegations, in their activity in the frame-

[95] Borivoje Pupić, "Delokrug odbora i komisija Savezne Skupštine odnosno njezinih vijeća," in Borislav T. Blagojević, ed., *Mesto i uloga odbora i komisija predstavničkih tela* (Beograd: Institut za Uporedno Pravo, 1969), p. 51.

[96] Marjan Vivoda, "Organizacija i način rada odbora Savezne i Republičkih Skupština posle donošenja Ustava SFRJ i Ustava socijalističkih republika," in Blagojević, *Mesto i uloga odbora*, pp. 96-106; and idem, "Zajednicke komisije Savezne Skupštine," in Blagojević, *Mesto i uloga odbora*, pp. 117-25.

work of the Chamber of Nationalities, must have before [their] eyes primarily the interests of [their own] republics, and only in the second place the interests of the whole; that is, the entire social community.'' Given the obvious conflicting interests of the republics, he concluded, ''it is possible to doubt the position that is useful to see in this chamber an integrative factor.''[97]

Moreover, the constitutional definition of the task of the Chamber continued to confuse both regional and nationality issues. Although now defined as ''representing the Republics and the Autonomous Provinces,'' the Chamber of Nationalities still was to be concerned with ''the equality of . . . peoples and national minorities.''[98] The Chamber, therefore, could be used legitimately as a forum for the expression of interethnic hostilities. Indeed, an analysis of the decision-making process in the Chamber of Nationalities during the period 1967-1971 carried out by an American political scientist confirms these views. Lenard Cohen suggests that

> instead of resolving conflicts, the new legislative process was reproducing faithfully the various features of the national question found outside the Federal Assembly. The representation of diverse regional and ethnic interests was being achieved in the parliamentary system, but without the reconciliation of attendant conflicts which affected the stability and survival of the Yugoslav state.[99]

By late 1968 and early 1969 the need for authoritative political leadership, immune from particularistic pressures and able to provide sober judgment, was clear. It also was clear that such leadership could be provided only by a revitalized central party organ. However, on the eve of the Ninth Party Congress in March 1969, an unusually candid—and highly critical—commentary on the continuing importance of party leadership to the operation of the political system appeared in *Politika*.[100] Although the party, according to this account, had successfully divested itself of the governing function at the enterprise and commune levels, it had not yet given up power at the republican or federal levels. At these levels,

> Self-managing bodies which ought to be the carriers of power—assemblies, executive councils, and other organs of government—almost always, when they have to make some more important decision, want to hear what the party, [that is,] its appropriate forum, thinks about it and, as a rule, that opinion will be accepted and the decision will be based on it.

[97] Nikolić, *Savezna Skupstina*, p. 39.
[98] *1963 Constitution*, amends. VIII sect. 1, XI sect. 2.
[99] Cohen, ''Conflict Management,'' p. 144.
[100] Miloš Mimica, ''Dvojnost vlast,'' *Politika* (Belgrade), 2 March 1969.

The party had stepped in to take control at each critical moment in the past year: the Belgrade student strike, the invasion of Czechoslovakia, and the riots in Kosovo. In these crisis situations the central party leadership had performed well. But the party leadership also was involved in "dilemmas which appear on the economic-social level," and it was precisely these issues on which it no longer was able to agree. As a result, this commentator suggested,

> The government, . . . accustomed to the fact that the party will jump in when the situation becomes critical, is not efficient enough and sometimes is indecisive even in situations when its action is essential.

The author of this commentary openly hinted that the solution to this problem lay in the divestiture of power by the party even at the federal level, and the transfer to the federal government of "the authority it ought to have."

On the eve of the Ninth Party Congress, when this commentary appeared, it seemed that that was exactly what was going to happen. As the leadership had decided earlier, each of the republican party organizations convened its own congress in advance of the federal one and had elected a certain number of its members to serve on the central organs of the party. Those elected to membership on the central Presidium—which was supposed to serve as an authoritative, policy-making body for the entire party—generally were not the most authoritative and powerful members of the republican organizations. Those members were elected to positions within their own republican party organizations.[101] If the Ninth Congress had unfolded as planned, that is, had these personnel assignments simply been "verified," there no longer would have been any central party organ with even a pretense to authority over the regional organizations. Moreover, there apparently would have been no formal executive body at the center of the party. The small secretariat of the Presidium envisaged in July 1968 had been eliminated from the draft party statutes submitted to the Congress.[102] In order to prevent this, President Tito acted on his own initiative to construct a more authoritative central party organ.

Immediately prior to the Congress, Tito held a series of private consultations with the leaders of the republican party organizations. At those meetings, he reported later to the delegates assembled in Belgrade for the Congress,[103]

> we arrived at the mutual view that it is necessary that we strengthen the center of the leadership of the League of Communists, and particularly

[101] Savez komunista Hrvatske (SKH), *Šesti Kongres Saveza komunista Hrvatske*, Stenographic Record, 5 vols. (Beograd: Komunist, 1969), 3: 273-92, 386-87; and SKS, *Šesti Kongres*, pp. 369-71.

[102] Martinović, *Deveti Kongres SKJ*, 1: 286-91.

[103] Ibid., pp. 49-50.

the Executive Bureau of the Presidium of the LCY, by having some current presidents and secretaries of the central committees or certain other leading comrades from all six republics come here.

This step was necessary, Tito explained, because "the new central leadership must be stronger in composition in order to be able to ensure the unity of the League of Communists and its authority." The fifty-two-member Presidium elected by the republican, provincial and army party organizations was too large and its members were too strongly subordinated to their republican and provincial constituencies to do the job. It was necessary also,

> because the League of Communists needs continuity. Some of us already have gotten on considerably in years, and in the highest leadership continuity has to be ensured, the experience of the older must be transferred to the younger.

Consequently, the new Executive Bureau of the Presidium would include "some younger comrades" and be composed of "two outstanding leaders from each republic and one from [each of] the autonomous provinces . . . together with the President of the LCY."

One witness to President Tito's speech reports that the actual words used at that moment were not "together with the President of the LCY," as appear in the official stenographic record of the Congress, but rather "and, of course, me."[104] This discrepancy highlights the difficulty of assessing the actions of the Yugoslav political leadership. Much of what occurs in any political system is determined by personalities; by relationships of personal trust, confidence, friendship, and authority among political actors. In Yugoslavia, among an elite which in large part was together for more than a generation and which was dominated by a single figure with immense personal authority, these factors played an enormously important role. Nonetheless, the evidence suggests clearly and strongly that the institutional, procedural, and personnel changes that were taking place reflected a conscious effort by members of the Yugoslav political leadership to develop a formula for the peaceful regulation of the conflicts that divided them, and to preserve the Yugoslav state intact.

Tito's action required the republican party leaderships to decide in advance of the federal congress both the kind of role they wished to see this new body play and who would be selected to serve on it.[105] The role envisaged for the

---

[104] Rusinow, *The Yugoslav Experiment*, p. 258.

[105] Members of the Executive Bureau were elected formally at the first session of the Presidium following the Congress. But since they were to be selected from among the membership of the Presidium, this required certain last-minute changes in the selections of regional representatives on the Presidium. These are reported in Martinović, *Deveti Kongres SKJ*, pp. 263-64.

new Executive Bureau varied from republic to republic and, as a result, so did the nature of the members selected to serve on it. Both the Croatian and Bosnian parties selected their two most powerful leaders to serve on the Executive Bureau—their party presidents and secretaries. The Macedonian party selected its president and a Macedonian who had spent his entire career in the federal party. The Slovenian, Serbian, and Montenegrin parties selected neither their presidents nor their secretaries. These parties selected individuals associated primarily with the federal party apparatus rather than the republics. The only exception was the selection by the Slovenian party of the then relatively unknown Stane Dolanc to accompany Edvard Kardelj into the Executive Bureau.[106]

Clearly, the new Executive Bureau was better suited than the full Presidium to fulfill the role of an integrative, leading organ for the party. It was smaller; it immediately enjoyed enormous prestige as the apparent institutional successor to President Tito; its membership was composed according to an agreed formula for representation; its members were released from other responsibilities and could focus on the solution of divisive political problems; and it was to make decisions as an independent, collegial body, taking into account the interests of all the republics and provinces. Krste Crvenkovski, elected to the new Bureau from Macedonia, reported that "in Macedonia, *as in other republics*, there were certain reservations about the new organizational forms of the leading organs of the LCY."[107] Apparently, these "reservations" reflected the fear on the part of some regional leaders that the creation of such a body inevitably would lead to a re-centralization of power within the party. However, several factors promised to prevent the Bureau from accumulating such power or even providing the unifying force for which it had been created.

First, the mixed backgrounds and uneven political stature of its members, and their relatively limited experience working directly with one another, made it unlikely that they shared the degree of mutual trust that would allow them immediately to overcome the conflicting interests that divided them. Second, the members of the Bureau could not simultaneously hold positions in their respective republican and provincial party organizations. The work of the Bureau, which was to meet at least weekly to discuss and dispose of political problems, required them to remain in Belgrade. Third, membership in the Bureau was determined not by cooptation or election by the other members, but by nomination of the regional party organizations. These conditions severely undermined the ability of even the most powerful Bureau members to influence, let alone control, events within their own republics, and required the politically less powerful members to be at least as responsive

---

[106] *Politika* (Belgrade), 17 March 1969.
[107] Ibid., 25 March 1969 (emphasis added).

to their respective regional party organizations as to the views of their colleagues on the Bureau. These conditions certainly undermined their ability to ensure the implementation in their respective regions of any agreement they might reach in the Bureau that infringed on regional interests. Finally, the responsibilities of the Bureau were so broad that almost every divisive issue fell within its domain. As a result, other institutions and organizations that in the past had acted to control conflicts within their own territories or organizations began to defer action until the issue had been discussed in the Executive Bureau. Consequently, the Bureau rapidly became overworked. Thus, in the words of a later party report on the work of the central party organs following this congress, despite Tito's attempt to prevent the disintegration of the central party leadership,

> the LCY was reduced to a coalition of republican and provincial organizations and the Presidium of the LCY to a place for mutual informing and consulting without obligation or responsibility for the realization of a mutually established uniform policy.[108]

The changes adopted at the Ninth Party Congress, in effect, institutionalized the existence of eight distinct blocs in the Yugoslav political system, each defined by reinforcing national, economic, and territorial-political cleavages, and led by its own communist party organization. A less clearly defined, but certainly no less important, bloc was composed of the central party-political leadership. It included members of the party leadership who had made their careers primarily in the center rather than a region, the most prominent among them being Tito and Kardelj, and prominent members of the federal government; party figures who had based their careers primarily in a regional leadership but were closely allied with and supportive of the center, such as Vladimir Bakarić of Croatia; and the leadership of the party organization in the military. Decisions in central political organs now were to be based on negotiations among representatives of these blocs.

By March 1969, it was clear that the interests of several of the blocs were in direct conflict on a number of critical policy issues and that the level of hostility between them was increasing on both the mass and elite levels. But, despite joint efforts to devise institutional and procedural provisions for the regulation of interbloc conflict and efforts by members of the central leadership bloc to mediate among them, their representatives could not establish the overarching cooperation by which the economic conflicts dividing them might have been resolved. Instead, their leaderships acted in ways that aggravated those conflicts. As a result, conflict between the blocs became dominated by the national cleavages that divided them. There was an explosion of inter-

[108] Emil Rojc et al., eds., *Deseti Kongres SKJ: Dokumenti* (Beograd: Komunist, 1974), p. 495.

nationality hostility and a concomitant breakdown of political institutions and processes. Communist elite politics began to resemble the politics character-istic of the interwar kingdom more closely than the politics of either the communist resistance movement or the first two decades of postwar rule.

Unlike the elites of interwar Yugoslavia, however, the legitimacy of the communists' claim to political power rested squarely on their successful suppression of inter-nationality conflict under the difficult conditions of war and revolution, and its continuing regulation in the postwar period, rather than on the representation of any one set of ethnic interests over the others. This was why the conservative opposition to reform led by Ranković was doomed to failure; even had it won the struggle for power inside the party itself, it was too closely associated with traditional Serbian interests to preserve social peace and thereby retain legitimacy. Changes since the ouster of Ran-ković, however, now made the task of preserving that peace more difficult.

Each of the regional communist leaderships would have to represent and defend the interests of its constituency if it was not to lose power to potential nationalist movements and their leaders. This required still further changes in the organization and operation of the party itself, and the broader political system—changes in the direction of further decentralization. But Tito and the other members of the bloc of central party-political leaders seemed unwilling or unable to recognize the extent to which power had already passed unal-terably to the regional leaderships, and were as yet unwilling to permit any further movement in this direction. For further decentralization might call into question the basic operating principles by which the Yugoslav party preserved its internal coherence in the face of social complexity and, as a result, retained power. Moreover, further governmental decentralization might call into question the continuing survival of Yugoslavia as a single state—without which, the *raison d'être* of the party ceased to exist. Hence, Tito's creation of the Executive Bureau, a rearguard action intended to recreate a "political center" along the lines of the pre-1966 Executive Committee. It apparently was not until this "solution" failed that Tito and his supporters at the center were willing to concede additional power to the regions and to experiment with new forms of party and state organization in the search for formulas by which to regulate inter-nationality conflict.

The success of this experiment required the regional leaderships to remain responsive to both regional pressures and central considerations. But, by the time it began, they had been affected by the social forces released following the ouster of Ranković and had become more responsive to the former than to the latter. It would require, therefore, the forceful application of central power and authority to restore the balance between them, and thereby re-impose social peace, and preserve communist power.

III. THE "YUGOSLAV CRISIS":
NATIONAL, ECONOMIC,
AND IDEOLOGICAL CONFLICT AND
THE BREAKDOWN OF ELITE COOPERATION,
1969-1972

The Ninth Party Congress of March 1969 was followed by a period of pro-
longed conflict both between and within the nine blocs into which Yugoslavia
had become divided. At the mass level, inter-nationality hostilities continued
to intensify and, by mid-1971, threatened to erupt in renewed fratricidal war.
Such war promised not only to tear Yugoslavia apart but to destroy several
of the republics and provinces, as well. Among the leadership, conflicts arising
out of the opposing economic interests of the regions were complicated by
the party's continuing commitment to the seemingly incompatible goals of
extending economic and political reforms on the one hand, and equalizing
the levels of development of the regions on the other. Each goal seemed to
preclude the other, but neither could be easily abandoned. Reconciliation of
conflicting regional interests was made even more difficult by the growing
subordination of individuals in central institutions to their respective regional
constituencies. Central decision-making bodies no longer could develop solutions autonomously and impose them directly but were dependent on the
regional leaderships both to ratify such solutions and to enforce them. However, organizational changes in the regions weakened the ability, and rising
nationalism among the peoples of Yugoslavia weakened the resolve of those
leaderships to do so.

Following the Ninth Congress, nationalist attention in Yugoslavia shifted
from traditional cultural concerns to the defense of regional economic interests. Inter-nationality conflict became linked to economic and ideological
issues, reinforcing existing divisions within the leadership based on continuing
disputes over the economic powers and policies of the federation. In response
to the stalemate produced by these divisions, the leadership redefined the
areas of decision making subject to the autonomous authority of central bodies,
the areas subject to joint decision making by regional representatives in central
bodies, and those subject to autonomous control by the individual regions.

This was accomplished by once again amending the constitution. However, unlike those adopted in 1967 and 1968, the 1971 amendments represented a fundamental redefinition of the character of the Yugoslav state.

Within a few months of their adoption, however, it became clear to the members of the central leadership and to some regional leaders that the agreement on which the amendments were based had failed. It did not resolve the major conflicts then dividing them and did not seem to provide a mechanism for the regulation of future conflicts. Moreover, it appeared to them that that agreement could not succeed unless certain conditions changed, and that these conditions were unlikely to change for the better unless they themselves acted to change them. Consequently, this coalition, under the renewed leadership of President Tito, acted together to impose the changes necessary to implement the agreement embodied in the 1971 amendments.

Their actions were precipitated by the threat of civil war and disintegration of the Yugoslav state posed by events in Croatia, and resulted first in the dramatic, forced resignations of the leading members of the Croatian political leadership in December 1971 and a widespread purge of the party and other social and political organizations in that republic. As a result, the entire period from the Ninth Congress to 1972 has come to be referred to as the "Croatian crisis." But the "Croatian crisis" should more accurately be called "the Yugoslav crisis," for its underlying causes were to be found not only in Croatia and in the behavior of Croatian political leaders but also in the behavior of other Yugoslav political actors and in conditions elsewhere in Yugoslavia; it was accompanied by widespread and dramatic changes in the organization and operation of the Yugoslav political system; and it began with the explosion of national discontent not in Croatia, but in Slovenia.

The League of Communists on The Eve of Crisis

In the League of Communists as a whole, the period between the Eighth Congress held in December 1964 and the Ninth Congress held in March 1969 was one of enormous changes not only in organization and procedure but also in membership. While the party did not change dramatically in total size, its composition changed in important ways. The proportion of members defined as "workers" declined steadily during this period, while the proportion of "employees," or white-collar workers, increased steadily. The number of members excluded from the party each year remained essentially constant during this period. The number of voluntary resignations of membership, however, increased steadily. More than fifty percent of both those who resigned and those who were excluded belonged to the broad social category "workers." However, "workers" constituted only about a third or less of the new members accepted during these years. At the same time, an opposite

84

and stronger process was taking place among members classified as "employees," or white-collar workers. As a consequence, the party gradually was changing from a party of the working class to a party of the white-collar, managerial, and intellectual strata.[1]

Resignations and exclusions changed more than the class composition of the party. They also reinforced the reformist orientation of the party. The increase in voluntary resignations after 1966 was in large part a reaction to the political reforms carried out in the post-Ranković period. The party's commission for membership affairs reported to the Ninth Congress that:

> A significant number of members resigned from the League because they could not comprehend that the basic force of the League is [found] in its ideo-political activity, and not in positions of power and command. In their opinion the League should decide more directly about all the more important questions. Such views lead individuals into conflict with the organization, because of which disciplinary measures are taken against them. Revolted by such a situation, unable to see the error of their positions, they decide to quit the League of Communists.[2]

Exclusions were motivated primarily by the failure of members to remain active or to pay dues. However, they also were "in part a result of the effort of the organization of the LC to free itself of members who for various reasons became a brake on contemporary processes in the League of Communists."[3] In this way, elements opposed to the political liberalization of the post-1966 period left the party in large numbers during the period preceding the Ninth Congress.

The August 1968 Soviet invasion of Czechoslovakia prompted a massive influx of new members into the party. Up to that point, the number of new members accepted each year had been declining. During the first six months of 1968 only 20,953 new members had been accepted. By December, however, that figure had grown to 145,487; almost thirteen percent of the total end-of-year party membership of 1,119,307. The 1968 enrollment consisted of generally younger persons, reversing a long-term trend toward the "aging" of the party. More than eighty percent of the new members accepted during 1968 were aged twenty-five or younger, and over thirty percent were students or working apprentices.[4]

The party became younger in 1968 not only in terms of the age of its members, but also in terms of the organizational experience of its cadres. More than seventy-five percent of the 1,093 delegates elected to the Ninth

---

[1] Martinović, *Deveti Kongres SKJ*, 1:214, 218, 219, 246.
[2] Ibid., p. 230.
[3] Ibid., p. 215.
[4] Ibid., pp. 218, 245-46.

Congress in 1969 occupied two or more socio-political positions. Yet ninety percent of them had never before participated at a congress of the Yugoslav party. Only eighteen percent had even participated at a republican party congress, and more than seventy percent of these had participated at only one such congress; probably one held only a few months earlier. The delegates also were surprisingly young. Fifty percent were twenty-eight to forty years of age. Eighty-two percent were aged forty-five or younger. But these delegates were not new to the party. Only about twelve percent of them had joined the party since 1963. Their lack of organizational experience was a reflection not of their youthfulness, but of the widespread turnovers that had taken place among middle- and lower-level cadres since 1966. This relative inexperience among the party's own cadres may have been another factor in Tito's decision to establish an Executive Bureau. For these young, untested cadres would be facing difficult political decisions in the years ahead.[5]

The same processes were taking place within each of the republican party organizations. In both Croatia and Serbia the proportion of workers among the party membership had declined steadily, and the proportion of "employees" had increased steadily in the period since 1964. Immediately following the Fourth Plenum in 1966, the Serbian reformist leadership undertook a limited purge of their party. They excluded 129 members from the party for opposition to the reform, and gave disciplinary "warnings" to 159 others.[6] Voluntary resignations during 1967 were almost double what they had been in 1965. The Serbian party's Control Commission made only oblique references to political motivations for such resignations in its report to the Sixth Congress of the Serbian League of Communists in November 1968. Similarly, the Croatian party's Control Commission down-played political motivations for the increasing number of resignations of its members in its report to the Sixth Congress of the League of Communists of Croatia in December.[7] But in both reports it was clear that opposition to the political reforms undertaken since 1966 had increased the rate of resignations.

All the republican party congresses were convened before final membership data could be compiled for 1968. But the Serbian party did report in November that "according to incomplete data, in the first nine months of this year 31,672 youths were accepted into the League of Communists of Serbia; of that, 23,851 just in the last three months."[8] Similar post-Czechoslovakia enrollments must have been taking place in other republics as well. These changes were making these republican parties, like the party as a whole, younger, more educated and less experienced.

[5] Martinović, *Deveti Kongres SKJ*, 2: 2-6.

[6] SKS, *Šesti Kongres*, p. 339.

[7] Ibid., pp. 341ff. SKH, *Šesti Kongres*, 1:161ff.

[8] SKS, *Šesti Kongres*, p. 276.

At the same time, organizational changes carried out in the republics during this period reduced leadership control over the general membership. The number of basic party organizations in the republics was reduced radically after 1967. In Croatia, the number of such organizations was reduced by 53.3 percent. From 1965 to 1968, the number of professional political functionaries in Serbia dropped from 510 to 303. In Croatia, their number fell from 773 to 539.[9] As a result, lower-level party functionaries became responsible for the supervision and control of larger numbers of party members. As can be seen from Table 3.1, below, a relatively large proportion of the membership in Croatia became concentrated in a relatively small number of local territorial organizations in urban areas.

Even more important, however, was the simultaneous establishment of a new type of party organization called—in Croatia—the inter-*općina* (commune) conference. Created in order to improve coordination between basic organizations on issues of mutual concern, these conferences interposed a layer of party functionaries between the central republican leadership and the basic party organizations. In Croatia, one of these conferences was created for each of eight regions and for the city of Zagreb.[10] Thus, not only did supervision of the party membership by professional cadres become more difficult during this period, but so did supervision of local functionaries by

TABLE 3.1

Organizational Change in the Croatian Party

Type of Party Organization	Number of Organizations			Membership After Reorg.	
	Before Reorg.	After Reorg.	Percent of Orgs.	Total	Percent of Total
Economic	3,854	1,778	46.6	96,370	44.7
Non-Economic	1,079	535	13.9	18,865	8.8
Secondary & Higher Ed.	192	68	1.8	7,617	3.5
Local Rural	2,318	1,134	29.6	41,790	19.4
Local Urban	769	321	8.4	50,857	23.6
Total	8,212	3,836	100.0	215,499	100.0

SOURCE: Savez komunista Hrvatske, *Šesti Kongres Saveza komunista Hrvatske*, Stenographic Records, 5 vols. (Beograd: Komunist, 1969), 1:90.

[9] Ibid., p. 362; SKH, *Šesti Kongres*, 1:102.
[10] Ibid., pp. 93-94.

the leadership. In Croatia, the central leadership of the republican party organization was weakened further by the unexpected removal to Belgrade of its two most authoritative members—Vladimir Bakarić and Miko Tripalo—to join the new Executive Bureau created by Tito at the Ninth Congress.

The Slovene Road-Building Crisis and the Breakdown of Elite Cooperation in the Government

Despite Tito's efforts to the contrary, power still resided in the republics following the Ninth Congress. That power was demonstrated almost immediately by the difficulty Mitja Ribičič, the newly designated president of the Federal Executive Council (premier), encountered when he undertook the task of negotiating with the republics and provinces over the formation of a new government. The leaderships of the republics could all agree on only one point: each was to have equal representation on the Council just as they had on the party's Executive Bureau. The larger republics no longer would enjoy more numerous representation on the Council, as they had had up to then.[11] There was little agreement, however, concerning who those members were to be or what positions they were to occupy.

The political leaderships of the republics clearly were reluctant to release their most capable cadres for service in the offices of the federation. Those they were willing to release generally were either older cadres who had to be moved out of the republics in order to make room for younger people, or "leftover cadres" for whom no position could be found in the republic. At the same time, capable cadres were themselves not anxious to give up a republican position for a federal one.[12]

The republics did, however, seek to place competent cadres in administrative and executive posts in the federal government from which they could influence economic policy. This led to intense interrepublican competition over these positions. Ribičič reported after about a month of negotiations that "he had spent more than half his time in discussion about the so-called first vice-president for current economic affairs and on discussion of certain positions in the economic secretariats [ministries] in the center." This competition suggested to Ribičič that the regional leaderships believed "it is really possible in our society, by taking over certain positions in some economic or administrative organs, to exert pressure on the division of resources."[13]

The process by which the federal government divided the resources at its disposal among the republics and provinces became the subject of a serious political crisis only a few months later, when dissatisfaction in Slovenia over

[11] *Politika* (Belgrade), 3 April 1969.
[12] Ibid., 10 and 19 March 1969.
[13] Ibid., 3 April 1969.

a Federal Executive Council (FEC) decision concerning the funding of road construction projects in that republic erupted in July in "a real wave of protest" that threatened the collapse of the federal government. The events of "the Slovene road-building crisis" demonstrate clearly the extent to which the federal government had become vulnerable to attacks from local, republic, ethnic, and economic forces; the rapidity with which such conflicts could take on interrepublican dimensions; and the extent to which federal decision makers had become subordinated to, and dependent on, their regional constituencies.

Modernization of the road network in Yugoslavia had received substantial support from the World Bank in the past. During 1968 and early 1969 each of the republics and provinces submitted proposals for road construction projects to the FEC for inclusion in the new Yugoslav application to the Bank for funding. At its session of 26 March 1968, the Council decided to submit three of these projects for funding. At its meeting of 17 July, the FEC submitted three more of these projects for funding. Certain road construction projects proposed by Slovenia were not included in either proposal. Their absence from the second group "was received [in Slovenia] with criticism and protests the likes of which cannot be remembered in postwar Yugoslav practice."[14]

Protest meetings were held in extraordinary sessions of commune assemblies, work collectives, and socio-political organizations in all areas of Slovenia. In the presence of members of the republican and federal assemblies and representatives of socio-political organizations, letters of protest to the Republican Assembly of Slovenia, the republican Executive Council, and the FEC were drafted, demanding immediate reversal of the decision not to submit the Slovenian projects for funding. At several meetings, it was proposed that "federal representatives of Slovenia resign their mandates if the Federal Executive Council does not change its decision." Political functionaries of several communes even went so far as to suggest publicly that "we in Slovenia are prepared even to put forward the question of confidence in the Federal Executive Council."[15] In addition, certain "chauvinistic" and "nationalistic" demands were expressed at these meetings. A careful reading of later criticisms of these meetings by leading party officials in Slovenia suggests that perhaps even separatist demands were raised.[16]

In response to these widespread demonstrations of popular discontent, the republican Executive Council met on 31 July. The Council issued a statement calling on the FEC to reverse its decision on the grounds that it had not been

[14] Ibid., 31 July 1969.

[15] Ibid.

[16] Separatist demands are suggested, for example, by the Slovenian party president's attack on "the illusory idea" of "a separate, socialist Slovenia," reported in *Borba* (Belgrade), 3 September 1969.

made in accordance with established procedures for issues affecting the interests of more than one republic. The Slovenian Executive Council received widespread support. The next day, a group of political functionaries met under the auspices of the republican conference of the Socialist Alliance of Slovenia and issued a statement of support that condemned "the practice and methods of decision making of the Federal Executive Council in the case of the construction of roadways" as "unacceptable." At the same time, the Management Board of the Chamber of Commerce of Slovenia convened an extraordinary session and issued a statement "in the name of the entire economy of the republic" demanding that the FEC change its decision immediately. A few days later the Slovenian Executive Council received the full support of the leadership of the republican assembly.[17]

The Slovenian party leadership, meeting in an expanded session of the Central Committee secretariat that included the president of the Slovenian party (Franc Popit) and the president of the Slovenian Central Committee's commission for socio-economic questions (Zvone Dragan), issued a more carefully balanced statement.[18] Probably uncertain of exactly what transpired in the Federal Executive Council, it began with what was, under the circumstances, a comparatively mild criticism of the Council:

> the problem which has arisen because of the recent decision of the FEC and similar problems, show that in Yugoslavia, as a multinational community, it is necessary to develop the method of patient, open and equal agreement making and mutual understanding. The practice which is seen in the recent decision of the FEC, however, . . . shows that that is not the situation. There have appeared, namely, old and out-lived methods.

Certainly fully informed of what was happening in their own republic, the Slovenian party leaders went on to suggest that public reaction to the decision, although justified, included "various nationalistic, chauvinistic, and other negative tendencies" that were problematic. Finally, they constructed their conclusion very carefully: "The secretariat thinks that it is essential that the Federal Executive Council once again and argumentatively discuss the project." In this way, the Slovenian party leadership carefully balanced their dual responsibilities to their republican constituency, on the one hand, and to their colleagues in the central party organs, on the other. By pointing out that certain nationalistic tendencies had been expressed, the Slovenian leadership emphasized the boundaries of acceptable behavior. By stopping short of calling for a reversal of the decision, they preserved their options for future action.

[17] Ibid., 2 and 5 August 1969.
[18] Ibid., 2 August 1969.

The degree to which members of the FEC were by this time more closely bound to their respective republican constituencies than members of the party leadership is reflected in the extremely carefully worded statement issued by Marko Bulc, a member of the Federal Executive Council from Slovenia who was on vacation in that republic when the popular protest meetings began. Isolated from his Council colleagues and confronted with obvious discontent in his own republic, Bulc was in no position to oppose either. Consequently, he made an essentially noncommittal statement to the press:

> The details of this decision of the Federal Executive Council are not known to me because I was not present at that session. It is difficult for me to believe that it was possible to accept such a decision, because at three earlier sessions of the Federal Executive Council, at which I personally was present, the proposal in which international help was anticipated for the construction of [these roads] always was accepted. . . . These decisions represented the agreed policy of the federation with the republics. If this time a different decision was accepted, then additional, new and documented argument for it was necessary, which is not known to me. I think it would be good to examine the whole thing again.[19]

Premier Ribičič, also a Slovene, was on vacation on the Slovenian coast at the time of these protests. On 31 July he met with a delegation of presidents of local commune assemblies and representatives of local socio-political organizations to discuss the decision.[20] Because of the seriousness of the continuing public protests, he met with newsmen the next day to issue a long statement defending the actions of the Federal Executive Council. It had become routine practice by this time for the Council to submit important issues to interrepublican negotiations prior to decision, and Ribičič emphasized that the decisions of the Council concerning proposals to the World Bank were made in accordance with the results of such negotiations. He argued that the actions of the Council were consistent with decisions "made in connection with this during the course of 1968 and most recently in March 1969" and "did not deviate from the principles that were adopted not only in the highest federal forums, but also in agreement with all republics; and that is the principle of parity for all . . . previously accepted projects."[21]

Ribičič acknowledged that at their sessions of 27 December 1968 and 13 March 1969 the members of the Federal Executive Council had agreed to submit seven proposals to the World Bank, including the Slovenian project. But he noted that the Council agreed to submit only those proposals that

---

[19] *Politika* (Belgrade), 31 July 1969.

[20] Ibid.

[21] This excerpt and all those that follow are from the text published in *Borba* (Belgrade), 2 August 1969.

fulfilled two major and necessary preconditions: "republican funds were secured and the proposal was prepared according to world norms." He pointed out that "projections for [the Slovenian project now in dispute] . . . were not completed, and because of that they were not considered." He explained further that

The Federal Executive Council did not find it necessary to consult once again with the republics because positions already had been agreed to earlier. The accelerated decision-making process [by which the decision was made not to submit the Slovenian proposal] was conditioned in the first place by the need to send quickly to the World Bank (at its request) proposals for projects. . . . Every delay could have had the effect of delaying for at least three months and possibly even for a longer time the adoption of a decision by the World Bank.

Ribičič attempted to mollify public anger by suggesting that the decision was not necessarily irreversible. The Slovenian road projects, he argued, "are the most serious candidates for the next allocation" of funds. And he pointed to "the possibility of a direct agreement among the republics whose roads have been proposed that one of them transfer their right to Slovenia." In addition, he noted, there were more formal methods for changing federal decisions. At its next regular meeting in the middle of August, the Federal Executive Council "will, in agreement with the Executive Council of Slovenia, seek a concrete solution if the arguments of the Executive Council of Slovenia are convincing."

The statement by Premier Ribičič did little to calm the situation. As he himself recognized,

The problem of construction of the road by itself did not cause the present dissatisfaction in Slovenia. It also concerns the fact that Slovenia, as the most developed republic, also most clearly feels the ever-present compromises and inconsistencies in the carrying out of the economic reform. . . . It should not be forgotten, however, that certain negative elements who seek and want to draw from the situation their [own] conclusion associate themselves with these positive pressures.

The resolution of this conflict, therefore, would require more than action by the central leadership. It would require a concerted effort by the Slovenian political leaders. But they were as yet unprepared to take such action.

The day after publication of Ribičič's statement, *Delo*, the major Slovenian daily, published a front-page editorial that promised a dramatic expansion of the scope of the conflict. This disagreement, *Delo* suggested, "does not concern only the two disputed sections [of road] but is primarily about material-financial relationships between Slovenia and the Federation." The editorial suggested that "the disputed road opened and sharpened a circle of questions which concern the position and relations of the Republic of Slovenia in the wider Yugoslav community, [and] which already have been current for a long time."[22]

Indeed, the scope of the conflict already was expanding, for the political leaderships of other republics were becoming involved in it. On 1 August, the Executive Council of Croatia "stated with regret that this important decision was taken without prior agreement with the republics, in other words, in a manner which differs from the normal and until now customary practice in such and similar situations."[23] On 4 August, the City Committee of the League of Communists of Skopje met in an expanded session to discuss the situation in Slovenia. It condemned events there and called for the intervention of central party organs.[24] The Skopje City Committee announced its position in a letter to the Executive Bureau of the party, whose contents were revealed a few days later. The letter was uncompromisingly supportive of the FEC decision and strongly critical of events in Slovenia. The Macedonian argument is worth presenting in some detail, for it reflects the simultaneous commitment of that underdeveloped republic's leadership to both the federalization of political power inherent in the reforms of the 1960s and the maintenance of a strong federal center. The letter read, in part,

> If some socio-political community [i.e., republic or province] is not satisfied with a decision of a federal organ, our system of self-management has regular channels through which disagreements can be overcome. However, in recent instances of pressure we see an absence of self-managing mentality in our political decisions, which can be seen in a clash between individual and mutual interests.
>
> Conflicts and polemics do not worry us . . . because they are inherent in a self-managing society. However, we are worried by the fact that in this instance, in these conflicts, tendencies are strongly present which, by directly non-democratic forms and by organized pressure, impose their own problems. . . . Tendencies to impose decisions under organized public pressure and by means of an ultimatum which makes it impossible for these decisions to be the result of a dialogue among equals are foreign to our system.
>
> There is no doubt that constructive criticism of the decisions of certain organs of the federation and the republics has a positive influence on their decisions. . . . However, if a decision of some representative or executive organ is based on the ostensible conclusions or resolutions of

[22] As cited, ibid., 4 August 1969.
[23] Ibid., 2 August 1969.
[24] Ibid., 5 August 1969.

a representative body in which all republics are represented, then organized public pressure against that decision, outside of these institutionalized forms, represents the misuse of selfmanaging democracy.[25]

In Serbia, *Nedeljne Informativne Novine* (*NIN*), the influential and widely read Belgrade news weekly, presented a highly critical commentary on the events in Slovenia. It conceded that "the policies, decisions, and methods of those who perform public functions" were legitimately open to public discussion, but argued that "it could not be said that that which socio-political organizations of Slovenia have done is normal and in the spirit of the principles which we support." The commentary then went on to place a more sinister interpretation on the events:

> No matter how much the extraordinary political meetings, protest letters . . . and threats of resignations . . . are presented as the spontaneous reaction of the Slovenian public, the impression is inescapable that this is the result of organized political pressure on the Federal Executive Council to annul a decision taken in a normal manner and by a normal procedure.[26]

These reactions, and especially the strong reaction of the Macedonian party leadership, put enormous pressure on the Slovenian party leadership to act. Yet they remained reluctant to intervene against the still-growing public protests. They insisted that the intervention called for by the Macedonian leadership was unnecessary "at the present time" and that:

> elected social organs, the republican assemblies and their executive councils, are in a position to . . . find a satisfying solution . . . and that it is necessary to give them full support in this and not to turn the whole thing onto a purely political track.
>
> . . . .
>
> In this concrete situation and as far as things stand now, it would be neither desirable nor in the spirit of our selfmanaging system for any party forum to interfere directly in the operational affairs of state organs. Instead of this, it is recommended that party organs and individual communists strive to create a better climate so that state and social organs could more consistently and responsibly solve all questions which are of interest for the realization of the goals of the reform and the economic-political equality of the republics.[27]

But by this time "elected social organs, the republican assemblies and their executive councils" already had committed themselves to positions that were

[25] Ibid., 8 August 1969.
[26] *NIN*, 3 August 1969.
[27] *Borba* (Belgrade), 6 August 1969.

difficult to reconcile with the position of the Federal Executive Council. With the next regular meeting of the FEC not scheduled for more than a week, with protests in Slovenia continuing, and with the Macedonian demand for action in hand, it was becoming difficult for the central party leadership not to act. But action by the party did not promise to be easy, for it was reported that "representatives of Slovenia, should it come to it, would be prepared to explain and defend their positions and demands even in the highest organ of the LCY." Just two days later, however, they were given the opportunity to do so.

On 7 August, under the chairmanship of President Tito, the Executive Bureau of the Presidium of the League of Communists of Yugoslavia met in an expanded session on the island of Brioni. In addition to the members of the Executive Bureau, the session was attended by the presidents of the central committees of the republican party organizations, the president of the Federal Assembly, the president and other functionaries of the Federal Executive Council, and the presidents of the republican executive councils. It constituted, in effect, a joint meeting of the party and government leaderships of both the federation and the republics. The introductory address was delivered by Premier Ribičič and consisted of an explanation of the Federal Executive Council's decision.[28] The meeting did not produce a dramatic confrontation between republican political leaderships or between the Slovenian leadership and the central leadership. Rather, it resulted in an anticlimactic show of support for the Federal Executive Council.

The explanation offered by Ribičič undoubtedly was similar to that adopted by the whole Council on 13 August and made public on 15 August. That explanation consisted of a long and detailed report on the series of decisions on this matter taken by the Council since early 1968.[29] "At the time of the adoption and submission of the [original] requests to the World Bank," the report explained, "it was certain that because of the amount of funds required, the entire program could not be realized in the framework of a single loan." Consequently, the FEC decided in late December 1968 to submit in April 1969 only those projects that met the World Bank's requirements for "technical and economic documentation making possible use of the loan in business year 1968-69." At the same time, the Council decided that "the remaining projects . . . , if they are completed by the end of September 1969, . . . will be included at that time." On the basis of this decision, the report continued, six projects including the disputed Slovenian project were submitted to the World Bank for funding. However, the Bank itself decided that "according to the preparedness of the projects themselves as well as the availability of funding at that time" only certain of the proposed projects qualified for

[28] Ibid., 9 August 1969.

[29] The following account is based on the text published in ibid., 15 September 1969.

funding. The Slovenian project was not among them. "The Federal Executive Council, at its session of 26 March 1969, adopted the World Bank's proposal that these sections [of road] be the object of the [next] loan."

The Federal Executive Council directed the federal secretariats for the economy and for finance to "take all necessary measures" to ensure that the remaining projects would be prepared in time for the fourth allocation of funds in September. Eight proposals, including the disputed Slovenian project, were prepared. But:

> In its letter of 30 June, which arrived at the responsible federal organs 11 July 1969, the World Bank . . . pointed out that in terms of their preliminary estimate of costs the eight announced sections of road were too wide to serve as the basis for the next loan, and requested that the Yugoslav government select projects within the framework of the announced limit of expenditures for the loan. The World Bank . . . made the arrival of its technical team, announced for the beginning of September, contingent on notification of the selection of projects, and on that notification reaching them by the end of July at the very latest.

The Slovenian project was eliminated a second time both because it was too expensive and because the proposal for it could not be completed before the revised, earlier deadline set by the World Bank.

Yugoslavia's application to the World Bank for funding for 1969, the FEC report continued,

> included some of the roads from the established program with the highest intensity of traffic, . . . and certain projects in the insufficiently developed areas with a lesser intensity of traffic, which is completely in accord with realization of the bases of economic policy for 1969 [adopted by the Federal Assembly], according to which it is necessary to give a certain priority for credits from the World Bank . . . to projects from those areas.

Therefore, the report pointed out, the Federal Executive Council "did not in any way change the already adopted and harmonized complete program . . . nor did it deviate from any part of this program." The Council concluded its report by pointing out that it intended to submit the remaining sections of the road construction program, "whose technical and economic documentation will be completed by September of this year," for funding in the next loan competition, "and will attempt to conclude that loan by the end of 1970."

The Executive Bureau supported the FEC decision as explained by Ribičič and issued a relatively short statement. The Bureau emphasized that "capable and efficient organs of the federation, which makes decisions autonomously within the framework of their competencies, correspond to the interests of all our peoples," and expressed the belief that "the controversial questions surrounding the financing of further road construction will be straightened out and successfully settled in the responsible federal organs and on the basis of agreement with the republics." The Bureau adopted a relatively low-key condemnation of the events in Slovenia, and pointed to a fundamental lesson to be learned from the crisis:

> The Executive Bureau emphasizes the importance of providing timely, objective, and detailed information to the working people about measures proposed or taken in all self-managing organs and political organizations, and especially in organs of the federation, considering the fact that decisions which they make have an impact on inter-nationality relations.[30]

Franc Popit, president of the Slovenian party, affirmed the Slovenian party leadership's commitment to uphold the decision of the Executive Bureau. At a later meeting of the Bureau he reported that in Slovenia people were coming to realize

> that the president of the Federal Executive Council as well as all other members of the FEC and representatives of the administration in the federation, must have an equal understanding for the interests of their own republic and for the interests of any other republic and that, understandably, they cannot be the exponents of partial interests.

But this realization did not come easily. Popit pointedly remarked that communal and republican party activists in Slovenia accepted the central Executive Bureau's findings only after reading the stenographic record of that meeting. "The reading of the stenographic record," he reported, "contributed to the calming down of the first reaction to the communiqué of the Executive Bureau."[31]

The Executive Council of Slovenia suggested later that the lack of full information played an important role in the Slovenian events. In its own report on the causes of the conflict,[32] the Slovenian Council explained that

> Since the sections of road . . . were not mentioned in the decision of the FEC and in no other form was there offered any explanation of why they were removed, the impression arose that the Federal Executive Council had changed the already agreed-on program. Such an impression arose especially because, on the basis of previous announcements, there dominated the belief that all remaining sections of road from the accepted program would be included.

[30] Ibid., 9 August 1969.
[31] Ibid., 3 September 1969.
[32] The following account is based on the text published in ibid., 6 September 1969.

97

But Ribičič's report to the party's Executive Bureau made it clear that no such change had been made. Indeed, the Slovenian Council went on to note that the announcement of the FEC revealed "certain important new circumstances which were not known earlier."

The Slovenian Executive Council followed the lead of the party's Executive Bureau by suggesting that "these disagreements and misunderstandings probably would not have arisen had all these questions been cleared up in prior consultations or at the session of the FEC of 16 and 17 July 1969." But it carried its own analysis of the reasons why this disagreement assumed crisis proportions so rapidly one step further. The Slovenian Executive Council laid the blame squarely on the shoulders of the political leadership of the republic. "In addition to all of this," the Council pointed out, "there came to expression defects in the work of representative and self-managing organs, including the republican Executive Council."

If a system based on "the method of patient, open and equal agreement making and mutual understanding" among regional leaderships is to work, each party to an agreement must enforce that agreement in its own constituency. The political leadership of Slovenia clearly had failed to do this, and it recognized its own failure:

> the [Slovenian] Executive Council states and regrets that, in the period from 22 July when Tanjug [the Yugoslav news agency] reported the news to 29 July when there appeared widespread reactions in the public and at meetings of selfmanaging organs, it did not repeatedly and more resolutely request from the FEC an explanation and clarification of the decision of 17 July with which it could have prevented the later development of events.

In explaining its failure, the Slovenian Executive Council observed that "political presssures make sober judgment difficult."

But in the period since 1966 political pressure had become an almost commonplace feature of Yugoslav politics. After the "Slovene crisis" had subsided, Premier Ribičič observed that "these pressures are not something new in our society."

> I am not the first president of the FEC who has been a target of his native republic. Stambolić [premier 1965-1967] also was such a target. We all know what the situation was like with comrade Špiljak [1967-1969], under what kind of difficult conditions he worked. And right at the beginning problems arose in relations between me and political organizations in my own native republic.[33]

[33] *NIN*, 21 September 1969.

Such pressures, he suggested, could be overcome through interrepublican bargaining prior to the adoption of policy. But even such bargaining would not avert conflict if the parties to these bargains could not be counted on to support them.

> From the very beginning, the Federal Executive Council was forced to confront its own positions with [those of] some republican executive councils and certain economic groups. We reconciled differences at consultative meetings with the presidents of the republican executive councils. We achieved at the outset a relatively high [level of] agreement. . . . But certain agreements [made] in the center and with the participation of the presidents of republican executive councils did not last very long because they depended on the authorization of the republican leaderships. . . . I think that we cannot work in the federation if we must verify again every decision which is in line with the realization of a policy, the realization of an assembly resolution, or which is the execution of an agreement that already has been reached with the republics, [that is,] if we do not have the necessary authority and trust in this respect.[34]

The Slovene "road-building crisis," Ribičič suggested, indicated that that "authority and trust" were lacking.

The Slovene road-building crisis demonstrates clearly that a policy decision that affects the constituent groups in a multinational state unequally can aggravate inter-nationality tensions even when made by an institution constructed on the basis of mutually agreed-on formulas of representation and participation and operating according to mutually agreed-on rules of procedure. It suggests, too, that other conditions must be present if the discontent generated by such a policy decision is not to find expression in ethno-national hostility. The political leadership of each national region must enjoy not only extensive control over the actions of both lower-level political leaders and the masses in its own region but also a high level of trust in both the leaders of the other national regions and the central leadership. This trust, in turn, must motivate the regional leaderships to use their control over their own regions to enforce decisions made at the center. As a political commentator for *NIN* observed shortly after the crisis,

> our democracy . . . requires generally accepted rules of behavior, rules of the political game, conventions to which all adhere. Not only because they are prescribed or legally sanctioned but because, understanding the meaning of federalism, we accept [the fact] that forums of the Federation

[34] Ibid.

also must make decisions and that it is in the mutual interest to carry them out.[35]

When either of these conditions is absent, the discontent generated by the unequal effects of a centrally made decision may become linked to, and find expression in, ethno-national hostility. When both conditions are absent, such linkage is highly likely to occur, as it did during the road-building crisis. Where there is suspicion and hostility between the leaderships of the ethnic regions, the aggravation of ethno-national tensions is inevitable. Events during 1969-1971—beginning with the road-building crisis—slowly transformed the relationship between the regional political leaderships from one based on mutual trust and confidence to one based on mutual suspicion and hostility. These mutual suspicions and hostilities were both a cause and a consequence of increasing policy conflicts between the regional leaderships and increasing ethno-national tensions among the masses.

Interbloc Conflict and the Growing Isolation
of the Croatian Leadership

During 1969, nationalistic feelings and activities were increasing among all the peoples of Yugoslavia. A strong revival of Serbian nationalism was taking place on the pages of a number of literary journals and within certain cultural institutions. During 1967 and 1968 the Belgrade literary journal *Književne Novine* had carried articles pointedly condemning instances of nationalism and chauvinism elsewhere in Yugoslavia, but from an only faintly disguised Serbian nationalist—indeed, chauvinist—viewpoint. During 1969 this journal was joined by the satirical Belgrade journal *Jež* in attacking post-Ranković political reforms such as the application of national and republican "keys," or quotas, to ensure proportional appointment of cadres to the staffs of federal institutions. Even the Belgrade political weekly *NIN* became involved in the resurgence of nationalism when in the summer and fall of 1969 it published a series of articles entitled *"Jugosloven—ko je to?"* (The Yugoslav—who is that?).[36]

This series examined the meaning of "socialist patriotism" for the Yugoslav peoples. It began with a review of recent sociological research on the national question, including some of the survey research cited above, in Chapter Two. These data were used to suggest that inter-nationality tensions and conflicts could be attributed not to nationality itself, but to "objective" social and economic differences that coincided with national ones. But the series then presented a wide range of often-conflicting personal statements by both private

[35] Ibid., 17 August 1969.
[36] Ibid., 8 June-2 November 1969.

citizens and public officials concerning their understanding of the meaning of "socialist patriotism." Some of these clearly contradicted the official positions of the party. There were expressions of intolerance toward the national minorities; resentment over the extent to which the expression of the national-cultural individuality of the minorities was supported and encouraged by official policy; and impatience with the apparent economic irrationality and inefficiency associated with the effective division of the Yugoslav economy into six separate republican economies. Most important, the concept of *jugoslovenstvo* was revived and presented as a positive basis for the integration of the Yugoslav peoples. These views were expressed in more than fifteen lengthy articles without critical commentary by either the general author of the series or the editors of *NIN*. The unacceptable nature of some of these statements from the official point of view was pointed out only at the end of the series, after it already had generated substantial public discontent outside Serbia.

Foremost among the organizational supporters of Serb nationalism was the *Matica Srpska*, the historical organizational base for Serb cultural activity. The Serbian Philosophical Society also became a center for Serb nationalist activity, as did the Serb cultural society in Croatia, *Prosvjeta*. The Serbian Orthodox Church, another strong organizational base of Serb culture, also became more active. At the universities in Priština (Kosovo) and Novi Sad (Vojvodina) Serbian nationalist student groups were organized and became very active. All these groups promoted certain common themes. Among them were the need to protect Serb culture from encroachment by Montenegrins, Macedonians, and Muslims, whose claims to enjoy their own distinct cultures were rejected by Serb nationalists; the need to protect Serbs outside Serbia from unequal treatment by the political leaderships of other regions and from physical assault by other groups, especially in Kosovo and Croatia; and the need to combine all the lands populated by Serbs into a single political unit. These themes were evident not only in publications and conferences sponsored by these groups and organizations but even in a number of books published in private editions by Serb authors.[37]

The resurgence of Serb nationalism continued to conflict with rising nationalist feelings among Albanians in Kosovo. During 1969, inter-nationality conflicts there focused on employment practices, language policy, and the election of management personnel in enterprises; elections in basic party organizations; and control over Priština University.[38] In Vojvodina, there was less conflict between Serb nationalists and the Hungarian minority than between Serb and Croat nationalists. Concomitant with a general increase in its

[37] SKS, Predsedništvo, *Aktivnost Saveza komunista Srbije u borbi protiv nacionalizma* (Beograd: Komunist, 1972), pp. 161-218.

[38] Ibid., pp. 37-41; and *Borba* (Belgrade), 19 September and 4 October 1969.

activity, the *Matica Hrvatska* had become very active among Croats in Vojvodina.[39]

In March 1969 the Zagreb weekly newspaper "for contemporary questions of society and culture," *Telegram*, published a highly politicized round-table discussion on the theme "language and reality."[40] This discussion revived most of the issues this same publication had raised in 1967 by first publishing the Declaration. The present action, in contrast, provoked a significantly less sharp reaction from the Croatian party leadership. However, the rising levels of Croat and Serb nationalism led President Tito to criticize harshly both the *Matica Hrvatska* and the *Matica Srpska* as nationalistic strongholds. In response, in May the Croatian party leadership cited several *Matica Hrvatska* regional journals and the literary journals *Hrvatski Književni List* and *Kritika* for unacceptable nationalistic content.[41] But no disciplinary action was taken against communists involved in these journals or the *Matica Hrvatska* organization itself. In June, the *Matica Hrvatska* leadership launched a counterattack against accusations that it was the sponsor of "antisocialist" and "nationalistic" activities. The *Matica* leadership issued a statement in which it agreed "with evaluations . . . which speak of the existence of nationalistic episodes," but directed attention away from them by emphasizing "the need for struggle against the causes of these events," which it identified as the then-current political issues dividing the republican political leaderships.[42] In July, *Kritika* published a 250-page special edition of twenty-two articles devoted to "the Croatian literary language and the question of variants." It reviewed the controversial history of attempts to develop a unified Croatoserbian/Serbocroatian language with two "variants."[43] Like the earlier discussion of "language and reality" in *Telegram*, this publication was explosive because it included a nationalistic Croat treatment of the language and political status of Serbs living in Croatia. In July, the party leadership once again criticized nationalistic excesses in the press. The Zagreb party organization criticized the editorial board of *Hrvatski Književni List* for having established "its own ideological and political character which is in opposition to the policies of the League of Communists and directly contrary to the basic interests of the Croatian people and all peoples of Yugoslavia."[44] But once again the Croatian leadership stopped short of applying disciplinary measures to the communists involved.

Nationalistic activity in Croatia and the apparent reluctance of the Croatian

---

[39] SKS, Predsedništvo, *Aktivnost SKS u borbi*, pp. 103-104.
[40] *Telegram* (Zagreb), 14 March 1969.
[41] *Politika* (Belgrade), 27 May and 4 July 1969.
[42] Ibid., 13 June 1969.
[43] Ibid., 6 July 1969.
[44] Ibid., 20 July 1969.

party leadership to take action against it were overshadowed during the summer and fall by events in Slovenia. But the problems posed by Croatian nationalism once again became a central issue in Yugoslav politics in November when Miloš Žanko, a Croatian deputy in the Chamber of Nationalities, a past critic of Croatian nationalism, and an individual associated with the central rather than the regional leadership, published a series of five lengthy articles in the Belgrade party daily *Borba*. He presented a detailed inventory of the increasing number of nationalistic activities in Croatia and emphasized the role of the *Matica Hrvatska* as the organizational base for what he called an antisocialist, nationalistic movement. He suggested in these articles that the nationalist revival in Croatia was supported by anti-Yugoslav forces abroad, and he criticized the leadership of the Croatian Party for its failure to take resolute action to suppress these activities or call communists in the *Matica* leadership to account.[45]

In the concluding article of the series Žanko proceeded from criticism of the Croatian party leadership to criticism of all the regional party leaderships for refusing to compromise in order to resolve the economic and political conflicts then dividing them.

> I am afraid that today many communists in our republics are not aware of the kind of harvest which is being prepared by those who, by their unprincipled opportunism or hasty approaches, resurrect the spirits of the old world. Communists in all republics should, therefore, invest much more effort so that the peoples of Yugoslavia more intensively come to agreement and more quickly come to a [mutual] understanding— even with, if it is finally necessary, mutual concessions, instead of becoming the executors or even organizers of imprudent pressures in the pragmatic service of momentary partial interests.
>
> Even the sharpest critic of the economic policy of federal organs should see from the discussion of state capital, old investment obligations of the federation, of illiquidity [and other issues], that such issues are too complicated and complex for us to be able to resolve them simply by pressure [tactics]. Solutions for certain questions, as already has been shown in the past, must be sought even in compromises; to the degree that these represent a step forward toward a final solution.
>
> . . . In practical politics it is necessary to have a sense of proportion. . . . The people who would, because of minor momentary calculations, lose [its] sense of its own long-term interests, or would sacrifice its own future for some illusion of the present moment, prepares its own defeat.[46]

[45] *Borba* (Belgrade), 17-21 November 1969.
[46] Ibid., 21 November 1969.

The implication of this argument was clear: the Croatian leadership was not capable of compromise because it had fallen subject to organized pressure from nationalist forces.

Since the fall of Ranković, the Croatian leadership had become increasingly intransigent in pressing its demands for further reform of the banking system, for changes in the foreign currency exchange and foreign trade systems, and especially for devolution of greater control over investment policies to the self-managing economic enterprises that generate capital. Since the early 1960s the Croatian leadership had had the support of other republican leaderships for its efforts to decentralize the economy and to win greater power for the republics by reducing the powers of the federation. Indeed, at the time of the 1968 constitutional reforms it was the Macedonian political leadership that was most outspoken on the latter issue.[47] Until the middle of 1969 the leaderships of Slovenia, Croatia, and the autonomous province of Vojvodina usually presented a solid bloc of "wealthy" regions opposed to the interests of the poorer regions of Bosnia, Montenegro, Kosovo, and Macedonia.

Conflict between the developed and the underdeveloped regions focused on the party's commitment to devolve onto self-managing enterprises greater control over the investment of their capital resources. Such increased control would be likely to result in an increased proportion of resources remaining in the developed republics for investment in modernization and expansion. Consequently, as a later Yugoslav analysis of this conflict suggests, the leaderships of "other, national, republican areas in Yugoslavia, whose economic structures are different from that of Croatia were less insistent" on the immediate fulfillment of this principle. They emphasized instead "another, similarly general principle which was built into the programmatic orientation of the LCY, and that is the principle of solidarity and help of the developed for the underdeveloped." These leaderships demanded the continuing "concentration of resources at the federal level and their redistribution to lesser-developed national, or republican areas." Thus,

> the tendency emerged for the emphasis, even confrontation of two principles which were included in the programmatic orientation of the League of Communists. Both were legitimate from the perspective of socialism and its development.[48]

By refusing to compromise its positions, the Croatian leadership isolated itself among the regional leaderships. The road-building crisis made the Slovenian political leadership acutely sensitive to the potential consequences of

[47] Slavko Milosavlevski, "Prilog pitanju daljeg razvitka političke organizacije jugoslovenske federacije," in Stankov, *Karakter i funkcije federacije*, pp. 70-79, but esp. 75 and 78.

[48] Ivan Perić, *Suvremeni Hrvatski nacionalizam* (Zagreb: August Cesarec, 1976), p. 52.

allowing interrepublican conflict to continue for very long. Consequently, Slovenian representatives in the central leadership grew increasingly reluctant to support even those Croatian positions which, if adopted, would have benefited Slovenia as well. Croatian demands for the retention of control over foreign currency earnings of hotel and other tourist enterprises in Dalmatia alienated the leaderships of agricultural regions that supplied those enterprises with foodstuffs and of mining areas that provided them with fuel supplies necessary to continue operation, who wanted to share in those earnings. The leaderships of other regions who might otherwise have supported Croatian demands for reform felt compelled, by the nationalistic coloration given to those demands by events in Croatia and by their own positions as "national" leaders, to oppose them.[49]

In a 1976 analysis of this period carried out at the Center for Social Research of the Central Committee of the Yugoslav party, Ivan Perić reports that increasing nationalistic activity in Croatia and the apparent failure of the Croatian leadership to contain it also contributed to the growing isolation of that leadership in higher party councils. The representatives of other republics, he suggests, withheld their own reservations concerning the role of the federation and expressed instead their reservations not only about the Croatian leadership and its positions concerning these matters but about political events in Croatia as well.[50] Thus, the Croatian party leadership was caught between pressure from nationalistic forces to become more radical in their demands, and pressure from the leaderships of party organizations in other republics and at the center to limit those demands. Perić argues elsewhere that, having lost effective control over the actions and demands of the nationalist forces, the Croatian leaders reacted to these pressures not by finding common cause with the party leaderships of other republics, but by moving closer to the positions of the nationalistic forces.

> Defending themselves against negative evaluations of political events in Croatia, they took joint and conciliatory positions toward many phenomena in Croatia, and they tolerated nationalistic views, proclaiming them to be somewhat strongly expressed national sentiments that should not disturb anyone.[51]

This reaction became especially pronounced following publication of the Žanko articles. Vladimir Bakarić opened the public counterattack on Žanko

---

[49] See, for example, the conversation with an unidentified Serbian leader reported in Rusinow, *The Yugoslav Experiment*, pp. 252-53.

[50] Perić, *Suvremeni Hrvatski nacionalizam*, p. 54.

[51] Ivan Perić, *Ideje "masovnog pokreta" u Hrvatskoj* (Zagreb: Centar za Aktuelni Politički Studij, 1974), p. 156.

in December 1969 with a major speech to the Croatian party leadership.[52] While Žanko had argued that nationalism was increasing, Bakarić argued "rather the opposite, [that] it is momentarily on the defensive." The danger of its revival, he conceded, continued to exist. But this did not require that the leadership of the Croatian party be replaced by "one put into place from outside, by intervention from outside," an action at which, Bakarić suggested, Žanko was openly hinting. Nor did it call for repressive measures against individuals and organizations in Croatia, actions, according to Bakarić, implied in Žanko's assertion that "everything that has been done has been empty phrases" and his call for "moving from words to actions." "If we do that," Bakarić warned, "we will arrive at such a situation that we will inflame nationalisms—not only our own, but all the others. Therefore, that is the worst thing we could do."

The central Executive Bureau, Bakarić reported, had already considered the situation in Croatia and had decided on an alternate course of action: to mobilize the League "and see what we can do," confident "that we have the force to overcome this thing, but that without greater mobilization and without greater clarification of these questions we will not succeed." These discussions, he continued, were followed by discussions among the Croatian leadership. Both leaderships, he reported, were confident that nationalist feelings in Croatia were a consequence of the continuing unresolved conflicts between the regions. The political leadership of Croatia "pointed out certain difficulties" in the hope of solving them, and the nationalists, he observed, "accepted these analyses and drew their own conclusions from them." In order to eliminate nationalistic phenomena in Croatia, therefore, it was necessary to resolve the ongoing interregional conflicts. Bakarić warned, however, that

> these are not small problems, there are several elements here: the transfer from the narrowest centralism to an entirely different economy, the construction of self-management, the struggle with remnants of the old [system], with material obligations of the past, etc., and it would be strange if that transformation of society *which is equal to revolution* unfolds without controversies, without conflicts, and without difficulties.

The text of Bakarić's speech was circulated among party activists throughout the republic for discussion at the tenth session of the Croatian Central Committee, which convened a few weeks later in January 1970. The tenth session was convened to call Miloš Žanko to account for his veiled accusations against the Croatian party leadership, and Žanko was, in fact, severely crit-

[52] The following citations are from the authorized stenographic text published in Milovan Baletić and Zdravko Židovec, eds., *Deseta Sjednica Centralnog komiteta Saveza komunista Hrvatske* (Zagreb: Vjesnik, 1970), pp. 108-10 (emphasis added).

icized and punished. But the tenth session was devoted to more than this. For the first time in the history of the party in Yugoslavia, a single republican party organization undertook to review "the historical moment" and to suggest—on its own initiative—the correct direction for the long-range development of Yugoslavia as a whole. Moreover, the Croatian leadership undertook this task without consulting the party leaderships of the other republics.[53]

Enlarging on the arguments introduced by Bakarić in December, Savka Dabčević-Kučar, who had become president of the Croatian party when Bakarić was called to Belgrade to join the Executive Bureau, opened the tenth session with a lengthy, rambling speech in which she suggested that nationalism should no longer be considered the main obstacle to progress. Rather, that obstacle now was unitarism—the insistence on central power at the expense of the republics and provinces. Together with Bakarić's December speech, her speech established the Croatian "party line" for the next two years. And it was to this speech and this session of the Croatian Central Committee that Croat nationalists would point during the next two years for proof of the legitimacy of their actions.[54]

Dabčević-Kučar argued that "unitarism is a mask behind which hegemonism hides its face . . . [and] proclaims as nationalism the concern and responsibility of the socialist republics for the development of the federation." In this way she subtly equated it with Serbian nationalism—historically associated with insistence on a strong centralized Yugoslav state and hostile to the weakening of that state to accommodate the national aspirations of the other Yugoslav peoples. She pointed out that "Unitarists do not want to accept the fact that there does not exist a unified Yugoslav people," and she criticized them for continuing to advance "the unacceptable phenomenon of Yugoslavism, which denotes some superior supranational phenomenon." As far as "Croatian chauvinism and nationalism" were concerned, Dabčević-Kučar argued that it "is fed primarily by difficulties, by open economic questions and conflict situations, [that] it rises up first of all on existing unresolved problems." Consequently, all that was necessary to defeat it was to resolve the issues around which the leadership was then deadlocked.

She insisted that "nationalism, although more aggressive and more vocal, is not increasing; . . . we have cut off a series of its roots and narrowed its space in relation to what it had been earlier." She pointed out that the Croatian Central Committee already had criticized several organizations for nationalistic activities, including the *Matica Hrvatska*, and she warned against going too far in this.

[53] Bilandžić, *Ideje i Praksa*, pp. 275-76.

[54] The following citations to this speech are from the text published in Baletić and Židovec, *Deseta Sjednica*, pp. 5-20.

I think some generalization which would *en bloc* reject everything the *Matica* has done would not be politically acceptable for the Central Committee . . . or [as a basis] for our political action; nor would it correspond to the real situation, although there have been certain actions which were not on the course of the party program, especially when individuals in the *Matica*, instead of a cultural institution, attempted to transform it into a sort of self-proclaimed political representative of the interests of the Croatian people and on that basis embarked on essentially political actions in other republics. Nevertheless, there are a great number of progressive members in the *Matica Hrvatska* who are for self-managing socialism. . . . The question of the struggle for political positions should once again be put before the communists in the *Matica* for whom, as for all members of the League of Communists, the political course of the League of Communists is obligatory. It seems to me, nevertheless, [that] the forces which exist in the *Matica*, the general disposition in our society, and the political platform of the Central Committee and the League . . . are sufficient to eliminate, by the action of communists and all positive forces, the possibility that various nationalistic and chauvinistic forces will put their stamp on the work of the *Matica Hrvatska*, even if temporarily or in individual articles.

She argued that in dealing with "views which relate to current social questions but do not coincide in their entirety with the evaluations of the political leadership" it "would be better" if

we develop a dialogue both in the League of Communists and in society, . . . [if] in our actions we rely more on politics, on the ideological and political offensive of our views, and not on the administrative shutting of the mouths of others, on constructive polemics, avoiding except when necessary direct intervention of party forums and especially state organs.

When Bakarić returned to the podium the next day to comment on Dabčević-Kučar's speech, he hinted strongly that one reason why the leadership had taken this position was that the time was now past when it could have taken more coercive action. "I would add something else," he said,

the *Matica Hrvatska* being mentioned [here] has more journals than earlier, and people who are more insolent today than they were earlier. We wanted to arrange the *Matica Hrvatska* differently . . . , [but] we did not succeed. To go on, two organizations were set up differently than we had thought and wanted, and were set up practically in defense of the Declaration on Language [of 1967] and on a nationalistic basis. That was the *Matica Hrvatska* and the Literary Society of Croatia. But even in the war every battle was not won. It is necessary to recognize here that we did not carry out that which should have been done and that is why we have not had success.[55]

This was an ominous admission of the relative weakness of the party in comparison to the *Matica*.

In attacking Žanko directly, Dabčević-Kučar repeated and expanded on the themes raised by Bakarić in December. But she added an even more damaging charge: "The formation of a group on unprincipled bases, the spreading of lies, insinuations and similar [actions] . . . that could grow into fractional activity." The charge of incipient fractionalism rendered Žanko subject to party disciplinary action, and this was used to remove him from his party post as permanent member of the Croatian delegation to the federal party Conference. Shortly thereafter he was stripped of his membership in the Chamber of Nationalities. As A. Ross Johnson has astutely pointed out, by this action the Croatian party leadership established a de facto imperative mandate for the delegates of the republics in the Chamber, and brought the relationship between the republics one step closer to confederation.[56]

More important than this, however, was the fact that the leadership of the Croatian party had founded its criticism of Žanko on the assertion that nationalism did not represent as great a danger to the party or to the system of socialist self-management as did unitarism—the vestiges of the old command economy, and the social and political forces that sought its restoration. The most significant remnants of unitarism were the economic policy-making powers of the federation. By declaring unitarism the greater danger, the Croatian party leadership was, in effect, mobilizing the forces of Croatian nationalism criticized by Žanko for an attack on the remaining powers of the federation. In so doing, the leadership asserted its ability to control the nationalists, to harness their forces to the course of self-management, and to prevent them from advancing extreme demands of their own. More than this, in her treatment of the relationship between the party leadership and those whose views did not coincide with the views of the party, and especially in her recommendations for party policy toward the *Matica Hrvatska*, Savka Dabčević-Kučar had rejected forcefully the position taken by the central party Presidium only a month earlier.

Bakarić's claim of support from the central leadership did not mean that that leadership was prepared to sanction the relaxation of party control over society. Indeed, at its Seventh Session, held two days after Bakarić's December speech, the Presidium heard Miko Tripalo—who had given up his position as secretary of the Croatian party to accompany Bakarić as Croatia's

[55] Ibid., p. 51.

[56] A. Ross Johnson, *Yugoslavia: In the Twilight of Tito*, The Washington Papers, Vol. 2 (Beverly Hills: Sage Publications, 1974), p. 12.

representative on the Executive Bureau—deliver a report in which he noted that "when conditions of crisis or sharper social conflicts appear" there arise not only strong desires "for a return to a role for the party as it was during the administrative period" but also attempts to turn the party into "a discussion club, or ineffectual organization which relinquishes to others the monopoly position it had enjoyed in the past." "In contemporary conditions of a relatively developed system of self-management and the creation of multiple centers of social decision making," he argued, "it is necessary to devote special attention to controlling the tendency to degrade the avant garde role of the League of Communists." The party, he reported, was opposed to "centers of decision making becoming ideologically and politically independent" and turning into "partner organizations to the League of Communists," because this could lead to situations in which "individual functionaries under the cloak of 'popular support' separate themselves from and oppose the League of Communists."[57] However, the tone and content of the tenth session of the Croatian Central Committee, including remarks delivered by Tripalo himself, were in clear opposition to these centrally agreed-on and adopted views.[58] Because of this, the session "was received with great suspicion in the Yugoslav public."[59]

The tenth session marked the beginning of a concerted assault by the Croatian leaders on the powers of the federation. They attempted to reduce those powers not by a direct attack, but by pushing through changes in federal cadres policies and decision-making processes intended to strengthen the ability of a single republic to prevent the federation from taking any action to which it was opposed. They won a partial victory a few months later, in April 1970, when the central party Presidium decided that, "as a rule, decisions in the federation should be taken on the basis of harmonization [of views] and agreement making among the republics." "Harmonization" of views [usaglašavanje] calls for a negotiating process aimed at the formulation of policies that satisfy the interests of all the republican and provincial leaderships; it precludes the adoption of any policy without the complete agreement [puna saglasnost] of all republics and provinces. Thus, the Croatian party leadership had won explicit recognition of a principle of unanimous decision making. The issues to which this principle was to be applied remained to be established.[60]

The Presidium also accepted Croatian demands for equalization of republican and national representation in all federal bodies. The Presidium agreed

<hr>

[57] SKJ, Predsedništvo, *Sedma Sednica Predsedništva SKJ* (Beograd: Komunist, 1970), pp. 8, 9, 12.

[58] For Tripalo's comments, see Baletić and Židovec, *Deseta Sjednica*, pp. 40-43.

[59] Bilandžić, *Ideje i Praksa*, p. 276.

[60] SKJ, Predsedništvo, *Osma Sednica Predsedništva SKJ* (Beograd: Komunist, 1970), p. 11.

"consistently [to] support the application of the principle of parity" in the selection of cadres for both "organs of the federation and leaderships of the socio-political organizations, *with deciding influence and responsibility in the resolution of cadres questions in organs and institutions of the federation belonging to the socialist republics and provinces.*" The criteria for determining "appropriate republican and national representation" also remained to be established.[61]

The party leadership was well aware of the additional strain these changes were likely to place on central decision making. Consequently, the Presidium conclusions included a reminder that the republican and provincial leaderships would now be responsible for "the state of relations between the republics and between the nations and nationalities," and a cautionary note about their behavior: "It is natural that they struggle for the satisfaction of the needs of the peoples of their republic, but it is similarly necessary that they strive in their own areas for full understanding of the needs and interests of others."[62] In the absence of such understanding, the principles of decision making just adopted were a formula for deadlock and disaster.

The principles adopted at this session necessitated further consideration of several important issues. Foremost among these was the task of defining the areas to which the "harmonization" process would be applied. Consequently, the Presidium charged its Executive Bureau and its commissions to consider, among other things, "relations between the republics and the federation; . . . the position and responsibility of the republics in the framework of the federation; the further carrying-out of constitutional principles concerning the character, functions, and competence of the organs of the federation . . ."; and "cadres policy in organs of the federation."[63] These issues became the central focus of intraparty debate during 1970, and the major public issues of the moment in Yugoslavia.

Cadres policies in federal institutions were a particularly sensitive issue. Heretofore the central political leadership had dealt with it behind closed doors. Now, however, as one commentary in *Borba* put it, "one of the so-called 'taboo-themes' from political life . . . which until recently was discussed, and about which decisions were made, in the offices of the highest functionaries, has been placed on the public agenda."[64] In response to the Presidium decisions, the Federal Assembly undertook to draft a document establishing the policy of parity in the election and appointment of cadres in the federation. Preparation of the document was carried out by two commissions of the Assembly, with the participation of representatives of each of

[61] Ibid., p. 13 (emphasis added).
[62] Ibid., p. 9.
[63] Ibid., p. 14.
[64] *Borba* (Belgrade), 1 July 1970.

the republics and provinces. These representatives quickly agreed on certain basic principles: (1) the republics and provinces would be represented equally; (2) the conflicting interests of the republics and provinces would be "harmonized" by constant social agreement making and prior reconciliation of views; (3) positions in the federation, including even the highest, would be accessible to cadres from all republics and provinces; (4) the republics and provinces would be responsible for the quality of cadres in the federation; and (5) the principle of parity [*pariteta*] would be applied to all positions to which functionaries were elected or appointed by the Federal Assembly and the Federal Executive Council.[65]

Agreement on these principles left considerable room for conflict. How far down in the federal bureaucracies was the principle of parity to be applied? Positions in the bureaucracies of the foreign ministry, defense ministry, and Federal Secretariat for Internal Affairs (security police) as far down as chiefs of individual offices, for example, were the subject of considerable discussion. There was disagreement over the means by which to prevent cadres from a single republic from occupying the same positions for a long period and thereby monopolizing certain functions. Questions also arose as to the precise operational meaning of "parity." Did it mean "equal" or "equivalent"? Did parity preclude proportionality as a means of ensuring the participation of the smaller national minorities? Proportionality was rejected by the representatives of the smaller republics. A representative of Montenegro, for example, argued that "it would not be the most appropriate solution to apply this principle according to the size of the population." On the other hand, a representative of Bosnia, one of the larger republics, argued that proportionality would permit the representation of the diverse nationalities within a single republic. And finally, the most serious conflict concerned the apparent overrepresentation of the republic of Serbia among cadres in the federal bureaucracies.[66]

The federal bureaucracies are located in Belgrade and draw heavily on the local Serbian population for staff. This results in an obvious overrepresentation of Serbs among them. An extensive study of the republican and national composition of cadres in federal organs carried out in 1969 by the Institute of Social Sciences in Belgrade confirmed this.[67] But, as can be seen from Table 3.2 below, it also revealed that that overrepresentation occurred primarily among professional staff [*stručni nosioci poslovanja*] and technical assistants [*pomoćno-tehničko osoblje*] who were not selected directly by the republics and provinces, but by the Federal Assembly or Federal Executive Council. Among decision makers [*rukovodeći kadrovi*] who were delegated

[65] Ibid.

[66] Ibid.

[67] Milan Matić et al., *Republički i nacionalni sastav kadrova u organima Federacije* (Beograd: Institut Društvenih Nauka, Centar za istraživanje javnog mnenja, 1969).

Table 3.2

National Composition of Cadres in Federal Institutions and Organizations, 1969

Type of Organ/ Type of Cadres	Total Cadres	Nationality (Percentages)							
		Serbs	Croats	Slovenes	Macedonians	Montenegrins	Others	Undecided	Unknown
State Administration									
Leading Cadres	259	39	19	10	8	15	4	5	—
Professional Staff	2,432	72	8	3	3	9	2	3	—
Govt. Commissions & Institutes									
Leading Cadres	16	44	6	6	13	25	—	6	—
Professional Staff	912	83	4	3	1	6	1	2	—
Judicial and Prosecutory									
Leading Cadres (Judges)	64	42	12	6	11	25	2	2	—
Professional Staff	70	79	9	1	1	6	3	1	—
Parliament and Govt.									
Members ⎫ Leading Staff ⎬ (Leading Cadres)	683	42	18	9	7	5	8	8	3
	131	36	18	13	11	16	2	3	1
Professional Staff	187	65	5	4	3	15	—	8	—
Socio-Political Organizations									
Members of Organs ⎫ Leading Staff ⎬ (Leading Cadres)	823	18	12	8	6	6	4	1	45
	46	48	11	6	9	15	2	9	—
Professional Staff	210	58	11	3	4	16	—	8	—
SUB-TOTALS									
Leading Cadres	2,022	32	15	9	7	9	5	4	19
Professional Staff	3,811	73	7	3	3	9	2	3	—
Technical Assistants	4,015	78	7	3	2	5	1	4	—
Total	9,848	67	9	4	3	7	2	4	4

Source: Milan Matić et al., *Republički i nacionalni sastav kadrova u organima Federacije* (Beograd: Institut Društvenih Nauka, Centar za istraživanje jzvnog mnenja, 1969), p. 73.

by the republics and provinces, Serbs were represented about proportionately to their share of the Yugoslav population. The higher proportions of Serbs among these cadres resulted primarily from the fact that Serbs were to be found among the cadres from several republics. The proportion of cadres from the republic of Serbia was not much greater than that of cadres from the republic of Croatia (Table 3.3, below), despite the fact that these data included cadres from the provinces of Kosovo and Vojvodina among those from Serbia.

In discussions of parity, representatives of Serbia took the position that "functionaries of the federation who are not delegated by the republic to a particular position cannot be counted in the cadres quota for that republic," because they are selected "without the knowledge or agreement of the republic." As one Serbian delegate put it, "we cannot accept these functionaries as our own. Ours, the republic's, are those whom we propose." This position was opposed by the representatives of all other republics and provinces.[68]

Solutions to these conflicts were negotiated among representatives of the party leaderships of the republics and provinces. The Presidium's Commission for the Development of the League of Communists had been charged in April with drafting the party's position. In early September the Commission finished its work and made its conclusions known to the central party leadership. Paradoxically, the Executive Bureau of the party made certain last-minute changes in the draft conclusion that strengthened the role of the republics. The Bureau emphasized that the principle of parity was to apply to "all organs of the Federation in which decisions are made that significantly affect the equality of a nation and nationality, [or] republic and province." The Bureau also suggested a solution to the conflict over Serb overrepresentation. "Only those candidates whom the republics and provinces propose," it suggested, "can be elected and appointed to political functions in the Federation." But at the same time it insisted that the Commission emphasize more clearly "that the principle of proportionality in the composition of professional staffs cannot be accepted." Consequently, the Commission adopted the position that, with respect to the composition of these staffs, "it is necessary to strive for the more equal achievement of representation of people from all the republics and provinces."[69]

One week later, Miko Tripalo, president of the Commission for the Development of the League, presented this formulation to the full Presidium at its eleventh session. He characterized it as a compromise between the position of the Serbian leadership and the position shared by all the other republican and provincial leaderships.

[68] *Borba* (Belgrade), 1 July 1970.
[69] Ibid., 11 September 1970.

TABLE 3.3
Republic of Origin of Cadres in Federal Institutions
and Organizations, 1969

Type of Organ/ Type of Cadres	Total Cadres	Republic of Origin (Percentages)					
		Bosnia	Montenegro	Croatia	Macedonia	Slovenia	Serbia
State Administration							
Leading Cadres	259	14	17	26	9	10	24
Professional Staff	2,432	13	10	17	5	3	52
Govt. Commissions & Institutes							
Leading Cadres	16	13	25	13	12	12	25
Professional Staff	912	9	7	10	3	3	68
Judicial & Prosecutory							
Leading Cadres (Judges)	64	12	25	19	11	6	27
Professional Staff	70	11	16	7	3	1	62
Parliament & Govt.							
Members ⎫ (Leading Cadres)	683	17	5	23	9	10	36
Leading Staff ⎭	131	14	14	20	11	13	28
Professional Staff	187	17	15	18	4	4	42
Socio-Political Organizations							
Members of Organs ⎫ (Leading Cadres)	823	16	10	21	19	13	28
Leading Staff ⎭	46	20	15	24	9	6	26
Professional Staff	210	16	14	18	6	4	42
SUB-TOTALS							
Leading Cadres	2,022	16	10	22	10	11	31
Professional Staff	3,811	13	9	16	4	3	55
Technical Assistants	4,015	13	6	19	3	2	57
Total	9,848	14	8	18	5	4	51

SOURCE: Matić et al., *Republički i nacionalni sastav kadrova*, p. 72.

In the conclusions [of the Commission] a position is taken on the need to achieve the presence of cadres from all republics and provinces in the professional staffs of the federation in a much more equal way than has been done up to now. In the beginning the opinion prevailed that the principle of proportionality should be applied to the composition of organs which are not constituted on the principle of parity. That is, the number of representatives in the professional staffs would be determined by the size of population of each republic and province. However, it was seen that such a position would have a negative effect on the presence in the federal administration of members of those republics which have a smaller population. Therefore the expression "more equal" is used, because now the overwhelming majority [of professional staff cadres] in the federal administration is from one republic.[70]

Tripalo carefully avoided pointing out to the full Presidium that this solution and, indeed, the entire document[71] represented not so much a compromise between Serbia and all other republics as a victory for his own republic, Croatia, won with the support of the smaller republics.

The final conclusions of the Presidium concerning cadres policy in the federation make no mention of nations or nationalities in the context of applying the principle of parity to federal institutions. Proportionality had been advanced by representatives of multinational Bosnia as a means for ensuring the representation of all the nationalities in each republic or province, and was consistent with the Presidium's own decision in April that it was necessary to ensure "appropriate republican *and national* representation." But proportionality was defeated by representatives of multinational Croatia by portraying it as an instrument for ensuring the dominant position of the largest nation—the Serbs. By eliminating nationality from consideration in the determination of parity, the Croatian leadership cleared the way for effective disenfranchisement on the federal level of the large Serb minority in Croatia.

In Croatia, discussion of federal cadres policy had been particularly vigorous and widespread. In mid-July the *Borba* correspondent in Zagreb reported that the discussion had "burst into flames." Already of wide interest, the issue had recently generated even greater public attention. Indeed, some political functionaries in the republic were reportedly " 'shocked' by the openness with which this until recently 'taboo-theme' of our society is now approached." The discussion of federal cadres policy became linked in Croatia to the question of federal decision making. On the latter question, "the view

[70] Ibid., 19 September 1970.
[71] The text appears in ibid., 30 September 1970.

prevailed that it is necessary to apply consistently the principle of joint positions, and not to make decisions on certain solutions by outvoting."[72] Here, too, the Croatian view was adopted by the central party leadership. The party's document on cadres policy in the federation suggested that, with respect to decision making in the foreign ministry and the Federal Secretariat for Internal Affairs, "it is essential to develop further the work of collegial bodies (composed on the principle of parity)."[73]

How both to achieve republican parity in federal institutions and to maintain the authority and effectiveness of the central government was an important problem. Continuing conflicts between republican and provincial representatives in key institutions such as the Coordinating Commission of the Federal Executive Council and the Chamber of Nationalities had paralyzed the federal government and the federal parliament. As a result, the split between the Croatian leadership and those of the other republics and provinces grew even wider. The cadres policy worked out by the party promised to expand the participation in state institutions of individuals acting as representatives of republican and provincial interests, thereby increasing the difficulty of forging interrepublican agreements in them. In an attempt to end the stalemate in the government and to reduce conflict in the party leadership, President Tito traveled to each of the republics and provinces during August to hold direct, private discussions with each of the regional party leaderships. The topic of these discussions was an idea he had developed in cooperation with "a few comrades from the highest leadership, after long thought about what should be done in order to avoid in the future various frictions."[74]

President Tito proposed the creation of a new collective state Presidency to be composed of highly authoritative individuals from each of the republics and provinces. The collective Presidency would provide both an arena for high-level resolution of interrepublican conflicts over government policy and an answer to the question of his own succession. After he had secured the support of the regional leaderships, Tito made the proposal public in a speech to the Croatian party leadership on September 21.[75]

Tito made it clear that this step was being taken in response to the pressure of ongoing events. The inability of the government to overcome interrepublican conflicts, he argued, necessitated the creation of an authoritative, integrative institution at the summit, composed of

[72] Ibid., 15 July 1970.

[73] Ibid., 30 September 1970.

[74] Introductory comments by President Tito at the twelfth session of the Presidium, 4 October 1970, in SKJ, *Aktuelni problemi daljeg razvoja našeg političkog sistema* (Beograd: Komunist, 1970), p. 129.

[75] Text in ibid., pp. 5-12. Cf. *Borba* (Belgrade), 22 September 1970.

people who . . . will not be republican advocates [*republikanaci*] higher up. They will be the best people from the republics, in whom you will have trust. They will have to be an independent factor which will resolve problems and not, as representatives of the republics, listen to what will come from them [the republics]. This relates not only to you but to all republics.

He also suggested that the creation of a state Presidency was necessary in order to liberate the central party leadership—the Presidium, and especially the Executive Bureau—from day-to-day involvement in governmental affairs, so that they "will be able to devote greater attention to the role of the League of Communists as the ideological directing force of socialist development."

By suggesting the creation of a state Presidency, Tito was in a sense recommending the separation of party and state that had seemed imminent on the eve of the Ninth Congress, eighteen months earlier. In effect, he was attempting to ease interrepublican conflicts by resuming the process of reform he had intervened earlier to halt. But by now the Croatian leadership had committed itself to a solution based on maximizing its autonomy in all areas, and the idea of an authoritative federal institution independent of republican influences or control was seen by them not as a concession to reform but as an attempt to re-centralize power.

Indeed, creation of the collective Presidency did suggest an attempt to concentrate power at the center, for Tito also asserted that "the most outstanding people of the League of Communists will be in it." Since 1966 the party leadership had remained organizationally distinct from the state administration. Although still deeply involved in governmental policy making, the party formally exercised its leadership through organs subject to the effective control of the regional party leaderships. Overlapping membership between the party Presidium and the collective Presidency would represent a return to earlier practices and, to the extent that that body enjoyed real power rather than influence, would concentrate power in the hands of individuals who were members of both.

However, creation of a collective state Presidency would reduce regional control over the exercise of central power only if its members ceased to act as representatives of regional interests, and this appeared unlikely. Nonetheless, Tito himself reported that,

When discussions about this reorganization began, there arose certain complaints in some places, a certain disorientation. It began to be said that this will be a kind of directorate, and similar [things].

He dismissed these as "stupidities" [*gluposti*]. But they were much more than that. They reflected a fundamental division between the Croatian party leadership and those of the other regions that precluded the kind of interregional and regional-federal cooperation that would be necessary if the new Presidency was to function as an integrative institution.

The proposal to establish a collective state Presidency was so much a part of the ongoing negotiations over federal cadres policy and reconsideration of the role, functions, and institutions of the federation that it did not generate a dramatic public response. But the political impact of this proposal—both official and unofficial—was dramatic. As President Tito suggested to the central Presidium just two weeks later,

> It is clear that this reorganization cannot be carried out without corresponding constitutional changes, by which would be specified the rights of the republics, their relationship to the federation and vice-versa. Namely, the role of the federation and relations between the Federation and the republics must be cleared up and specified in the Constitution.[76]

This proposal, in effect, placed on the agenda the entire political order of the Yugoslav state. It provided the Croatian leadership with an opportunity to break the deadlock over federal policy by amending the constitution to remove areas of contention from the competence of the federation entirely.

The process by which the constitutional changes prompted by this proposal were formulated is examined in greater detail in the next chapter. Here, it is sufficient to note that that process took the form of complex interregional negotiations focused on redefining the relationships between the republics (and provinces) and the federation, on reducing the independent power and functions of the federation, and on reorganizing federal institutions and prescribing new rules for decision making in them. A less controversial element in these negotiations was discussion of the continuation of the economic reforms of the mid-1960s. These discussions focused on expanding the autonomous power of self-managing economic enterprises and extending the principle of self-management to additional spheres of social life. There was comparatively little conflict over the formulation of constitutional amendments dealing with the latter issues. Almost all public attention was focused on the more directly political amendments, although in the post-crisis period the changes embodied in the amendments concerning self-management would assume vastly increased importance.

The process of drafting the amendments unfolded on two levels. The first consisted of discussions among constitutional and legal experts representing their respective republics and provinces. Although there were serious differences in views among these individuals, their discussions proceeded relatively quickly and smoothly. Their task was to record, not to reconcile divergent

---

[76] SKJ, *Aktuelni problemi daljeg razvoja*, p. 129.

views. Reconciliation of conflicting views was to occur at another, higher level of the process, among a group of politically powerful representatives of the republics and provinces. At this level, disputes over the organization of state institutions became linked to current political conflicts between the regions over specific federal policies. This made the reconciliation of opposing views on either set of issues still more difficult. In effect, the conflicts then paralyzing the political process were translated into the language of constitutional reforms and reproduced in the amendment process.

The policy disputes dividing the regional leaderships and differences over constitutional formulas for the organization and operation of the state became even more difficult to resolve because the constitutional amendment process opened the door to public discussion of issues which heretofore had been excluded from the public domain. Unlike the period of the Croatian Declaration and the Serbian Proposal, the regional party leaderships now either were no longer willing or were unable to enforce the boundaries of these discussions. As a result, nationalist forces throughout Yugoslavia could use discussions of constitutional questions and later discussions of draft amendments to the federal and republican constitutions to offer highly provocative counterproposals and to raise highly explosive issues.

Nowhere in Yugoslavia was this process more pronounced than in Croatia. There nationalist forces—both Croat and Serb—were well-organized and politically active. The Croatian nationalist leadership appeared to enjoy widespread popular support and was able to exert enormous political pressure on the party leadership. At the same time, the party leadership itself was divided over how to react to these forces.

In the aftermath of the December 1971 purge of the Croatian party leadership, the Croatian Central Committee established an investigatory commission to examine the causes of the nationalist upheaval in Croatia. The report of that commission, delivered in May 1972, provides a detailed account of the organizational growth and increasing activity of nationalist forces in Croatia and a remarkable analysis of the internal politics of the Croatian party elite in the period from October 1970 to January 1972.[77] It discusses the nature of authority relationships within the party and the operation of the party's control mechanism, and it documents the subversion of those relationships and that mechanism by nationalist forces. Until this report was delivered, many of the events that occurred during this period could not have been understood fully. Included in its more than 300 pages is a substantial amount of material—extracts from verbatim transcripts of closed party meetings, records of secret activities of party leaders and organizations, and nu-

[77] SKH, CK, *Izveštaj o stanju u Savezu komunista Hrvatske u odnosu na prodor nacionalizma u njegove redove (Izveštaj usvojen na 28. sednici Centralnog komiteta Saveza komunista Hrvatske)* (Zagreb: Informativna služba Centralnog komiteta Saveza komunista Hrvatske, 1972).

merous documents, reports, and analyses of events in nonparty organizations and institutions—never before revealed. The report is surprisingly objective in its account of events and, except for its unfaltering criticism of the actions of those party leaders forced to resign in December 1971, candid in its analyses of them. It is one of the most important sources for the study of this period in Croatian and Yugoslav politics.[78]

The "Croatian Crisis" and the Breakdown of Elite Cooperation in the Party

Development of the Croatian crisis was conditioned by the rise of an organized Croatian nationalist movement. The *Matica Hrvatska* provided the organizational core of that movement. Long before the proposal to amend the constitution, its leadership and its publications had actively supported and advanced Croatian nationalism. But in November 1970, the *Matica* announced a stepped-up membership drive and a program of increased activities. According to the report of the Croatian party's investigatory commission, the *Matica* had at that time thirty territorial branch organizations with a total of 2,323 members. By the end of 1971, it had expanded to fifty-five branch organizations, sixteen commissions, and thirty-three initiative committees, with a total of about 41,000 members. The opening of new *Matica* organizations were well-publicized, well-attended, and highly politicized events. They were attended by functionaries of the *Matica* who delivered highly nationalistic speeches and, frequently, by representatives of local socio-political organizations, including the party and its mass front organization, the Socialist Alliance. They sometimes also were attended by higher political functionaries of the republic. The participation of local and republican officials gave an aura of official sponsorship to the expansion of the *Matica*. These events also attracted "some people whose behavior in the course of the national liberation struggle had been problematic." These included "a certain number of people who clearly decided against the socialist order and the LCY" and even some who "had been convicted because of participation in unfriendly ranks."[79]

The *Matica* also expanded by establishing organizations in large economic enterprises. The investigatory commission reported that these *Matica* organizations often used the financial, material, and technical resources of these enterprises to support their own propaganda activities. These included more than the distribution of nationalist literature among employees. These *Matica*

[78] For a parallel report on this period, see Mira Suvar, ed., *Sedmi Kongres Saveza komunista Hrvatske*, stenographic record, vol. 1 (Zagreb: Centralni komitet Saveza komunista Hrvatske, 1974), passim.

[79] SKH, CK, *Izveštaj o stanju*, pp. 70-72, 150-56.

organizations frequently insisted on ethnic "head-counts" of employees to determine whether non-Croats (usually Serbs) were "overrepresented" in the workforce, and demanded "adjustments" in the ethnic composition of managerial, administrative, or other personnel. Such "adjustments" required personnel changes that created opportunities to place people sympathetic to the nationalist cause into positions of authority.[80]

Expansion of the *Matica* was accompanied by changes in the structure and operation of its central leadership—the executive, administrative, and main committees. The Croatian party commission reported that responsibilities in these committees were divided into functional "portfolios" and assigned to individual members, thereby creating within the *Matica* leadership a "shadow government" for Croatia. At the same time, the *Matica* leadership imposed strict discipline on its organizations and individual members. It began even to oppose the right of the party leadership to contact party members working in *Matica* organizations without first informing the central *Matica* leadership. In this way, the central *Matica* leadership began to function as a "parallel central committee" for a potential nationalist "party."[81]

The *Matica Hrvatska* also stepped up its publishing activities. By September 1971, it had increased the number of its regional journals for "culture, literature and social questions" from the nine that had existed in November 1970 to thirteen, and it had established irregularly published journals in five additional cities in Croatia.[82] These publications provided local forums for the presentation of highly nationalistic treatments of contemporary political, cultural, and linguistic issues. In addition, the *Matica* commenced publication of a weekly republic-wide newspaper, *Hrvatski Tjednik*, in April 1971. Officially, *Hrvatski Tjednik* was "a newspaper for cultural and social questions" intended to fill the cultural void created when the Zagreb weekly *Telegram* ceased publication in March 1971 because of financial difficulties.[83] *Telegram* did publish highly controversial political material on several occasions. But these were exceptional events in the life of that publication. *Hrvatski Tjednik* had an entirely different character. Careful review of the contents of every issue (except number 16, which was banned by court order) shows that from the outset *Hrvatski Tjednik* functioned as a forum for the expression of extreme Croatian nationalism. By October 1, it had achieved a circulation of 100,000. At the same time, *Vjesnik*, the Zagreb daily, had an average circulation of 101,000.[84] To demonstrate rapidly growing popular support for its positions,

[80] Ibid., pp. 160-63, 271-73.

[81] Ibid., pp. 157-59.

[82] *Hrvatski Tjednik*, 10 September 1971.

[83] Ibid., 16 April 1971.

[84] Ibid., 1 October 1971; and Federal Institute for Statistics, *Statistical Pocketbook of Yugoslavia 1972* (Beograd: Federal Institute for Statistics, 1972), p. 110.

the editors of *Hrvatski Tjednik* proudly displayed a circulation figure of 100,755 in the next issue.[85]

Nationalistic publishing in Croatia was not the exclusive domain of the *Matica Hrvatska*. The Society of Economists of Zagreb began publication in May 1971 of a highly nationalistic biweekly—*Hrvatski Gospodarski Glasnik*—devoted to "economic-political questions." It was dominated by nationalistic analyses of the relative position of the Croatian republic and Croatian enterprises in the Yugoslav economy, many of them written by economists active in the *Matica Hrvatska*.[86] The journal of the Literary Society of Croatia (*Kritika*) and the journal of the association of independent writers of Croatia (*Hrvatski Književni List*), identified by the Croatian party two years earlier as nationalist forums, continued to publish highly nationalistic material. In the spring of 1971 these were joined by a newly established journal of Zagreb University (*Hrvatsko sveučilište*) and the already-existing journal of the League of Students of Croatia (*Studentski List*).[87]

At the same time, the Serbian cultural society in Croatia, *Prosvjeta*, was expanding its organization and activities. Up to 1971, it had consisted of five local committees. During 1971 that number increased to thirteen. The founding of those new committees was accompanied by activities similar to those which accompanied the opening of new *Matica Hrvatska* branches. The nationalist themes simply were Serb rather than Croat. *Prosvjeta* also expanded its publishing activities. Its monthly journal for education and culture was transformed into an openly nationalist journal. In early 1971 *Prosvjeta* established a weekly publication for Serbs in Croatia staffed largely by Serb nationalists from Belgrade and Novi Sad. In its post-crisis report, the Croatian party's investigatory commission concluded that

> it could not be said that it [*Prosvjeta*] grew into a political organization to the degree that was the case with the *Matica Hrvatska*. However, the fact is evident that important forces arose in that organization which pushed it directly onto a nationalistic platform.[88]

The transformation of *Studentski List* from an ordinary student newspaper into a forum for extreme Croatian nationalism was a result of the dramatic takeover of Croatian student organizations by nationalist elements. According to the report of the Croatian party's investigatory commission, the core of a nationalist student movement in Croatia was established when a "committee of 50" was organized in the dormitories of Zagreb University during 1970.

[85] *Hrvatski Tjednik*, 8 October 1971.
[86] Summaries of *Hrvatski Gospodarski Glasnik* appear in *Hrvatski Tjednik*, 18 June, 2 and 16 July, and 24 September 1971.
[87] SKH, CK, *Izveštaj o stanju*, pp. 181-86.
[88] Ibid., pp. 233-38.

These students received material and political support from a number of functionaries of the *Matica Hrvatska*, from some university faculty and even from some functionaries of the League of Communists of Croatia. On December 21, elections for the post of student pro-Rector of Zagreb University were held. The candidate supported by the university party organization was defeated by a "spontaneous" candidate who was non-communist, a practicing Catholic, a nationalist, and a member of "the committee of 50." His election marked the beginning of open, organized nationalist activity among Croatian students. This activity increased in frequency and intensity throughout January and February of 1971, while intense interregional negotiations were taking place over the constitutional amendments then under preparation. In late March and early April, the nationalist student leadership organized itself formally and, in an impressive show of physical and political force, took control of the Zagreb University Student Federation in a manner that one Western observer described as a "coup." A short time later nationalist students took over the leadership of the League of Students of Croatia.[89]

The rise of open nationalism in the student press of Croatia, the publications of the Croatian writers' and literary societies, and in the publications of the *Matica Hrvatska* was accompanied by a more restrained but still open rise of nationalism in the Croatian mass media nominally under party supervision.[90] According to the investigatory commission, a small group of nationalistically inclined editors in key positions in the *Vjesnik* publishing house, including the general editor of the enterprise and the editor-in-chief and political editor of the Zagreb daily newspaper *Vjesnik*, used their authority to increase the nationalistic content of the newspapers published by *Vjesnik*. They monopolized policy making in these newspapers and controlled their content by writing certain material themselves, by determining which reporters would write about what topics, and by reworking and adding to texts prepared by others, all, of course, normal senior editorial functions. Under the leadership of its own general director, Radio-Television (RTV) Zagreb—the radio and television "network" for the Croatian republic—tripled its current events coverage in 1971. Most of this coverage was devoted to events in Croatia. Coverage of events elsewhere in Yugoslavia was reduced to "symbolic" levels, and joint programming with radio and television stations in other regions of the country was reduced sharply.

The newspapers of the *Vjesnik* publishing house and the broadcasts of RTV Zagreb encouraged the growth of nationalist sentiments among the masses by selective and one-sided reporting of policy conflicts between the republics,

[89] Ibid., pp. 169-74; and Dennison I. Rusinow, "Crisis in Croatia," 4 vols., *American Universities Fieldstaff Report* Southeast Europe Series, Vol. 19, Nos. 4-7 (Hanover, N.H.: American Universities Fieldstaff, 1972), 3: 3-8.

[90] The following account is based on SKH, CK, *Izveštaj o stanju*, pp. 241-52.

by emphasizing "incidents" with interrepublican and inter-nationality dimensions, by publicizing the activities of the *Matica Hrvatska* and the nationalist student leadership, and by using nationalistic publications such as *Hrvatski Tjednik* and the publications of the student and youth press as sources for the preparation of news copy for broadcast. Some reporters on *Vjesnik* newspapers and some employees of the RTV Zagreb news division served at the same time as functionaries in *Matica Hrvatska* or worked for the nationalistic *Matica* publication *Hrvatski Tjednik*.

The emergence of open nationalism in the mass media led to a perceptible change in the character of Croatian political life in the spring of 1971. A Western observer of this period has described the change as it was felt on an individual level in Croatia. It was:

> atmospheric and difficult to describe: an exponential rise in intensity, in the magnitude of the catalog of real or rumored wrongs and in the occasions on which the catalog was volunteered, in sudden detailed knowledge about kinds and values of exploitation or about the number of Serbs who are directors of Croatian enterprises, commanders of Croatian regiments, or to be found in Croatian factories, on Croatian railroads, or on the Zagreb police force.[91]

The conflict between Croat and Serb nationalisms also changed the nature of Yugoslav politics in general. As a later Yugoslav analysis of the period describes it,

> Every current issue: economic, social, cultural, and others . . . was treated as an aspect of the national question in Yugoslavia. The order of things up to then was completely reversed. The national question ceased to appear or to be treated as a phenomenological form with certain social content. On the contrary, every economic, social, cultural and other aspect of life began to be presented as a form with national essence.[92]

The appearance of nationalist ideas in the semi-official press was in large part the result of a split in the Croatian party leadership over the question of how to react to the growing strength of nationalism in Croatia. The general director of the *Vjesnik* publishing house and the general director of RTV Zagreb were both members of the Croatian party's Central Committee and in close contact with the party leadership. According to the report of the investigatory commission, Savka Dabčević-Kučar, president of the party, Pero Pirker, secretary of the Croatian executive committee, and Srečko Bijelić,

[91] Rusinow, "Crisis in Croatia", 2: 14.
[92] Perić, *Ideje "masovnog pokreta"*, p. 121.

president of the Zagreb city committee were attempting to use the force of Croatian nationalism to win political concessions from the leaderships of the other republics and provinces. Consequently, in direct conversations in October 1970 between representatives of *Vjesnik*, RTV Zagreb, and the party, these leaders moderated the criticisms of nationalist tendencies in the mass media raised by other members of the party leadership. They used the authority of their positions as leaders of the party to prevent discussion of these issues by the party organizations in *Vjesnik* and RTV Zagreb, and thereby prevented the organization of internal opposition to the growing nationalist content of the mass media. In this way, they reinforced the control of the general directors over their enterprises, and these directors used their control to lend overwhelming support in the media to these party leaders' positions on critical political issues and to mobilize nationalist sentiments in Croatia around the formation of a "mass movement" in support of them as personalities.[93]

The "mass movement" in Croatia, also known as the "national" or "popular" movement (the word *narodni* carries both meanings in Croatian and may be translated either way), was less an organized movement than a widespread upsurge of nationalist emotions and activities in the populace. The *Matica Hrvatska* leadership and nationalist student leadership worked together closely to control and direct those emotions and activities. But nationalism had grown by the spring of 1971 far beyond the control of any one organization or leadership. By then there were widespread incidents of interethnic violence and hostility both in Croatia and elsewhere in Yugoslavia. Spontaneous marches, demonstrations, and episodes of vandalism with openly nationalistic or ethnic characteristics, as well as individual confrontations between local politicians in ethnically mixed areas, were being reported almost daily in the press. The reports of them varied dramatically between the nationalistic Croatian press and the increasingly alarmed Belgrade newspapers.

The rapidly growing strength of the "mass movement" was unsettling to some members of the Croatian party leadership. That leadership had been united in late 1969 when it chose to emphasize unitarism as the major obstacle to further progress in Yugoslavia. But there had been subtle differences in conception between Vladimir Bakarić, the authoritative leader of the Croatian party since the prewar period, and the younger leaders he had trained and elevated to positions of power in that party, especially Dabčević-Kučar, the president of the party, and Tripalo, his colleague on the central party's Executive Bureau and the only member of the younger leadership whose personal reputation and authority within the Croatian party approached that of Bakarić himself. In constructing his attack on unitarism, Bakarić had carefully warned of the difficulty of the road ahead and had specifically cautioned against an

---

[93] SKH, CK, *Izveštaj o stanju*, pp. 241-52.

alliance with "those who have created a 'parallel central committee' in the *Matica*."[94] But these warnings were ignored by the younger leaders who organized and controlled the tenth session of the Croatian Central Committee in January 1970. They apparently were confident that they could control the more extreme elements among the nationalists and use popular nationalist sentiments as leverage against the leaderships of other regions in order to win further concessions on both substantive policy and constitutional issues. By early 1971, the growing strength of Croatian nationalism and of the *Matica Hrvatska* organization led "some members of the Executive Committee and certain comrades from the political leadership of Croatia" to insist that the president of the party reaffirm the party's opposition to nationalism. By the February 12th meeting of the Croatian party's Executive Committee, a serious split in the leadership already was evident. According to the party's investigatory commission, the policy of leniency toward manifestations of nationalism advocated by Dabčević-Kučar and Tripalo was supported by a number of critically placed cadres. Among them were Pero Pirker (secretary of the Executive Committee), Dragutin Haramija (president of the republican Executive Council [premier]), Marko Koprtla (member of the Executive Committee), Srečko Bijelić (president of the party Conference of Zagreb), and Ivan Šibl (president of the republican veterans' organization). These state and party functionaries rapidly became the major proponents of Croatian nationalist positions on the current issues of the day in Yugoslavia.[95]

The months that followed this meeting were characterized by continually increasing nationalist activities in Croatia. March and April was a period of intense nationalist activity among Croatian students, the *Matica Hrvatska*, and *Prosvjeta*. Yet the Croatian party leadership took no decisive action against the nationalists. Instead, those leaders who had committed themselves to an alliance with Croat nationalist forces used their authority to protect and support them. In the words of the Croatian investigatory commission:

> A narrow group in the leadership of the LCC [League of Communists of Croatia] succeeded in putting into effect their own political line by the force of their positions in the leadership, by means of [their] control over the means of mass communications, by selectively informing and politically manipulating members of the LCC, as well as by direct reliance on certain 'trusted' functionaries in some commune and intercommune leaderships of the LC, in leading organs of some other sociopolitical organizations, in some organs of government, and in some work organizations.[96]

[94] Baletić and Židovec, *Deseta sjednica*, p. 109.
[95] SKH, CK, *Izveštaj o stanju*, p. 68.
[96] Ibid., p. 137.

Early in March draft texts of the constitutional amendments prepared in response to the proposal to establish a collective presidency were submitted to the central Presidium for discussion and approval. In his report to the Presidium, Edvard Kardelj, chairman of the coordinating commission responsible for drafting the amendments, acknowledged that negotiations over the amendments dealing with the political order had been characterized by sharply divergent views and intense conflicts among the representatives of the republics and provinces.[97] As will be shown in greater detail in the next chapter, the solutions finally adopted in these amendments reduced the independent powers of central institutions to a minimum. Specific procedural and organizational changes were adopted to ensure the participation of representatives of all the republics and provinces in the formulation of federal policy. Even routine decisions in the remaining areas of federal competence were to be carried out on the basis of interregional consensus. These changes increased the decisional load of the regional leaderships and made them politically responsible for the day-to-day operation of the federation. Even the independent authority of the Chamber of Nationalities was reduced in favor of direct representation of the regional leaderships in the federal policy-making process.

These amendments reflected almost complete acceptance of the Croatian leadership's positions on the future organization of the Yugoslav community. Consequently, the central leadership and the leaders of the other republics and provinces expected that their adoption would quiet nationalist unrest in Croatia and contribute to the resolution of outstanding interregional policy disputes. Instead, submission of the draft amendments to public scrutiny was followed by still sharper interrepublican conflict and yet more intense internationality conflicts not only in Croatia, but throughout Yugoslavia.

In Serbia, discussion of the draft amendments provided a framework for the expression of extreme nationalist positions. At a public discussion organized by the Law Faculty section of the Association of University Instructors, for example, one participant suggested that the increased autonomy of the republics and provinces embodied in these amendments represented a particular danger for the Serb nation.[98] He argued that the Serb nation was "already in an unequal position with respect to the other nations in Yugoslavia" and that the proposed constitutional amendment would result in "its complete disintegration." He lamented the fact that "the borders of the present Socialist Republic of Serbia are neither the national nor the historical borders of the Serb nation" and that the Serb nation was divided among several of the republics. Moreover, he asserted that "not in one of these republics can

[97] Savo Martinović, ed., *Ustavne promene: Šestnaesta sednica Predsedništva SKJ (Dokumenti)* (Beograd: Komunist, 1971), pp. 9-63.

[98] Cited in Bilandžić, *Ideje i Praksa*, pp. 287-88.

it live properly." Consequently, he called on the Serb nation "to struggle for its own dangerously threatened national identity and integrity." This constituted a clear call for the re-drawing of internal regional boundaries and the creation of a large Serbian republic comprising all territory inhabited by Serbs. The explosiveness of this proposal was reflected by the almost immediate arrest and imprisonment of its initiator. In Croatia, announcement of the amendments did not in any way decrease the level of nationalist activity. Indeed, Miko Tripalo observed that:

> Knowing the mood, I can say that the public in Croatia is dissatisfied with the existing situation and that it seeks radical change. However deep the proposed changes are, we think that they are minimal.[99]

The failure of the draft amendments to calm the political atmosphere even after six weeks of public discussion provoked an angry response from President Tito. Speaking in Priština to the political leadership of Kosovo, Tito delivered an exceptionally frank and emotional warning to the leaderships of all the regions that the time had come for decisive action to end the conflicts paralyzing the party and government. In order to emphasize the importance of the warning, the Yugoslav press agency included in its report of the speech indications that it had been interrupted at several critical points by applause from the audience—a style of reporting rare in the Yugoslav daily press:

> behavior in the League of Communists is not good, [Tito observed,] and I am not satisfied. I must say that that hurts me terribly. You know that I have been at the head of the Communist Party, that is, the League of Communists, for a long time. I think that up to now we have not had a situation such as we have today in the League of Communists. But as long as I am in this position, as long as the membership wants to support me, I will strive to establish order in the League of Communists. We must have unity. However, we have today those who violate it, even though they too speak about unity. Well, good; for once let's see who is really for unity in action and who violates it, destroying in this way our community.[100]

This was an unmistakable call for a showdown within the party itself, and it was greeted with "powerful applause" from his listeners. As the leaders of Kosovo, the most underdeveloped region of the country, they were acutely aware of the high costs of stalemate in the party leadership. They applauded, too, when Tito promised that that showdown would not be long in coming.

Tito made it clear that the urgency of the situation required strong measures.

---

[99] Cited in Perić, *Ideje "masovnog pokreta"*, p. 118.

[100] This and all following citations are from the text published in *Borba* (Belgrade), 16 April 1971.

Among them, he suggested, might be "administrative measures"—the Yugoslav political euphemism for purges. "I know," he said, "that there will be cries of protest that those are undemocratic procedures. . . . But," he asked, "is it possible to proceed differently when such behavior is concerned, especially if [it is] communists [who] are acting this way?"

Up to now we have been very liberal. I never was a supporter of such liberalism. You know that in my own experience I have had many instances of fractionalism and many other negative phenomena. But we always resolved them successfully, because we had the support of the vast majority of the membership. . . . We decisively approached those who did not stand on the line of the Party and who did not support its decisions. We have to act that way today, too, without regard [for the fact] that such a broad democratization of our life has come to pass. Because even under conditions of democracy there must exist some factor which regulates relations in society.

Tito made it clear whom he expected to provide that factor: "Who else can be responsible for all that but we communists," he asked. "We must conduct ourselves this way. And those who do not behave this way," he warned, "are outside the League of Communists." This open threat of a purge of those who were not adhering to the party line was greeted with "long-lasting applause."

In Tito's view, two fundamental tasks lay before the party leadership. First, "we must adopt the amendments as soon as possible." Second, "we must deal with the question of . . . behavior and relations within the League of Communists." Therefore, he announced, "I soon will convene the members of the Presidium and the other most responsible people from the republics and provinces so that we can deal with everything about which I have spoken." And, he added, "we will not split up as long as we do not agree. We must achieve that [agreement], because the situation demands it." At this point, too, he was interrupted by applause.

The Presidium met in an expanded session—its seventeenth—on the island of Brioni for three days at the end of April. In addition to the fifty-two members of the Presidium itself, participants included the presidents of the provincial party committees, the secretaries of the executive organs of the republican and provincial party organizations, the secretary of the party organization in the army, the presidents of socio-political organizations in the federation, representatives of the Federal Executive Council, and the presidents of the republican and provincial Assemblies, the federal Conference of the Socialist Alliance, the trade union Council, and the republican Executive Councils. Almost one hundred people attended. In effect, the meeting brought together almost the entire top elite of the state and party. The agenda for the meeting had been set by President Tito in his Priština speech.

It was widely anticipated that this meeting would produce dramatic denunciations and perhaps even purges of key members of the party leadership. After all, Tito had said in Priština that "today it was asked that it be told at once—who are the ones who destroy that unity. I will certainly say so one day and I will not wait long." But these expectations were not fulfilled. The session produced a set of official "conclusions" that startled the Yugoslav public not by their drama, but rather by their simplicity. The political leadership apparently could agree only to three general positions: First, the draft amendments, which by this time had been public for two months, should be adopted as soon as possible. "That is one of the essential conditions for overcoming the present political and economic difficulties."[101] Second, the political leadership of the country would have to act more cooperatively and responsibly in order to resolve the conflicts then dividing it. The first step would be for regional representatives to enter into negotiations in good faith:

> in the solution of all controversial questions it is necessary to create a working atmosphere of agreement making and to realistically and argumentatively present opinions and views and to represent interests [in order] to carry out their harmonization at sessions of political forums and other bodies.

Once agreement had been reached, each leadership would have to act responsibly. "One of the conditions for the united action of the LCY," the Presidium concluded, "is responsibility of federal, republican, and provincial leaderships in the formation of policy and in the carrying out of jointly passed decisions." In what was the most sharply worded passage in the conclusions, the leadership assembled at Brioni acknowledged that:

> the failure to support agreed-on positions and decisions in the work of certain political, state and other bodies has contributed to the worsening of the political situation . . . , caused distrust in relations and has brought forth the same reactions and conduct in others.

Third, the Yugoslav political elite agreed that nationalism had become a serious threat to the continuing survival of the socialist order, for it had provided "the basis for the coming together of all anti-communist forces." The Presidium conclusions, therefore, obligated the regional leaderships to undertake "a more decisive and concrete struggle against all forms of nationalism in one's own area." Noting that "serious ideo-political errors and

---

[101] This and all following citations are from the text published in Savo Martinović, ed., *Kako ostvarujemo dogovor: posle XVII sednice Predsedništva* (Beograd: Komunist, 1971), pp. 5-10.

instances of opposition to the course of the LCY have been manifested in certain media of information and journalism," the Presidium specifically required the regional leaderships to take appropriate action to bring them under closer control. In describing the discussions carried out during the session, the "conclusions" said only that they had been "detailed and open." Contrary to usual practice, no other materials from the session were made public.

Two days after the meeting ended, President Tito talked about it at some length during a May Day speech in Labin, which he characterized as "a kind of report" on the session. He indicated that "there was much said about inter-nationality relations" and that there had been "sharp discussions." But he emphasized that "it was entirely that kind [of discussion] which it had to be, and, in the end, on all questions which were before the League of Communists, unity was achieved." In language strikingly more forceful than that used in the official conclusions, Tito reiterated the need for elite coherence and for greater party control over nationalist forces.[102]

There was widespread dissatisfaction following the Presidium meeting over both the fact that the leadership had not singled out specific individuals or party organizations for criticism, and the fact that the proceedings of the Presidium session had been kept secret. In his concluding remarks to the Second Congress of Self-Managers in Sarajevo a few days later, Tito acknowledged that "there is quite a bit we could not say" publicly, and went on to explain "why we could not and why we did not dare." He reported that "there was no self-criticism there, or there was very little," and observed caustically that "it looks like our people do not suffer from that disease."

> If we had published everything that was said there, then we would have added to the general psychosis which has been created artificially in our country, especially in the big cities; such an uproar and discord that we could not have achieved anything by it. We would have caused still greater confusion than there already is.[103]

A few days later, the party secretary of Slovenia explained to the Slovenian Central Committee that the secrecy surrounding the discussions was the result of an explicit agreement among the participants, motivated by a reason entirely different from those mentioned by Tito:

> At Brioni we agreed that after the session of the Presidium we will not cite the stenograms or explain personal and other nuances in the positions and proposals. The reason for such a decision is, first of all,

[102] Text, ibid., pp. 11-21.
[103] Text, ibid., pp. 29-36.

the uniform view that it is our task to add to and specify the positions depending on our concrete conditions.[104]

Thus, discussions at the seventeenth session of the Presidium apparently did not unify the regional leaderships as completely as Tito was suggesting. In fact, those leaderships had negotiated a certain degree of freedom for regional adjustments of central policy. It is not surprising, therefore, that Tito, in his public speeches immediately following the session, attempted to add more force to the decisions. At Labin he suggested that those whose actions did not conform to the spirit of the decisions would be purged.

> I call on the people in responsible positions in the economy, in banks, and in the other sectors of our economic life—and there, in the main, are communists—to behave in the way ordered by the decisions of the League of Communists and not how they themselves decide. . . . In the contrary [event], we will proceed against them decisively. But not so that we simply exclude such persons from the League . . . and they still remain in their positions . . . , they also will go from their positions and not just from the party.[105]

And in his speech to the Congress of Self-Managers Tito assured his audience that, unlike in the past, such action would be taken in the future.

> Abroad, and not only abroad but even here all sorts of things are said. For example, immediately after the session of the Presidium . . . and my speech in Labin, I heard that some foreign newsman told how he had spoken in Belgrade with some reporters and some people from higher circles . . . [who said] that Tito already has threatened many times in the past and now threatens again, but that it was all an empty gun in the past and that it always will be the old way again in the future. But no, it will not be an empty gun, we have plenty of ammunition. . . . We will know how to stop the people who confuse us and disrupt our socialist development. You can be sure of that, comrades.[106]

Indeed, Tito moved quickly and quietly to ensure his supply of both guns and ammunition. He met a little more than a week later with the federal secretary for national defense (his close political ally, Nikola Ljubičić), the commanders of both the regular army and the territorial defense forces, the chiefs of the republican and provincial people's defense staffs, the president of the league of reserve officers, and certain members of the central political elite. It was reported publicly at the time only that "President Tito talked in

[104] Ibid., p. 109.
[105] Ibid., pp. 17-18.
[106] Ibid., p. 32.

a lengthy speech about the future tasks of the armed forces, about the tasks of the League of Communists after the seventeenth session . . . and about the current international situation."[107] The Croatian party's investigatory commission revealed later, however, that he had "spoken very sharply and concretely about the danger, the anti-self-managing class essence, and the major centers of nationalism in Yugoslavia and Croatia." He warned specifically that the *Matica Hrvatska* "had formed itself into an alternative political party."[108]

Tito emphasized in his post-Brioni speeches that adoption of the constitutional amendments would place full responsibility for the future course of events directly onto the shoulders of the republican and provincial political leaderships.

> But we will see how the responsible people in the republics will work when greater competence is transferred to the republics. . . . Up to now we have spoken about the negative consequences of etatism in the federation, in the federal government, the Assembly, etc. Now let's see how it will be in the republics.[109]

The test of those leaderships began almost immediately with the round of regional party meetings following the seventeenth session.

In Bosnia, the conclusions of the Presidium received the enthusiastic support of the party leadership. Party secretary Hamdija Pozderac emphasized to his Central Committee that "the taking of even administrative measures" was approved of by the Bosnian party membership. This strong support was in part a consequence of the enormous pressures being put on that multinational republic by nationalists in Croatia and Serbia. Pozderac reported that demands had been raised for "the formation of national institutions," and that these demands "meant the destruction of the community, brotherhood, and unity already created by existing institutions." The creation of "national institutions," he was convinced, "would have led . . . to the disintegration of Bosno-Hercegovinian society." Bosnian party president Branko Mikulić reported that nationalist activity elsewhere had led in Bosnia to "intrigue and the sowing of doubt in certain functionaries and even [whole] leaderships of other republics." This, in turn, had led to suggestions that the Bosnian party form an alliance with the organizations of certain republics aimed against those of others. Even within the Bosnian party itself divisions were beginning to form on the basis of the nationality issue.[110] Similarly, strong support for the Presidium's conclusions, and veiled suggestions that the real problem lay

[107] *Borba* (Belgrade), 21 May 1971.
[108] SKH, CK, *Izveštaj o stanju*, pp. 75, 142.
[109] Martinović, *Kako ostvarujemo dogovor*, p. 34.
[110] Texts, ibid., pp. 57-74; see also *Borba* (Belgrade), 16 May 1971.

in some other republic, were evident at the meetings of the Slovenian, Serbian, and Macedonian Central Committees following the seventeenth session.[111]

The Croatian party leadership convened the twentieth session of its Central Committee to discuss the Brioni decisions. Savka Dabčević-Kučar noted in her opening remarks that "those of us who participated at the session have been asked frequently about the discussions which took place at it." She confirmed that "the discussion was sharp," but reassured the Central Committee that the Croatian leadership had defended Croatian positions faithfully:

> After all, if we did not represent in the Yugoslav center the interests, positions, and concepts of our own area, our socialist republic, and our League of Communists, we could not be real partners in the active and responsible search for joint socialist solutions with others.

Despite the strongly worded remarks delivered by Tito at Labin and Sarajevo, Dabčević-Kučar focused most of her opening remarks on a defense of the actions of the Croatian party leadership in the period prior to the seventeenth session. She asserted that "our political course and our mass base . . . is socialist, it is on the line of the . . . League of Communists." Consequently, she argued, the Croatian party must "deepen" its mass base, "acquiring new allies in the active struggle for self-managing socialism." She followed this with an even more provocative suggestion:

> Pressure and support of the widest public which is interested in the successful performance of these tasks on a socialist and self-managing course, which is less inclined toward concessions, particularly in cadres solutions, will be a great help and support to us and that is why I plead for still greater publicity even in these questions; not only because that is a postulate of our democratic development, but because that is also our need.[112]

This was a call for increasing public action independent of the Croatian party and directed against the central leadership. Precisely this strategy of mobilizing popular support in one's own region against the center—the basis for which inevitably would have to be in large part nationalism—had been roundly condemned two years earlier in the wake of the Slovene "road-building crisis." By adopting this position now, Dabčević-Kučar was expressing clear opposition to the spirit of the Brioni decisions.

At Brioni, the political leaderships of the regions and the central leadership had agreed to a policy of re-imposing party control over society. In formal

---

[111] See texts in Martinović, *Kako ostvarujemo dogovor*, pp. 93-106 and 107-25, but esp. 96, 114; and *Borba* (Belgrade), 15 and 16 May 1971.

[112] This and following citations are from the text in Martinović, *Kako ostvarujemo dogovor*, pp. 75-87.

compliance with these decisions, Dabčević-Kučar devoted a portion of her introductory remarks to criticism of "the tendency toward devaluation of the role of the party . . . [and] denial of everything which has been carried out up to now in socio-economic, cultural, and political life," Croat chauvinism (which she characterized as "the elimination of every socialist and class character from the understanding of the national question, a separatist approach, [and] intolerance and hatred toward others"), and Serb chauvinism. Because the Presidium had made it obligatory, she adhered quite closely in her speech to the Presidium's position concerning "ideo-political errors and opposition to the course of the LCY." In the strongest passage of her remarks, she affirmed the opposition of the Croatian party to "tendencies and attempts by individuals to transform certain cultural institutions into political centers with indications of opposition to the course of the League of Communists."

> Such individuals must not be permitted to attempt to transform cultural institutions into political organizations with a non-socialist orientation. It is logical to expect that these institutions base their cultural and national activity on a socialist platform, orientation and determination, and that they move more openly into confrontation with such tendencies and individuals. It is the obligation of communists to come decisively to accounts with these [individuals] in the area in which they are active. We do not dare tolerate such phenomena.

But, when she exercised her right as president to summarize the sense of the meeting, Dabčević-Kučar made it clear that she and the others in control of the Croatian party did not view these tendencies as widespread, and were not about to embark on a wholesale purge of Croatian cultural institutions. She also "warned against declaring as unfriendly that which is not."[113]

Dabčević-Kučar's summary was an obvious attempt to restrict the scope of party action against nationalist forces in Croatia. While she suggested in her concluding remarks that there were only "certain differences in nuances in some political evaluations of some discussants," contemporary reports of the proceedings and the retrospective report of the Central Committee's investigatory commission suggest that those differences were very deep. The Belgrade press reported that certain members of the Croatian party leadership had been outspokenly critical not only of nationalist forces and their activities but also of the behavior of other members of the leadership itself. Characteristically for this period, the reporting of this criticism in the Zagreb press was highly selective. The Belgrade newsweekly *NIN*, for example, reported that Josip Vrhovec and Jure Bilić—both members of the Croatian party's Executive Committee—had been among the critical speakers. Each had de-

---

[113] Text of concluding remarks, in ibid., pp. 87-91.

nounced nationalist forces as chauvinistic and separatist in intent. Bilić denounced the drift toward what he called "national communism" in the Croatian party.[114]

Borba provided extensive coverage of both the hour-long speech by Dušan Dragosavac (also a member of the Croatian party's Executive Committee), in which he denounced both the *Matica Hrvatska* and *Prosvjeta* as institutional bases of "anticommunist chauvinism," and the comments of Jakov Blažević (president of the Croatian Assembly and member of the central Presidium), in which he denounced nationalist forces as the "allies of unitarism."[115]

The conclusions adopted by the twentieth session reflected both the renewed strength of the antinationalist members of the Croatian party leadership and the growing uselessness of official party pronouncements as means of controlling the rising tide of nationalism in Croatia. "The Central Committee of the League of Communists of Croatia," the conclusions read,

> *insists* on a decisive ideo-political confrontation with all those ideas and actions—*both within its own ranks and in society*—which are contrary to the development and affirmation of our socialist revolution, which negate its continuity and devalue the role of the League of Communists. . . . By the carrying-out of our program we must deliver the most effective blows to [nationalistic, chauvinistic, unitaristic and bureaucratic-technical tendencies and interests]. . . .
>
> Communists, leaderships, and working people in cultural, artistic [and] educational institutions and organizations, in the mass media, [and] journalistic and publishing activities are obligated [*dužni*]—where and when activities and ideological concepts of individuals and groups who are alien to our ideology and policy . . . appear—*to thwart decisively and make impossible* such activity and their executors.[116]

The strongly antinationalist tenor of these conclusions contrasted sharply to the positions adopted at the tenth session and in the period since and the nationalist Zagreb press reacted quickly. *Vjesnik*, the Zagreb daily, reported critical comments only by Dragosavac—the only Serb among the members of the Croatian party leadership. Dragosavac then came under bitter attack in *Hrvatski Tjednik*.[117] The executive committee of the *Matica Hrvatska* used the pages of *Hrvatski Tjednik* to defend itself against "insinuations" by party leaders that it was pursuing policies contrary to the party platform in a statement carefully worded so as to project precisely that opposition. The editorial

---

[114] *NIN*, 16 May 1971 as cited in Rusinow, "Crisis in Croatia", 3: 13-14.
[115] *Borba* (Belgrade), 15 May 1971.
[116] SKH, CK, *Izveštaj o stanju*, p. 290 (emphasis added).
[117] *Hrvatski Tjednik*, 11 June 1971.

board of that newspaper openly equated attacks on the *Matica* with attacks on Croatian self-consciousness in general.[118]

Throughout April, May, and June, *Hrvatski Tjednik* was filled with articles advancing symbolic and substantive demands. Articles called for the rehabilitation of Croatian literary and political/historical figures looked upon with disfavor by the party; for the enforcement of the "purity" of the Croatian language; for the restoration of the pre-communist Croatian national flag, shield, etc.; for ethnic "proportionality"—meaning Croat dominance—in governmental and economic institutions in Croatia; and for widespread radical changes in the Yugoslav economic system. Such demands also were raised in numerous other publications of the *Matica* during this period and in privately published authors' editions of extremely nationalistic works circulating in Croatia. Moreover, the nationalist student movement used discussions of the federal constitutional amendments to raise demands for independent international economic relations for the republic; division of the banking and foreign currency exchange systems by republic; application of a republican "key" to the military officers' corps; use of Croatian as the language of command in Croatia; and home-basing of Croatian recruits.[119]

Among the nationalistic publications, *Hrvatski Tjednik* followed contemporary political developments most closely and published the most numerous attacks on actions and decisions of the party, governmental agencies, and individual politicians. It even went so far as to suggest the need for convening an extraordinary congress of the Croatian party "in order to secure for 'the progressive part' of the leadership of the Central Committee full support and the ability to carry out effectively the policy which it represents."[120] In almost every case, nationalistic positions, activities, and demands were legitimized by invoking the authority of the tenth session of the Croatian Central Committee. On the pages of *Hrvatski Tjednik*, the tenth session remained the most authoritative statement of Croatian party policy.

The obligatory positions adopted at the seventeenth session of the central Presidium and the twentieth session of the Croatian Central Committee seemed to require severe sanctions against party members who participated in the activities of the *Matica Hrvatska* during these months, and the adoption of strong measures against the *Matica* organization itself. But these did not happen. Instead, according to the later report of the Croatian investigatory commission, certain members of the Croatian party leadership in authoritative positions acted in a directly contrary fashion. Members of the Croatian leadership met publicly and privately with functionaries of the *Matica* to discuss current political issues. "Functionaries in the central committee" prevented

[118] Ibid., 28 May and 4 June 1971.
[119] Ibid., 28 May 1971.
[120] SKH, CK, *Izveštaj o stanju*, p. 76.

138

distribution to the Croatian party membership of the text of Tito's private speech to the military leadership, for its distribution to all organizations of the reserve officers' corps in Croatia already had "contributed to stopping the penetration of nationalism into its ranks." "Some leading functionaries" of the Croatian party even expressed support "in unofficial conversations" for the idea of convening an extraordinary party congress.[121]

By this time, however, a majority of the members of the Croatian Executive Committee were convinced that the party had to take concrete measures against nationalism. Therefore, "with the support of some comrades from the remaining part of the political leadership of Croatia"—a veiled reference to the participation of individuals not formally members of the Croatian party leadership, such as Bakarić—they called for the convening of a special consultative meeting between the republican party leadership and all presidents and secretaries of commune and intercommune organizations of the Croatian party.[122]

Despite the fact that the group seeking to impose sanctions on the nationalists constituted a majority of the top leadership, it could not impose them immediately. In the short run, it was able only to control the party agenda and use its majority to force through binding party directives aimed at establishing more strongly antinationalist guidelines for the action of local organizations. Even to present its views to the Croatian party membership it had to struggle against deeply entrenched norms of party discipline and the effective organizational instruments for their enforcement that remained under the control of the minority. The antinationalist majority could not make its positions known to the Croatian public because the mass media remained under the effective control of nationalists or elements allied to members of the party leadership who remained sympathetic to nationalist positions—or, at least, continued to believe that they controlled the nationalists rather than vice-versa and that nationalist pressure could be used to win further political concessions. Ultimately, the antinationalist majority in the Croatian leadership was able to win control of the party only because it could appeal to a powerful outside arbitrator—Tito.

The conflict between the minority group of Croatian leaders who occupied the key positions of authority and control in the party and the majority group of leaders who occupied positions of authority without direct control over the operation of the party received a full airing at the consultative meeting called for by the Executive Committee majority. The meeting was held June 22 and 26 in Zagreb and was attended by the members of the Croatian party's Central Committee, members of the Executive Bureau of the central party Presidium, "a wide circle of the most responsible leaders" from the republican Assembly

---

[121] Ibid., pp. 75-79.
[122] Ibid., pp. 79-80.

and Executive Council, and the "republican leaderships of socio-political organizations."[123] According to the Croatian investigatory commission, "these discussions revealed the full depth and sharpness of the conflicts in the political leadership."

The main topic of discussion was "the danger of a one-sided orientation against unitarism, with neglect of action against nationalism and chauvinism . . . even though the activity of nationalists . . . has assumed a more organized and increasingly aggressive form." In relation to this, there also was discussion of "the tendency to seek an alliance in the struggle against unitarism with advocates of nationalistic ideas." There was discussion of the fact that:

the most outstanding advocates of nationalism have developed wide activity, but among the highest leadership of the central committee of the LCC and in some party leaderships in the field there are diametrically opposite evaluations of their activity. . . . [N]ationalistically oriented persons in many areas are accepted and presented as the most consistent fighters for the policy of the Central Committee . . . and especially for the positions of the Tenth session.

There also was discussion of "the danger that everyone who points out incidents of Croatian nationalism is marked as a unitarist," including even members of the Croatian party's Executive and Central Committees, "with the goal of discrediting them." And, finally, there was discussion about "the appearance of two lines and two directives in local party organizations."

This meeting was held behind closed doors. Information about it was made public only in the later report of the Croatian investigatory commission. That report suggests that the meeting was rancorous, and that the Croatian leadership split into two clearly defined factions. Even more important,

Those comrades who related critically to the phenomena presented [in the meeting] and placed them into an organized system of unfriendly activity felt like, and were presented, especially by the most responsible functionaries of the Central Committee, as advocates of ideas and actions opposed to the Tenth session and the policy of the Central Committee of the LCY.[124]

It was now clear to the majority of the Croatian leadership that the time had come for decisive action.

The conflict of views expressed at this meeting marked the beginning of a behind-the-scenes factional struggle within the Croatian party leadership. In an attempt to win that struggle at the outset, the majority called on the support

---

[123] All citations to this meeting are from the report, ibid., pp. 80-81.
[124] Ibid., p. 82.

of President Tito. He came to Zagreb a week later, called for a closed meeting of the political leadership of the republic, and on 4 July delivered a powerfully critical, deeply emotional, highly personal, and apparently spontaneous speech to them. He was, in his own words, "very angry" and promised that "the meeting will not last long." According to the text reconstructed by the Croatian investigatory commission from the notes of Croatian Executive Committee members in the antinationalist majority,[125] he began by demanding more resolute action by the Croatian party, suggesting that the nationalist movement included counterrevolutionary forces and that "decisive class struggle" was required. Those who were not prepared to undertake such a struggle, he warned, should resign from their party positions.

He reported that he had received information about "the situation in Croatia" and that, in his judgment, it was "not good." Although the "explosion of nationalism" was taking place "in all the republics," he admonished the Croatian leaders, "now it is worst in yours." Despite the fact that the party itself was divided and that some of its leaders were opposed to such action, Tito assured his Croatian audience that he was prepared to act on his own if necessary. "There is quite a bit of power against me," he told them, "but I will not give up now when the situation is like this."

Tito's further comments make it clear that, despite a growing preoccupation with the international security of Yugoslavia, he had been kept fully informed about events in Croatia. He was, he told the Croatian leadership, deeply worried by the intensity of interethnic hostilities already manifest in Croatia and by the failure of the party there to control the activities of nationalist organizations. He was well aware of the symbolic demands raised on the pages of *Hrvatski Tjednik* and was distressed that the Croatian party had failed to act to control their consequences. And he chastised the Croatian leadership for having permitted ethnic head-counting to take place in Croatian factories "among the working class." But he was especially worried by the potential re-emergence of the kind of fratricidal war that had taken place during the German occupation:

> Relations between Serbs and Croats are not good here by you. Because of the troubles, Serbs in some villages are standing vigil and are arming themselves. Pro-*ustaša* and pro-chetnik elements are now gathering. . . .
> Do we want to have 1941 again? That would be a catastrophe.

He warned them that "The nationalists now are taking everything away from you."

Tito demanded that the Croatian party leadership act immediately and he was very specific about what needed to be done. He urged "the prohibition

---

[125] The reconstructed text appears in ibid., pp. 82-88.

of political activity" by both the *Matica Hrvatska* and *Prosvjeta*. "In a socialist society," he argued, "socialist organizations should develop culture and education, and not those who are against socialism." He criticized the Croatian leadership for their failure to act against the enemies of socialism and for preparing to "accept *en masse* into the Party those who are forecasting a hot fall." "Fall will be hot," he warned his listeners, "but for them—I personally will take care of that."

Tito also displayed, however, a lingering faith in the bonds that tied all the members of the communist political leadership together. "Come to your senses, comrades!" he urged them, "It is not necessary to enter into a campaign but it is necessary to cut the roots of all those who are against socialism." He emphasized the need to re-establish ideological unity in the party. Those with views different from the party's should be eliminated from it and sent to the Socialist Alliance, where "democratic centralism does not have to prevail." Inside the party, "democratic centralism must be respected strictly" and the force of a disciplined party must be turned toward "the struggle against the class enemy." Even his faith, however, had limits. The international situation was such, Tito insisted, that continued failure by the Croatian leadership to act would compel him to take action instead, and he made it quite clear that he would not hesitate.

> Others are watching this. Are you aware of the fact that others immediately will be present if there is unrest? But I will establish order with our Army before I will allow others to do it. . . . The League of Veterans is united, if it is necessary once again to take up arms. We really will allow people to fight again for that for which they already fought once before.
>
> . . . .
>
> It would be blindness and unpolitic to think that this will go easily or that you will solve this by some negotiations with them. A scalpel is needed here [and] I will not renounce it, be sure that I will not.

Tito acknowledged that his own efforts up to then had been unsuccessful. "It has been so difficult for me recently that sometimes I do not know what to do. I warn, but people in the leaderships do not accept, people do not like criticism." In order to guarantee success now, he warned, "I will have to go public," and he cautioned the Croatian leadership that "I know that I will have the workers on my side."

According to the report of the Croatian investigatory commission, a lively discussion ensued during which "the members of the [Croatian] leadership who later submitted their resignations" attempted to minimize the threat posed by nationalism and the activities of nationalists in Croatia. In the end, however, "Tito's criticism . . . was accepted by everyone as a warning and an obligation to sharpen the struggle against nationalism and to take concrete measures against its advocates and their activities." This apparent acceptance of his criticisms led Tito to abandon his plan to go public with them. "Under the impression of these deep contradictions among you," he observed at the end of the meeting, "I thought that I would come out publicly and openly. However, now I will not." His primary reason for not going public at this time was not, however, his confidence in the Croatian leadership. Indeed, he noted that "the discussion has confirmed my fears." It was instead the international situation that dictated maintenance of the façade of party unity.

> Since the seventeenth session [of the Presidium] foreign countries have been waiting [to see] whether the process of disintegration of Yugoslavia will be halted. I will not come out publicly now, because they would say Yugoslavia is not capable of surviving. We do not dare to give to the foreign world arguments about our disunity.[126]

He made it clear that it was the Soviet Union that posed the threat of intervention.

The struggle within the Croatian party leadership continued even after Tito's July 4 speech. The majority within the Croatian leadership intent on implementing Tito's recommendations demanded that the sense of the July 4 speech be communicated "objectively" to the delegates to the fourth meeting of the Croatian Party Conference, to be held in Zagreb on the twelfth and thirteenth of the month. It was agreed that the information would be presented at the end of that meeting. However, "Pero Pirker presented information about the discussion of the Croatian political leadership with comrade Tito . . . so generally, superficially, and inadequately that a significant number of those present were not satisfied."[127] As a result, the secret struggle between the opposing factions within the Croatian party leadership intensified.

Late in July, under pressure from the Executive Committee majority, the Zagreb city organization acceded to President Tito's demand for the exclusion from the party of two of the most prominent *Matica Hrvatska* activists and authors of nationalistic economic and political tracts—Marko Veselica and Sime Djodan. But Srečko Bijelić, president of the Zagreb city Presidium and a member of the nationalist-oriented faction, used his authority and the support of Tripalo and Dabčević-Kučar to moderate the charges against them. Their

---

[126] Ibid., p. 88.
[127] Ibid., p. 89.

exclusion from the party did not result in the loss of their university teaching positions and was not accompanied by any action against the *Matica Hrvatska* organization itself. At the same time, nationalists in the leadership of the intercommune and commune-level party organizations for Dalmatia convened secret sessions to mobilize support for nationalist attacks on individual members of the leadership majority, including for the first time even Bakarić. These attacks were communicated to the nationalist minority in the party leadership directly and were not made known to the majority. Indeed, the fact that these meetings and communications had taken place was not generally known until much later.[128] Other attacks on members of the majority appeared with increasing frequency in the nationalist press.

The exclusion of Veselica and Djodan prompted the nationalist student leadership—with whom they had closely cooperated—to put forward a series of openly political demands. Among these were a demand for inclusion in party decision-making forums "at all levels" and an ominous demand for the formation of "student military territorial units."[129] The majority in the Executive Committee responded by condemning the student movement as "in essence, anticommunist." They circulated an official letter to this effect to all intercommune and commune organizations in Croatia. "In order to prevent individuals . . . in the field from falsely interpreting and falsifying the positions of the Executive Committee," the majority "insisted" that Pero Pirker, secretary of the Committee and a central figure in the nationalist faction, sign this letter.[130] The majority followed this action by convening a "consultative meeting" of the Croatian party leadership and the presidents and secretaries of the executive organs of the intercommune and commune party organizations two weeks later, on August 2. At this meeting the majority proposed the adoption of a strongly antinationalist "Program of Activity." But the nationalist minority was able to moderate the document by introducing the assertion that "bureaucratic etatistic" forces still represented an "equal danger." Nonetheless, the "Program of Activity" remained a highly critical account and condemnation of the tactics, strategies, activities, and organization of the nationalist movement in Croatia.[131]

The "Program of Activity" was intended to serve as an authoritative and obligatory statement of the Croatian party's position concerning nationalism in Croatia and, therefore, as a guide for action at all levels of the party. But "in those places where the [nationalistic] fractional group had a certain in-

---

[128] Ibid., pp. 90-94.
[129] *Hrvatski Tjednik*, 23 July 1971. See also ibid., 20 August 1971.
[130] SKH, CK, *Izveštaj o stanju.* p. 96.
[131] Edited text, ibid., pp. 291-97.

fluence and had assumed certain leaderships of the LC, the Program neither reached basic [party] organizations nor was accepted as obligatory for the action of communists."[132] During August and early September the Executive Committee majority conducted a bitter struggle to impose its control on intercommune and commune-level party organizations in Croatia. In the process,

> mutual trust between the majority of the Executive Committee and the other then most responsible functionaries of the Central Committee, already weakened in earlier confrontations over principles, deepened to the edge of crisis and to the point that real unity of action and cooperation no longer was possible.[133]

In mid-September President Tito toured Croatia as part of a larger tour commemorating the thirtieth anniversary of the Yugoslav revolution, and delivered lengthy public speeches in several locations. Unlike his secret July speech to the Croatian party leadership, these public speeches were much less critical of events in Croatia.

> In Zagreb and in a good mood on the final evening of the tour, he offered a toast to his hosts. The enthusiasm he had seen reminded him, he said, of the Partisan spirit of the wartime National Liberation Struggle and the first postwar years, with the same positive socialist orientation. Nowhere had he found evidence of nationalist deviation in this enthusiasm and so he must conclude that reports of "nationalist excesses" dominating the Croatian atmosphere were exaggerated.[134]

With these speeches and this toast, Tito delivered a stunning blow to the efforts of the Croatian majority to impose the Program on the Croatian party and encouraged the nationalist minority and the nationalist movement.[135]

Later in September, Soviet party Secretary Leonid Brezhnev paid an official visit to Yugoslavia at the invitation of President Tito. In July Tito had warned the Croatian leadership that the failure to establish order in Yugoslavia might prompt Soviet intervention. Soviet press coverage of Yugoslavia immediately preceding the visit referred ominously to the existence of conflict and opposition to socialism from domestic forces in Yugoslavia. Because the Soviet justification for the invasion of Czechoslovakia was built on the premise that socialism in that country had been in danger, these press reports contributed

[132] Ibid., p. 99.
[133] Ibid., p. 103.
[134] Rusinow, "Crisis in Croatia", 4: 1.
[135] See, for example, the report of his toast in *Hrvatski Tjednik*, 23 September 1971.

to a noticeable heightening of tension in the Yugoslav party leadership. Nonetheless, Brezhnev's departure was followed by an escalation of nationalist activity in Croatia and by increasingly open conflict between republican party leaderships.

These conflicts now began to be expressed openly in the pages of Belgrade and Zagreb newspapers. Since the time of the Žanko articles of 1969 there had been marked differences between the tone, style, and content of Belgrade and Zagreb reporting of Yugoslav political affairs. But in each of these regional capitals these now escalated into open attacks on developments in the other region. On 2 October *Politika* published extensive excerpts from the Croatian Program, which heretofore had circulated only on a restricted basis among Croatian party functionaries. On 8 October *Hrvatski Tjednik* attacked the *Politika* action. The following week the Belgrade weekly *NIN* began a series of interviews with Croatian leaders that emphasized the obvious differences of interpretation between them.

The adoption of twenty-three amendments to the federal constitution in June necessitated the amendment of the republican and provincial constitutions. Discussion of changes of the constitution of the Croatian republic provided a context in which Croatian nationalists could advance far-reaching demands for the creation of an effectively separate state. For eleven weeks, starting with the issue of 10 September, *Hrvatski Tjednik* contained articles discussing the proposed changes in the Croatian constitution. In them, the editorial board proposed radical changes of its own, and reported the even more extreme proposals of other nationalist organizations such as the Croatian Writers' Society, student organizations, and the *Matica Hrvatska*. Mass meetings organized during this period to discuss the amendments often were transformed into nationalist rallies. At meetings in late October, students rejected the officially proposed amendments to the Croatian constitution. They disputed the right of those who had "trampled" on the constitution and on human rights "for twenty-five years" to determine the new constitution and called for separate United Nations membership for each of the Yugoslav republics.[136]

Early in November the majority in the Croatian Executive Committee made a last-ditch effort to gain organizational control of the party. The Croatian Central Committee was scheduled to meet on November 5th. According to the investigatory commission report, the majority attempted to persuade Savka Dabčević-Kučar to allow them to present publicly to the Central Committee a report "in which the situation in the LCC and in the leadership . . . would be presented objectively." But she insisted on presenting her own more

[136] Ibid., 5 November 1971; and SKH, CK, *Izveštaj o stanju*, p. 177.

general report instead, and restricted the role of the Executive Committee in its preparation. "Two or three days before the session she explained to the [members of the] Executive Committee what she intended to include in the report, and then on the eve of the session read a still incomplete report [to them]." In this way, the commission observed, "[their] influence on its content was reduced to a minimum." But even during these last-minute discussions, members of the majority faction in the Executive Committee "offered particular criticism" of Dabčević-Kučar's treatment of the "mass movement." They

> pointed out that such a critical ideological question should not go before the plenum [Central Committee] without prior thorough discussion and reconciliation of opinions, and that in this instance it was even more necessary because in the "Program of Activity . . ." adopted at the consultative meeting of 2 August 1971 the nationalists' thesis about some new kind of "unified national movement" was criticized and because this was the first session of the Central Committee since that meeting and the discussion with comrade Tito in July.[137]

Bakarić was among those protesting the contents of Dabčević-Kučar's intended report. Following his move to Belgrade to join the new central Executive Bureau in March 1969, he had not been directly involved in the internal affairs of the Croatian leadership. Early in 1971, however, he became involved on a limited basis when, he reported later, "comrades in the [Croatian] Executive Committee told me that there did not exist an identity of views among them and that there was no possibility for them to act." Dabčević-Kučar's report prompted him to intervene in Croatian party affairs directly.

> I protested [the fact] that she was approaching this plenum in this way. I stated that something was happening; that an organization is being created inside the party which is strong, which has its own discipline, its own intentions, and which has a different program than the program of the party, so that certain [party] organizations obviously were connected to that movement and were of the opinion that discipline is directed toward the movement and not toward the League of Communists.[138]

Because of his protests and those of the majority of the Croatian Executive Committee, the investigatory commission reported, it was agreed that Dabčević-Kučar would present the idea of a "mass movement" "only as a

[137] Ibid., p. 105.
[138] *Borba* (Belgrade), 8 December 1971.

personal opinion in the context of a review of the general political mood in Croatia," and that only those parts of her speech "which represent a basis for further political action by the LC on the carrying-out of the constitutional amendments and the solution of questions of social policy" would be submitted to the committee for adoption. It also was agreed that the Program adopted at the August 2nd meeting would be submitted to the Central Committee.

In fact, the two-day meeting unfolded completely differently. The long rambling speech by Dabčević-Kučar in which she recognized and approved the "mass national movement" in Croatia was adopted "unanimously" in its entirety, and the Program was not adopted at all, despite an open demand to do so by Jure Bilić.[139]

The breakdown of this agreement led Bakarić and the majority in the Executive Committee once again to seek a solution outside the Croatian Party. For now it was clear that, despite their efforts over the summer and into the fall, the Central Committee remained under the firm control of those leaders who sought to use nationalist pressure as a political weapon or had themselves given in to that pressure. A few days after the Central Committee session, Dušan Dragosavac met with President Tito and "in the name of the majority in the [Croatian] Executive Committee informed him of the course of events in Croatia since his [Tito's] meeting with the Executive Committee in July."[140] Bakarić later reported that Tito, "parallel to and simultaneously with our own initiative, took his own initiative." Tito "had read the newspapers, did not know everything that had happened among us, but felt that something was not in order here, that a movement was developing here which had doubtful political goals and that he had to say something about this."[141] But an American writer who interviewed Tito in May 1972 suggested a different source of Tito's information. He reported that, at about the same time, "Yugoslav army leaders showed Tito suppressed TV reels of Croatian Communist mass meetings, with only Croatian flags and with Croatian nationalist and anti-Tito slogans, songs, shouts, and signs. Then Tito struck."[142] Whatever the source of his information, Tito was not able to act immediately because of an official visit to Romania scheduled for 23 November.

Two days after the meeting between Tito and Dragosavac, the nationalist president of the League of Students of Zagreb openly and dramatically called the Croatian party leadership to account during a meeting organized to discuss the proposed amendments to the Croatian constitution. According to a report

---

[139] SKH, CK, *Izveštaj o stanju*, pp. 105-106.

[140] Ibid., p. 107.

[141] *Borba* (Belgrade), 8 December 1971.

[142] Cited by Rusinow, "Crisis in Croatia", 4: 11.

in *Politika* the next day, he declared that "a dirty and behind-the-scenes game is being played, calculating on bringing a confrontation between Tripalo, Savka, Pirker, Šibl, and Bijelić—consistent fighters for the interests of the Croatian nation—and all that is progressive in Croatia, in order to divide them from the Croatian people." And he warned that "Insofar as the responsible functionaries named above do not understand and do not see through this game, it can happen that they will lose the confidence of the nation."[143] He followed this with demands for separate Croatian membership in the United Nations, for the elimination in Croatian schools of language study other than the study of Croatian, for the formation of a separate Croatian army based in Croatia and using Croatian as the language of command, and for the use of whatever means necessary to defend the economic interests of the Croatian republic. But he noted that even "if the regulations we are proposing are adopted, that still does not mean that the struggle for full Croatian sovereignty is really won and completed."[144]

Within a few days of these meetings, the nationalist leadership of the Croatian student movement, apparently informed of Tito's intention to "strike" after his return from Romania, organized a strike of their own. On the afternoon of 22 November between two and three thousand students[145] gathered in the Zagreb student center for a meeting called by the Zagreb student leadership to declare a strike "because of the continual prolongation of the resolution of problems connected with the foreign exchange system [which is] unsuitable to socialism, and the banking and foreign trade systems." Not included in the declaration of the strike was a series of additional demands voiced at this meeting: for constitutional affirmation of Croatian as the official language of Croatia; for the transfer of the Yugoslav Admiralty to Split; for home-basing of Croatians serving in the army; and for the designation of Croatian as the language of command in Croatia. It was nonetheless clear to all present, however, that the strike was to have a wider purpose than simply to force modification of the foreign currency exchange system.[146] That evening a meeting of the League of Students of Zagreb—attended by forty-eight representatives of student organizations, including the "hometown clubs" of students from Kosovo, Vojvodina, and Macedonia and the Slovenian member of the Coordinating Committee of the Association of Yugoslav Leagues of

[143] *Politika* (Belgrade), 18 November 1971, as cited in Rusinow, "Crisis in Croatia", 4: 12-13.

[144] *Politika* (Belgrade), 18 November 1971.

[145] The number is reported as 2,000 in *Borba* (Belgrade), 23 November 1971, and 3,000 in *Hrvatski Tjednik*, 3 December 1971.

[146] Text of the declaration in *Hrvatski Tjednik*, 26 November 1971. Report of the meeting in *Borba* (Belgrade), 23 November 1971.

Students—unanimously endorsed the strike. The next evening the League of Students of Croatia convened to endorse the strike and call for its extension to other university centers in the republic.[147]

By dawn on Tuesday [the 23rd] faculties of Zagreb University throughout the city were picketed and students and professors arriving for classes were told of the strike and, when necessary, prevented from entering their classrooms. Observers who were present say that it was one of the best organized such actions they had ever seen.[148]

The first few days of the strike were marked by its spread to other campuses and by continuing endorsements from various student groups. Expressions of support for the strike were accompanied by expressions of support for the "progressive" leadership of the Croatian party (especially Savka Dabčević-Kučar) and by attacks on the "unitarists, class enemies, and enemies of the freedom of the Croatian people" in the leadership of the party. Dušan Dragosavac, Josip Vrhovec, Milutin Baltić, Ema Derossi-Beljajić, Čedo Grbić, and Jure Bilić were specifically mentioned by name.[149] A few meetings of workers also endorsed the strike, but student attempts to solicit worker support generally failed in the face of party-led resistance. By the fifth day of the strike, evidence of organized opposition to the strike began to appear in Zagreb in the form of placarding. These efforts were accompanied by strong condemnations of the strike by a variety of local party organizations and the Reserve Officers' Corps of Zagreb.[150] By 1 December strike-breakers led by party functionaries began sporadic action. In Rijeka, however, the strike met strong resistance from the start. It set off a fierce and sometimes violent struggle involving students, party functionaries, and the local press.[151]

Fragmentary evidence suggests that the nationalist student leadership had been preparing the strike for some time and that it would have been called for about 1 January even had the majority in the party leadership not appealed to Tito.[152] The call for a strike more than a month earlier than planned appears to have been a last-ditch effort to force the minority faction still in control of the Croatian party and apparently still sympathetic to the nationalist cause to use its authority to declare the party openly in opposition to the central

[147] Ibid., 24 November 1971; and *Hrvatski Tjednik*, 26 November and 3 December 1971.

[148] Rusinow, "Crisis in Croatia", 4: 13.

[149] *Hrvatski Tjednik*, 3 December 1971.

[150] *Borba* (Belgrade), 26 November 1971.

[151] See the reports in *Hrvatski Tjednik*, 26 November 1971, and *Borba* (Belgrade), 26 November 1971, and the chronology in *Hrvatski Tjednik*, 3 December 1971.

[152] Rusinow suggests this in "Crisis in Croatia", 4: 14. See also the report on student activity in Rijeka in *Hrvatski Tjednik*, 3 December 1971.

leadership and in alliance with the nationalist "mass movement." It did not work.

The Croatian party leaders knew that they no longer could hope to control the openly nationalist leaderships of the *Matica* and the student movement. Indeed, the growing stridency of the nationalists since July demonstrated the party's inability even to influence the behavior of the more outspoken nationalist leaders. The strike confirmed all the worst fears Tito had expressed to them in his secret speech in July. In probable anticipation of his reactions, they moved quickly to distance themselves from the strikes. Television Zagreb, strongly under the influence of Tripalo, Dabčević-Kučar, and Pirker, immediately was critical of the call for a strike. The evening news commentator noted that the party leadership had been waging "a very successful struggle" for transformation of the foreign currency system, and likened the strike to use of a battering ram on an open door.[153] Koprtla and Bijelić, attending the plenum of the League of Students of Croatia on the twenty-third, "appealed to the students to refrain from the action they had begun, because objectively it . . . damages the efforts of the socio-political leadership of the Republic for the solution of the problem." Beginning with the Zagreb city organization, party organizations under their control opposed the strike as "a direct action against the policy and course of the League of Communists of Croatia!"[154] The leadership even went so far as to distribute in the streets of Zagreb a special edition of the *Bulletin of the Central Committee*—normally restricted to circulation among party cadres and intended to inform them of the work of the Committee and its organs—containing the leadership's critical views concerning the strike.[155] But it was too late. Tito summoned them almost immediately to a private confrontation.

On 30 November, with the strike still in progress in Croatia, the entire Croatian Executive Committee and the leaders of all Croatian socio-political organizations, the republican Assembly, and the Executive Council assembled in Karadjordjevo in response to the summons from President Tito. According to the report of the Croatian investigatory commission, the nationalist minority in the Croatian leadership "tried to explain and justify the negative tendencies and events in Croatia simply by [reference to] the general situation in Yugoslavia and the slow resolution of economic, socio-economic and other systemic problems," and attempted to "minimize their political significance."[156] These discussions lasted twenty hours.[157] Unlike July, however, Tito no longer was prepared to wait for them to act on their own:

[153] *Borba* (Belgrade), 23 November 1971.
[154] Ibid., 24 November 1971.
[155] Ibid., 1 December 1971.
[156] SKH, CK, *Izveštaj o stanju*, p. 112.
[157] *Borba* (Belgrade), 3 December 1971.

I must say *and I will say tomorrow* that I do not stand behind your policy, because you have not justified the trust which I sought from you. You have not acted in full measure as we had talked.[158]

The central party Presidium's twenty-first session was scheduled to meet the next day and provided the forum in which Tito could make his views clear not only to the entire party leadership but to the Yugoslav public as well.

For the first time since the Slovene road-building crisis of 1969, the agenda of a Presidium meeting was devoted entirely to discussion of conditions in a single republic.[159] The Presidium meeting was attended by the secretaries of the executive organs of the republican central committees, the presidents of the provincial committees, the secretary of the party organization in the army, the president of the central party statutory committee, the president of the FEC, the president of the federal youth organization, and representatives of the Socialist Alliance, the federal council of the Trade Union Federation, and the federal committee of the Veterans' Organization. The group was somewhat smaller than that assembled for the seventeenth session in April, but certainly no less powerful. Tito delivered the opening speech. He began by announcing that he had met with the Croatian leadership the previous day and night to discuss "the current situation." He then reported on that meeting and gave his views.[160] The strike in Croatia, he insisted, was "counterrevolutionary activity." "A group of already known negative people exists here," he suggested, "which stands behind it." At the meeting with the Croatian leadership, he reported, "there was strong criticism and I said openly that they were to blame for not having undertaken anything effective in order to prevent that strike." "It is lucky," he observed, "that the working class in Croatia is sufficiently conscious," because those who had organized the strike had attempted to "pull it into [the strike], too."

He then reiterated many of the views and complaints he had expressed in July. "Antisocialist, antiself-management elements" had penetrated the press ("especially the *Matica Hrvatska* press"); "a so-called revolutionary committee of fifty exists . . . which directs all these activities" ("but I call it 'counterrevolutionary' "); and "the *Matica Hrvatska* is the center" of this activity. He attacked the idea of a "mass movement" as a label covering "various lumpen proletarians, counterrevolutionary elements, various nationalists, chauvinists, [and] dogmatists," and as a "fiction" that is "absolutely for condemnation." Tito made it clear that he had said all this before, in Zagreb in July. But, he observed, because his views were not made public

---

[158] SKH, CK, *Izveštaj o stanju*, p. 112 (emphasis added).

[159] *Politika* (Belgrade), 9 December 1971.

[160] All citations to this speech are from the text published in *Borba* (Belgrade), 3 December 1971.

at that time "there was a lot of guessing about what I actually had said." This time he would not make the same mistake.

Tito stated his opposition to the course pursued by the nationalist minority in the Croatian leadership in unequivocal terms:

> Already yesterday I denied that I stand behind such a policy. And here today I say that I do not stand behind such a policy. And I shall not stand for it should a similar policy come to pass in other republics. I shall not and cannot; I must look out for the interests of our entire country and the principles of the League of Communists of Yugoslavia. And this time the public, too, must know that I do not stand behind this.

He then went on to note that even now there appeared to be a certain reluctance among the Croatian leaders to admit their errors. It was, Tito reported, "a two-thirds majority" of the Croatian leadership that agreed with him in the discussions of the prior day and, therefore, one-third that still held out against him. Consequently, he suggested the expulsion of "people who should have been outside the party a long time ago" and the dissolution of "those organizations which slipped to the side of those who are engaged in counterrevolutionary undertakings." He took the first step in this direction by having the recording of his opening remarks broadcast on radio and television throughout Yugoslavia during the afternoon and evening of 2 December, while the Presidium session was still in progress.[161]

At the close of the meeting Tito again addressed the group.[162] During the two days of discussion, "there had been self-criticism here, even from the side of the comrades from Zagreb," and "certain questions were treated very well [and] self-critically." He conceded that nationalist unrest "happened earlier, too, in various areas such as you mentioned—in Slovenia, in Serbia, and in Kosovo." "But," he continued, "this which has happened in Croatia is the most drastic example, which really knocked us in the head." Therefore, the major burden of action remained with "the comrades from Zagreb."

Tito expressed full confidence in the ability of the Croatian leadership to act. But he pointedly repeated some of the demands he had expressed in his opening speech. And, in order to restrict the options available to the Croatian party leaders and Croatian nationalist organizations, he decided—at the suggestion of Kardelj—to distribute the complete materials from this Presidium meeting to the Croatian party membership for full discussion.

These measures reflected a lack of trust in the willingness and ability of the Croatian party leaders—Dabčević-Kučar, Pirker, Tripalo, and the other

---

[161] Rusinow, "Crisis in Croatia", 4: 16.

[162] All citations to this speech are from the text published in *Borba* (Belgrade), 4 December 1971 (emphasis added).

members of the minority faction in that leadership—to fulfill the tasks required of them. But they also reflected a conviction among some members of the central leadership—never publicly identified—that the root of the crisis lay in the introduction of too much independence of action into the operation of the republican organizations.

This conviction led to a reconsideration of the organization and operation of the party. Tito agreed that changes in the operation of the party would be necessary.

> We must specify exactly and clearly what the competencies of the highest forum of the LCY are and what kind of rights it has toward the central committees of the Leagues of Communists of the republics. . . . The Presidium of the LCY of course has its own specified rights, because it is responsible for the development of all of Yugoslavia, and not just certain parts. . . . [W]hat would it be if the Presidium of the LCY did not have the right to criticize, let's say, a central committee of a republic; if it did not have the right to familiarize itself in advance with the materials for a conference or session of the central committees of the republics?
>
> . . . The leadership of the League of Communists of Yugoslavia should be acquainted with what is happening there. Its members should be acquainted with the basic material of these sessions, especially when critical issues which affect the entire Yugoslav community are concerned. And, when necessary, members of the leadership of the LCY should even attend these sessions.

Several times, however, Tito carefully pointed out the limits that had to be placed on strengthening the accountability of any single republican leadership to those of the other republics and on the restoration of central authority. He agreed that within the forum of the League, communists in one republic have "the right to criticize certain things and events in another republic," because "that is only well-intentioned." But, he cautioned, "as soon as a finger is pointed at another republic *through the press or in another way*, or a republic is criticized *in public* from the side of another—that is not good and should not be." Although he asserted the authority of the central leadership, he cautioned that "I am not now for repeating the old way, for *only* administrative measures." But he also conceded that "we must make use of these." Summing up, he argued that

> Our democracy is misused too much. *I do not agree that we have too much democracy*. But, against the opponents of such a community, a democratic community, those measures must be taken which will be most effective, including even administrative ones.

Tito continued to believe that the Croatian leadership would heed his warning and take action; that the members of that leadership who had erred for so long would cease to do so. Indeed, in the wake of the public broadcast of his 2 December speech, the Croatian student leadership already had called an end to the strike. But the days immediately following the twenty-first session proved Tito's confidence to have been misplaced. The minority faction in the Croatian leadership failed to carry out the tasks assigned to them and continued to use Croatian party forums—such as the Zagreb city party Conference and certain intercommune organizations in Dalmatia—to adopt positions in opposition to those adopted by the central leadership. Nationalists in local party organizations, enterprises, socio-political organizations, and the media began "a game with telegrams" in which they expressed strong support for Savka Dabčević-Kučar and only formal support for the positions adopted at the twenty-first session.

In response, the majority in the Croatian Executive Committee moved to consolidate their control. Almost immediately, they notified all intercommune organizations that "the Executive Committee is taking over collective leadership and direction of all political activity until the [next] session of the Central Committee" and that "directives and information cannot move by other channels, except via the Executive Committee."[163] On 6 December they issued a public statement that was sent at the same time to all commune and intercommune organizations. In it they stated that a meeting of the Committee had been held "with the presence of . . . Savka Dabčević-Kučar" to discuss action to implement the conclusions of the twenty-first session. The Committee noted that "in some areas" there was a tendency "to throw the emphasis on . . . division and differentiation of individual leading personalities, instead of on . . . the carrying out of the positions and evaluations from the speech of comrade Tito." As a result, "the danger exists that things will be led in a different direction and the whole action will be killed." Consequently, the Committee ordered that

> the positions and conclusions from the speeches of comrade Tito as well as the conclusions of the Presidium be studied and worked on in all organizations immediately, and without waiting for materials from the twenty-first session.[164]

The next day Bakarić, now leading the majority in the Croatian party leadership directly, delivered a major public speech attacking the concept of a mass movement and criticizing the Croatian leadership for failing to adhere to clear-cut positions adopted by the central leadership as much as a year

---

[163] SKH, CK, *Izveštaj o stanju*, p. 120.
[164] Ibid., pp. 309-10.

earlier. At the same time, supporters of the antinationalist majority sharing the platform with him called for the resignations of Savka Dabčević-Kučar, Pero Pirker, and Marko Koprtla, accusing them by name.[165] This public naming of names was accompanied by a decision of the Executive Committee majority to distribute to the full membership of the Croatian party the sten- ographic notes of the 30 November secret meeting between Tito and the Croatian leadership.[166]

The next day the Executive Bureau of the League of Communists of Yu- goslavia issued a public invitation "to those communists, especially to mem- bers of leaderships, who are not prepared to struggle sincerely and consistently for the positions adopted" at the twenty-first session "to give up their positions on their own in a democratic manner." In the event that such resignations were not forthcoming, the Bureau emphasized that "the bodies which elected them are responsible for replacing them." So that there could be no doubt about its intent, the Bureau declared specifically that:

> the Central Committee of the League of Communists of Croatia, in which the Presidium of the LCY has shown confidence, is invited at its next session to evaluate the behavior of its members, especially those elected to leading positions, and to ensure unity on the basis of the conclusions of the twenty-first session of the Presidium.[167]

This open call for the resignation or removal of the Croatian leaders discredited by their association with nationalist forces—backed-up by Tito's long-stand- ing, but now unspoken promise to use even the army, if necessary, to ensure that it was carried out—marked the end for Dabčević-Kučar, Pirker, and Koprtla, all of whom resigned at the next session of the Croatian Central Committee on 12 and 13 December. The resignation of Miko Tripalo from the Executive Bureau was announced at that meeting, as well. The meeting was *not*, however, characterized by denunciations of the nationalist leaders. On the contrary, as Dennison Rusinow has reported,

> It was a dignified performance by all concerned. It was also a prear- ranged scenario with a specific purpose, designed to set the tone of the debate to come and to warn the members of the Central Committee . . . that the kind of violent attacks on fallen leaders that have usually char- acterized Communist parties, including the [League of Communists of Yugoslavia] . . . would be out of place.[168]

[165] *Borba* (Belgrade), 8 December 1971.

[166] SKH, CK, *Izveštaj o stanju*, pp. 110, 123.

[167] *Politika* (Belgrade), 9 December 1971.

[168] Rusinow, "Crisis in Croatia", 4: 20-21. However, cf. Tito's comments reported in *Politika* (Belgrade), 19 December 1971.

Their resignations caused mass nationalist demonstrations in Zagreb. These lasted for several nights and resulted in the arrest of 550 demonstrators—most of them university students. But just as the majority had followed their leadership for so long, these ex-leaders now faithfully adhered to the new course charted by the group now in control of the Croatian party. The principles of party discipline would prove to be as effective a weapon, if not more effective, in the hands of the new leadership as they had been for the old.

Resignations of other high-ranking members of the party and governmental leaderships of the republic soon followed. According to the report of the Croatian party's investigatory commission, twenty-three Croatian party organizations containing 715 members were reorganized during the period 3 December to 30 April. In the same period, disciplinary action was taken against 947 party members and sixty-nine persons who were not members of the party "because of participation in or contribution (by their behavior) to the development of nationalistic and fractionalistic activity." The new leadership excluded 741 individuals from the party, removed 131 from their positions, and pressured 280 others to resign.[169] Some of the more prominent members of the nationalist leadership suffered extreme abuse and later were made to stand trial for "counter-revolutionary activity."[170]

Almost all of the individuals against whom disciplinary actions were taken were Croats. As can be seen in Table 3.4, relatively few Serbs were punished. Over 80 percent of those punished were located in three of the principal cities of Croatia: Zagreb, Osijek, and Split (Table 3.5). These individuals also were concentrated among the political and intellectual elite of the republic. As Table 3.6 demonstrates, over 80 percent of those punished were technical, professional, and white-collar workers, leading individuals, or paid functionaries. Although concentrated geographically and in a few social strata, these individuals were at the same time widely dispersed among socio-political and other organizations in the republic (Table 3.7), a reflection of the extent to which nationalism had penetrated the regime's own official organizations. The relatively small number of individuals actually punished in the aftermath of what was in fact a massive upsurge of nationalist activity (947 individuals constituted only 0.4 percent of the Croatian party membership in 1971) and their relative concentration in leading positions of Croatian society suggests that the post-crisis party leadership—both in Croatia and at the center—viewed the events in Croatia as a clear case of the failure of the elite, and especially the party leadership, to perform its leadership and control functions.

[169] SKH, CK, *Izveštaj o stanju*, p. 127.

[170] See, for example, the account of Sime Djodan's fate in the preface to Sime Djodan, *The Evolution of the Economic System of Yugoslavia and the Economic Position of Croatia* (New York: Journal of Croatian Studies, 1973).

TABLE 3.4
National Composition of Individuals Punished
in Wake of "Croatian Crisis"

| | Type of Punishment | | | | |
	Exclusion	Replacement	Resignation	Total	Percent
Croats	656	122	258	1,036	89.9
Serbs	43	3	8	54	4.7
Others	7	—	6	13	1.1
Unknown	10	6	5	21	1.8
Undecided	25	—	3	28	2.4
Total	741	131	280	1,152	100.0

SOURCE: SKH, CK, *Izveštaj o stanju*, p. 128.

TABLE 3.5
Regional Distribution of Punished Individuals

| Inter-*općina* Organization | Type of Punishment | | | | |
	Exclusion	Replacement	Resignation	Total	Percent
Bjelovar	22	3	18	43	3.7
Gospić	10	—	—	10	0.9
Karlovac	15	—	9	24	2.1
Osijek	228	40	83	351	30.4
Rijeka	44	15	11	70	6.1
Sisak	29	4	21	54	4.7
Split	171	33	60	264	22.9
Varaždin	9	—	6	15	1.3
Zagreb	213	36	72	321	27.9
Total	741	131	280	1,152	100.0

SOURCE: SKH, CK, *Izveštaj o stanju*, pp. 127-28.

TABLE 3.6
Socio-Economic Position of Punished Individuals

| | Type of Punishment | | | | |
	Exclusion	Replace-ment	Resignation	Total	%
Workers	85	7	7	99	8.6
Peasants	7	—	2	9	0.8
Technical & Professional	320	55	83	458	39.8
(Engineers, Technicians,					
Economists & Lawyers)	(80)	(16)	(25)	(121)	(10.5)
(Scientists, Culture,					
Educators & Health)	(96)	(16)	(37)	(149)	(12.9)
(White Collar Empl.)	(144)	(23)	(21)	(188)	(16.3)
Leading Individuals	188	23	108	319	27.7
Paid Functionaries	17	2	65	84	7.3
Students	56	10	7	73	6.3
Pensioners	43	5	7	55	4.8
Others	25	29	1	55	4.8
Total	741	131	280	1,152	100.0

SOURCE: SKH, CK, *Izveštaj o stanju*, p. 129.

TABLE 3.7
Organizational Memberships of Replaced and Resigned Functionaries[a]

Organization[b]	Replaced	Resigned
The Party	43	85
(Central Presidium		
& Conference)		(3)
(Central Committee)		(9)
(Repub. Conference)		(5)
(Commune & Basic Orgs.)	(43)	(68)
Socialist Alliance	19	43
Youth League	14	26
Trade Union	2	16
Veterans' Org.	15	13
Government	29	85
Judiciary	2	7
Work Orgs.	44	52

SOURCE: SKH, CK, *Izveštaj o stanju*, pp. 128, 265.

[a] Does not include 28 individuals "suspended from combat responsibility
. . . as reserve commandants of battalions, political commissars, etc."

[b] Not mutually exclusive.

Lessons of the "Croatian Crisis"

President Tito, the central party leadership, and the leaders of other regional party organizations, as well as the majority in the Croatian party leadership, consistently attributed worsening political conditions in Croatia to the failure of political leadership in that republic and not to the inadequacy of procedural rules and institutional arrangements for central decision making and policy formulation. The performance of central institutions in the period immediately following the crisis provides strong support for this contention. In the first seven to eight months of 1972 alone, for example, the interrepublican committees created by the 1971 amendments for the formulation of federal policy in those areas in which the interests of the republics and provinces conflicted successfully completed 120 interrepublican and provincial agreements on issues over which the regional leaderships had earlier been deadlocked.[171] Only two weeks after the resignations of the Croatian leadership, the Federal Executive Council announced the conclusion of an interrepublican agreement on reform of the foreign currency system that raised retention quotas from 7 to 20 percent (45 percent for tourist industry enterprises) and established an internal foreign currency market in Yugoslavia, thereby conceding to the two central demands of the Croatian nationalist movement.[172]

This acceleration of the decision-making process was achieved within the institutional framework established by constitutional amendments adopted prior to and during the period of crisis. The success of these institutional and procedural provisions for decision making can, therefore, be attributed in large part to the fact that the "Croatian crisis" had sensitized Yugoslav political leaders to the dangers inherent in certain forms of behavior. In a number of surprisingly candid accounts of the events in Croatia, members of the political leadership and political analysts with close connections to that leadership have identified some of the specific behaviors they perceived as having undermined the effectiveness of decision making during the period of the crisis. Two of the most important of these are Ivan Perić's studies of the ideas of the mass movement and of contemporary Croatian nationalism.[173]

Perić argues that the views expressed by the Croatian leadership on critical issues, although not necessarily "deviations from a class, self-management orientation," "opened space for opposition nationalistic forces to build their own platform, and to give to that platform a false socialist and self-managing facade." In effect, he criticizes that leadership not so much for the positions

---

[171] Bilandžić, *Ideje i Praksa*, p. 291.

[172] *Politika* (Belgrade), 28 December 1971.

[173] Perić, *Ideje "masovnog pokreta"* and *Suvremeni Hrvatski nacionalizam*; cf. Ema Derossi-Beljajić, "Karakteristika i dimenzije idejno-političkih devijacija u Savezu komunista Hrvatske," *Naše Teme* 14, 1 (1972): 1-20.

they formulated as for the fact that "nationalistic opposition forces" were able to use them to buttress their own.[174] Perić criticizes the former Croatian leaders more directly when he suggests that the application of "continuing pressure" on the central leadership and the leaderships of the other republics and provinces "remained an essential component of the understanding of the members of the replaced group about Yugoslavia and the activity of Croatia as a state within it." "For them," Perić argues, "the only problem lay in the insurance of leadership and control over the activity of actual or potential pressure groups."[175] However, the Croatian political leaders "could not secure and maintain the position of exclusive representative of the nation." Nationalist forces became "the advocate of action and pressure by citing the national interest; substantiating it by proving and emphasizing directly economic problems." Under such pressure, Perić argues, political leaders "either are checked by these forces, which 'radicalize' the problem, or enter into an open or tacit alliance with them."[176]

The Croatian leadership's loss of control over "actual or potential pressure groups" threatened the party as a whole with the loss of control over the introduction of change in the system. The party had to maintain a monopoly over innovation in order to protect, and assert, the continuing validity of the principles on which its own legitimacy—and power—rested. Perić uses Tripalo's statement of March 1971 (cited earlier), implying that Croatian public opinion would determine the extent of change necessary, to focus his argument. "Knowing the mood," Tripalo had stated, "I can say that the public in Croatia is dissatisfied with the existing situation and that it seeks radical changes. However deep the proposed changes are, we think that they are minimal." Perić argues that:

> to the extent that these changes are thought of as the result of the recognition in the League of Communists that the organization of the federation, and interrepublican relations within it, must be changed . . . , then to that extent there can not be put forward the question of any kind of minimum. There can be as much change as is, on the basis of the recognition of the League as a whole and in the interest of further socialist development, necessary to carry out.[177]

Change, even radical change, had to be carried out under the banner of continuity. If the party leadership were to carry out changes in order to meet some kind of minimum, "then that demonstrates that they are carried out under the pressure of certain forces outside the League and that it is possible

[174] Perić, *Ideje "masovnog pokreta"*, p. 132.
[175] Ibid., p. 119.
[176] Ibid., p. 212.
[177] Ibid., p. 118.

for that pressure to continue with the advancing of new demands which exceed that minimum." Perić concludes from this that "those who emphasize the question of a minimum in a certain way distance themselves from the League of Communists of Yugoslavia as a whole and identify with the forces that exert pressure, or very closely approach these forces."[178]

This strategy may have been the only one the Croatian leaders could devise to preserve their positions in the republic without resorting to the repressive measures that they and the rest of the communist political leadership had rejected earlier. Perić notes that by the summer of 1971 the nationalistic press in Croatia had insisted on the right of the movement, "as an independent force," to evaluate political functionaries and choose from among them.[179] In effect, the Croatian party leadership slowly was losing power to an alternative elite composed of the interlocking leaderships of the *Matica Hrvatska* and the student associations of Zagreb and Croatia, and other Croatian nationalist organizations.

By 1971, Perić argues, the Croatian leadership was being evaluated by this powerful alternative elite in terms of "the national interest" of Croatia, which had to prevail "in every instance, in every undertaking. Nothing can be done of value for others which would simultaneously be against Croatia." Moreover, even though these evaluations were carried out "by bourgeois nationalistic forces outside the League of Communists," he observes, "this does not mean that it did not find a corresponding echo in the League, as well." During the period of nationalist fervor in Croatia, the leadership of the party "formulated positions and conclusions" over a wide range of important issues not directly affecting relations between the republics or between the nationalities and "sent them to [party] organizations and to the membership and obligated them to take corresponding action, to adopt appropriate behavior." However, these did not find "an appropriate response among the membership at the base of society." In other words, the Croatian leadership was losing control not only over the nonparty nationalist activists but also over local party organizations, and even on issues not directly related to the national question![180]

Perić criticizes the Croatian leaders for having attempted to break the deadlock in the central leadership by carrying the dispute to the public. In 1968 this had been avoided by referring deadlocked issues to the next session of the central party Presidium. Perić cites a 1968 report on the decision-making process in the Central Committee of the Yugoslav party, delivered to the Croatian Central Committee by Savka Dabčević-Kučar, in which she

[178] Ibid.
[179] Ibid., pp. 234-38.
[180] Perić, *Suvremeni Hrvatski nacionalizam*, p. 67.

acknowledges that proposals put forth by the Croatian representatives were rejected by all other republican representatives. She reported, too, that the conflict was resolved by moving it to the higher, smaller and more authoritative Presidium.[181] By 1971, however, the disposition of the Croatian leadership had changed. By then, Dabčević-Kučar was prepared to insist under identical circumstances that "there is no one who could prevent us from giving basic information about this [conflict] not only to the [Croatian] party membership, but to the public, as well."[182]

For Perić, this is clear evidence that the Croatian party leadership had accepted the idea that it "was not obligated to obey the norms of behavior which were valid for the League as a whole, or all of the parts of that whole." Dabčević-Kučar's threat raised the possibility that a republican leadership might mobilize its own "national" public opinion as "support for their own positions and to initiate pressure against the state and party leaderships as well as against the party organizations of other republics."[183] Moreover, this pressure would be in support of "positions which the political representatives of other republics or nations in the federal leadership could neither comprehend nor accept."[184]

Perić contends that this is precisely what occurred. Savka Dabčević-Kučar raised a series of demands at the same time that "interrepublican bodies established on the level of the federation were beginning to discuss and seek solutions to them." Moreover, not only did the Croatian leaders expose unresolved conflicts within the party to public scrutiny but they also continued to raise issues for which solutions had already been formulated by representatives from all republics. This, Perić asserts, can only be understood as an effort to deepen interregional conflict.[185] In this way, the Croatian leadership struck at the root of the party's ability to admit and maintain a diversity of views and, at the same time, to reconcile them.

These analyses suggest that if the leadership of Yugoslavia was to prevent another such crisis in the future it would have not only to resolve the outstanding "objective" economic conflicts between the national-territorial blocs into which the country had been divided but also to review, and if necessary, change the character of five broad sets of relationships: those among bloc leaders in the central party organs; between the central party leadership bloc and the regional leaderships; among the leaders within each bloc; between each of the regional bloc leaderships and their respective party organizations; and between individual communists and the social organizations and insti-

---

[181] Ibid., p. 54.
[182] Perić, *Ideje "masovnog pokreta,"* p. 194.
[183] Ibid., pp. 194, 195.
[184] Perić, *Suvremeni Hrvatski nacionalizam,* p. 119.
[185] Perić, *Ideje "masovnog pokreta,"* p. 119.

tutions of which they are a part. The communist leadership of Yugoslavia would have to reestablish mutual trust and confidence, and rebuild a community of shared values among the regional leaderships and their representatives in the central organs of the party—i.e., among themselves—that would override the particularistic interests of their respective regions, and thereby motivate them to cooperate. All the members of each regional leadership, and not just those engaged in interregional negotiation, would have to share this trust, confidence, and community of values, for each of these leaderships was internally divided by economic, ideo-political, and, in certain regions, ethnic lines of cleavage. The communist leadership of Yugoslavia also would have to ensure the confidentiality of negotiations among the regional leaderships, at least in their early stages, so that leaders could forge compromises without irritating mass sensitivities and thereby engendering mass pressure. Finally, the communist political leadership also would have to ensure that compromises, once struck, would be enforced. To do so would require that leadership to restore the power and authority of central party organs in relation to each of the regional leaderships, as well as the predominance of each of the regional leaderships over their respective organizations. And, if these changes were to result in reduced levels of inter-nationality hostility and social conflict at the mass level, the existing relationship between individual communists and the other social organizations, institutions, and self-managing economic enterprises in which they worked or participated would have to be reversed. Individual communists would have to exercise influence in those organizations, institutions, and enterprises on behalf of the positions of the League, rather than vice versa. Such changes would be easier to carry out if the economic conflicts between the regions were resolved. If those conflicts continued, however, such changes would ease their resolution. The two tasks were closely interconnected.

Not surprisingly, therefore, the coalition of central and regional leaders that assumed control under the direction of President Tito in December 1971 moved to resolve "objective" conflicts and to reshape the structure and character of the party itself. At the same time that it pressed the interrepublican committees of the government to accelerate the resolution of outstanding interregional conflicts over federal economic policy, the coalition carried out changes in the party that closely approximated those outlined above. In his concluding remarks to the twenty-first session of the central Presidium, Tito had emphasized the right of that body to supervise the operation of the regional organizations. One week later, Stane Dolanc pursued this theme further. During a frank discussion of the organization and operation of the Presidium with the editors of the party's organizational journal, *Komunist*, Dolanc argued that the joint leadership of the League of Communists of Yugoslavia can not be deprived of the possibility, right, and responsibility to follow continuously, to analyze, and to direct the entire course of events in the League of Communists and in the country.[186]

In order for it to be able to do so, however, certain changes in the organization and operation of the central organs were required.

Following the twenty-first session, Tito took over direct, personal supervision of the work of the Presidium and, until the second Conference of the party late in January, the operation of its Executive Bureau as well. At the second Conference, the Bureau, which thus far had failed to perform the integrative leadership function for which it had been created at the Ninth Congress, was reorganized. "In order [to enable it] to act and make decisions more successfully," the Bureau was reduced in size from fifteen to eight members, plus the president of the League (Tito). Each of the republican and provincial organizations now was represented equally, by a single member. This change was intended by Tito and those who supported him to be a step toward the re-creation of an authoritative "party center" capable of reviewing and giving directions to the activities of the regional organizations. However, the members of the Bureau still were to be determined by their respective regional organizations, and because not even the regional leaders who supported Tito were anxious to transfer predominant authority to the center, the new Bureau was composed of individuals generally less powerful than their predecessors.[187]

Nonetheless, the new Bureau was strengthened by certain internal changes in its operation. Whereas operational responsibilities in the previous Bureau had rotated among the members bimonthly and decisions had been made on a collegial basis, individual members of the new Bureau were assigned responsibility for specific policy areas. Stane Dolanc, who had been chairman of the Bureau during the weeks of crisis in November and December and had proved himself both a capable party administrator and loyal supporter of the coalition led by Tito, was appointed secretary of the Bureau and was made responsible for overall supervision of its work.[188] As a result, while the members of the Bureau still were subject to the greater authority of their regional leaderships, they now could operate more effectively as the executive organ of the Presidium—that is, of the Tito-led coalition in it. At the Tenth Congress in 1974, new party statutes assigned the Executive Committee (successor of the Bureau) formal authority "to supervise and ensure the execution

---

[186] *Politika* (Belgrade), 9 December 1971.

[187] SKJ, *Druga Konferencija Saveza komunista Jugoslavije* (Beograd: Komunist, 1972), p. 4.

[188] Rojc et al., *Deseti Kongres SKJ*, p. 498.

of adopted decisions" of the Presidium.[189] This solution appeared to be a compromise between the Tito coalition, intent on reestablishing a strong "party center" and certain regional leaders intent on preserving the autonomy of their organizations.

By itself, even a strengthened Executive Bureau could not function as a strong "party center"; and this Executive Bureau, which was still subordinate to the regional leaderships, certainly could not. If such a center was to be reestablished, the unity and authority of the larger Presidium itself—that is, the unity of the regional leaderships and their representatives assembled as a group and the authority of their joint decisions for each individual regional party organization—would have to be restored. At the time of the second Conference in January 1972, those leaderships and their representatives remained divided on specific issues, and reluctant to accept any reduction of their own autonomy.

At the time of the second Conference, only a few weeks after the forced resignations of the Croatian leadership, the central coalition led by President Tito apparently was as yet unable, unprepared, or unwilling to confront publicly in any detail the organizational and operational problems in the party that had led to the crisis or to recommend concrete remedies for them. As a result, the report to the second Conference on the work of the Presidium in the period between October 1970 and January 1972 is remarkably vague and somewhat contradictory.[190] The spokesman for the party's commission for the preparation of a conference document on the future tasks of the party reported that the members of that commission, representing their regional organizations, had a great deal of difficulty synthesizing their divergent positions on specific questions. As a result, "many positions in the draft of the Action Program are not completely worked out and have not achieved the necessary [degree of] concreteness."[191]

At the twenty-first session, the Presidium had emphasized "the full responsibility of all communists of Yugoslavia, but primarily of the central committees of the republics and the provincial committees, each in its own area, to initiate decisive ideo-political action against antisocialist phenomena . . ." and to create

improved political conditions for the functioning of the constitutionally established democratic institutions of society and the system of agreement making, for the sake of faster solution of systemic and other open questions of the development of society, in order to overcome controversies

[189] Ibid., p. 355.
[190] SKJ, *Druga Konferencija SKJ*, pp. 439ff.
[191] Ibid., p. 431.

in the solution of economic problems, *as well as in the more consistent carrying-out of the program and policy of the League of Communists.*[192]

But the regional representatives who composed the Presidium remained silent as to precisely how this was to be achieved. The coalition led by Tito clearly saw the restoration of central authority in the party as the requisite first step in this direction. That restoration, however, continued to be opposed by still-powerful regional leaders.[193] Even after nine months of effort, Tito and his supporters were compelled to admit that "acceptance of the positions and conclusions [of the twenty-first session] has been translated only slowly into action. . . . It is obvious that even in the ranks of the League of Communists there have been attempts to blunt the edge of the adopted positions."[194]

The Purge of the Serbian Party and the Reaffirmation of Central Authority

Even as the Tito-led coalition began its attempt to restore central authority in the party, it was met with strong resistance from the party leadership of Serbia.[195] Early in January 1972, before the second Conference was convened, the Tito-led coalition began to call for the strengthening of "democratic centralism" in the party, with the emphasis on "centralism." The Serbian leadership, in contrast, began to emphasize that "one of the most important lessons" to be learned from the Croatian crisis was "the problem of democratism in the League of Communists, especially at its summit." The Serbian insistence on the making of "principled decisions" under conditions that the Tito-led coalition saw as calling for immediate, practical action was interpreted by the coalition as resistance to central authority.[196]

Despite Tito's warning at the second Conference to the effect that "we cannot have some party centers that would do what they want to, even contrary to the interests of whole," and that "there has been and continues to be some of that in Serbia," the Serbian leadership continued to resist implementation of the more authoritarian relationship between party and society called for by

[192] *Borba* (Belgrade), 3 December 1971 (emphasis added).

[193] For a partial account of this resistance see William Zimmerman, "The Tito Succession and the Evolution of Yugoslav Politics," *Studies in Comparative Communism* 9, 1 and 2 (1976): 72-74.

[194] *Nova inicijativa u SKJ*, second edition (Beograd: Komunist, 1975), p. 8.

[195] The following account of the resistance by the Serbian leadership to re-centralization of authority in the party is drawn from a surprisingly frank, lengthy (30-page) account drawing on previously secret materials, including reports and transcripts from closed meetings of the Serbian leadership and Central Committee, published in three installments in *NIN*, 8, 15, and 22 April 1973.

[196] Ibid., 8 April 1973.

Tito and his supporters. However, with the offensive against the Croatian nationalist deviation under way, the central leadership was reexamining some of the substantive issues underlying the conflicts of recent years. "Serious questions" were raised concerning the banks, foreign trade companies, and other factors. "It was awaited with great interest what would now be done in Serbia, first of all in Belgrade, with respect to the great concentration of banks and foreign trade concerns in the capital." When the Serbian leadership failed to take any action to bring these organizations under closer party supervision, "it began to be said in some places that the political leadership of Serbia was prepared to stand in defense of the interests of these organizations" against criticism from other regional leaders and the central leadership.[197]

The Serbian leadership's continuing failure to establish closer party control over other social, economic, and political organizations in that republic prompted Tito to meet with them in April to discuss the situation. At this meeting, he insisted on "a strengthening of the struggle and work of the party" and on "a sharpening of the militancy of party organizations." He emphasized that "there are quite a few enemy centers in the University, in publishing houses, and other areas" and that "it is necessary to act against them as against counterrevolutionaries." In this way, he equated the challenge to party authority in Serbia with that which had just been defeated in Croatia. Tito accused the Serbian leadership of inaction, of failure to distance itself from enemies of the party, of failure to expel such people from the party or mobilize the public against what he insisted on calling "counterrevolutionaries."

The Serbian leaders reacted to this criticism in much the same way as the Croatian leaders had reacted to Tito's critical, July 4th speech in Zagreb. Serbian party president Marko Nikezić defended the party as being in line with central policy. At a Serbian Central Committee meeting two days later, party secretary Latinka Perović reported on the meeting in a manner that "softened the critical forces of the meeting and the words of Comrade Tito." She asserted that the discussion with Tito had "affirmed our general orientation," and she resisted demands from members of the Committee for distribution of the stenographic records from that meeting to the entire party leadership and all party *aktivs*. Thus, just as the Croatian leadership had done the previous July, the Serbian leadership now attempted to strengthen their control over their party organization by monopolizing first-hand information about judgments delivered by President Tito behind closed doors.[198]

However, just as the Croatian leadership had been divided, so the Serbian leadership was similarly divided. Party and leadership meetings held in April, May, and June 1972 suggested the emergence of "a direct confrontation of

[197] Ibid.
[198] Ibid.

positions" in the leadership. "For more attentive readers," certain "symptoms of disagreement" were evident even in the reports of those meetings that had been public. At closed meetings, the differences were more obvious.[199] One group of party leaders, led by Nikezić and Perović, felt that "the enemy is not so strong as much as we are weak," while another "thought that oppositional forces were more organized and more aggressive than was believed, that they were putting forward their own programs, and attempting to transform certain institutions into bases for their legal activity." This latter group, led by the president of the Serbian parliament, Dragoslav Marković, "insisted that the League of Communists must turn toward more decisive and concrete action" aimed at restoring party control. The former group, however, in control of Serbian party policy by virtue of their positions, insisted that "the main danger for the League was not on that side but the other—to begin to return to the past, to old methods."[200]

These differences intensified during July. Early in the month a closed meeting of the republican political leadership was convened to continue discussions of the situation. At that meeting, the leadership disagreed over the danger posed by "the class enemy" in Serbia and over the meaning of "democracy" in the party and society. Serbian supporters of the Tito-led coalition criticized the policies of the republican party leadership as "liberalistic and opportunistic" and warned of the strength of nationalist forces in the republic. Dragoslav Marković, in particular, complained that "every plea for the organized offensive approach of conscious socialist forces, and even the application of legal and constitutional . . . measures of force, is characterized as Rankovićism and Stalinism." He criticized the Serbian party leadership for its lack of control over the press, for the weakening of its ties to the central party leadership, and for its "insufficient valuation of some of comrade Tito's views on conditions in Serbia."[201]

Nikezić, Perović, and their supporters, however, did not accept this criticism. They defended their efforts to oppose "alien ideologies," asserted that the party did not have particular responsibility for the press but must oversee it jointly with the Socialist Alliance and parliament (Perović dismissed the entire subject as "not a priority question"), and suggested that efforts to resolve the situation concerning banks and foreign trade firms were not being delayed but rather were meeting with resistance. Nikezić suggested that the criticism from within the Serbian leadership itself constituted an attempt to break up or "betray" Serbia, and warned against over-dramatizing the situation.[202]

[199] Ibid.
[200] Ibid., 15 April 1972.
[201] Ibid.
[202] Ibid.

Following this meeting, a factional struggle appears to have broken out within the Serbian leadership similar to the one that took place in Croatia only a year earlier. Nikezić, Perović, and their supporters tried to use their powerful positions in the party to suppress any attempt to oppose them. Unlike the party leaders in Croatia, however, they could not prevent their opponents from using their own organizational bases as forums from which to press their positions. Thus, for example, Marković's republican parliament became an arena in which discontent with party policies was now expressed openly. By mid-July open discussion of "a struggle for power" and "factionalism" in the party leadership was taking place even among members of the Central Committee. Some evidence suggests that, in response to their declining ability to contain this internal opposition, the leaders of the Serbian party began during the summer to lay the foundation for a purge of their opponents. In the meanwhile, however, they continued to portray events in their republic in the best possible light before central party leaders.[203]

In September, Perović reported on the political situation in Serbia to the Executive Bureau of the central party Presidium. She characterized the situation as completely normal and suggested that the widespread interest in events in Serbia evident among other party leaders was exaggerated.[204] By this time, however, the coalition under Tito's leadership could no longer be dissuaded from intervening directly in Serbian affairs. They were determined to establish those conditions that events in Croatia had taught them were necessary for the continuing survival of the country as a unified political system under communist control.

In mid-September, the Executive Bureau, on the initiative of Tito, Bakarić, Kardelj, and others,[205] drafted a letter sharply criticizing party work since the twenty-first session and renewing the call for increased central authority in the party. Apparently, the coalition did not yet have the support of a majority of the Presidium membership, for the letter was signed by Tito, as president of the party, and Dolanc, as secretary of the Executive Bureau, but was not submitted to the Presidium as a whole for approval until *after* it had been circulated to party organizations for discussion—a breach of standard procedures, if not of party rules.

The letter began by pointing out that weaknesses in party work continued to be primarily the result of leadership failures. These included

inconsistencies, hesitations, and ineffectiveness in the implementation of adopted conclusions . . . , differing criteria and various levels of intensity in action on the carrying-out of the political positions of the

---

[203] Ibid.
[204] Ibid.
[205] Reported by Tito during an interview two weeks later. *Nova inicijativa*, p. 27.

LCY . . . [and] instances of ideo-political and operational divisions all
the way up to attempts at the revival and strengthening, in old and new
forms, of fractional activity and of the struggle of cliques for positions
of authority.[206]

In order to strengthen "the unity and operational capabilities of the League
of Communists," the Executive Bureau advanced a series of "demands"
calling for more self-critical evaluations by party members of their performance in the party, the exclusion of members who failed to adhere to policy,
and the reaffirmation of the "centralist" features of democratic centralism.
The Bureau emphasized the responsibility of regional leaderships for the
implementation of party policies. It demanded "decisive opposition to every
tendency which leads to the ideological and political disintegration of the
LCY, to its transformation into an unstable coalition of republican and provincial organizations, and to the division of the working class according to
national and republican membership." It argued that:

> The equal participation of all the leagues of communists of the re-
> publics and provinces in the construction of joint policy also means their
> equal responsibility for the implementation in practice of decisions adopted
> by democratic means, their equal responsibility for the results of the
> policy of the LCY.

At the same time, it asserted the responsibility of the Presidium and Executive
Bureau to "discuss regularly all those questions from the experiences and
activities of the leagues of communists of the republics and provinces which
affect the policies and practices of the LCY as a whole," and to do so by
"direct inspection of the implementation of adopted decisions." The Bureau
acknowledged that "up to now there has been quite a bit of weakness in this
respect." But it committed itself to "create such a method of work and
immediately take the measures necessary for changing this situation."

The Bureau also demanded that regional party leaderships "intercede directly and concretely" to ensure that party members hold all key positions
in important social institutions, including "leadership responsibilities in the
economy, the area of education, the information media, public administration,
the judiciary, the prosecutor's office, [and] the organs of control and security." The Bureau "presented as an immediate task" the convening of party
meetings in all social and political institutions, including the media, "to expel
from leading positions all those who do not accept the political course of the
LCY, to prevent writing which is opposed to the policy of the LC, and [to
prevent] fractional activity in the press." Individual party members were

---

[206] This and all following citations are from the text, ibid., pp. 7-14.

required to "strengthen their activity in organs of self-management, state organs, and socio-political organizations" in order to implement party policy.

In closing, the Bureau delivered its most authoritarian directive since the "invitation" issued in December to the Croatian Central Committee to evaluate the performance of its leaders. The Bureau stated that

All organizations of the League of Communists are *obligated*, on the basis of the positions expressed in this letter, to evaluate critically their own ideo-political practice, [and] to define in precise form their own obligations and tasks.

In the context of a campaign to assert central authority and to reestablish the limits of party policy, this provided a formal basis for direct intervention by the central leadership in the affairs of the regional party organizations.

The letter was distributed to all party organizations on 2 October. On 8 October, a lengthy interview with President Tito, conducted by one of the editors of the Zagreb daily *Vjesnik* was published.[207] In this widely reprinted and distributed interview, Tito emphasized the themes contained in the letter. He stressed that "there must be unity of thought and of action in the League of Communists so that it can function as it must." But he also made it clear that this did *not* mean a return to a Stalinist system. "What is the essence of unity of thought and of action?" Tito asked rhetorically.

It isn't any kind of turning backward, to some Stalinist or I don't know what kind of other concept. It is something completely different. . . . It does not mean that [communists] command, but rather that on the basis of a correct evaluation of the situation they make decisions which then are valid when the majority accepts them [and] at that time they are obligatory for all. This is the essence of democratic centralism and it is absolutely necessary in an organization such as the League of Communists.

The problem, Tito suggested, was that "there are still certain areas in some republics in which democratic centralism is incorrectly understood and resisted." Too much emphasis has been placed in recent years on "democratization" at the expense of party discipline and authority, or "centralism." He complained that:

already on the eve of the Sixth Congress, but especially afterwards, there arose a kind of euphoria of democratization of everything and everyone, up to the point that the role of the Party was reduced in all important domains of social life. Only the task of ideological direction was left to it. Of course, the Party has this role, but that is not sufficient. It must

[207] Ibid., pp. 15-38.

have within its ranks such members and such discipline that it could ideologically direct the masses and prevent the class enemy from taking over positions such as it already has today in various forms in our country.

"In the base of the League of Communists there is no disunity," Tito argued, "I am deeply convinced of that." The blame for these problems, he insisted, lay mainly with "some of our leadership" who "have . . . not [been operating] in a party manner." These leaders, he suggested, "have around themselves, both outside the party and inside the party, the support of certain opposition elements who are in various social positions, in the universities and in other areas." Consequently, he reported, "we are sending to [party] organizations a letter which we adopted at the last session of the Executive Bureau, which I proposed and, together with the secretary [of the Bureau], signed." This was, he noted, "the first step by which to proceed," and "everyone agreed" that it was necessary. However, Tito himself suggested that "everyone" did not include all members of the central leadership:

Among those of us who led the revolution, who were united in the war, there is no disagreement. We see things the same way. But, there are others who have come from unhealthy intellectual environments, from the non-socialist intelligentsia. They are the ones who now are resisting us.

This last comment, about the social origins of the leaders opposing the reaffirmation of central authority within the party and of party authority in society seemed to be a lightly veiled reference to the Serbian party leaders.

The Serbian party leadership received the letter October 2nd and convened a meeting of all central committee members and commune party secretaries October 3rd to discuss it. At that meeting, Perović presented its contents in such a way as to minimize their importance. The same approach was followed by the republican leadership of the Socialist Alliance, and key journalists and editors in the mass media countered the letter's demands for greater party discipline with expressions of concern for the preservation of democracy and respect for established procedure in the party. Institutions under the influence of Marković and the other supporters of the Tito-led coalition acted "more successfully" to implement the letter. Thus, two distinct "lines" began to emerge in the Serbian party in October.[208]

Party Secretary Stane Dolanc had reported at the time the letter was released that, to ensure compliance with its demands:

a team from the Presidium of the LCY will go into all republics, provinces, and army party organizations where it will transmit the agreed-

[208] *NIN*, 15 April 1973.

on positions and the letter . . . , [and] where it will familiarize itself with the state of affairs in connection with that which we have decided.[209]

On 9 October President Tito, Stane Dolanc, and Kiro Gligorov met with the political leadership of the Serbian republic in a closed meeting. In his opening remarks, Tito reminded the Serbian leaders that the meeting had been called "to see which are the elements that prevent work inside the party organization from developing as it should, so that sometimes things happen that are not in harmony with our principles."[210] He noted that relations between the central Presidium and the Serbian party leadership had not been good, but he cautioned his listeners that further decentralization "would be a mistake." "The party," he insisted, "needs to be more united."

In the face of apparent skepticism on the part of some members of the Serbian leadership, Tito argued that the "class enemy" really existed and had been especially active in the past two years. Moreover, "some leaderships" were falling subject to pressure from "outsiders." Consequently, he insisted, "we must put the situation in the League in order and remove from the party those who do not agree with our line." He therefore demanded that "all comrades say everything here," that the meeting "proceed to clarification" of the situation inside the Serbian party. And he reserved the right to speak at the end of the meeting "about the issues I will hear here, and to give my opinion."

The discussion that ensued lasted four days. Exactly what transpired during it remains unclear even today. The evidence suggests that the Serbian leadership divided into two distinct groups: one whose judgments of the situation in Serbia and the work of the Serbian party leadership were even more critical than those of Tito, and another that "categorically rejected" this criticism. This interpretation is supported by rumors that circulated in Belgrade during these discussions to the effect that the Serbian party leadership had successfully resisted Tito's effort to reassert control over their party. But the evidence is too limited to permit a more detailed description and analysis. However, after a four-day recess, the meeting reconvened to permit President Tito to exercise his right to "give his opinion" about what he heard. His remarks, published in the open press the next day, provide important insights into what had transpired.[211]

Tito began with a lengthy criticism of the failure of the Serbian leadership to implement party policy. After some general criticism of that leadership's failure to pursue "a decisive struggle for the implementation of that line on

[209] *Nova inicijativa*, p. 73.

[210] This and all following citations are taken from the report in *NIN*, 15 April 1973.

[211] The following citations are from the text reprinted in *Nova inicijativa*, pp. 39-50 (emphasis added).

all fronts," he turned to specific shortcomings. He accused the leaders of being "more liberal, both in ideo-political confrontation and with respect to the policy of criminal prosecution, pronouncement of sentence, and even presentation in the mass media." He accused them of permitting "nationalistic and other phenomena in the press, popular publications, and publishing activity," and of tolerating "ultra-leftists," on the basis of "the theory that these are people who ideologically are for self-management but just are unrealistic and have illusions." He also warned them "about the fact that the treatment in the Belgrade press of events in other republics—despite repeated warnings and protests from certain republics—has remained in great measure unchanged, and that it has not contributed to better mutual understanding." That reporting was creating the impression that conservative forces were at work elsewhere, while in Serbia "progessive forces are leading the battle for socialist democracy."

Once again, Tito vigorously denied that he was attempting to return the party to its Stalinist past. He insisted that the demands now being advanced by the central leadership had always been the party's course. But his condemnation of the policies of the Serbian party had not gone unopposed. Indeed, he himself indicates that during the previous four days of discussion his views had been opposed by a majority of those present:

> when discussions take place about the line of the Party, its results and weaknesses, then *the number of discussants for or against a certain thesis or evaluation of the situation is not the deciding factor* for the revolutionary determination and assessment of where it is necessary to go and what is necessary to do. . . .
>   . . . As far as people turning critically to the weaknesses about which I spoke briefly in my introductory talk is concerned, *already in the beginning I saw that the discussion was taking a completely different direction than the one I had wanted.*

The discussion had shown, Tito argued, "that there is a not small number of comrades to whom I have listened, I am thinking in the first place of leading ones, who are immune to such virtues as self-criticism." He had expected these individuals to "turn self-critically to their own work" during this meeting and to acknowledge that they advanced "formulations which are contradictory" and had engaged in "direct and indirect polemicizing with my and not only with my views on various problems." But, Tito reported with protestations of regret, that did not happen.

In response to this opposition Tito gently reminded the Serbian leadership that he had recourse to outside support if it was needed. "Why was this meeting held? Is the situation in the LC of Serbia good or not?" "I think, *as does the majority, not only those who are sitting here but outside also,* that the situation is not good." In view of the warnings he had delivered to the Croatian leadership during the course of 1971 and had made good on in December—now known in detail to the party membership and general public as the result of both the twenty-first session and publication of the report of the Croatian investigatory commission—there was no need to be more explicit.

Tito then suggested that the discussion he had listened to for four days was "*not about how to eliminate everything which prevents ideological and operational unity in the implementation of the general line, but [rather] about who will defeat whom [ko će koga]*." And he chastised the Serbian leaders for the rumors that had spread across Belgrade during the course of the meeting.

> Already before we even completed [our] work, across Belgrade it began to be said that those who were criticized were victorious, and not those who did the criticizing, and that with such [critics] it will be necessary to settle accounts. Such behavior is not in accord with the behavior of a real Communist no matter from which side it comes. . . . Look comrades, if we were to allow ourselves to settle accounts within the League of Communists in a way which has the mark of fractionalism, then we would come into still greater difficulties. I think that the majority of members of both the LCY and LCS [League of Communists of Serbia] also think this way about this and that they expect something completely different from us. We must settle accounts with those who stand on the other side of the barricade, with the class enemy.

Tito acknowledged that "some comrades have spoken here about the danger of a split in the LCS," but he did not agree that this was likely. "That disagreement exists is exactly correct," he conceded, "but primarily among the responsible comrades and not in the membership. It could come to a split if things were to proceed by the path of fractional struggle." "But," he warned, "we cannot permit that." "As far as a purge of the ranks . . . is concerned," he suggested "that must be done in the process of carrying out the discussion now before [the party leadership]."

At the end of his remarks, Tito "suggested" that the Serbian party meet to discuss "certain personnel changes in leading bodies" of the party. Publication of these remarks the next day in the press thus constituted an open call for the replacement of the Serbian party leadership. This was not achieved easily, however. When the Serbian Central Committee convened in closed session five days later, there was strong resistance among the membership to accepting the resignations offered by party president Marko Nikezić and party secretary Latinka Perović. Despite the fact that it was clear these resignations were being offered under pressure from Tito and that Tito was expecting to meet with members of the Serbian party secretariat and the presidents of the provincial committees for Vojvodina and Kosovo to select new party leaders, members of the Central Committee demanded further discussion of the issues in contention between the central leadership and the Serbian party. Despite repeated pleas by members of the secretariat for acceptance of the resignations, and a plea by Nikezić himself for their acceptance, the Central Committee accepted them only after that acceptance was distinguished procedurally from any decision concerning the future policies of the party or election of a new president and secretary.[212]

The Committee then adjourned to permit the secretariat and provincial presidents to meet with President Tito and Stane Dolanc. This group undoubtedly reported to Tito on the depth of resistance in the Serbian Central Committee, for they later informed the Committee that Tito believed there was "no hurry" to elect new leaders; this could wait "two or three days" while wider consultations were carried out. When the Serbian Central Committee reconvened in closed session two days later, "lively discussion" and strong resistance to the change of leadership continued. Not until three additional days had passed, during which further consultations with Tito had taken place and he and his supporters had undoubtedly exercised enormous pressure on the Serbian leadership, did the Serbian Central Committee finally accept the nomination of a new president and secretary. Thus, ten days of behind-the-scenes maneuvering and pressure were required even after open publication of Tito's critical remarks and ultimatums to the Serbian leadership before he and his supporters were able to impose a new leadership on that party.[213]

Ten months earlier, Tito had been able to force the resignations of the Croatian leadership not only because the Croatian executive and central committees had been divided over the policies of their leaders but also because the failures for which he held the Croatian party's leaders responsible were manifest in a phenomenon clearly alien to the official ideology of self-management: nationalism. The forced resignations of the Serbian party's leaders engendered considerable unified opposition in the leadership and Central Committee of that party because the failures for which these leaders were held responsible were manifest in phenomena not clearly alien to the official ideology: autonomous action by self-managing institutions. Consequently, while the forced resignations of the Croatian leadership signaled a decisive rejection of nationalism and affirmation of the political role of the party in society, the forced resignations of the Serbian leadership signaled a decisive reaffirmation of the authoritative role of the central leadership in the party.

Following the forced resignations of the Serbian party's president and

[212] *NIN*, 22 April 1973.
[213] Ibid.

secretary, the new leadership of that party conducted "a decisive struggle against phenomena and tendencies of liberalism and technocratism" in which "numerous cadres changes were carried out in the Central Committee, in the leadership of socio-political organizations [and] of the League of Communists of Serbia, [and] in the city organization of the LC of Belgrade."[214] By the end of February 1973, almost 300 individuals were removed or had resigned from leading positions in the party and other organizations.[215] By the end of the campaign, more than 1,000 individuals had been excluded from the party.[216] Similar "struggles" were conducted in other regions throughout the period 1972-1974 in the form of a campaign to restore "the principles of democratic centralism."

In Vojvodina, supporters of the Tito coalition conducted "a struggle with anarcho-liberalism and opportunism, [with] fractionalism and groupism" in the LCV. These tendencies had been manifest, according to the later account prepared by the Tito leadership for the Tenth Party Congress in 1974, in

> deviation from the principles of democratic centralism [in the form of] opposition by the liberalistic-fractionalistic leadership of the LCV to the positions of the higher leadership [of the LCY], defensiveness toward criticism of weaknesses, and the settling of accounts with critics from the base.

The leadership of the Vojvodina party organization also was accused, among a long list of other things, of fractional activity in alliance with the former leaders of the Serbian party; of "opposition to revolutionary continuity and an insistence on the conflict of generations"; and of "neglect of the class criterion in cadres policy and its privatization and monopolization." The latter charges suggest that the leadership of the Vojvodina party organization was actively promoting its own younger and more highly educated cadres to positions of responsibility heretofore monopolized by members of the "partisan generation." Such cadre changes were likely to increase any tendency toward independence in the Vojvodina organization and strengthen the autonomy of its leadership. But the reassertion of central authority by the Tito coalition meant that "all those who came into conflict with the revolution, revolutionary practice, and line of the LCY . . . were removed from responsible positions."[217] The removal of the president and secretary of the pro-

---

[214] Rojc et al., *Deseti Kongres SKJ*, p. 386.

[215] *NIN*, 22 April 1973.

[216] SKS, CK, *Izveštaj o aktivnosti Saveza komunista Srbije i radu Centralnog komiteta izmedju šestog i sedmog kongresa* (Beograd: Komunist, 1974), p. 18. This source contains a decidedly less complete, but still interesting account of the confrontation between the Serbian and central leaderships (pp. 28-36). For an indictment of the purged leadership, see pp. 37ff.

[217] Rojc et al., *Deseti Kongres SKJ*, p. 387.

vincial party committee, however, required six weeks of political struggle. The Tito-led coalition in the central leadership mobilized veterans and other socio-political organizations in the province to demand their resignations until they had enough support to force them at a provincial committee meeting in December 1972.[218]

In Macedonia, too, the independence of views in the regional organization and of its leaders came under attack. There, supporters of the central coalition conducted "an intensified struggle . . . for the decisive liquidation of fractionalism, groupism, and elitism in the ranks of the LC and in socio-political life as a whole," and against:

> unacceptable theories about a party of the so-called social elite which relies solely on the intelligentsia and highly-skilled part of the working class, "theories" about the so-called elite role of the intelligentsia and attempts to create artificial confrontations between the working class and intelligentsia, and even "theories" about the creation of "a new social block" in society.

Within the Macedonian party organization itself, "a decisive fight was begun against tendencies which lead to polycentrism and to 'partnerism' toward the League of Communism." That fight resulted in "certain personnel changes in the leadership organs of the LC of Macedonia."[219]

In Kosovo, the central coalition supported the Albanian leadership of the provincial party organization in a struggle against "nationalism in all its forms." As a result:

> a number of members of the LC were excluded; some cadres changes were carried out; [and] sharper administrative measures were taken against a number of nationalistic elements from the media and some cultural, educational, and political institutions.

In both the Croatian and Montenegrin party organizations during this period, supporters of the Tito coalition waged a "struggle" against both nationalism and "conservative-bureaucratic forces which offered an alliance in the struggle against nationalism, but . . . from positions of neo-Stalinism and other ideologies rejected by the League of Communists."[220]

Only the Bosnian party organization and leadership appears not to have carried out personnel changes under pressure from the center. The report to the Tenth Congress that described the "struggles" and leadership changes in other regional organizations does *not* report either such a struggle or such leadership changes to have taken place in Bosnia. Instead, it reports that:

[218] *NIN*, 22 April 1973.
[219] Rojc et al., *Deseti Kongres SKJ*, pp. 389-90.
[220] Ibid., pp. 387-88.

in the execution of the conclusions of the Twenty-first session of the Presidium of the LCY and the Letter, the activity of the organization and organs of the League of Communists of Bosnia and Hercegovina . . . became even more organized, more energetic, and more successful.

Unlike the critical descriptions of other leaderships and party organizations, the policies and action of the Bosnian leadership were described as "resolute," "decisive," "clear," "principled," and "uncompromising," all laudatory terms in the Yugoslav political vocabulary.[221]

The Bosnian leadership controlled a multinational republic composed primarily of Serbs, Croats, and Muslims and which was subject to the conflicting territorial and cultural claims of both Serb and Croat nationalism. Consequently, that leadership was compelled to develop policies that recognized and accommodated but carefully controlled the expression of distinct national identities, and which discouraged and combatted divisive nationalism. The Bosnian leadership was particularly hostile to the rise of nationalism in Croatia and Serbia, to nationalism's penetration into Bosnia, and to its toleration by the Croatian and Serbian party leaderships. The Bosnian leadership also appears to have been more sensitive than those of other regions to the need for maintaining the activist, ideological character of the party, especially at the level of basic organizations. And, as the leadership of an underdeveloped republic, the Bosnian party leaders were compelled to support federal policies and party positions calling for the interregional transfer of resources. This made them likely to support the reestablishment of strong federal centers in both the state and the party and to oppose the more decentralist inclinations of the Serbian, Vojvodina, and Macedonian leaderships. As a consequence, the policy preferences and actions of the Bosnian leadership very likely coincided during this period with those of the Tito coalition, earning the high praise it received.

These "struggles" to reassert central authority in the party resulted in personnel changes in the central organs of the party far exceeding the number permitted under party statute. By the time of the Tenth Congress in May 1974, thirteen individuals whose election to the fifty-two-member Presidium had been verified at the Ninth Congress in March 1969 had either died (2 individuals), taken up positions in the state that precluded simultaneous membership in the Presidium (9), resigned under honorable conditions (1), or been rotated out of the position from which they had been elected to the Presidium in the first place (1). Ten other members had resigned "because of conflict with the course of the LCY and on the demand of [their] central and provincial committees." These included the leaders of the Croatian party forced to resign in December 1971, the leaders of the Serbian party forced to resign in October

[221] Ibid., pp. 388-89.

1972, and members of the Slovenian, Macedonian, and Vojvodina party leaderships forced out by the Tito coalition in the wake of the "letter." The apparently voluntary resignation of an additional member of the Presidium was listed in the report delivered to the Tenth Congress among the resignations of those "in conflict with the course of the LCY," bringing to eleven the number of individuals who resigned as the result of conflict with the dominant Tito coalition. The individuals elected by the regional party organizations to fill their places in the Presidium all were either obvious clients or supporters of members of that coalition.[222]

The central party Presidium and Executive Bureau also were strengthened by the long-delayed implementation of the May 1969 decision to establish a Center for Social Research attached to the Presidium. The Center gave the central leadership for the first time an internal professional social research staff to provide it with policy-relevant analyses. The Center was funded by an increase in the proportion of income from party dues allocated to the maintenance and operation of the central party organs in the period following the twenty-first session.[223]

Changes in the structure, composition, and operation of the central party organs during 1972-1973 were accompanied by changes in the structure and operation of lower-level party organizations. A recent history of the party reports that during the period between the second Conference and the Tenth Congress

> Large organizations with several hundred members of the party, in which there wasn't sufficient possibility for the individual action or responsibility of individual members, were broken up and numerous smaller organizations were established in which there is a greater possibility for each member to express his own activity and to receive a more precise assignment.[224]

Basic party organizations were established for each of the numerous small production units ("basic organizations of associated labor") into which each large self-managing work organization had been divided as a consequence of the "workers amendments" adopted in 1971. Smaller, more functional organizations were established within local territorial communities, and provisions for practical coordination among communists living in the territory of each community were improved.[225] The principle of reducing the size of

[222] Ibid., pp. 488-89.

[223] Ibid., pp. 452, 538; and SKJ, *Druga Konferencija SKJ*, pp. 520-21.

[224] Pero Morača et al., *Istorija Saveza komunista Jugoslavije: Kratak pregled* (Beograd: Rad, 1976), p. 314. Citations to this volume all are to the final chapter written by Dušan Bilandžić, which covers the period from the purge of Ranković to the Tenth Party Congress.

[225] Rojc et al., *Deseti Kongres SKJ*, p. 449.

basic organizations was applied even to the party organization in the army, where the number of basic organizations and the number of party sections approximately doubled, while the number the party conferences comprising one or more garrisons declined.[226] In order to improve coordination between and the class orientation of these more numerous smaller organizations, the central party leadership ordered the establishment in each commune of *aktivs* composed of "worker-communists" from the basic party organizations.[227]

Following the ouster of Ranković, and especially in the period following the Ninth Congress, the active involvement of party organizations in the operation of other social and political organizations had declined rapidly. At the Tenth Congress it was reported that

In many non-economic work organizations, [and] organs and organizations of socio-political communities, basic organizations of the LC were abolished, so that the activities of these organizations and organs and the development of self-managing relations in them remained outside the organized influence of the LC.[228]

Indeed, the rise of an organized nationalist movement in Croatia was largely attributed to the failure of local party organizations and individual communists to exercise influence on behalf of the party over the other institutions and organizations in which they participated. In the period following the twenty-first session, the central leadership ordered the establishment of basic party organizations in "the organs and organizations of the federation" in order to allow individual communists in them "to mobilize better and more directly for the carrying-out of the positions and policies of the LCY and to devote greater attention to the issues on which the more successful work of the organs and institutions of the federation depends."[229]

These changes were accompanied by efforts to improve the flow of information between basic party organizations and the central party organs. In his introductory speech to the Tenth Congress's commission for the development of the League, Stevan Doronjski emphasized that "it is necessary decisively to overcome the practice of so-called informal consultation and intervention between the membership and the leaderships of the LC . . . which created the possibility for manipulation of the membership and the division of the leadership of the LC from basic organizations."[230] The central leadership extended the past practice of holding conferences, consultative meetings, seminars, and other forms of joint meetings between leadership bodies and

[226] Ibid., p. 465.
[227] Ibid., p. 449.
[228] Ibid., p. 447.
[229] Ibid., p. 449.
[230] Ibid., p. 105.

lower-level functionaries or groups of specialists to include the holding of such meetings with the memberships of several local party organizations, thereby increasing direct contact between the party summit and its base.

The personnel and organizational changes carried out as part of the campaign to restore "the principles of democratic centralism" were extensive. The resultant turnover in party cadres was reflected in the previous congress participation of the delegates elected to the Tenth Congress in May 1974. As can be seen in Table 3.8, 90 percent of the delegates had never participated in a congress of the Yugoslav party before, and only a little more than 16 percent had ever participated in a republican party congress. Yet almost 29 percent of the delegates held positions as functionaries in the party, the state, or a socio-political organization. The similarity of these figures to those for delegates elected to the Ninth Congress in 1969—and the fragmentary evidence available on admissions, expulsions, and resignations of party members in the intercongress period[231]—suggests that the party, which had undergone extensive cadres turnover in the wake of the ouster of Ranković, experienced a turnover of similar proportions in the post-1971 period.

TABLE 3.8
Previous Congress Participation of Delegates Elected
to the Ninth and Tenth Party Congresses

	Ninth Congress (1969)		Tenth Congress (1974)	
	Number	%	Number	%
Yugoslav Congresses				
None	985	90.1	950	90.3
One	63	5.8	47	4.5
Two	19	1.7	25	2.4
Three or More	26	2.4	30	2.9
Republican Congresses				
One	140	12.8	105	10.0
Two	25	2.4	28	2.7
Three or More	33	3.0	40	3.8
Total Delegates	1,093		1,052	

SOURCE: Martinović, *Deveti Kongres SKJ*, 2: 5; and SKJ, *Deseti Kongres Saveza komunista Jugoslavije*, Stenographic Records, 4 Vols. (Beograd: Komunist, 1975), 4: 314.

[231] SKJ, *Druga Konferencija SKJ*, pp. 49-92; and Rojc et al., *Deseti Kongres SKJ*, pp. 520-21.

However, while personnel and organizational changes during this period were extensive, and the authority of central party organs relative to that of the regional party leaderships undoubtedly was strengthened, the campaign to restore "the principles of democratic centralism" did not involve complete rejection of the principles of decision making that had evolved in the party since 1966. The report on the future tasks of the party delivered in January 1972 to the second Conference struck a careful balance between the need to strengthen the ability of central party organs to review and control the activity of both regional leaderships and local organizations, on the one hand, and the need to preserve and protect the autonomy of the regional party organizations, on the other.[232] Even the Executive Bureau "letter" of September 1972 that marked the beginning of the campaign conceded that "it is necessary to oppose every attempt to transform democratic centralism into bureaucratic centralism, into the imposition of views without prior democratic discussions . . . , into the rule of narrow groups."[233] At that time, President Tito had emphatically rejected any "turning back" to Stalinism. Even the report to the Tenth Congress emphasizing the need for strenthening unity and central authority in the party affirmed "the equal participation and identical responsibility of republican and provincial organizations in the construction and execution of the unified policy of the LCY."[234]

The direct participation of representatives of the republican and provincial organizations in the central institutions of the party was reaffirmed not only by the fact that those institutions were composed of individuals nominated by the regional organizations according to an agreed formula of representation but also by the operation of the institutions themselves. The new Executive Bureau, for example:

> began the practice of [holding] expanded sessions with the presidents of the central and provincial committees of the LC, with the secretaries of the executive organs of the central and provincial committees [and] the Conference of the LC in the Army, and with representatives of the organs and socio-political organizations in the federation, at which all questions of wide political and social significance are discussed.[235]

Indeed, even the decision of the central leadership to establish party organizations in the organs and institutions of the federation was made only after consultation with the regional leaderships.[236]

The re-centralization of authority within the party in 1972-1974 did not

[232] SKJ, *Druga Konferencija SKJ*, p. 426.
[233] *Nova inicijativa u SKJ*, p. 10.
[234] Rojc et al., *Deseti Kongres SKJ*, p. 448.
[235] Ibid., p. 497.
[236] Ibid., p. 460.

include the transfer to central organs of control over regional cadres assignments. The new party statutes adopted at the Tenth Congress retained the principles of composing central party organs of members elected by their respective organizations according to a formula agreed to in advance among the regional leaderships. The formula for the composition of central party organs remained "equal representation of the republics and corresponding representation of the provinces." A new element in the formula adopted in 1974, however, was the addition of a provision for "the corresponding representation" of the party organization in the army.[237] This reflected the increased political importance of the military during this period, arising out of its support for Tito and the antinationalist coalition during the "Croatian crisis," the occupancy by military officers of several key positions in the government's heretofore civilian internal security apparatus, and its role as the only remaining "all-Yugoslav" integrative organization.[238]

Nor did the re-centralization of authority within the party result in the organizational expansion of the central party organs. As can be seen from Table 3.9, the number of cadres employed by the central party organs did not increase dramatically during this time and, in fact, remained relatively small throughout the entire period since 1965. The support staff employed by the larger regional organizations far exceeded that available to the central leadership.

The strengthening of the central party leadership was carefully circumscribed by efforts to maintain the autonomous authority of the regional party organizations. The Tenth Congress, for example, replaced the party Conference, which had been established at the Ninth Congress in 1969 as the most authoritative decision-making body of the party between congresses, with a more conventional Central Committee. Whereas three-quarters of the 280 members of the party Conference had been elected anew by commune-level party organizations before each of its sessions, the membership of the newly reestablished Central Committee was to remain unchanged between congresses and included only 165 individuals.[239] Both the smaller size and stable membership of the new Central Committee strengthened its autonomous authority. But that membership continued to be elected by the regional party organizations. Similarly, the members of the smaller and more authoritative central Presidium elected at the Tenth Congress were determined by the regional party organizations. The presidents of each of the regional party organizations continued to be members of the Presidium by virtue of their positions.

[237] Ibid., pp. 354, 355.

[238] See A. Ross Johnson, *The Role of the Military in Communist Yugoslavia: An Historical Sketch*, Rand Paper No. P-6070 (Santa Monica: The Rand Corporation, 1978).

[239] Rojc et al., *Deseti Kongres SKJ*, pp. 354, 561-62.

TABLE 3.9
Cadres Employed by the Republican and Yugoslav Party
Organizations, 1965-1973 (End-of-Year Figures)

Party Organization	1965	1966	1967	1968	1969	1970	1971	1972	1973
	Functionaries and Other Socio-Political Workers								
Bosnian	231	187	155	145	124	140	146	161	158
Croatian	254	207	369	139	123	180	158	162	212
Serbian	510	419	368	286	267	277	270	291	345
Slovenian	143	119	75	74	85	85	99	102	119
Macedonian	52	110	98	101	41	43	44	46	60
Montenegrin	121	48	47	46	31	33	31	34	44
Yugoslav	58	19	11	13	14	13	14	15	15
	Professional Staff								
Bosnian	345	330	331	346	358	387	395	423	448
Croatian	345	388	133	390	463	499	432	476	484
Serbian	977	923	998	1,025	1,017	1,006	1,036	1,034	1,064
Slovenian	137	130	122	124	121	157	151	159	186
Macedonian	73	145	147	140	198	203	196	186	189
Montenegrin	161	74	91	81	87	94	74	86	97
Yugoslav	88	131	137	148	189	213	205	198	199

SOURCE: Rojc et al., *Deseti Kongres SKJ*, pp. 556-58.

Thus, while the Tito-led coalition established the right of central organs independently to determine their own internal organization and operation, to expel individuals from their ranks, and to remove regional leaders from office, it did not establish the right of central organs independently to appoint either their own members or the leaders of regional organizations. That appointment power, as well as the power to control cadres appointments in lower-level party organizations, remained in the hands of the regional leaderships. Even after the Tenth Congress, the central party organs continued to be made up of individuals appointed by, and therefore responsible to, their respective regional or military party organizations.

Moreover, the Tito-led coalition did not abandon the principle of consensual decision making based on interregional consultation and "harmonization" of positions that had evolved since 1966. Indeed, following the Tenth Congress, that process became a central element in the effort to restore cohesiveness to the central party leadership. Nor did that coalition abandon the principle of consensual decision making in the state and government embodied in the 1971 amendments. It moved ahead with the already scheduled consideration of additional constitutional changes—the so-called "second phase" of the reforms undertaken in late 1970.

The coalition did, however, amend the decision-making process in one important respect: it reestablished President Tito as the ultimate arbiter of political conflict. He was empowered informally to establish the limits on discussion and debate and, if necessary, to intervene in the routine decision-making process to enforce them. His role, however, was seen as exceptional, a status confirmed by the unprecedented provision in the 1974 constitution granting him the status of president of the Republic for life, coupled with a later article providing that on his death that office would cease to exist.

IV. THE SEARCH FOR A
REGULATORY FORMULA: WRITING THE
1971 CONSTITUTIONAL AMENDMENTS
AND THE 1974 CONSTITUTION

The Yugoslav crisis was played out in large part in the language of constitutional reform. The communist political leadership attempted to regulate interbloc conflicts by altering the formal division of authority between center and region and by changing the organizational and procedural provisions for decision making at the center. To do so required that they amend the federal constitution.

Instances of constitutional change present dual opportunities to study a political leadership's search for a formula by which to regulate the conflicts that divide its country. First, they produce explicit statements of the formal "rules of the game" agreed to by the "players" involved. Where a succession of such changes has been carried out, it is possible to identify changes in those rules over time. It is also possible to infer changes in the cast of players themselves. Changes in the structure of the state, in the bases of representation in its institutions, in the distribution of powers and responsibilities in it, and in the provisions for making decisions ordinarily reflect changes in the relationships among the politically most powerful and important groupings, or even changes in the power or importance of the groups themselves. Second, the processes by which constitutional reforms are prepared are themselves cases of political decision making. As such, they are very likely to reflect existing organizational and procedural principles and to presage those they produce.

The individuals who drafted the twenty-three constitutional amendments adopted in Yugoslavia in June 1971 were compelled to deal with many of the same issues, the same conflicts, that confronted the political leadership at that time. Many of them were, in fact, members of the central or regional leaderships, and it was difficult for them to separate constitutional issues from substantive ones. The decision-making practices by which those amendments were drafted thus closely paralleled the practices characteristic of the broader political process. Similarly, the individuals who drafted the new constitution adopted in 1974 also were members of the central and regional political leaderships, and the preparation of that constitution was an important element in the postcrisis reaffirmation of central political authority. As a result, both the process by which that constitution was drafted and the provisions of the constitution itself reflected the character of the broader political decision-making process of the postcrisis period during which it was prepared.

In this chapter, the process by which conflicts were resolved during the preparation of the 1971 amendments is examined as a case study of the general pattern of conflict resolution in the political system during the period of crisis. It is used as a basis for explaining both the origins of the institutional and procedural provisions for decision making established by those amendments and the reasons why they failed to regulate interbloc conflict. The operation of federal institutions established by the 1971 amendments and the process by which the 1974 constitution was drafted are then examined as cases of postcrisis conflict resolution and decision making. Differences between the decision-making process in this later period and that by which the 1971 amendments had been drafted are examined in terms of the "lessons" learned from the earlier crisis, and in this way are used to trace the leadership's search for formulas by which to regulate the conflicts that divided them.

The 1971 Drafting Process

By the summer of 1970, national, economic, and ideological conflicts between the regions had paralyzed the decision-making institutions of the state. In an attempt to break this deadlock, Tito consulted with "a few comrades from the highest leadership" and together they decided to establish a collective state Presidency. It was to be composed of "the best people from the republics," but they were not to function as "republican advocates." Rather, they were to function as "an independent factor" that would resolve current and future interregional conflicts in the interest of the Yugoslav community as a whole.

Tito himself suggested that creation of a collective state Presidency was also an attempt to provide for his own succession. "Much has been written," he pointed out, "[to the effect] that Yugoslavia will disintegrate when I go." He conceded that his death "could cause a very difficult crisis. Because, the question then would be posed who will take my place." He concluded, therefore, that "We have to carry out this reorganization precisely so that our Yugoslav socialist community would not come to such a crisis."[1]

Tito's discussions with "a few comrades from the highest leadership" should not be seen, however, as an urgent attempt to settle the succession

---

[1] SKJ, *Aktuelni problemi daljeg razvoja*, p. 7.

question. Rather they must be seen primarily as an attempt by him and his closest colleagues in the communist party leadership to devise some means of resolving the conflicts that had deadlocked the system and of providing for their continuing regulation in the future. Indeed, at the eighth session of the Presidium in April 1970, at the same time that it acceded to Croatian demands for consensual rules of decision making and regional parity in federal institutions in the hope of achieving a short-term resolution of those conflicts, the leadership had already committed itself to reexamining both relations between the republics and the federation and constitutional provisions for the organization and operation of the federation itself in the hope of devising a mechanism for their longer-term regulation. In order to carry this out, a "special working group" of the Presidium was established under the chairmanship of Edvard Kardelj. The group was composed of representatives from the republics and provinces and was to work on problems in two areas: relations between the federation and the republics, and "the structure of federal organs, their mutual relations and the system and method of decision making in them."[2]

Kardelj presented a report on the work of this group to an expanded session of the central Executive Bureau in September 1970, only four days after Tito publicly proposed the creation of a collective state Presidency.[3] Not surprisingly, Kardelj reported that the group had concluded that current political problems called "for a better and more effective means to secure the necessary harmonization and coordination of positions and interests in the formulation of joint policy." The group also agreed on the clear need to transfer certain functions from the federation to the individual republics and "to strengthen the independence and responsibility of [federal] executive organs" in those areas that remain in their competence. The working group found that the proposal to create a collective state Presidency most directly involved questions about the structure of the federation and "relations between assemblies and politico-executive or administrative organs." Consequently, Kardelj observed, "solutions to questions from these areas, including here constitutional changes as well, must be adopted simultaneously, in 'one package,' so to speak."[4]

The changes anticipated by the working group at this point, Kardelj continued, focused on the structure, competencies, and method of decision making in the federation. He noted that "it is obvious that we will not solve the most significant problems which now appear in relations between the feder-

[2] Ibid., p. 16.

[3] *Borba* (Belgrade), 26 September 1970.

[4] This and all following citations to this speech are from the text in SKJ, *Aktuelni problemi daljeg razvoja*, pp. 15-53 (emphasis in original).

ation and the republics if we limit discussion to *the methods of adopting federal decisions.*" Rather, Kardelj suggested, it was necessary to focus instead on "what the organs of the federation make decisions *about*, and *what kind of organs* those decisions require."

It was generally agreed that all areas of joint interest not subject to the autonomous decision-making authority of the federation should be subject to "mutual cooperation and coordination between the republics." Kardelj pointed out, however, that despite this agreement "it is not only possible, but certain that conflicts of interest will occur" even in these areas. Consequently, he argued, "it will be necessary to provide appropriate forms of conflict resolution, agreement making, temporary solutions, and even arbitration, which in certain situations . . . could perhaps even be obligatory." Only in this way would it be possible to "ensure unconditionally that the organs of the federation really will be in a position to carry out effectively those functions which will be established as functions of the federation."

A major point of contention in these discussions, Kardelj reported, was the question of a republican "veto"—an idea which, he noted, "has its supporters in present discussions." He made it clear that he personally opposed the adoption of such a veto as the general principle of decision making in the federation.

History demonstrates that state systems which have been based on the right of veto as a general principle have experienced a very bad historical fate. And not only that. We have opposed [the idea] that the many rule by majority over the few. But the right of veto is in fact the "majoritization" [*majorizacija*] of each against all [others], because it practically excludes every democratic means of decision-making and leads to the most crude confrontation of pressure against pressure. And conflicts of such type sooner or later inevitably must lead to the restoration of this or that kind of state compulsion, hegemonism, or political absolutism.

In order "to avoid such unavoidable consequences," he suggested, "the functions of the federation really must be reduced to the real and necessary framework . . . of the joint interests of the people." Only in this way would it be possible "to insure that organs of the federation will be in a position to fulfill their functions and make decisions in a democratic way and by democratic means, and that also means by majority votes."

The ability to make certain decisions by majority vote, Kardelj argued, "does not mean that organs of the federation do not have to consult with the republics and with self-managing organs in our society." However, the carrying out of such consultation was a procedural question and not a systemic one. The federation, he insisted, is not and would not dare to be a kind of "super-state," . . . rather [it must be] a form of inter-nationality integration. . . . The fact that the federation also must adopt, within the sphere of its functions, obligatory decisions behind which stands the force of the state, does not contradict such an understanding [of it], because when people and nations agree on joint work and cooperation they also accept certain mutual obligations as well.

The discussion that followed Kardelj's report revealed continuing disagreement between the regional leaderships about decision making in the organs of the federation. Each of the discussants made it clear that he was speaking not as an individual member of the central leadership, but as a representative of the views of his regional organization. Those views had been determined in earlier discussions by the regional leaderships of an advance copy of the report. Speaking for the Macedonian leadership, Kiro Gligorov expressed mixed support for the positions taken by Kardelj. But, recalling the April decisions of the Presidium, he emphasized the necessity of ensuring republican control over federal policy making despite the fact "that introduction of the institution of a veto carries within itself very great dangers and in fact can mean the inability of a society to constitute itself and make decisions."[5] Macedonian opposition to majority decision making in federal organs was supported strongly by Savka Dabčević-Kučar, representing the views of the Croatian leadership. She acknowledged that "warning about the danger which is inherent in [the right of] veto is completely justified, especially a veto which would be applied in all the conflictual, ongoing situations of our political and social life." But she argued:

There also is an enormous danger, and it would not be acceptable, if rule by majority prevailed [ako bi se vršila majorizacije] on the most important political questions which are of interest to certain nations or republics. . . . We must find such a solution . . . which will not allow outvoting on key, I repeat, key questions.[6]

Croatian opposition to the idea of majority decision making in the federation and support for the introduction of a republican veto was part of the strategy established at the tenth session of the Croatian Central Committee in January. That strategy called for increasing the autonomous authority of that republic at the expense of the federation and maximizing Croatian control over the remaining decisional authority of the federation. The Croatian leadership continued to pursue that strategy at the third Conference of the Croatian party in October. Pero Pirker, secretary of the party, reaffirmed Croatian support

---

[5] Ibid., p. 75.
[6] Ibid., p. 85.

for the "application of the principle of parity to the composition of the SFRY [Socialist Federal Republic of Yugoslavia] Presidency and all other organs of the federation that significantly influence common matters" and Croatian opposition to majority-rule decision making.

> We are not for a veto in the organs of the federation, but we particularly emphasize our negative position toward the possibility of making decisions on the basis of a majority [*majorizacija*], especially when decisions are being made about basic questions for all the peoples, and especially each one of them [individually].

But Pirker, a central figure in the emerging nationalist faction in the leadership of the Croatian party, went one step further. He also suggested that

> it is necessary to throw out the long-rooted idea that one is always responsible [*zadužen*] and called on [*pozvan*] to protect the interests of Yugoslavia, because that has the tone of demands for a federation as some kind of authority above the nations.[7]

This formulation was more extreme than any offered in meetings of the central organs of the League, and it called into question the Croatian leadership's commitment to the preservation of the Yugoslav state.

Both the Macedonian and the Croatian leaderships had presented their positions in the central party organs in a manner that emphasized apparent agreement with Kardelj's report. Both seemed to concede the need for majority decision making in routine matters. But both were reluctant to concede many questions to the domain of "routine matters." The Serbian leadership, on the other hand, appeared inclined to assign most issues to the domain of "routine matters." On critical issues, it suggested, unanimity was a matter of course. Marko Nikezić, president of the Serbian party, suggested to the central Executive Bureau that "on certain matters there has to be unanimity . . . or there will not be the kind of community we want if it were necessary to vote on these things." However, he argued, "when a regular act is concerned, we are protected by [the fact] that parity exists. Not even in these circumstances is decision making by majority vote perfect, but all other means of decision making are less fair."[8]

Just as the Croatian leadership presented its position more forcefully in Croatia than in meetings of the central party organs, the Serbian position was presented more forcefully by Dragoslav Marković, then president of the Serbian Assembly, in a public meeting in Belgrade on the eve of the Executive Bureau meeting. He began by suggesting that the Serbian leadership "strongly

---

[7] *Politika* (Belgrade), 6 October 1970.

[8] SKJ, *Aktuelni problemi daljeg razvoja*, p. 98.

supports the position that . . . the functions of the federation should unconditionally be reduced to those which are in the joint interest of all the nations
and of the working people of Yugoslavia.'' He then went on to insist, however,
that the Serbian leadership

> consider[s] it essential that . . . when the functions of the federation are
> established, there must also be efficient, independent and strong organs
> of the federation that will be responsible for the execution of these
> functions. Our position starts from the point that *federal organs are
> neither exclusively nor primarily a place for interrepublican negotiation,
> but are independent* organs of the federation. . . .
>
> . . . .
>
> *As far as interrepublican negotiation is concerned,* . . . we think that it
> is of fundamental interest for the cohesion of Yugoslavia, but that *it must
> occur on those questions that are in the independent competence of the
> republics*. However, when the competencies of the federation are in
> question, when its functions are concerned, then there must be inde-
> pendent and responsible organs that will execute these functions. There-
> fore . . . *when the functions of the federation and its organs are in
> question, there can be no place for either the right of veto by the republics
> over the decisions of federal organs or an imperative mandate for rep-
> resentatives in the federation.*[9]

His remarks placed the Serbian leadership in direct opposition to the positions
of the Croatian and Macedonian leaderships and to the general direction of
changes in decision making since 1966.

Disagreements between the regional leaderships over the structure, composition, and mode of decision making in the federation continued at the
twelfth session of the Presidium, on 4 October.[10] The Presidium endorsed
Tito's proposal to create a collective state Presidency and ''the basic concept,
place, and character of this new organ of the federation'' as presented in
Kardelj's report. But this, of course, meant that no agreement had as yet been
reached on the composition or mode of decision making of the proposed
Presidency or its relationship to other organs. Nor had any agreement been
reached concerning precisely what its functions were to be. In fact, the leadership had apparently agreed on very little other than to create a collective
Presidency. Consequently, the Presidium emphasized ''the need to work out
the functions of the SFRY Presidency together with the precise establishment
of the relationship between the republics and the federation, the competencies
and structure of the organs of the federation'' and a number of other fun-

---

[9] *Borba* (Belgrade), 25 September 1970 (emphasis added).
[10] SKJ, *Aktuelni problemi daljeg razvoja*, pp. 129ff.

damental questions concerning the organization and operation of the feder-ation.[11] The month of October was devoted to consideration of these issues by the regional party leaderships and to negotiations between them. Late in October, these negotiations resulted in a major shift in the position of the Serbian leadership.

The state and party leaderships of Serbia, the autonomous provinces of Vojvodina and Kosovo, and of Belgrade convened a joint meeting late in October to announce that "it is essential that in the coming period the functions of the federation be reduced exclusively to those areas which represent the previously jointly established, united, and direct interest of all the nations and nationalities of Yugoslavia." By itself, this represented no significant change. However, they went on to propose:

> it is essential to emphasize that this simultaneously assumes [the fed-eration] will be freed of all functions [concerning] the distribution of special material resources which serve for the financing of investments and the expansion of production in general, except those which serve for the financing of the accelerated development of the insufficiently developed republics and provinces.[12]

This formulation represented a dramatically restricted conceptualization of the role of the federation in the Yugoslav economy from the position taken earlier by the Serbian leadership. It constituted a major concession to the interests of the Croatian and Slovenian leaderships, and appeared to be aimed at resolving the conflict over federal economic policies that had deadlocked the regional leaderships. According to the Serbian proposal, "the federation no longer would [be able to] seize resources directly from the economy." It pointed out that "precisely the function of the federation up to now in this respect, because of the differing interests of the republics, has been one of the causes of . . . interrepublican disagreements." Therefore:

> the federation no longer should have such economic functions . . . as the financing of investment, the granting of beneficial interest rates, the subsidizing of exports [and] shipbuilding . . . , the granting of premiums and penalties, the financing of scientific research work and similar things.[13]

However, while conceding in all these areas and more, the Serbian leadership remained absolutely committed to the retention by the federation of the in-dependent authority necessary to "secure the unified market" and to "ensure [the availability of] material resources for the accelerated development of the insufficiently developed republics and provinces." The latter position reflected

[11] Ibid., pp. 167-68.
[12] *Borba* (Belgrade), 23 October 1970; full text in *Politika* (Belgrade), 23 October 1970.
[13] Ibid.

Serbian interest in receiving support from the more developed republics for the development of Kosovo, and represented a natural basis for agreement with the Bosnian, Montenegrin, and Macedonian republics. It also retained some basis for insisting on the establishment of a relatively strong and autonomous decision-making center in the federation, capable of both adopting certain policies contrary to the short-term interests of the developed republics and enforcing them.

Serbian agreement to reduce the economic functions of the federation still left the nature of decision making in federal organs as a major point of contention between the regional leaderships. On this issue the Serbian leadership offered a more limited concession. They adopted the position that:

> in principle, in all their areas of responsibility, the organs of the federation must make decisions independently. Therefore, prior consultations . . . represent only a method of work. The competencies for which the passage of some decision requires the agreement of all republics and provinces may be established by the constitution, but the number of such questions should be kept to a minimum. In the event that some republic or province does not give [its] agreement to such questions, a special procedure should be established for final passage of a decision.[14]

This position contrasted sharply with those taken by the Croatian and Macedonian leaderships. But the next day Slavko Milosavlevski, secretary of the Macedonian party organization, seemed to respond to the Serbian proposal. He began by criticizing the view expressed earlier by the Serbian leadership that equal representation of the republics in federal decision-making organs "by itself is a completely sufficient guarantee of the equal treatment of every republic" and the view expressed earlier by Kardelj (and implicit in the Serbian position) that "the most rational means of decision making in the federation is the general democratic rule of decision making by majority." These positions, he argued, did not take into account "at least two things":

> First, that even in other democratic societies in which the national factor is not present there is deviation from that rule, [when] a rule of the so-called qualified absolute majority is established. And second, that ours is a multinational society and at least theoretically, but surely also in practice, outvoting at the expense of the vital interests of one or more nations is possible.

However, he went on to suggest that this "does not mean that we are insensitive to the dangers which come from demands that the full agreement of all republics and provinces be [made] necessary for all questions about which

[14] Ibid.

decisions are made in any organ of the federation.'' Although he reiterated the Macedonian position that "unbridgeable difficulties would be created in the life of our federation to the extent that fundamental relationships can be changed in it without the agreement of all its members,'' he then conceded that "the difficulties will not be fewer if in ongoing relationships the spirit of trust, mutual negotiation, and maximal harmonization of interests is missing.'' Consequently, he announced that the Macedonian leadership had decided to "accept the possibility of passing decisions on some questions by relative or absolute majority as a condition for the normal work of the federal political organism.'' This concession, couched in terms of confidence in the mutual trust among regional leaderships, brought the Macedonian position closer to the position taken by the Serbian leadership and held out the promise of an interregional agreement on federal decision making.[15]

In this way, despite continuing differences over the principles of decision making to be adopted, the month of intraparty discussion and debate following Tito's Zagreb speech proposing the creation of a collective Presidency did establish a tenuous consensus on the broad outlines of organizational changes to be implemented along with the establishment of the Presidency. With interregional conflict on substantive issues intensifying, the debate over constitutional principles could not be allowed to preoccupy the central party leadership for very long. Consequently, the Joint Commission of All Chambers of the Federal Assembly for Constitutional Questions was convened on October 28 to take over actual preparation of constitutional amendments. The Joint Commission for Constitutional Questions served as an organizational link between the Federal Assembly, which was constitutionally responsible for the preparation and adoption of constitutional changes; the party leadership, which was politically responsible for such changes; and the political and legal scholars who would be called on for expert assistance in their preparation.[16]

The Joint Commission, following the guidelines established in the conclusions of the party Presidium and by the intraparty discussion and debate which followed, decided that priority would be given to "the establishment of the SFRY Presidency and its relationship to other organs in the federation,'' and to determining "the functions of the federation and mutual relations [among] the federation, republics and autonomous provinces.'' It also decided:

> Questions concerning socio-economic relations that in the last three years have been at the base of all the disagreements behind which stand

---

[15] *Borba* (Belgrade), 24 October 1970.

[16] Sekretarijat za informativnu službu Savezne Skupštine, *Organizaciona struktura Savezne Skupštine, Saveznog izvršnog veća i ostalih organa federacije* Biblioteka Savezne Skupštine 6, no. 5 (Beograd: Prosveta, 1969): 18-19.

unresolved systemic questions—and among them especially is [the question of] the economic functions of the federation—must also be placed on the agenda as a priority.[17]

"The major work on preparation of theses and proposals for the resolution of the priority issues" was to be carried out by working groups of the Commission. Working groups were created for the organs of the federation; for relations between the federation, the republics, and the autonomous provinces; and for the economic functions of the federation. These groups were constituted with equal representation of the republics, the provinces, and the military.[18] Although clearly a task under close party supervision, constitutional reform was in fact a state function. The military was the single state institution that transcended regional and national divisions (however imperfectly) and that could, therefore, be expected to represent and defend "all-Yugoslav" positions in these working groups. All other members of these groups were required to transmit the positions of their respective republic or province, and remained in "constant contact" with them during the process of drafting the amendments.[19]

The working groups were composed of parliamentary and governmental functionaries, legal scholars, and some politicians. The scholars selected were politically well-connected and in most cases very well-known individuals. Most of them had written extensively on legal and political issues prior to their selection, and most continued to do so both during and after the drafting process. Their public writings and their comments on constitutional issues during public discussions of the draft amendments reflect very closely the discussions in the working groups.

The task of those groups was not to reconcile the conflicting views of the regions. Rather, it was simply to record them as alternative formulations of particular constitutional provisions.[20] Reconciliation, or "harmonization," of

[17] *Informativni Bilten Savezne Skupštine* [henceforth: *IBSS*], No. 32 (November 30, 1970), p. 26.

[18] Ibid., pp. 26-28; and *Borba* (Belgrade), 7 November 1970.

[19] Martinović, *Ustavne Promene*, p. 214. In addition to the sources cited, the following account of the drafting process is also based on interviews with individuals who participated in the work of the coordinating Commission and its working groups, conducted by the author during 1975 and 1976. The author also had access to a series of volumes of excerpts from the stenographic records of these groups, prepared for limited circulation to federal and regional party and state officials, which provided helpful insights into the nature of their work. Some of these volumes included: *Projekat: Promene Ustava SFRJ izvršene u periodu 1970-1973 godine* vol. II "Politički sistem" (No. 1, "Karakter jugoslovenske federacije"; No. 2, "Funkcije federacije"; No. 6, "Funkcije federacije i način odlučivanja u federaciji i ustavom utvrdjeni položaj i funkcije društveno-političkih organizacija"; No. 10, "Skupštinski sistem—deo prvi"; No. 11, "Skupštinski sistem—deo drugi") (Beograd: Institut za političke studije Fakulteta Političkih Nauka, 1970-73).

[20] *IBSS* 32, pp. 26-28; and SKJ, *Ustavne promene*, p. 213.

conflicting views on the proposed amendments was to take place in another, more authoritative body created by the Joint Commission—the coordinating Commission. The coordinating Commission was created:

> with the task of coordinating the positions and proposals of the republics and autonomous provinces. . . . This commission [also] would coordinate the work of the working groups of the Commission . . . and function so that the President of the FEC and representatives of the federal forums of socio-political organizations would be invited to its sessions and participate in its work. . . . Before the presentation of the proposals of the working groups to the [Joint] Commission . . . the coordinating Commission would discuss their proposals and evaluate whether they are ready for consideration in the [Joint] Commission and whether political harmonization has been carried out in advance.[21]

According to the records of the Domestic Documentation Service of the Federal Assembly, the task of the working group for organs of the federation was completed in only three sessions, held November 4 and 20, and December 30, 1970. The work of the group for relations between the federation, republics, and provinces required more sessions, but was completed in less time (sessions of the group were held on November 4, 12, and 24, and December 7-10, 11, and 18, 1970). Not surprisingly, the work of the group for economic functions of the federation took the longest time and was completed only after consideration of a set of comments and opinions on its work produced by the coordinating Commission during a lengthy session on the island of Brioni in mid-January.

The coordinating Commission was composed of "three representatives from [each of] the republics and two from [each of] the provinces."[22] Its twenty-two members were selected "on the basis of the proposals and agreement of appropriate organs of the republics and autonomous provinces."[23] Milentije Popović, president of the Federal Assembly and of the Joint Commission, noted that "the people selected for it hold the kinds of functions that enable them to transmit the positions of their republics and provinces and, in the course of work, to harmonize views."[24] In fact, the coordinating Commission included seven of the fifteen members of the party's central Executive Bureau and thirteen of the fifty-two members of its Presidium. Kardelj served as its chairman. Clearly, it constituted the most authoritative decision-making body in the drafting process.

The coordinating Commission exercised considerable control over the activity of the working groups. It set the initial agenda for each group and

[21] *IBSS* 32, p. 27.
[22] *Borba* (Belgrade), 7 November 1970.
[23] *IBSS* 32, p. 27.
[24] *Borba* (Belgrade), 7 November 1970.

proposed a set of guidelines for the preparation of amendments in each area.[25] The drafts produced by the working groups at each stage were circulated first to the coordinating Commission for review. Changes suggested by the Commission served as the basis for the further work of the working groups.[26] The changes made by the Commission often were extensive and ranged from the exercise of ideological control to mechanical adjustment of particular formulas or procedures, to what a participant in the work of one group called "changing an entire concept when conflict existed."

The coordinating Commission convened its first full session in mid-December, after the working groups had prepared preliminary versions of the amendments for its consideration.[27] It did not meet again, according to the records of the Federal Assembly's Domestic Documentation Service, until mid-January 1971. At that time, it convened for several days on Brioni (January 11 and 13-16). One product of this meeting was a series of "comments and opinions" on a preliminary version of the amendments concerning the economic functions of the federation that provided the basis for completion of the work of the working group for the economic functions of the federation. This meeting was followed by a series of meetings of the Commission "in narrow composition" [u užem sastavu] (January 19-20 and February 5 and 8). There are no public accounts of the membership or activities of this group. The fact that these meetings were convened following the first working meeting of the full coordinating Commission and prior to the last meeting at which the draft amendments were approved for submission to the Joint Commission suggests that the "narrow coordinating commission" functioned as a more authoritative and perhaps politically more homogeneous decision-making group within the larger Commission. It is not unlikely that it was composed of the seven members of the Commission who also were members of the party's Executive Bureau. The full coordinating Commission met again on January 26 to consider draft amendments prepared by the working group for the organs of the federation.[28] And it completed its work during three days of meetings in early February (9-11).

The actual work of the coordinating Commission "lasted, with short breaks, about a month." Kardelj, its chairman, reported in an interview on the occasion of the conclusion of its work that this was "significantly longer than was anticipated." He attributed this to the fact that "the Commission . . . attempted to carry out a more fundamental political harmonization of positions and . . . that process . . . demanded more time."

[25] Martinović, *Ustavne promene*, p. 212.
[26] Ibid., p. 213.
[27] Ibid.
[28] Ibid.

Although in the beginning there were differences in opinions, during the course of the long-lasting, many-sided, and open discussions and exchanges of opinions in the coordinating Commission political agreement was achieved with respect to the solution of all the basic issues contained in the approaching constitutional changes.

Of course, as always in such situations, in order for agreement to be reached, in certain instances it was necessary that we agree to the acceptance of certain "middle" solutions. The constructive and democratic atmosphere that dominated the discussions made it easier for the members of the Commission to understand better the arguments of others and to take them into account when they took their own final position. Nevertheless, I can assert that we did not make unprincipled compromises.[29]

At the sixteenth session of the central party Presidium a little more than two weeks later, Kardelj again described the work of the coordinating Commission in very similar terms. But this time he indicated somewhat more conflict than was suggested by his earlier remarks.

An atmosphere of democratic and constructive discussion was established in the coordinating Commission, in which all problems were discussed openly [and] without any kind of restrictions. Precisely this [atmosphere] enabled us to find joint solutions for all the essential questions that were made the task of the . . . Commission, although in certain cases that was achieved by both great effort and compromise solutions. I do not believe that at this moment we could have achieved such a result in so short a time by any other method.[30]

Kardelj reported to the Presidium that the members of the Commission had

to take into account the fact that in relations between the nations or republics of Yugoslavia there are not only differing, but even certain *objectively* contradictory interests. . . . It is obvious that these objective contradictions cannot be overcome with ideological formulas, and even less by state coercion alone through the federation. On the contrary, the excessive use [*hipertrofija*] of such force could lead the federation into an extremely serious political crisis.

"That is why," Kardelj continued,

we turned primarily to the method of negotiation [*dogovoranja*] and agreement making [*sporazumevanja*] among the republics. Because in such direct negotiations by the republics, on the occasion of the har-

[29] *IBSS*, No. 42 (February 20, 1971), pp. 2-3.
[30] Martinović, *Ustavne promene*, p. 11.

monization [*usaglašavanje*] of their interests, it will be easier to find appropriate forms of mutual compensation in situations when someone's legitimate interests are affected.[31]

As the statements of the regional leaderships cited earlier would suggest, the decision to apply the principle of decision making by interregional negotiation and agreement making to federal organs caused considerable controversy among the members of the coordinating Commission. Kardelj reported to the Presidium that "even on this question there were many discussions and many disagreements in consultations with responsible republican bodies." However, "a compromise solution was discovered, and it received the agreement of all the republics."[32]

Kardelj also noted that during the course of the Commission's deliberations it became clear that "because of the differing effects of common economic policy, it will be not possible in every instance to satisfy all interests." Therefore, the Commission recommended the establishment of "a system of compensations . . . [to be] understood not only and not even primarily in the form of financial resources but also [in the form of] other definite measures that will secure the reconciliation of material relations." How this system would work, however, remained in dispute. Kardelj reported that

> There were many discussions and disagreements—in my opinion, more than this problem deserves—about the questions whether compensation should apply only to work organizations or to republics and regions as well.

"These disputes," he suggested, "are more the consequence of the present mistrust than [of] doubt in the principle itself."[33] He concluded:

> whether we recognize this principle or not, that problem will always be the object of negotiation and agreement making among the republics or else there will not be unified economic policies. In fact, such already is the situation even today, so that some call it "haggling and bargaining." But in essence that is the normal method of agreement making of the republics . . . with respect to the problems caused by the unified economic policy of the federation because of the unequal position and interests of the republics.[34]

Kardelj's report to the sixteenth session of the Presidium suggests that the decision-making process by which the members of the coordinating Com-

[31] Ibid., p. 29.
[32] Ibid., p. 54.
[33] Ibid., p. 52.
[34] Ibid.

mission reconciled the conflicting positions of the regions involved compromises achieved at great effort. That "effort" entailed the acceptance and unrestricted discussion of conflicting interests arising out of "objective differences" between the regions; the renunciation of both solutions based on coercion and solutions inspired only by ideological formulas in favor of solutions based on pragmatic "haggling and bargaining" over concrete issues; and the acceptance of the principle of reciprocity, to be implemented by means of a system of economic and political "compensations." However, it is important to note that these compromises concerned the establishment of rules of procedure, and not the formulation of common policies.

The devolution of still greater decision-making power to the regional leaderships, which these amendments embodied, by itself may be considered a "substantive" decision, especially in view of the earlier resistance to such change. For it also entailed the transfer to the republics of capital resources heretofore controlled by the federal leadership and the adoption of new principles of procedure for their disbursement—most importantly, with respect to funding for the accelerated development of the underdeveloped regions. However, while these amendments may have established the principles of procedure by which common policies henceforth were to be made, Kardelj's reference to "the present mistrust" among the regional leaderships as the cause of much of the disagreement in the first place suggested that they still remained far from agreement on what, precisely, those policies were to be.

The organization and procedures adopted for the drafting process reflected the leadership's prior commitment to the decision-making principle of harmonization through interregional negotiation. The institutions and procedures for federal decision making established in the amendments produced by that process, in turn, reflected that organization and those procedures. Krste Crvenkovski, a member of the coordinating Commission, the central Executive Bureau, and the Macedonian party leadership suggested to the Presidium that the experience of the members of the Commission in harmonizing positions on the draft amendments indicated that the institutional and procedural formulas for conflict resolution contained in the amendments themselves could be made to work if the individuals engaged in them behaved as did the members of the coordinating Commission. Interregional harmonization of interests, he argued, "passed the test of full maturity [*položio ispit pune vrelosti*] on this occasion. . . . It has been shown not only not to be a delaying [factor], but to be an accelerating factor and an efficient method [of decision making]." He described the experience of the Commission and the lessons it suggested:

It can be said that—while sniping at each other from our bunkers . . . whether they are republican, provincial, economic, or federal . . . —

differences among us appeared far greater. That situation is completely understandable. . . . But I think that in the long run we should understand and accept one thing. We are dealing with diverse nations, with the presence of numerous nations and nationalities in this country. . . . I especially cheer the opinion of comrade Kardelj that these things should not be resolved on the basis of some ideological schemes. Rather, it is much more necessary to respect and to attempt to get into the interest of others. [*i pokušavati de se udje i u interes drugih.*]

But Crvenkovski concluded with what appears to be a hint that at least some members of the leadership continued to be dissatisfied with the compromises that had been necessary to forge an agreement on the amendments, and he suggested that this might be a source of trouble in the future.[35] Indeed, creation of a collective Presidency composed of individuals from each of the republics and provinces represented the application to the state of the principles of organization, representation, and decision making that had evolved in the party since the ouster of Ranković; and it was a mistake to think that their extension to the state would by themselves contribute to the solution of interregional conflicts over federal policy. For they had neither improved the cohesiveness of the party leadership nor increased the conflict-regulating capacity of central party organs. In fact, it could have been argued that their adoption had exacerbated conflict between the regional party leaderships and had debilitated the central party organs. Given "the present mistrust" and "sniping" between the regions that had made agreement on procedure so difficult to achieve and, apparently, so tenuous, it was unrealistic to expect agreement on substance to follow as long as each regional leadership was unwilling or unable "to respect and to attempt to get into the interest of others."

The 1971 Amendments[36]

The product of these negotiations was a series of 22 amendments[37] that substantially altered the nature of formal political relations in the state and laid the foundation for extensive changes in relations in the workplace. The most striking feature of these amendments was the radical reduction of federal

[35] Ibid., p. 133.

[36] All citations of the amendments are from the official English-language text; Secretariat of Information of the Federal Executive Council, *Constitutional Amendments XX-XLII* (Belgrade: Prosveta, 1971).

[37] Later to become twenty-three with the division of a single amendment into two separate ones in order to emphasize the importance of "self-managing agreement making" (*samoupravno sporazumevanje*) and "social negotiation" (*društveno dogovaranje*); the latter also can be translated as "social agreement making."

authority embodied in them. Amendment twenty-nine divided the "common interests" of "the nations, nationalities, working people and citizens" into those realized through the federation "with the participation, on terms of equality, and the responsibility of the Republics and Autonomous Provinces"; through "direct cooperation and agreements" among the republics, provinces, communes, and other territorial communities; through self-management agreements, social contracts, and other forms of voluntary association among organizations; through "the activity of socio-political and other organizations . . . "; and through individual activities of citizens. Amendment thirty limited the role of the federation to ensuring "the independence and territorial integrity" of the country, including determination of the basic principles of national defense, organization and command of the military, the conduct of international relations, and the protection of state security; regulating the "basic rights of working people in associated labor"; regulating "contractual and other obligatory relations regarding the sale of goods and services"; regulating basic ownership, property, and material relations pertaining to commerce, and copyright matters; laying down "the basic principles concerning social planning" and drafting the social plans of Yugoslavia, including among other things regulation of the monetary, foreign exchange, credit and banking systems, trade and other economic relations with foreign countries, and the crediting of accelerated development in the economically underdeveloped republics and provinces; and the provision of a number of standardization services such as ensuring an accurate and uniform system of weights and measures.

Amendment thirty-three established prior consultation, interregional bargaining, and harmonization of regional interests as the basic principles of federal decision making with respect to "the money system and money issue; the foreign exchange system, external trade, and credit relations with other countries; tariff and non-tariff protective measures; social control of prices of goods and services; crediting accelerated development in economically underdeveloped Republics and Autonomous Provinces; the determination of the revenue of socio-political communities . . . ; [and] the system, sources and total volume of funds for financing the federation." Federal regulations for the implementation of policies in these areas also were subjected to interregional bargaining and harmonization of positions. The Federal Executive Council (FEC) was required to "ensure the adjustment of stands with the competent republican and provincial agencies through the Republican and Provincial Executive Councils" on draft legislation in these areas prior to its submission to the Federal Assembly. To ensure such adjustment, the FEC and the executive councils of the republics and provinces were empowered to establish "interrepublican committees" as arenas for interregional bargaining in specific areas.

Kardelj acknowledged to the party Presidium that such bargaining had already become common practice in the formulation of joint economic policy. Jure Bilić, chairman of the working group for relations between the federation, republics, and provinces, not only acknowledged to the Joint Commission of the Federal Assembly that "such is the practice even now," but also suggested that by these amendments "we wanted only to establish in constitutional law and to institutionalize [*institucionalizirati*] the system of negotiation and harmonization of positions among the republics and provinces." He meant by this that the adoption of this amendment should not be seen as a source of interregional friction, but he acknowledged that interregional conflicts, "and sometimes even crises," had arisen in the past because federal organs operating informally according to such rules "were not sufficiently effective in the search for a solution to the harmonization of the differing interests of individual republics and provinces." He implied, therefore, that his working group really had no other choice for the organization of federal decision making. "No kind of majoritization in the adoption of decisions in federal organs will in future be effective," he admitted, "as long as the interests of the basic subjects of the federation [the republics and provinces] are not harmonized by mutual negotiation and agreement."[38] A pessimistic observer, therefore, might have suggested that this amendment held out little promise of improving the effectiveness of the federal decision-making process.

The organizational and procedural provisions for federal decision making contained in amendment thirty-three also reflected the organization and operation of the drafting process itself. In the post-amendment period, the division of functions between the Federal Executive Council as a whole, its own Coordinating Commission, and the interrepublican committees was identical to the division of functions between the Joint Commission, the coordinating Commission, and the working groups during the drafting process. Amendment thirty-three required that the interrepublican committees of the FEC be composed "on the principle of equal representation of the Republics and a corresponding representation of the Autonomous Provinces." The members of these committees were to be "delegated by the Executive Councils of the Republics and the Executive Councils of the Autonomous Provinces." This formula for "parity" also was applied to the collective Presidency, the Federal Executive Council, and the Constitutional Court. In somewhat modified form, it was applied even to "the commanding staff and promotion to higher commanding and leading posts" in the military; amendment forty-one required that "the principle of the most proportional representation of the Republics and Autonomous Provinces shall be applied" to these positions.

Amendment thirty-six established the collective Presidency proposed by

---

[38] Martinović, *Ustavne promene*, p. 200.

Tito in September. Aleksandar Fira, chairman of the working group for the organs of the federation, reported that the precise number of members of the Presidency had aroused considerable interregional disagreement in both his working group and the coordinating Commission. Different proposals for representation of the republics and provinces in the Presidency, calling for either two representatives from each republic and one from each province or three from each republic and two from each province, prevailed at different times during the course of their work. The draft finally submitted by the coordinating Commission to the Joint Commission called for two from each republic and one from each province. Fira reported, however, that

> at its last session the coordinating Commission decided to inform the [joint] constitutional commission . . . that . . . Bosnia . . . , Vojvodina and . . . Kosovo had reservations and wanted the number of members of the Presidency to be determined so that each republic elects three representatives, and [each of the] . . . provinces two. . . . They emphasized that three representatives from the republics and two from the provinces were thought to secure, or was the only [way] possible to secure the adequate national composition and representative structure of the Presidency, while not damaging the effectiveness of its work.[39]

The Presidency was in the end composed according to the formula suggested by Bosnia, Vojvodina, and Kosovo. This decision was consistent with the constitutional mandate of the Presidency, which required it to ensure both the harmonization of the views of the republics and provinces and to ensure the equality of the nations and nationalities. It corresponded precisely to the formula on the basis of which the coordinating Commission itself had been created.

The Presidency was to include the presidents of the republican and provincial assemblies, two members elected by each of the republican assemblies, and one member elected by each of the provincial assemblies. Tito, as president of the Republic, also was to be a member. This brought the total membership to twenty-three. The Presidency was assigned all the powers of a head of state. But this organ was created to serve a broader and more important purpose. As Kardelj explained to the party Presidium, the Presidency was intended to serve as "an active and integrative factor of stability for the political system," as a "factor of political cohesion in the center." It was intended to serve as "one of the advocates of unity, an organ that would react quickly to important problems and ease their solution by the path of political harmonization and initiatives." And it was to do so not through formal action in the form of government acts or decisions, "but primarily as

---

[39] Ibid., p. 218.

a political factor." Its members were to "work on the basis of adjustment of views." Kardelj explained that "each one of its members, although an authentic representative of an individual republic, also will take into account the needs and interests of others, that is, of the joint interest and needs of the entire social community." Therefore, he suggested, the "real function" of the Presidency "will come to expression precisely at the time when it will be unified in the taking of positions."[40]

The 1971 amendments were not limited to changes in the organization and operation of federal political institutions. According to Kardelj, the members of the coordinating Commission:

> found it impossible to restrict ourselves to bringing order, so to speak, into the state aspects of federation relations, or rather of relations among the republics, without laying down principles to consolidate the self-management and socialist position of the working man and of the basic organization of associated labor.[41]

Consequently, the Commission drafted a series of amendments (twenty-one through twenty-four) by which principles of organization and decision making in self-managing enterprises and social organizations were established. These amendments marked the beginning of a radical reorganization of the system of self-management that would culminate in the adoption in 1976 of a major new federal law on self-management, commonly referred to as the "second constitution."[42] They also reflected an effort by the members of the coordinating Commission to root the changes adopted for the political system in an ideological foundation. In a sense, they were an attempt to make the "base" of Yugoslav society conform to its "superstructure."

Kardelj pointed out in his report to the Presidium that "the proposed draft constitutional amendments are not fully completed in a technical sense."

> At present we are carrying out only a part of the constitutional changes. Complete coordination of relations and the institutions of the constitutional system will be possible only when we carry out the remaining changes which the present, first phase of constitutional changes makes necessary. Therefore, some provisions of the proposed amendments are insufficiently systematically worked out or are half-measures.[43]

Even the institutions and procedures established for the harmonization of positions among the republics and provinces during federal decision making—the central focus of the amendments—remained open to further adjustment.

[40] Ibid., pp. 56-57.
[41] Ibid., p. 41.
[42] The Associated Labor Act.
[43] Martinović, *Ustavne promene*, p. 12.

"It goes without saying," Kardelj reported, "that it is necessary to reach for the most suitable and . . . most efficient procedure for coordination. It is likely that the procedure proposed in the amendment [thirty-three] is capable of improvement."[44] Indeed, the institutions and procedures established by that amendment provoked continuing controversy not only during public discussions of the draft amendments but also among the individuals who participated in their preparation and within the political leadership itself, and especially between regional leaderships.

The coordinating Commission submitted the draft amendments to the Joint Commission of all chambers of the Federal Assembly for constitutional questions early in March 1971. That Commission approved them and submitted them for public discussion and debate. Organized public discussions of these amendments frequently were used by nationalists as forums for the expression of extremist sentiments. But these discussions also permitted the expression of less provocative, but no less conflictual, views by individuals who were close to or were members of the regional political leaderships and the groups that prepared the draft amendments. Individuals who participated in the preparation of the 1971 amendments reported during interviews conducted in 1975 and 1976 that many of the position papers prepared by regional representatives in the working groups eventually found their way into public print in the form of articles and polemics.

Late in March 1971, for example, a major symposium was organized on the topic "federalism and the national question."[45] Several participants in the drafting process attended this conference and delivered papers on topics relevant to the constitutional reform. A major issue during the discussion was the probable success of the provisions for federal decision making contained in the draft amendments. Several participants from different republics expressed strong reservations about both the de facto republican veto established by amendment thirty-three and the apparently overlapping functions of, and uncertainty of relations between, the Presidency, the Federal Executive Council, the interrepublican committees, the regional executive councils, and the Chamber of Nationalities of the Federal Assembly. The most extensive direct criticism was offered by a Belgrade law professor who did not participate directly in the drafting process, Balsa Špadijer. He suggested that constitutional provisions for federal decision making should be based on "two fundamental principles."[46]

---

[44] Ibid.

[45] Proceedings reported in Jovan Djordjević, ed., *Federalizam i nacionalno pitanje* (Beograd: Savez udruženja za političke nauke Jugoslavije, 1971); and *Arhiv za pravne i društvene nauke* 17, nos. 2 and 3 (1971): 318-67.

[46] Ibid., pp. 356-57.

First, that in Yugoslavia today the harmonization of positions of the republics and provinces, or nations and nationalities, is necessary on vital questions. Second . . . , that today in Yugoslavia a federal center is needed that will be dynamic, autonomous, responsible, and efficient.

Rather than striking a balance between these principles, it seemed to him that the draft amendment reflected an extreme position.

I have the impression that at the moment when [the amendment regulating federal decision making] . . . was prepared we really were under a negative impression, or a negative estimate, of the functioning of existing federal organs; that a fear of majoritization existed. . . . However, from fear of majoritization we went to another extreme with the introduction of [a form of] absolute majoritization. [And] that majoritization, in fact, according to the constitutional amendment [and] to the extent that that proposal is adopted, is that one [republic] is able to majoritize [*majorizira*] all [others].

But, to the extent that opposition to a form of majority rule that permits one republic or province to be outvoted by all others is justified, he argued, it is necessary to oppose the opposite extreme, as well. For, he continued:

this introduction of the veto, in fact, creates a situation of uncertainty, blockade, and probably will lead to certain political pressures, manipulation, and probably will reflect very negatively on the functioning of federal organs.

In this way, as this mechanism of negotiation is established, the role of the Presidency and even the role of the Federal Assembly is, to a considerable degree, derogated. In fact, as experience already is showing us now, we are creating an interrepublican/provincial committee out of the Federal Executive Council, which probably will have a negative effect on the operation of federal organs.

He suggested instead that

Harmonization . . . must be concentrated in only two centers in the federation: in the Chamber of Nationalities and the [state] Presidency. This harmonization should be [carried out] in the framework of a special procedure, with a qualified majority, which will ensure the protection of the vital interests of the republics and provinces.

Similar reservations were offered by Montenegrin economics professor Brana Ivanović and Macedonian law professor Evgeni Dimitrov, both members of the working group for the organs of the federation, and by Majda Strobl, a

Slovenian law professor and member of the working group for the assembly system, created in December 1970.[47]

A more severe criticism of the organizational and procedural provisions for federal decision making contained in the draft amendments was presented by Jovan Djordjević in a polemical pamphlet published in March 1971 as "a contribution to the debate about the constitutional changes" and entitled *Federalism, the Nation, Socialism*.[48] Djordjević was then, and remains today, the most well-known political scientist and authority on constitutional law in Yugoslavia. He is the author of a series of texts on the constitutional and political systems established by the successive sets of constitutional reforms and is reputed to have been the primary author—with Edvard Kardelj—of the 1963 constitution. At the time of the 1970 decision to amend the constitution, he was a member of the Constitutional Court of Yugoslavia. The Serbian leadership selected him to represent Serbia on both the working group for organs of the federation *and* the working group for relations between the federation, republics, and provinces, making him the only individual to participate in the work of more than one working group simultaneously. Both the similarity between the views expressed in the pamphlet *Federalism, the Nation, Socialism* and those expressed by members of the Serbian political leadership, and impressions and observations on the nature of the 1971 drafting process gathered during interviews with participants in it suggest that this pamphlet represents a public statement of at least the initial, if not the preferred, bargaining position of the Serbian political leadership. The views expressed in this pamphlet suggest that agreement on the provisions for federal decision making contained in the 1971 amendments was achieved only after significant concessions by that leadership.

As a legal scholar, Djordjević began his polemic against the provisions of the draft amendments by defining three closely related, but distinct, categories of politico-legislative functions: "pure federal functions (of general interest) [(*od opšteg interesa*)] . . . , matters of common interest [*od zajedničkog interesa*] to the republics, [and] matters of common interest of a special category [*od zajedničkog interesa posebne kategorije*]." He then criticized application of the principle of harmonization to decision making on matters of "common interest of a special category" and especially to matters of "general interest."[49]

As far as matters of general interest were concerned, he argued:

> the execution of these functions is not only the right but also the responsibility of the federal system of government and therefore their

[47] Ibid., pp. 359-60, 361-62, 350.
[48] Jovan Djordjević, *Federalizam, Nacija, Socijalizam* (Beograd: Privredni Pregled, 1971).
[49] This and the following citations are to be found in ibid., pp. 73-74, 82-87.

formulation and execution cannot be—from a legal perspective—conditioned by any kind of prior, additional, or similar agreements or votes of the republics. And—viewed theoretically and rationally—any right of veto is particularly beyond possibility.

This did not, in his view, preclude either consultations between the federal and regional governments on "controversial questions" or regional participation in the "regulation" and "implementation" of policies in these areas. "But," he reiterated, "matters of general interest for the federation as a whole are the right and obligation and therefore full responsibility of the federal organization."

This position, Djordjević insisted, "does not mean pleading [for], or the existence of, a kind of abstract opposition of the *apparat* of the federation, and thereby for the 'definition' of general interests as 'supranational' or 'suprarepublican.' " But his clear emphasis on the independent authority of the federation contrasted sharply with the principles embodied in the draft amendments. Djordjević insisted, too, that "general interests presume the transcendence of individual interests (even when [those interests] are republican [ones])." To achieve such transcendence, he implied, required certain changes in "the character of the organs that concretely define these functions." One such change, he argued, involved the function or role of regional representatives in federal institutions, and he used the Chamber of Nationalities to illustrate his point. "From the right of a republic to elect the members of the Chamber . . . through its own assembly," he observed, "the idea is derived that these representatives are delegates of the republic or republican assemblies, and sometimes in practice only of the highest forums of the League of Communists of the republics." In contrast, Djordjević argued that the Chamber of Nationalities was instead an institution of the *federation*. The republics and provinces were represented in it "for the sake of securing their equality and preventing majoritization." But this did not mean, in his view, that it was "a creation of the republics which is inserted into the structure of the federation."

Djordjević suggested that application of the principle of parity in the representation of the republics and provinces be restricted to federal institutions that make "political decisions." He acknowledged that "in the present situation of internal political relations, and in general, representation of the republics and provinces in organs of the federation is inevitable and justified," and that "the principle of parity has its political rationality in the composition of political bodies; as has been provided for the SFRY Presidency and Federal Executive Council and the 'government' as a whole (secretaries, undersecretaries, and similar functionaries)." But he objected to the "absolutization and schematic transfer of the principle of parity to . . . all organizations and services of the federation.'' This would lead, in his view, ''to the transformation of federal institutions into interrepublican [institutions] and thereby cause conflicts, excessive voting, passivity and incomplete decisions.'' Moreover, rigid application of the principle of parity would be unfair ''in view of the significant differences in the size and proportion of population between individual republics.''

Djordjević thus vigorously opposed the principle of unanimous decision making embodied in the draft amendments.

> Unanimity in conditions of a heterogeneous society, and especially a society in which the majority and minority, or various minorities, still wage a struggle over decisions, . . . would introduce a veto by the back door and thereby distort its nature. Unanimity would come into conflict with the efficient and necessary passage of decisions because, as a rule, a decision of some kind is better than none at all. Finally, it is not impossible that in such circumstances unanimity would mean either the domination of the powerful or a frustrating struggle by the progressive majority. . . .
>
> Therefore, unanimity and the veto are extremely exceptional and disputed categories, and still less are accepted instruments of decision making.

The principle of majority rule, he argued, is ''not just the only efficient but also the only politically justified [principle] in situations in which there . . . is no full homogeneity of interests, goals, and knowledge. . . .''

On all these points, however, Djordjević and the Serbian political leadership that he represented in the drafting process were compelled to concede. The amendments adopted in June 1971 closely corresponded to the positions advanced by the Croatian leadership and its representatives and strongly supported by the leadership of the Macedonian republic. The amendments did, however, maintain the integrity of the Serbian republic. Albanian pressure for elevating the status of Kosovo from an autonomous province within the Serbian republic to a separate republic was only partially accommodated by the effective equality of the regions established by provisions for representation and decision making in federal organs and the interrepublican committees. Kosovo was to remain, at least symbolically, part of Serbia.

The 1971 amendments also included a provision for the adoption of ''temporary'' federal legislation by a qualified majority rule in the event that interregional agreement could not be achieved on an issue which, in the view of the collective Presidency, required action. This represented something of a concession to Serbian demands. However, the procedure outlined in amendment thirty-three required that a proposal for a temporary measure first be submitted to the Chamber of Nationalities for a vote by delegation. Only if such a measure failed to receive a majority in each delegation could the Presidency move that the proposal be passed by simple majority. Consequently, the procedure seemed designed to emphasize interregional differences rather than to submerge them, thereby affirming regional power as much as limiting it.

The Failure of the 1971 Amendments

The constitutional drafting process was undertaken in an attempt to break an interregional deadlock over federal policies by developing new institutions and procedures for decision making. The amendments adopted in 1971 focused on the division of authority between the federation and its constituent units, the formulation of general principles and formulas for federal decision making, and on the creation of specific institutional arrangements for putting these principles and formulas into practice. Consequently, their success may be measured in terms of the degree to which interregional conflicts were, in fact, resolved through the routine governmental decision-making process established by the reforms, without resort to extra-systemic solutions or to modification of the decision-making process itself.

A temporary lull in open political conflict and decrease in political tensions during the late spring and early summer of 1971 suggested even to the most sensitive observer of Yugoslav affairs that perhaps a successful mechanism for the regulation of conflict had, in fact, been established.[50] But the analysis presented in the previous chapter suggests that conflict between the regional leaderships simply had temporarily been moved behind the closed doors of the highest organs of the central and regional party organizations. By the criteria set out above, the 1971 amendments clearly failed to regulate conflict. Their adoption necessitated amendment of each of the republican and provincial constitutions. As a result, public debate of highly sensitive and conflictual issues resumed in the Fall at an even higher level of intensity. The adoption of these amendments also called into question—as the critics cited above suggested they would—the role of the Federal Assembly, and its Chamber of Nationalities in particular. The legislative institutions of the federation were rendered almost entirely superfluous to the continuing political conflict between the regions. None of the issues dividing the regional leaderships during the Spring and Summer could even be discussed by the members of the Assembly until the process of interregional negotiation in the interrepublican committees established by the amendments was completed, and those

[50] See, for example, Paul Shoup, "The National Question in Yugoslavia," *Problems of Communism* 21, 1 (1972): 18-29.

negotiations rapidly became deadlocked. Nor did adoption of the amendments ease tensions among the regional party leaderships. And finally, the central leadership was compelled in December to resort to an extra-systemic solution to the "Croatian crisis."

While they may have failed in practice, the organizational and procedural provisions for decision making contained in the 1971 amendments did create a number of structural conditions for the successful operation of a system of conflict regulation based on interbloc negotiation. The amendments provided for the participation of all the regions in decision-making bodies whose decisions directly affected them; for consensual decision making; and for an alternative, non-consensual decision-making mechanism in cases of deadlock. The decision-making process by which they were prepared suggests that the regional leaderships accepted the differences which divided them as basic realities which could not be changed, at least not in the short term; that they were able, in these amendments, to identify and differentiate between activities properly subject to joint decision making and those subject to their respective autonomous control; that they appeared to be dedicated to the formulation of decisions with which all could concur; and that they seemed to accept the principle of reciprocity in decision making. These are all attitudes and behavioral orientations that would be expected to contribute to the eventual successful resolution of the still-outstanding substantive conflicts that divided them.

However, other characteristics of the drafting process made their resolution still more difficult. The overlapping membership of the coordinating Commission and the party leadership, for example, meant that members of the Commission who were at the same time members of the Executive Bureau or Presidium of the party could not easily isolate discussions of constitutional issues from discussions of specific policy questions. The initiation of constitutional reform transformed conflicts over substantive policies into conflicts over principles, and thereby intensified them. Conversely, continuing disagreement and distrust arising out of conflicts over substantive policy issues spilled over into discussions of constitutional principles. Continuing conflict over substantive policy delayed adoption of the amendments until determined pressure from President Tito forced recalcitrant regional leaders to accept them. But, despite the adoption of general principles of procedure, the regional leaderships continued to be unable actually to come to agreement on issues they themselves had assigned to joint control. For they lacked the mutual trust and confidence necessary to give real meaning to their professed commitment to reciprocity, and thereby make a system of consensual decision making work. Indeed, there is reason to doubt whether the formulation of unanimous decisions by regional representatives in the coordinating Commission was as much the behavioral manifestation of a mutual commitment to consensual decision making as it was evidence of the Croatian leadership's success in imposing its views on the others. Finally, the open criticism of the amendments by members of the working groups that drafted them and the open admission by the political leadership that it might be necessary to change the provisions of these amendments in the future if they did not work out suggest a relatively weak commitment to the agreements they embodied. In fact, there seems to have been a relatively low level of commitment among the Croatian leadership to the maintenance of the Yugoslav state at all. These factors help to explain why adoption of the amendments in June did not avert the crisis of December.

It is important to emphasize, however, that the failure of the regulatory mechanism embodied in the amendments to resolve the ongoing conflicts plaguing the system cannot be attributed solely to inadequacies in the institutions and procedures they established. That failure must be attributed primarily to the failure of the regional leaderships to respond to increasing internationality tensions and hostility at the mass level by increasing cooperative behavior at the elite level. For the institutions and procedures for federal decision making established by the 1971 amendments remained substantially unchanged in the period following the crisis; and, when the process of constitutional change was resumed in 1972, the organizational and procedural characteristics of the drafting process also remained substantially unchanged. Yet, despite the fact that regional representatives in federal decision-making institutions and in the groups drafting the new constitution continued to advance sometimes radically opposing proposals, under the conditions of renewed interregional elite cooperation characteristic of this period, these conflicts were successfully resolved.

Conflict Regulation and Decision Making in the Federation in the Post-Crisis Period

The new federal bodies established by the 1971 amendments were organized, and functioned, largely according to the formulas for representation and decision making prescribed in those amendments. Deviations from those formulas tended not to contradict, but to conform to the principles underlying them. Even already existing federal institutions, unchanged by the amendments, were reorganized or adopted new decision-making practices to conform to those principles. These adjustments had hardly been implemented, however, when the draft of a new integral constitutional text was ready. Thus, the federal decision-making process established by the 1971 amendments was relatively short-lived. It constituted, in effect, a transitional period in the Yugoslav political system; a period during which the principles embodied in the amendments were tested in practice and, finally, revised in the form of a new constitution.

The twenty-three-member collective Presidency was the institutional embodiment of the principles underlying the amendments. It was composed according to the formula calling for "equal representation of the republics and corresponding representation of the autonomous provinces," but operated on the basis of almost complete interregional political equality. Tito, as long as he remained president of the Republic, was to function as president of the Presidency. Otherwise, the positions of president and vice-president were to rotate among the regions annually. The autonomous provinces were assigned a symbolically inferior status in the Presidency by virtue of both the fact that they had fewer representatives in it and the fact that their representatives would alternate in a single turn in the rotation for president and vice-president. But their actual political status was equal to that of the republics. The amendments required the Presidency to make decisions "on the basis of adjustment of views of its members." Although this formulation permitted a variety of decision-making practices, the Presidency emphasized in its report on the first eighteen months of its operation that

in its actions up to now the Presidency has worked and made decisions on the basis of harmonization of the views of its members, which has been accepted as the leading principle in its work.[51]

Under these conditions, the fact that the autonomous provinces were represented by fewer individuals did not reduce their ability to advance and defend their interests.

During the first year-and-one-half of its existence, "the Presidency was in the situation that it made a decision by voting in only one instance." On this occasion it had to approve the adoption of a proposed federal law as a "temporary measure." But the Presidency used its power to authorize such measures only reluctantly. In February 1972, for example, it rejected a request from the FEC for such action, and "suggested to the Federal Executive Council that it attempt once again in agreement with the republics and provinces to find an appropriate solution, and if that is not achieved, the Presidency will discuss the question at one of [its] future sessions."[52]

The principle of "equal representation of the republics and corresponding representation of the autonomous provinces" also was applied to the support staff of the Presidency. During the first year of its operation, the Presidency established, according to this principle, councils composed of "members of the Presidency and other functionaries in the federation, republics, and au-

[51] *IBSS*, No. 107 (February 20, 1973), p. 4.
[52] Ibid., pp. 3, 10.

tonomous provinces." These councils reviewed issues before they were presented to the Presidency for its consideration. Often, during their deliberations, "the interest of each republic or province . . . came to expression . . . and their mutual and joint interests [were] harmonized." In this way, the work load of the members of the Presidency itself was reduced. These councils also "supervised the implementation of the positions of the Presidency."[53]

As required by the amendments, the Federal Executive Council also was organized according to the same principle of representation, with three of its members drawn from each republic and two from each province. However, the July 1971 law reorganizing the FEC also applied this principle to the appointment of functionaries in the federal bureaucracies. It called for the "equal representation of the republics and corresponding representation of the autonomous provinces" in certain specific categories and in the total number of positions. These were to include all "positions of significance for the implementation of the legal equality of the nations and nationalities of Yugoslavia." The specific positions encompassed by this formulation were defined in another, later "decision" of the Federal Executive Council, taken in cooperation with the executive councils of the regions. In federal administrative organs, they included the secretaries, undersecretaries, and assistants of secretaries in the federal Secretariats; the directors and assistant directors of federal Administrations; the heads and assistant heads of the state security service in the federal Secretariat of Internal Affairs, the counselors of the federal secretary for foreign affairs, and the heads of administration in the federal Secretariats for internal affairs and foreign affairs; and, the directors and assistant directors of all federal Directorates and federal Institutes. In the foreign service, these positions included the chiefs of diplomatic and consular missions and permanent missions to international and regional organizations.[54] Only the federal Secretariat for National Defense was exempted from this "decision."[55]

As required by the amendment mandating their creation, the statute reorganizing the FEC also called for the new interrepublican committees to be composed on the basis of "equal representation of the republics and corresponding representation of the autonomous provinces." But the FEC, in agreement with the executive councils of the regions, decided to establish five such committees composed on the basis of equal representation of all the regions. Interrepublican committees were established for development policy, for the monetary system, for foreign trade and the foreign currency exchange system, for the market, and for finance—that is, for each of the broad policy areas that had been the focus of interregional conflict in the preceding four

[53] Ibid., p. 4.
[54] Službeni List 27, No. 32 (1971): 609ff.
[55] Ibid., 27, No. 56 (1971): 985.

years and to which amendment thirty-three had applied the principle of decision making based on interregional "adjustment of views." The committees were to consist of a president drawn from the membership of the FEC and one member from each of the republics and provinces. The regional representatives were to be appointed by their respective regional governments. Unlike the members of the collective Presidency and the FEC, however, members of the interrepublican committees were required to represent the particular positions of those regions. The "decision" establishing the committees, however, also required these representatives to take into account "the interest of the social community as a whole."[56]

The interrepublican committees were created to take over the role played since 1967 by the Coordinating Commission of the FEC. The title "Coordinating Commission" was retained by another, more authoritative group within the FEC, composed of the president (premier), vice-presidents, and some members of the FEC, and the presidents of the regional executive councils. That group became a kind of super interrepublican committee, and functioned as the primary decision-making group of the Council.[57]

In the period between their creation and the forced resignations of the Croatian leadership in December 1971, the interrepublican committees fell subject to the same political stalemate that had paralyzed the earlier Coordinating Commission. After the December crisis, however, their effectiveness as arenas for the resolution of interrepublican conflicts over federal policy increased dramatically. When agreement between the republics and provinces could not be reached by these committees, by the Coordinating Commission of the FEC, or by the Federal Executive Council as a whole, the conflict was referred to the Presidency for resolution. Such referrals occurred only rarely; twice during 1972. During its first eighteen months, the Presidency was unable to resolve an interregional dispute, and was thereby compelled to authorize the adoption of a "temporary measure," only once.[58]

In deliberations of the interrepublican committees, the representatives of the FEC took positions largely determined during prior deliberations of the permanent commissions of the Council. These commissions were composed of a president and at least two additional members drawn from the FEC, and other individuals drawn from functionaries in federal organs and organizations, including the Council and its professional staff, the Federation of Trade Unions, the Federal Chamber of Commerce, "and other work associations and other organizations which carry out activity on the entire territory of Yugoslavia."[59] In this way the Council ensured that interests that cut across

[56] Ibid., 27, No. 37 (1971): 689.
[57] Ibid., 30, No. 21 (1974): 604ff.
[58] *IBSS* 107, p. 3.
[59] *Službeni List* 27, No. 37 (1971): 691; cf. ibid., 28, No. 33 (1972): 655ff.

regional boundaries would be represented in the preliminary discussion and preparation of federal draft legislation and legislative proposals. The members of the FEC who participated in the work of the interrepublican committees generally counterposed the "all-Yugoslav" interests and views developed in the permanent commissions to the more particularistic interests and views advanced by the representatives of the regions.[60]

This tendency to advance the general interest and the fact that representatives of the FEC participated in the interrepublican committees on an equal basis with those of the regions were reflected in a concept common among regional and federal politicians and administrators and among politically sensitive individuals outside of government and politics: the notion of the FEC as the "ninth republic." The statement has two implications: the representatives of the FEC were equal in status and power in interregional negotiations to the representatives of a republic, and there exist eight republics—not six—in addition to the FEC. The latter suggests that, while the representation of the autonomous provinces in the Federal Executive Council may have been numerically inferior to that of the republics, in power-political terms they had achieved equality.

In the period from September 1971 to February 1973, the interrepublican committees considered 293 issues. Only 18 of these could not be resolved by them and were referred to a higher level.[61] However, the successful operation of these committees as arenas for interregional negotiations raised serious questions about the role of the Federal Assembly. As early as June 1971, that is, even before the committees were formally established, a political commentator for *Politika* observed that as the Federal Executive Council becomes "less and less the highest executive-political organ in the country, and more and more an interrepublican coordinating body for the harmonization of positions," the Federal Assembly and its Chamber of Nationalities, in particular, is left without a role to play in federal decision making.

> Judging by practice up to now, although it has been only a short period, it is difficult for anyone to change that about which the republics have agreed and decided, which they have harmonized at the federal summit (really, in the federal government) to the last detail. The Chamber of Nationalities will want that least of all, because the republican delegations in it, viewed realistically, could not have positions different from those which republican delegates in the federal government had. Besides everything else, both the one and the other originate from the original policy of the republic and that is, as can be seen now every day, united and obligatory for all.

[60] Stjepanović, *Upravno pravo SFRJ*, p. 163.
[61] *NIN*, 1 April 1973.

With the establishment of interrepublican committees, the Chamber,

> more frequently than earlier, will have to make decisions about that on which the republics and provinces already have harmonized [their] views, so that *de facto*, the decision already has been made. That will be the situation particularly with respect to the key questions of the political and socio-economic system.[62]

This judgment was confirmed in January 1972 by Mijalko Todorović, then president of the Federal Assembly. Six months after the creation of the interrepublican committees, he observed in a meeting of the Assembly leadership that all decision-making power seemed to have accrued to the FEC and the interrepublican committees. He complained that "members of the Assembly are not sufficiently included in the first phase of work, in the process of conceptualizing a particular policy."[63] Policy issues "are presented to the members of the Assembly only when definite solutions have [already] been adopted in the interrepublican committees." As a result:

> a certain passiveness dominates among the members of the Assembly, because there exists the opinion that the Federal Assembly has been pushed into the background, that it is powerless and that it is not worth much effort to become involved in the solution of certain questions.

Todorović also complained that the actions of the Federal Executive Council itself had constrained the Assembly. "It is not only that representatives of the . . . Council frequently do not participate in the work of Assembly committees," he argued:

> but also [that] the atmosphere is such that between members of the government and the members of the Assembly bodies there has been established the relationship of "author" and his "critics." In this way, the members of the Assembly have been prevented from creatively influencing the carrying out of a particular policy or the formulation of certain acts.

The effect of these changes, he suggested, was to alter the character of federal decision making in the period since the Croatian crisis.

> contacts between representatives of the republican and provincial assemblies and representatives of the Federal Assembly are more rare, presidents of committees of the republican and provincial assemblies rarely come to sessions of corresponding committees of the Federal Assembly,

[62] *Politika* (Belgrade), 12 June 1971.

[63] This and the following citations of this talk are from the text in *IBSS*, No. 74 (February 10, 1972), pp. 3-4.

and so on. Cooperation also has been weakened between the Federal Assembly and [both] socio-political organizations in the federation and the Federal Chamber of Commerce; which, in contrast to the earlier situation, do not show much interest in the work of the Federal Assembly. Because of the new position of the Federal Executive Council and the interrepublican committees, the interest of these organizations has shifted toward the Federal Executive Council and the interrepublican committees, and the opinion prevails that the locus of work on the resolution of contemporary socio-economic and other issues is in the . . . Council and the interrepublican committees. . . . All this suggests that the interest of republican and provincial assemblies in cooperation with the Federal Assembly is falling because the harmonization of the interests of the republics and provinces is being channeled through the Federal Executive Council and the republican executive councils.

Todorović proposed a solution to the predicament of the Assembly and the other "interested social factors" that had been shut out of the federal decision-making process. He suggested:

the work of the interrepublican committees should be public and open toward all these factors so that they . . . could be actively included in these agreements. This relates especially to the committees of the . . . Federal Assembly, which should be included in discussion of all preliminary materials during the course of the procedure for the harmonization of positions [and] informed about the progress and result of the work of the interrepublican committees, make their own contribution, and influence the speeding-up of the procedure of harmonization.

Publicizing the work of the committees, however, was incompatible with their successful operation. The deliberations of the interrepublican committees were kept confidential in order to facilitate candid presentation of, discussion about, and negotiation over the positions of the republics and provinces.[64]

Unlike the federal and republican executive councils and the state Presidency, the interrepublican committees were not required to inform the public of their work. Consequently, no detailed reports of their work appeared in the public press. Public accounts were limited to reports of the achievement of particular agreements. Although the committees were required by law to keep minutes of their meetings, those records were required only to include "data about the members of the committee who attended the session and about the questions which were discussed at the session, as well as the conclusions about each question which is discussed at the session," and to record whether or not agreement among the regions had been achieved on

[64] *NIN*, 1 April 1973.

each question. "If agreement is not achieved, the positions of the members of the committee from each republic and province are to be recorded in the minutes."[65] Consequently, for those issues on which committee agreement eventually was achieved, the initial differences between the regions never would become a matter of public record. Their submission to the Federal Assembly or its committees, in contrast, would entail press coverage of the issue. Recent experience suggested that this also raised the prospect of a potentially inflammatory public debate in the assembly chambers.

In the period from September 1971 to February 1973, the issues that could not be resolved by the committees included eighteen of the politically most explosive ones, relating to interregional allocations of capital resources and economic cooperation. Among the specific policies in dispute were the crediting of development of the underdeveloped regions, reform of the foreign trade and currency exchange systems, and reorganization of the national bank and unified monetary system. As one committee chairman put it, these problems were "completely understandable because it is not some kind of caprice that is in question, but money!" He suggested that "if the republics and provinces had sufficient resources for their own needs and for the financing of general obligations, harmonization would be carried out far more simply." Of the eighteen issues, eight were resolved by the Coordinating Commission of the FEC, nine by direct negotiation between regional executive council presidents, and only one required referral to the Presidency.[66]

President of the Federal Assembly Todorović suggested that in instances when the interrepublican committees "do not function satisfactorily [*dovoljno efikasno*]," the Federal Assembly could provide "significant help" in the resolution of interrepublican conflicts.[67] However, the submission of such issues to the Federal Assembly would have been unlikely to have contributed to their resolution. Just as the members of the regional delegations in the Chamber of Nationalities would be unlikely to oppose a settlement agreed to in advance by the leaderships of their respective republics and provinces, so they would be unlikely to agree in the name of their regions to a settlement opposed (or not yet approved) by those leaderships. For they, like the members of the interrepublican committees, were obligated to represent the interests of their respective regions, and those interests were defined by the regional leaderships represented directly in the interrepublican committees. Moreover, if arbitration of such an issue were to be successful, it would have to be provided by an organ that not only was less subject to pressure from the regions but also occupied a higher and more authoritative position in the system. During this period the Assembly and its working bodies constituted

[65] *Službeni List* 27, No. 37 (1971): 690.
[66] *NIN*, 1 April 1973.
[67] *IBSS* 74, p. 3.

a lower, less authoritative level of decision making than the interrepublican committees.

The importance of extra-parliamentary consultations in federal decision making was reinforced in July 1973 when the Federal Executive Council, in cooperation with the executive councils of the regions and the Presidency, established "Federal Councils" (*Savezni saveti*) for "questions of the socio-political system" and for the economy.[68] These councils were an important innovation in the decision-making process for they provided institutional arenas for direct consultation and negotiation between both representatives of the regional political leaderships and representatives of socio-political organizations and interests that cut across regional boundaries. The Council for the socio-political system was to be composed of a president to be selected from among the members of the FEC, a number of members of the FEC and the regional executive councils, representatives of socio-political organizations on the level of the federation, and "outstanding educational and scientific workers." The representatives of the executive councils and socio-political organizations were to be named by their respective organizations. The Council for the economy was to be composed according to the same formula, with the addition of a representative of the Federal Chamber of Commerce (*Savezna Privredna Komora*).[69]

The mandates of these councils were sufficiently broad to allow them quickly to develop very comprehensive domains of concern. The Council for questions of the socio-political system

> reviews questions of the construction and further development of the socio-political system established by the constitution; discusses proposals of laws and other acts from the competency of organs of the federation by which are determined basic relations in the socio-political system; discusses these relations, and gives its opinions and proposals about them to the FEC.

The Council for the economy

> discusses questions of the construction and further development of the economic system established by the constitution, coordination of the economic development of Yugoslavia and the execution of established economic policy, [and] coordination and direction of the work of federal organs of administration and federal organizations in the area of eco-

[68] These *saveti* were established as explicitly political institutions and should not be confused with two other councils within the FEC which provide only expert (*stručni*) staff assistance—the Federal Legal Council (*Savezni pravni savet*) and the Federal Economic Council (*Savezni ekonomski savet*).

[69] *Službeni List* 29, No. 41 (1973): 1256-57.

nomics; discusses proposals of laws and other acts from the competence of organs of the federation by which basic relations in the economic system are determined; discusses the carrying out of policy in the economy; develops positions on these questions, takes the initiative, and gives proposals for their implementation.

Either council could be called into session on the demand of the Federation of Trade Unions, the Presidency, the FEC, or any of the executive councils of the republics and provinces. And each was responsible for its work to the Federal Executive Council.[70]

The establishment of these councils reflected the growing concern of the central political leadership with strengthening the role of integrative forces in the political system. It also reflected the continuing commitment of the central leadership to the institutionalization of prior consultation in the federal decision-making process, and its use as a mechanism for both the short-term resolution of specific conflicts and the longer-term regulation of the broader conflict relationship between the regions. These councils soon became the most authoritative policy-making bodies in the federation other than the central party organs and the Presidency.

As a result of the growing success of extra-parliamentary consultations, the Federal Assembly appears to have played no significant role in interrepublican negotiation over formulation of federal policy in the period following the Croatian crisis. In November 1972 Todorović and the leadership of the Assembly issued instructions concerning the procedure for decision making with respect to legislation which, according to amendment thirty-three, required interregional agreement. They called for the Assembly to discuss "variants" provided by the FEC for "preliminary proposals" for legislation not yet agreed on in an interrepublican committee. They did not permit the Assembly to discuss actual legislative proposals, or drafts, unless they already had received the approval of the republics and provinces. If the approval of a region was withdrawn after the Assembly had begun consideration of such a proposal, the Assembly was to cease consideration of it. Even legislation proposed by organizations other than the FEC required the approval of the appropriate interrepublican committee before the Assembly could consider it.[71]

Thus, during the period from the forced resignations of the Croatian leadership in late 1971 to the adoption of a new constitution in 1974, the Yugoslav political system was ruled by an elite cartel consisting of the leaders of the regional party organizations, the somewhat-strengthened central organs of the party, the state Presidency, and the executive organs of the federal, republican,

---

[70] Ibid.
[71] *IBSS*, No. 100 (December 10, 1972), pp. 4-5.

and provincial governments. The broad outlines of policy in areas subject to joint decision making were determined by republican and provincial representatives in the central organs of the party. The particulars of those policies were negotiated by republican and provincial representatives in the interrepublican committees and the Federal Executive Council. The expression of cross-cutting political, economic, and social interests was encouraged by providing institutional channels for their expression in the permanent commissions of the Federal Executive Council. And the Council, in turn, provided indirect representation of these interests in interrepublican negotiations. But direct participation in actual interregional bargaining was carefully restricted to members of the regional and federal leaderships, and their delegated representatives. Only in July 1973, with the creation of the "Federal Councils," was the range of participation in the bargaining process expanded. Even then, however, lower-level members of the political elite such as members of the Federal Assembly continued to be excluded from meaningful participation, and the activity of the masses and their involvement in discussions of public policy were closely controlled by the mass political organization under the reinforced control of the regional and central leaderships, the Socialist Alliance.[72]

Interregional conflicts over joint policy continued during this period. But these now took place under a much more comprehensive—and protective—cloak of secrecy. Only the consensually derived solutions became public knowledge. When conflict on a particular issue persisted, it was resolved by referring it to a higher and more authoritative body. In the rare instances when these bodies were unable to devise a solution acceptable to all the regions, the Federal Executive Council, Presidency, and Federal Assembly acting in concert were empowered to employ a special procedure for the adoption of a temporary solution, based on nonconsensual decision making. The successful operation of this system was conditioned by the restoration of elite control resulting from both the campaign to restore central authority in the party itself, described in the preceding chapter, and a concomitant campaign to restore party authority in society.

The central political coalition led by President Tito was convinced that the principles of representation and decision making embodied in the 1971 amendments, and the organs created to implement them, would successfully regulate political conflict if the cadres in them behaved in a manner consistent with the successful operation of a system based on interregional negotiations.[73] Consequently, following distribution of the Executive Bureau's letter in October 1972 and the subsequent purges of the regional party leaderships and

[72] Ilija Vuković, *Socijalistički Savez Radnog Naroda u političkom sistemu SFRJ* (Beograd: Savremena Administracija, 1975), passim, but esp. pp. 227ff.

[73] Rojc et al., *Deseti Kongres SKJ*, p. 432.

central party organs, the Bureau and representatives of the regional organizations agreed on the establishment of a uniform cadres policy. "The continuing implementation" of that policy, however, was entrusted to separate regional cadres commissions,[74] an indication of the continuing tension in the leadership between regional autonomy and central authority.

In July 1973, the Executive Bureau, in cooperation with representatives of the regional party organizations and "with communists who work in representative and state organs in the republics, provinces, and federation," worked out guidelines for the behavior of party members in state organs and other political institutions.[75] These guidelines were very likely reflected in the "Resolution on the current ideo-political tasks of the League" adopted at the Tenth Congress in May 1974. That document emphasized that the party as a whole, but especially individual communists in the leading organs and institutions of the republics, provinces, and federation and in interrepublican bodies, were:

> responsible for the further advancement and development of relations and forms of mutual cooperation, agreement making, and understanding [among] the republics and provinces on joint interests, for their equal participation in decision making about the joint interests of the working people, nations, and nationalities in the federation . . . , for the effectiveness of agreement making on the level of the federation, and for the faithful carrying out of agreed policy.

To fulfill these responsibilities, individual communists in these bodies

> must, with respect to the making and carrying out of decisions, always also have in view the entirety of interests of our Yugoslav socialist community and [must] constantly and persistently struggle against all forms of particularism, egoism, narrow-minded interpretation of the interests of one's "own" republic, province or economic branch or group.

But they could not go too far, for they also were required to struggle "simultaneously against the phenomenon of bureaucratic and unitaristic centralism and hegemonism."[76] The establishment of separate basic party organizations and *aktivs* in the organs and institutions of the federation, subordinated directly to the central party organs, provided an organizational framework through which the coercive authority of the party could be applied to enforce these principles.

Two additional targets of the central leadership's effort to reassert party authority were the universities and the mass media. After the second Con-

[74] Ibid., p. 458.
[75] Ibid., p. 460.
[76] Ibid., pp. 237-38.

227

ference in January 1972, representatives of the regional and military party organizations responsible for political-propaganda work met with the Executive Bureau to develop a joint position on "the activity, position, and role of the media, and informational activity in general." The mass media continued to be the topic of extensive discussion among the higher party leaderships and between the party and other socio-political leaderships throughout 1972. Despite these discussions, however:

> The agreed and established policies and ideological measures were not carried out persistently. And in those places where it was started, the struggle by communists was not sufficiently stubborn and concrete, [and] quickly fell into anemia, opportunism, and apathy [*nezamjeranje*].[77]

Only after distribution of the Executive Bureau's letter in October did the effort to establish closer party supervision over the media achieve success. Late in 1972, "important cadres changes in the press, in radio and television, and in journals, publishing enterprises, and cultural institutions were carried out so that the influence of the LCY in the system of public information as a whole was strenghtened."[78] Individuals who had been opposed to the party line or resistant to the reassertion of party authority were removed from "leading positions" in the media, and replaced by "people who were ideo-politically clearly determined, loyal to the course of the LCY, and capable." As a result, party organizations in the editorial boards of newspapers and other media now influenced editorial and cadres policy "in much greater measure."[79]

The reestablishment of party supervision over the mass media in 1972-1974 did not, however, end the reporting of controversial social and political issues and interregional political conflict. Rather, it resulted in an important change in the character of such reports. Instead of emphasizing the conflicting positions of the regional leaderships on a given issue, as had often been their practice prior to 1972, the media began to emphasize the efforts of the leaderships to reconcile their positions. Particular emphasis was placed on the successful operation of the institutions and procedures established by the 1971 amendments and on the unifying force of the party. The accounts of interregional conflicts were no less detailed than during the earlier period; they simply were no longer openly partisan and they carefully projected confidence that the eventual reconciliation of views through routine political processes was inevitable. This contributed to a markedly calmer political atmosphere in Yugoslavia.

The party leadership's assault on the universities and intelligentsia was the

---

[77] Ibid., p. 468.
[78] Morača et al., *Istorija SKJ: kratak pregled*, p. 315.
[79] Rojc et al., *Deseti Kongres SKJ*, p. 469.

central feature of its effort to improve "ideological education and theoretical work" in the party. At the Tenth Congress, the leadership admitted that "for years" the party had devoted insufficient attention "to the development of theoretical work, Marxist social criticism, propaganda, and to the development of institutions which deal with social research and the training of cadres." It also had neglected the ideological training of the broader membership. That task had been relegated to secondary institutions such as workers' and people's universities and evening political schools, and these went about their tasks with relatively little guidance from party leaders. Moreover, the content of this training was "quite general, lifeless [and] divorced from the burning problems of society." As a result, "naked pragmatism began to dominate the content and activity of many organizations and leaderships of the League."[80] Since the ouster of Ranković, and especially since the Ninth Congress, a host of political views, theories, and ideologies developed both in Yugoslav society as a whole, and in the party itself.

Among the major targets at the Tenth Congress were Croat and Serb nationalisms, various forms of "liberalism" and "anarcho-liberalism," "technocratism," and "etatism" (or "unitarism"). The growth of these ideologies was viewed by the central leadership as a challenge to the party's political monopoly. By reemphasizing the need for "ideological education and theoretical work" and its supervision and control by the party, the leadership hoped to combat these ideologies both by restricting their dissemination and by revitalizing the ideology of self-management and thereby the party as its defender.

In some cases, however, the campaigns to improve "ideological education and theoretical work" and increase party control over personnel appointments in key institutions took the form of more direct action. In his analytical history of the *Praxis* group of philosophers in Yugoslavia,[81] for example, Sher has described in detail the application, beginning in late 1972 and continuing through the Tenth Congress in 1974, of "moral-political" criteria—including adherence to the party "line"—to the evaluation of the performance of university professors. This party-led attack on the independence of the universities in Yugoslavia, and especially on the historical independence of Belgrade University, included the manipulation by the party of institutional structures and rules of procedure within the university and the republican legislature in order to establish direct control over academic appointments. The party leadership then used its control over university appointments to deny teaching jobs to the proponents of ideological positions they found unacceptable.

In May 1972 the central Executive Bureau, "in cooperation with the ex-

[80] Ibid., p. 450.

[81] Gerson Sher, *Praxis: Marxist Criticism and Dissent in Socialist Yugoslavia* (Bloomington: Indiana University Press, 1977).

ecutive organs of the central and provincial committees and the commission of the Presidium of the LCY for ideological questions and theoretical work,'' organized a consultative conference on ideological work in the party. The purpose of this conference was "to contribute to a harmonized evaluation of the situation of ideological life, to a more organized ideological struggle, and to point out certain of the basic causes of disunity in the League."[82] However, just as in the case of efforts to unify cadres policies and assert party control over social institutions, little concrete action was taken to harmonize, organize, and unify the ideological struggle of the party until after distribution of the Executive Bureau's letter and the subsequent changes in the regional leaderships. Shortly thereafter, however, each of the republican central committees established its own "Marxist center":

> to follow systematically events in theory and the social sciences and to achieve the organized influence of the League of Communists on the directions of social research [and] the use of its results in the practice of the LC, the programming of ideological work, [and] its organization and direction.[83]

Coordination of the work of these regional "Marxist centers" was to be achieved in the Center for Social Research attached to the Presidium.

One Yugoslav academic who experienced the work of these "Marxist centers" first hand likened their operation, somewhat hyperbolically, to the Spanish Inquisition. As he described the process, these centers functioned in the mid-70s as censorship boards for the academic and intellectual communities. A manuscript had to be approved by the board of such a center before it could be published. These boards examined manuscripts not only for unacceptable ideological content or ideological implications but also for the absence of explicitly ideological statements which they felt were appropriate or necessary. Where such a board found the former, the author could be subjected to intense ideological examination by its members. Where such a board found the latter, it could "suggest" that the appropriate statements of ideology be added in order to permit publication. It was, according to his account, entirely within the power of these boards to prevent the publication of any manuscript.

This same individual reported that the Marxist centers of the republics are under the firm control of the republican party leaderships, and that the coordination exercised by the central Presidium's Center for Social Research was minimal. Indeed, distinct differences of views between the regional academic and intellectual communities on important issues continued to appear

---

[82] Rojc et al., *Deseti Kongres SKJ*, p. 451.
[83] Ibid., p. 452.

in public print. The distances between those views, however, substantially narrowed as the result of the necessity to adhere relatively closely to a common ideological language, and differences between regions no longer could be exacerbated by the independent publication of inflammatory polemics. It continues to be the case, however, that works published in one region may prompt criticism or protests in that or other regions—either publicly or privately within the party leadership—and may even be withdrawn. This suggests that the censorship exercised by the "Marxist centers" is neither comprehensive nor uniform. It also suggests that the political leaderships of the regions continue to hold conflicting views on ideological issues and that those leaderships maintain a vested interest in seeing the continuation of debate on such issues— a debate which the central leadership is unwilling or unable to restrict.

The campaigns to restore central authority in the party and party authority in society should not be allowed to overshadow the fact that governmental decision making during the years 1972 and 1973 was characterized by a constant tension between central authority and regional autonomy. Just as in the party, each move to strengthen the former was balanced by another to protect the latter. This tension is very clear in the decision-making process by which the 1974 constitution was drafted. Implementation of the 1971 amendments confirmed what their critics had suggested even before they were adopted: that they undermined the position of the Federal Assembly. The fate of the Assembly, therefore, became a central issue during preparation of the 1974 constitution, and the competing proposals for resolution of this issue indicated the tensions between center and region. The way those proposals were reconciled reflected the character of the existing system and foreshadowed the character of the system that would be established by the new constitution.

Drafting the New Constitution

The "second phase" of constitutional reform—preparation of a new integral constitutional text—formally began in July 1971 with the appointment of a new coordinating Commission. A later official review of the organization and operation of the constitutional drafting process reported that the new Commission "was formed on the principle of representation of all the republics and autonomous provinces" and suggested that it was "composed of the most authoritative of their political representatives."[84] But the new Commission as a whole was considerably less authoritative than its predecessor. Although Kardelj continued as its chairman, it contained fewer members of the central party Presidium and Executive Bureau and was composed largely of the

---

[84] *IBSS*, No. 93 (September 30, 1972), p. 4.

presidents of the regional assemblies.[85] As a result, fewer members of the new Commission were directly involved in the intensifying political struggle then taking place in the party leadership, and the new Commission could separate constitutional questions from substantive ones more effectively than its predecessor. At the same time, members of the central and regional party leaderships released from direct participation in the drafting process could concentrate all their energies on the directly political conflict, which was then reaching crisis proportions. The new coordinating Commission was composed of two representatives from each republic and one from each province, giving it only fourteen members in comparison to its predecessor's twenty-two. And the projected period in which it was to complete its task was considerably longer than that of the old Commission.[86]

All these changes were likely to increase the effectiveness of the Commission as a constitution-drafting body. But the second phase of the drafting process could not proceed in any meaningful way until the larger political conflict that would determine the course of political development in Yugoslavia was resolved. In fact, the new coordinating Commission did not convene its first session until September 1971 and could not begin serious work on the preparation of a new constitution until early February 1972—that is, until after the forced resignations of the Croatian party leaders and the convocation of the January 1972 party conference.

The organization and operation of the constitutional drafting process during the postcrisis period was almost identical to that which had taken place in the context of intense conflict. At its first session the new coordinating Commission decided that regional leaderships would "review once again" the membership of working groups that had been created in December 1970 and March 1971 to prepare proposals for longer-range changes in the constitutional order.[87] This review did not, however, result in extensive changes in the composition of the working groups. This probably was because those groups had been composed of functionaries and specialists drawn from a lower level of the Yugoslav elite than those who had served on the other groups. They were, therefore, less directly involved in the ongoing political struggle.

The working groups that set out to draft the new constitution were composed according to the same principles as their predecessors. Each of the republics and provinces and the military named a single representative to serve on each working group. However, unlike the earlier period, the membership of some of the groups:

> was expanded by a certain number of functionaries and socio-political workers. In addition, representatives of working bodies of socio-political

[85] *IBSS*, No. 58/59 (July 30-August 10, 1971), p. 4.
[86] Ibid.
[87] *IBSS*, No. 60 (September 20, 1971), p. 4.

and other organizations on the level of the federation and a certain number of functionaries from the Federal Assembly and other federal organs and organizations participate in the work of certain working groups.[88]

This change reflected the central leadership's greater concern during the post-crisis period with ensuring the supervision of key political and social organizations and processes by reliable cadres. The inclusion of representatives from the military in the membership of working groups during the second phase also reflected this concern. Military representatives earlier had been excluded from participation in the groups working on long-range changes. The participation of military representatives in these groups is reported only in early 1972—*after* the military had assumed a more important and more directly political role in the system. The concern to ensure political supervision extended even to the new coordinating Commission itself. The sessions of the new Commission were attended by "a representative" of the Executive Bureau of the central party Presidium in addition to the three Bureau members who were simultaneously members of the Commission.[89] He, unlike the others, could represent the party without reference to the interests of any of the regions.

This greater concern also was reflected in a decision taken at the new Commission's first working meeting in the postcrisis period, held 8-10 February 1972. At that meeting the new Commission decided, in accordance with an agreement between the president of the Joint Commission for constitutional questions of the Federal Assembly and the president of the Federal Conference of the Socialist Alliance, "to create a special coordinating group with the task of studying questions of the role of socio-political organizations in our political system." This group was composed of "representatives of all socio-political organizations."[90] After several months of work it produced a draft thesis proposing new constitutional provisions strengthening the authority and responsibility of the trade unions, the Socialist Alliance, and the party.[91]

The operation of the working groups during the second phase was almost identical to that of the corresponding groups during the first phase. All materials prepared by the working groups were sent automatically to the constitutional commissions of the republican and provincial assemblies. At the same time, the members of the working groups participated in the work of the commissions of their respective regional assemblies. In this way, "it was ensured that the working groups . . . would be acquainted with the positions and opinions of the corresponding working groups in the . . . republics."[92]

[88] *IBSS*, No. 77 (March 10, 1972), p. 2; cf. *IBSS* 93, p. 5.
[89] *IBSS* 93, p. 4.
[90] *IBSS* 77, p. 4; and *IBSS* 93, p. 5.
[91] *IBSS*, No. 92 (August 1-September 1, 1972), pp. 55-56.
[92] *IBSS* 93, p. 6.

On the basis of the views expressed by the republics and provinces, "almost all working groups prepared draft materials that contained basic problems in connection with the constitutional regulation of areas in their responsibility."[93]

The relationship between the new coordinating Commission and its working groups also was identical to the relationship that had existed during the earlier period. The Commission considered the preliminary material prepared by its working groups and offered its criticisms and suggestions. "After consideration of these materials at a session of the coordinating Commission, drafts or pre-drafts were worked out of theses for constitutional regulation of issues from corresponding areas."[94] In order "to secure a constructive exchange of opinions and freedom of discussion," the new coordinating Commission decided at its first postcrisis working session:

> that in their reports on the work of the coordinating Commission the press and other information media will report about the themes and issues discussed, and about the opinions and alternatives on particular problems, without quoting the positions of the Commission or the positions of its individual members.[95]

Such a policy not only permitted more freedom of discussion within the Commission itself, and thereby increased the likelihood that representatives of the regions would be able to develop formulas to reconcile their divergent interests, but also decreased the likelihood that reports of such discussions would exacerbate tensions and conflict on the mass level. This decision reflected the general policy toward press reporting of political events in Yugoslavia adopted in the aftermath of the Croatian crisis.

The new coordinating Commission met again in April 1972 on Brioni to review the progress of the working groups on preparation of a new integral text of the constitution. In addition to the members of the Commission, this meeting was attended by the president of the Federal Assembly and its Joint Commission for constitutional questions, the vice-president of the Assembly, the president of the Federal Conference of the Socialist Alliance, representatives of the leaderships of socio-political organizations and the army, and the chairmen and members of the working groups of the Commission. In a later report on this session,[96] the leadership of the Federal Assembly noted that "although this session was concerned with . . . the most sensitive and most controversial problems," there were "no significant differences" among the regional representatives "in principled approach." Nonetheless, the As-

[93] *IBSS* 77, p. 3.
[94] Ibid.
[95] *IBSS* 93, p. 7.
[96] This and the following citations to this report are from the text in *IBSS*, No. 83 (May 10, 1972), pp. 2-3.

sembly leadership's report also suggested continuing interregional conflicts over "the structure and competence of the future federal assembly." Although the participants "moved significantly closer to one another" at this meeting, "certain differences did remain."

The Assembly leadership reported that the coordinating Commission had agreed

> that there must be a chamber of the republics and provinces in the federal assembly, similar to the present Chamber of Nationalities, [and] formed on the principle of equal [*paritetne*] representation of the republics and provinces. The members of this chamber, however, would not be elected by the republics and provinces as up to now, but rather by their self-managing bases directly.

The Assembly leaders also reported that "more important differences" were evident concerning whether a second parliamentary chamber was required and "whether, in the future, it could make decisions on issues that . . . [the 1971] constitutional amendments assigned to direct decision making by the republics and their mutual negotiation through the interrepublican committees."

This suggests that the interrepublican conflict over the organizational and procedural provisions for federal decision making characteristic of the first phase of constitutional reform in 1970 and 1971 continued during the second phase in 1972 and early 1973. As a result, the new coordinating Commission found that, in order to reconcile opposing views on this issue, it was necessary first to review the federal decision-making process established by the 1971 amendments. Consequently, the Commission decided at the end of its April meeting on Brioni

> to complete discussion of questions concerning the structure and competence of the future assembly at one of [its] future sessions, since in the meantime a special working group will study the issues [concerning] the carrying-out of the functions of the federation . . . as well as the method of decision making in the federation on these issues.

On 28 May 1972, the coordinating Commission created a special working group for the functions of the federation and the method of decision making in it. According to documents of the Joint Commission, the group was composed of a single representative from each of the republics and provinces and from the military, under the chairmanship of the vice-president of the Federal Assembly and its Joint Commission. Of the ten members of this group, five had been members of either the working group for the organs of the federation or the working group for relations between the federation, republics, and provinces during the first phase of the reform. However, among those not called on to participate was Jovan Djordjević, who had been a member of both earlier groups. One individual who participated in the work of the group for the functions of the federation and later assumed a high staff position in the Federal Assembly explained the absence of Djordjević by suggesting during an interview conducted in 1976 that Djordjević "thinks the old way. He does not understand how things are in the new federation, the new Yugoslavia." Although something of an exaggeration, this statement does reflect accurately the fact that the positions expressed by Djordjević and cited earlier in this chapter had been completely rejected at the time this group was formed.

The new coordinating Commission convened its next session in Belgrade from 19 to 23 June to discuss draft and preliminary draft theses prepared by the working groups. The special working group for the functions of the federation presented a preliminary draft thesis on the execution of certain functions of the federation and the method of decision making concerning them. A later report on this session suggests that both the special working group and the Commission as a whole had been wrestling with a fundamental problem concerning the Federal Assembly, and especially its Chamber of Nationalities:

> Namely, after [the 1971] . . . constitutional changes, the Federal Assembly, on the proposal of the FEC, passed decisions about economic and financial issues . . . [by] starting from agreements between the republics and provinces that had been concluded in the interrepublican committees. Consequently, the members of the Federal Assembly arrived in the situation that they were formally voting for these decisions, and carried social and political responsibility for them, although neither they nor the Assembly had any kind of influence in the preparation of these decisions and measures.[97]

Several different views were expressed during discussion of this problem. It was suggested, for example, that, in the future, decisions on issues requiring interregional agreement (i.e., those enumerated in amendment thirty-three) should be made separately, but on a coordinated basis, by the individual assemblies of the republics and provinces. In this way, it was argued, "the present dualism which results from the temporary retention of the old position of the Federal Assembly in conditions of the new method of decision making in the federation would be eliminated." However, it also was suggested that "the Federal Assembly would be a more appropriate and more efficient place for harmonization of the positions of the republics as well as for discussion and adoption of identical texts of . . . acts." Support for retention of a separate federal legislature composed of representatives of the republics and provinces

---

[97] *IBSS*, No. 88/89 (June 30-July 10, 1972), p. 4.

also was motivated by "fear of the complexity and lengthiness of the procedure of coordination of decisions in the republican and provincial assemblies themselves."[98]

The coordinating Commission as a whole, composed primarily of the presidents of the regional assemblies, adopted the position that federal decision making in areas requiring interregional agreement:

> would begin with an agreement in the appropriate interrepublican committee on the need for passage of a certain law. The working out of the proposal would then be entrusted to some permanent or ad hoc specialized body and then, as a proposal for the passage of a law, the republican and provincial assemblies would discuss it. After that it would be returned to the interrepublican committee for final harmonization of positions. Later it would come to the republican and provincial assemblies for adoption, and the SFRY Presidency would carry out only the proclamation of the adopted law.[99]

By adopting this position, the Commission was advocating a dramatic reduction of the autonomy of the federation and a concomitant increase in the authority of the regional assemblies. For this formulation did not provide for the existence of a separate legislative chamber at the federal level composed of representatives of the regions. In addition, while the Commission recommended retaining provisions for the adoption of "temporary measures" in the absence of interrepublican agreement, it was proposed during discussion "that, in the event that agreement is not achieved by the expiration of such a measure, the republics could resolve the controversial question in their own way for their own territory."[100] The latter proposal, however, was reserved for further discussion and did not become part of the Commission's official recommendation.

Kardelj conceded in April 1973 that even during the second phase of constitutional reform:

> With respect to the structure of the Federal Assembly, in the beginning of work and in the coordinating Commission there came more or less to expression quite different and sometimes even fundamentally contradictory understandings.[101]

These contradictory understandings of the future organization and process of federal decision making were clearly evident in the draft theses prepared by

[98] Ibid.
[99] Ibid.
[100] Ibid.
[101] Edvard Kardelj, *Osnovni uzroci i pravci ustavnih promena* (Beograd: Komunist, 1973), p. 106.

the working groups and circulated among functionaries of the federation and of the regional assemblies during August 1972.[102] The draft thesis prepared by the working group for the assembly system contained two alternative formulas for the organization and operation of the Federal Assembly. The first variant called for an assembly composed of two chambers: one to be a chamber of the republics and provinces composed of delegations of the regions, and a second to be a chamber of "associated labor" composed of delegations of working people in self-managing enterprises, organized into "basic organizations of associated labor." The chamber of the republics and provinces was to be responsible for all questions affecting the interests of the regions, as defined in amendments thirty-two and thirty-three. The chamber of associated labor was to be responsible for all questions affecting the working people of Yugoslavia. Both chambers were to be equally responsible for passage of social plans, the federal budget and "other general acts." Each of the regions was to be represented in the chamber of the republics and provinces by an equal number of delegates. The number of delegates in the chamber of associated labor was to be proportional to the number of persons employed in organizations of associated labor. The second variant called for a single-chamber Federal Assembly composed of delegations of the republics and provinces, each comprising an equal number of delegates. On questions requiring the agreement of all the republics and provinces, this chamber was to pass decisions by a unanimous vote of all *delegations*. The position of each delegation was to be determined by a majority vote of its members. On issues not in the jurisdiction of the republics and provinces, decisions were to be adopted by majority vote of all *delegates* in the chamber. These proposals, however, were preceded in the draft thesis by a note from the working group advising readers that the final organization and operation of the federal assembly undoubtedly would be affected by the positions adopted by the special working group for the functions of the federation in its proposals.[103]

Given the composition of the special working group, it is not surprising that it proposed the elimination of any federal legislative body composed of representatives of the regions. It called instead for federal decision making on issues requiring interregional agreement to be carried out by the regional assemblies acting independently. A decision would be considered adopted when it had been adopted by all the regional assemblies.[104] This proposal represented the further development of the principles of federal decision making already endorsed by half the group's members when they drafted the 1971 amendments, and conformed to the position adopted by the new coordinating Commission in April 1972. But the coalition in the central party leadership

[102] Texts in *IBSS* 92.
[103] Ibid., pp. 62-64.
[104] Ibid., p. 67.

that had supported Tito's intervention in Croatia was now reasserting central authority in the party and attempting to revitalize the central organs and institutions of the state. The proposal by the special working group stood in stark contrast to those efforts. Consequently, the new coordinating Commission, under Kardelj's chairmanship, was compelled to develop a formula for the organization and operation of federal decision making more appropriate to the current political environment.

Kardelj suggested later that the divergent positions of the republics and provinces and the contradictory proposals of the working groups "were reconciled on a solution which in fact is very different in form from all initially proposed variants."[105] In reality, the Commission merely constructed a compromise solution that included elements of the earlier proposals, but which also strengthened the independent position of the federation. Kardelj reported that the coordinating Commission decided that the republics and provinces had to be represented in the federal decision-making process by both "delegations of organizations of associated labor and other self-managing communities" and "the responsible organs of the republics or autonomous provinces." The former would "make decisions in the federation primarily about [issues in] the independent authority of organs of the federation," and the latter would "make decisions in the federation primarily when the constitution requires the agreement of the republics and provinces." With respect to the latter, he suggested, however:

> it is clear that for efficient work and the speedy and more responsible solution of mutual problems it is essential that delegations originate directly from republican assemblies. It also is obvious that they can operate successfully only on the basis of an explicitly imperative mandate, that is, [on the basis of] the agreement of the assemblies which they represent.

These provisions were obvious concessions to regional autonomy.

This formulation corresponded quite closely to the first alternative included in the draft thesis prepared by the working group for the assembly system. One important difference between that proposal and the formula described by Kardelj, however, was the application of the principle of parity to both the chamber of republics and provinces and the chamber of associated labor. Application of the principle of parity to the chamber of associated labor protected the developed republics against the eventual conversion by the underdeveloped regions of their expanding populations into political power. But it also contradicted the idea of a single, unified working class in Yugo-

---

[105] This and following citations of Kardelj's comments are from the texts in Kardelj, *Osnovni uzroci*, pp. 107-13.

slavia, for it meant the permanent division of that class along national-territorial lines. This contradiction reflected the continuing concern of the leadership to develop workable, rather than "ideologically correct," formulas, even during the postcrisis period of renewed emphasis on the ideological strengthening of the party.

The organizational and procedural formulas for the Federal Executive Council adopted by the coordinating Commission, in contrast, deviated significantly from the principle of parity. Under the new constitution, the Council, Kardelj observed, "will be a somewhat narrower body than it is now . . . [and] will be composed primarily of only the heads of individual activities or the executors of coordinative functions between activities." He explained that parity:

> is not appropriate to an expert-political body such as the Federal Executive Council must be, because its members are not in that body in order to represent the positions and interests of individual republics or provinces—that is the task of the delegations of the republics and provinces in the Assembly. Members of the Federal Executive Council and functionaries in it must execute the decisions of federal organs in a qualified way and with equal moral-political responsibility toward all the republics and provinces.

Relaxation of the principle of parity in the staffing of the executive organs of the federation and emphasis on the independence of federal functionaries closely corresponded to the broader political campaign to strengthen the independence and effectiveness of federal policy-making bodies that was being waged by the central political coalition under the leadership of Tito. These changes reversed the powerful tendency toward regionalization of the Federal Executive Council evident during the late 1960s and institutionalized in the provisions of the 1971 amendments, and approached the more balanced formulations suggested by the critics of those amendments. However, while the provisions of the 1974 constitution corresponded more closely to the positions taken by Djordjević and other critics of the 1971 amendments, they do not represent an abandonment of the principles embodied in those amendments. Indeed, with respect to the staffing of the Federal Executive Council, Kardelj pointed out:

> while parity . . . is not necessary here, it is completely obvious . . . that in the election of members of the Federal Executive Council and functionaries of federal administrations in general, it is of course necessary to ensure that cadres from all the republics and provinces always will be represented in them. In order to ensure that principle, the draft constitution provides that the SFRY Assembly must elect a certain smaller

number of members of the Federal Executive Council on the basis of equal representation of the republics and provinces; that is, according to the principle of parity.

The compromise formulations devised by the coordinating Commission during late 1972 and early 1973 reflected a continuing commitment by the central political leadership to the principles of decision making based on interregional negotiation and consensus embodied in the 1971 amendments, tempered by a renewed emphasis on interregional cooperation, elite control, and central authority. Changes introduced into the organizational and procedural provisions for federal decision making with the adoption of the 1974 constitution reflect the efforts of the central leadership to implement the lessons learned in the aftermath of the Croatian crisis. It is not surprising, therefore, that some of them closely corresponded to the changes carried out in the drafting process itself that also had been motivated by those lessons. Indeed, during interviews conducted in 1976, several participants in the federal decision-making process readily pointed to the drafting process as the model on which the organizational and procedural provisions of the new constitution had been based.

But the 1974 constitution, prepared during 1972 and 1973, also reflects the practical experience gained by the central political leadership by operating under the formulas for federal decision making established by the 1971 amendments. Organizational and procedural changes contained in the new constitution attempted to correct the obvious deficiencies in that process. As such, they represent the culmination of a continued search by the leadership for a successful mechanism to regulate political conflict. The high degree of continuity between the provisions of the constitution and those of the earlier amendments suggests that the basic organizational and procedural characteristics of that mechanism had already been worked out by 1971. Two additional years of intensive effort were required, however, to establish the requisite norms of elite behavior and the conditions of elite control that made it possible to fulfill them. By the Tenth Party Congress in May 1974, those efforts were essentially completed. The record of interregional negotiation and federal decision making since 1974 suggests that the party rules adopted at that congress, and the constitution proclaimed in February 1974, are the formal provisions of an agreement by which the leadership of Yugoslavia finally established a system of overarching elite cooperation for the regulation of regional, economic, and nationality conflict.

V. THE REGULATORY FORMULA
IN PRACTICE: DECISION MAKING
IN THE FEDERATION SINCE 1974

The political order established with the adoption of a new constitution in 1974 retains the essential characteristics of the system that had been developing since 1966. It preserves the division of Yugoslav society into distinct ethno-territorial blocs, and broad areas of political decision making continue to be carried out on the basis of interbloc negotiation and consensus. Indeed, some of the organizational and procedural changes introduced in 1974 contributed to the further institutionalization of these characteristics by eliminating problems and anomalies evident during 1972 and 1973. Unlike the period up to 1972, however, the central leadership in Yugoslavia has since 1974 once again become a powerful actor in the decision-making process, and it has used that power to facilitate the resolution of interbloc conflicts.

The restoration of central power and authority was in large part the product of President Tito's forceful intervention in the early 1970s. The central government continued to benefit from his support, and the support of the coalition of party leaders that he led, right up to his illness and death in 1980. Not even while Tito was alive, however, did central power ever completely dominate the regions. Yugoslav politics in general, and political decision making in the federation in particular, continued to be characterized during this period by a persistent tension between central and regional power. The formulation of central policy, therefore, depended more on the ability of the federal leadership to mediate among, and reconcile, the particularistic and often conflicting interests advanced by the regional leaderships than on its power to overrule them. The death of President Tito in May 1980 thus necessarily raised the question whether the central government in Yugoslavia could long continue to oppose the centrifugal forces of regional power.

This chapter describes the organizational and procedural provisions for federal decision making established by the 1974 constitution and examines how interregional conflicts over federal policy have been resolved since its adoption. It focuses in particular on the role of central leadership in the resolution of such conflicts, and especially on the role of the Federal Executive Council. It identifies factors and conditions that appear to have contributed to the successful resolution of interregional conflicts and others that appear to have made their resolution more difficult. In this way it suggests some of the strengths and limits of the established formula for the regulation of interbloc conflict in Yugoslavia and the conditions necessary for their continuing regulation in the post-Tito period.

The 1974 Constitution: Organizational and Procedural Provisions for Federal Decision Making[1]

The 1974 constitution established a complex organizational framework for facilitating continuous, extensive interbloc consultation and negotiation over the formulation of federal policies. Most of this framework was in place prior to the drafting of the new constitution and was simply incorporated into it, thereby preserving the general principles of representation, participation, and decision making in federal organs embodied in the 1971 amendments. The division of decision-making authority between the federation and the regions remained essentially unchanged from that contained in the 1971 amendments, and federal policies in all areas affecting vital regional interests, and especially regional economic interests, continue to require interregional consensus for adoption.

The Collective State Presidency. The new constitution calls for the Presidency to be composed of one representative from each of the republics, the provinces, and from the party, thereby abandoning the principle of "equal representation of the republics and corresponding representation of the provinces" in favor of simple equality. This reduces the Presidency from twenty-three to nine members. The presidents of the regional assemblies are no longer included in the new Presidency, giving it a distinctly more authoritative and more "federal" character by removing individuals who occupy positions in lower-level organs, and who inevitably would be more responsive to regional than to "all-Yugoslav" interests. The smaller size, increased authority, and more "federal" character of the new Presidency make it a potentially more effective organ for the resolution of conflicts that cannot be resolved in the other organs of the federation.

The equality of the autonomous provinces symbolized by their equal representation in the Presidency is reinforced by their functional equality. The rules of procedure adopted by the Presidency in February 1975 allocated each of the representatives of the provinces a separate turn in the rotation of the

---

[1] All citations to the 1974 constitution are to the official English-language translation. Dragoljub Djurović et al., *The Constitution of the Socialist Federal Republic of Yugoslavia* (Belgrade: The Secretariat of the Federal Assembly Information Service, 1974).

vice-presidency of the Presidency.[2] The inclusion of the president of the League among the members of the Presidency reflects the strengthened position of the central political leadership—and especially the party leadership—relative to the leaderships of the regions in the postcrisis period. In 1970 Tito had suggested that the larger Presidency then under consideration should include representatives of socio-political organizations at the federal level. But he had to withdraw his suggestion in the face of strong opposition from the regional leaderships. Now, however, these leaderships either could not, or did not want to, oppose such a decision. Thus, the status of the party as a constituent part of the federation distinct from, and equal in importance to, the territorial units was symbolically affirmed.

Under the new constitution, the function of the Presidency remains "to realize the equality of the nations and nationalities" and to "achieve adjustment of the common interests" of the regions. While this formulation suggests that the Presidency may become involved in a very broad range of concerns, a highly placed adviser to the Presidency reported during a 1976 interview that the work of the Presidency is limited to "only the key, strategic questions." Agendas for the forty-five sessions held during 1974 and 1975, he reported, included 170 separate items.

Decision-making practices in the Presidency remained unchanged by the adoption of a new constitution. The Presidency continues to make decisions on the basis of the "adjustment of views" of the regions. Its rules of procedure provide for certain decisions to be adopted by simple majority while others require a two-thirds majority.[3] However, the same adviser to the Presidency cited above reported that "the principle of work [of the Presidency] is that without complete agreement there cannot be a decision, [or in other words] unanimity" ["*princip je rada da bez potpune saglasnosti nema odluka-jed-noglasnost*"]. Thus, the Presidency continued to operate on the general principle of consensual decision making in the period following the adoption of the new constitution. Reflecting on these principles for a moment, this adviser to the Presidency suggested further that the process of decision making prescribed by the new constitution is the same as that by which the constitution itself was drafted.

According to this adviser, a second principle of procedure in the Presidency during this period was manifest in extensive consultations between the Presidency (and especially its working bodies) and groups likely to be affected by a decision under consideration. The Presidency's rules of procedure called for it to "cooperate with" and "rely on the initiatives, proposals and suggestions of" the Socialist Alliance, the League of Communists, the Federation

[2] *Službeni List* 31, No. 12 (March 7, 1975): 275.
[3] Ibid., p. 273.

of Trade Unions, the Veterans League, and the Youth League.[4] Most such cooperation and communication takes place through the working bodies of the Presidency. But consultation does take place at some sessions of the Presidency itself. The rules of procedure adopted by the Presidency permit the participation at sessions of the Presidency of representatives of other socio-political and self-managing organizations, and especially of the Federal Assembly, the FEC, and the individual presidencies of the regions. In practice, according to this adviser, the president of the FEC (premier) and the secretary of the Executive Committee of the League attend "as a rule," the presidents of the Federation of Trade Unions and the Socialist Alliance attend "regularly," and representatives of the republics and provinces attend only when the Presidency calls "an expanded session."

The constitution prohibits members of the Presidency from holding "any other self-managing, public, or other social function, except functions in socio-political organizations." One of the lessons learned by the leadership in the wake of the Croatian crisis was that the removal of individuals elected to central organs from involvement in the day-to-day affairs of their constituencies carries the potential effect of isolating them politically and thereby reducing their local influence and power. The loss of such influence and power, in turn, reduces the effectiveness of the central organ as an arena for the resolution of conflicts between those constituencies. To avoid this, the rules of procedure adopted by the Presidency require that its members "constantly and regularly be informed about conditions in the country and particularly about inter-nationality relations and relations between the republics and autonomous provinces," and provide that members of the Presidency "also have the right to seek reports and explanations about other questions about which familiarity is necessary in order to carry out the function of a member of the Presidency."[5] The political influence of the Presidency was reinforced by the fact that its members were, during the period following adoption of the new constitution, at the same time members of the party Presidium.

The Federal Executive Council. The new constitution and the federal statutes implementing its provisions preserve the structure of the Federal Executive Council that had evolved since 1967, and especially since 1971. The constitution applies the principle of "equal representation of the republics and corresponding representation of the provinces" to the Council, but also requires that nationality be "taken into account" in the selection of individuals for leading positions in the federal administration that entail ex officio Council membership. The latter provision had been incorporated in the 1963 consti-

[4] Ibid., p. 271.
[5] Ibid., p. 275.

tution, at a time when the republican and provincial party organizations were considerably less powerful than they are now, but nationality was nonetheless an important basis of division within the political leadership. The incorporation of both principles in the 1974 constitution reflects the continuing importance of both region and nationality in the current period.

In an interview conducted in 1976, one highly placed member of the Council proudly observed that, while the Federal Assembly underwent extensive organizational change, "the FEC did not change" as a result of the adoption of the new constitution. The constitutional provisions concerning the FEC did, however, change in at least one important respect. In a reflection of both the changed role of the Council in the post-1971 period and the growing realization among regional political leaders that central political institutions had to be strengthened, the new constitution affirms the independence of the FEC from regional pressures. It states:

> Members of the Federal Executive Council and officials in federal administrative agencies and federal organizations shall be responsible for the execution of policy and the enforcement of statutes, other regulations, and enactments exclusively to federal agencies, and *in the performance of this function may not receive directions or orders from the agencies and officials of other socio-political communities, nor may they follow such directions and/or orders* (emphasis added).

This provision did not mean, however, that the Council no longer functioned as an institutional arena for interregional bargaining.

The Council and its committees and commissions continue to be composed of representatives of those organizations or institutions likely to be affected by, or interested in, federal policies. The permanent commissions of the Council are composed of representatives of federal organs and organizations and socio-political organizations on the level of the federation, and the interrepublican committees are composed of one member of the FEC (who serves as president of the committee) and one representative delegated by each of the regional executive councils.[6] Although the constitution mandates creation of the interrepublican committees for the purpose of securing regional agreement on rules and regulations adopted by the Federal Executive Council for the *implementation* of legislation passed by the federal parliament with the agreement of the regional assemblies, these committees also serve as arenas for interregional negotiation during the *preparation* of such legislation.[7]

The rules of procedure adopted by the Council in 1975 do not specify the

---

[6] *Službeni List* 31, No. 47 (September 26, 1975): 1299, 1306.

[7] Cf. ibid., p. 1306; Miodrag Zečević, ed., *Ustav Socijalističke Federativne Republike Jugoslavije: stručno objašnjenje* (Beograd: Institut za političke studije FPN and Privredni Pregled, 1975), p. 519; and *Politika* (Belgrade), 28-30 November 1980.

precise membership of its Coordinating Commission, but the same functionary cited earlier reported that the Commission is composed of members of the Council selected on the basis of *equal* representation of the republics, provinces, and the FEC. The president of the Council is empowered to invite representatives of other organs and organizations on the federal level to participate in the deliberations of this body when appropriate.[8] The Coordinating Commission functions as the Council's central decision-making body. It carries out preliminary discussions of "all the more complex things," makes decisions in the name of the entire Council on certain issues, and serves as an arena for the resolution of conflicts that cannot be resolved in the interrepublican committees. Thus, the organization, operation, and function of the Commission appears to have remained relatively stable since it was first established in 1967.[9]

The permanent commissions and interrepublican committees within the FEC provide formal channels for the expression of political interests. This functionary of the Council suggested that, as a result, "the Council is open to all factors and all factors may send [their] opinions to the FEC." Consequently, one of the great "difficulties" in the operation of the Council has been that there are "so many opinions." One way in which the Council deals with this problem, he suggested, is by restricting the issues included on the agenda prepared for each three-month period. Setting the agenda is viewed by the FEC, the executive councils of the regions, and others as an explicitly political process. Not surprisingly, therefore, its preparation entails an elaborate process of consultation and negotiation between the Council and the executive councils of the regions and others. Thus, the FEC operates, in the words of this functionary, "not [simply as] a collector, but [as] a selector" of issues ["*ne kolektor, nego selektor*"].

The Federal (Social) Councils. In December 1974, the two "federal councils" (*Savezni saveti*) created in July 1973 as arenas for direct participation in the preparation of federal policies and legislative proposals by representatives of organizations and interests that cut across regional boundaries were replaced by four new councils. The new constitution does not explicitly provide for the creation of these bodies. They are defined by federal statute as "joint organs" of the FEC, the state Presidency, and other organs and organizations on the level of the federation. Each organ or organization that participates in the work of a council names its own representative to it. Members of the Council for International Relations and the Council for the Protection of the Constitutional Order are appointed by the Presidency. The president of the

[8] *Službeni List* 31, No. 47: 1297.

[9] For a summary analysis of council decision making, see *Politika* (Belgrade), 28-30 November 1980.

FEC and the federal secretaries for internal affairs (security police), national defense, and foreign affairs are ex officio members of the latter council. Members of the Council for Questions of the Social Order and the Council for Economic Development and Economic Policy are appointed by the FEC "from among the ranks of scientific and expert workers, in agreement with the organs and organizations which participate in the work of the Council." In each of the four councils, a member of the FEC serves as president, and the presidents of parallel bodies in the republics and provinces are ex officio members. The actual number and composition of members of each council may vary, depending on the issues under consideration.[10] But one highly placed functionary in the Federal Assembly, in an interview conducted in 1976, described the membership of these councils as generally "the most authoritative people." In many cases, he suggested, "they are the same people who wrote the [new] constitution." As a result, he observed, "they do not make [official] decisions, but . . . . "

Like those of their predecessors, the competencies of these new councils are extremely broad. They may discuss any issue raised by the organs and organizations that participate in them. But each has a particular area of responsibility. The Council for questions of the social order, for example,

> discusses questions concerning the achievement and further construction of the social order established by the SFRY Constitution, proposals of laws and other acts in the competence of organs of the federation by which are determined basic relations in this area, and other particularly important questions for these relations.[11]

Each of these councils is required, "in the framework of its sphere of operation," to "work on the principle of harmonization of positions."[12]

The operation of these federal councils was discussed in some detail by Anton Vratuša, then vice-president of the FEC and president of the Council for Questions of the Social Order, in a June 1975 interview published in *NIN*.[13] According to Vratuša, in discussions in the councils for both questions of the social order and economic development, it had proven "impossible to divide systemic questions from questions of development and ongoing economic policy." In discussions of the five-year plan then just beginning, for example, it was

> impossible to develop the shape [*dati fizionomiju*] of the plan without the construction of at least the basic elements of the system of [social] planning. . . . But . . . it is not sufficient just to pass a law on the

---

[10] *Službeni List* 30, No. 66 (December 27, 1974): 2002-04.

[11] Ibid., p. 2004.

[12] Ibid., p. 2002.

[13] *NIN*, 15 June 1975.

planning system. It is necessary also to prepare together with this social agreements in the sphere of at least some of the most important areas of production.

Consequently, although these councils had been created to resolve conflicts over specific policy proposals, they rapidly expanded their activity to include discussion of broader, more far-reaching "systemic questions."

The membership of these councils, Vratuša reported, included representatives of the SFRY Presidency, the party Presidium, and the highest organs of the Federal Assembly, the Federal Conference of the Socialist Alliance, the Federation of Trade Unions, and the Chamber of Commerce. The republican and provincial leaderships, he added, "usually come to an agreement about the composition of participants in the republics. Otherwise, the council would be too clumsy a body." He emphasized that membership in the councils was not individual. Rather, "certain institutions, as participants in the work, send . . . those whom they think are the most competent to deal with the questions on the agenda." The councils function, he reported, as "consultative organs of the most responsible forums of the federation, republics, and provinces."

The work of the councils focuses on "the harmonization of positions on fundamental issues" and takes place under the protection of limited public exposure. The sessions of the councils for questions of the social order and for economic development, which were the occasion for Vratuša's interview, took place over a period of several days in the seclusion of Brioni. Press coverage of the meetings was carefully controlled; those newsmen permitted to attend these sessions, Vratuša reported, "enter into this task in order, in their own way, to contribute creatively to the implementation of the constitution," and not simply to "observe."

The creation of these councils, Vratuša suggested, was part of a general effort to increase both the effectiveness of federal decision-making institutions and their "independence from pressure." "As far as the reconstruction [of the federation] is concerned," he observed, "I would say that the point is the restoration of social authority to the state administration." When asked whether, given the authority of their members, these councils "are slowly taking over power," Vratuša objected that "that is not exactly correct."

> But it is correct [he continued] that the positions taken by the councils have more and more influence. And that is their basic role. In fact, through them is achieved the means of carrying out the leading ideological and political role of the League of Communists.

However, when asked whether the agreements reached in the councils were obligatory for the participants, Vratuša acknowledged that "in fact, the authority of the councils is moral. based on their composition."

The composition of the federal councils reflects the post-crisis policy of emphasizing cross-regional factors and interests in the federal decision-making process. Whereas interrepublican committees provide arenas for interregional governmental consultations and the permanent commissions of the FEC provide arenas for consultation between transregional economic interests and the federal government, the federal councils are arenas for direct consultations among the socio-political leaderships of the regions, the federation, and transregional organizations. These became powerful political institutions in the period following adoption of the new constitution, and now constitute one of four major arenas for the resolution of political conflicts in the federation.[14] The others include the Presidency and the Federal Executive Council, and the reorganized federal parliament, especially its Chamber of Republics and Provinces.

In July 1979, new federal legislation changed the name of these councils to "Federal Social Councils" and reduced their number to three: one for questions of the social order, one for economic development and economic policy, and one for international relations. Protection of the constitutional order, a term meaning the preservation of internal security, thus became the sole domain of the Presidency, through its own internal advisory council. The basic character, composition, and mode of operation of the federal (social) councils remained unchanged by this legislation. Even more important, their role in federal decision making continued to grow. Yugoslav decision makers and the Yugoslav press sometimes continue to refer to the "federal social councils" simply as the "federal councils."[15]

The Federal Parliament. The most radical changes incorporated in the new constitution concern the organization and operation of the Federal Assembly. In a symbolic change, intended to suggest both the absence of a "federation" distinct from the republics and provinces acting in concert, and the existence of a "Yugoslav" whole, the Assembly was renamed "Assembly of the So-

[14] For some recent analyses of the role of these councils, see Dragoljub Djurović, ed., *Zapažanja iz rada Veća republika i pokrajina Skupštine SFRJ* Biblioteka Skupštine SFRJ, 14, 6 (1977), pp. 87ff; and Milun Perović, "Skupština i političko odlučivanje (prilog izučavanju i analizi procesa političkog odlučivanja u Skupštini SFRJ)," (1980) unpublished manuscript, pp. 289ff. [This is a revised version of the author's doctoral dissertation: "Proces političkog odlučivanja u Skupštini SFRJ," (Belgrade University, Fakultet Političkih Nauka, 1979). It is one of the finest empirical studies of political decision making in the federation produced in Yugoslavia. The author is a functionary of the Federal Executive Council and has made extensive use of sources not readily available even to the most determined foreign scholar. I am indebted to him for sharing his knowledge of the system with me, and for making this manuscript available to me.]

[15] The legislation by which the "federal councils" became "federal social councils" is contained in *Službeni List* 35, No. 34 (July 20, 1979):1069-72.

cialist Federal Republic of Yugoslavia.''[16] However, following common Yugoslav practice among both the general public and functionaries and delegates in the Assembly itself, it shall be referred to here as the SFRY Assembly or, in most cases, the Federal Assembly, except when this formulation would be confusing.

The constitution defines the Assembly as both the highest expression of the self-management system and ''the supreme organ of power within the framework of federal rights and duties.'' It is divided into only two chambers: a Federal Chamber, and a Chamber of Republics and Provinces. The new Federal Chamber replaces the functionally based chambers first introduced by the 1963 constitution, and the socio-political chamber introduced by the 1968 amendments. The domain of the Federal Chamber includes all areas of autonomous federal authority. The Chamber of Republics and Provinces is the successor to the Chamber of Nationalities. The domain of this chamber includes all areas of federal policy subject to joint decision making by the republics and autonomous provinces. The change of name of this chamber also carries symbolic meaning. The ''blocs'' composing the Yugoslav system of interbloc negotiation are in this way defined as primarily *territorial* communities. Nationality still must be, and is, ''taken into account'' in the composition of certain institutions, but participation in those institutions now is defined in terms of territorial, not national identity.

The constitution stipulates that the Chamber of Republics and Provinces

> shall ensure the adjustment of stands of the Assemblies of the Republics and the Assemblies of the Autonomous Provinces in spheres in which it passes federal statutes and other enactments on the basis of agreement with these Assemblies.

Among other things, this includes adoption of the social plans of Yugoslavia; formulation of federal monetary, fiscal, tax, foreign exchange, trade, tariff, price, and market policies; formulation of policy for crediting the accelerated development of the underdeveloped regions; determination of the federal budget and the system and sources for financing the federation; and ratification of most international treaties. The Chamber of Republics and Provinces was conceived explicitly as an arena for interregional bargaining and the regulation of interregional conflict. Hence, these areas of decisional responsibility include all those issue areas that in the past generated the most conflict. The Chamber also has autonomous decisional authority in a number of areas. The most important of these are the passage of ''temporary measures''; the formulation of policy for the enforcement of federal statutes, regulations, and

---

[16] Zečević, *Ustav SFRJ: stručno objašnjenje*, p. 477.

other enactments passed by it; and supervision over the work of the Federal Executive Council and other federal administrative agencies.

The internal organization of the Chamber was determined by both the constitution itself and the rules of procedure adopted by it in December 1974.[17] The constitution provides that the Chamber be composed of twelve delegates elected by the Assembly of each republic from among its own members, and eight elected by the Assembly of each autonomous province from among its members, for a total of eighty-eight delegates. Individuals elected to these delegations retain their membership in their respective regional assemblies. In this way, delegations to the Chamber of Republics and Provinces constitute organizational and communications links between the regional assemblies and the federal center. In fact, they are required by the constitution to keep their respective regional assemblies fully informed about the work of the Chamber.

On issues subject to joint decision making by the regions, delegations are required to represent the positions of their respective assemblies. Decisions on such issues are considered adopted only when they have received the approval of each delegation. In effect, the regions have been granted veto power over federal policies in areas subject to joint decision making. However, the Chamber may adopt a law on "temporary measures" by a two-thirds majority of all *delegates*, and it may adopt any measure on issues within its independent sphere of competence by a simple majority of all delegates present.

The Chamber's rules of procedure stipulate that "every delegation shall have a chairman." These chairmen represent their delegations in meetings of the leadership of the Chamber, in debates on the Chamber floor, in relations with their respective regional assemblies, and at other times. They also preside over meetings of their delegations, coordinate the representation of delegation views in the working bodies of the Chamber, and ensure the provision of staff services to their delegations. Professional and technical assistance to the delegations is provided by the staff of the Chamber itself. The chairmen also carry out the interdelegation communication and cooperation called for by the rules of procedure.

The constitution empowers the Chamber to set up committees and other working bodies to carry out interregional negotiations. It also requires that these bodies be composed on the basis of "equal representation of the republics and corresponding representation of the autonomous provinces," and that representatives of the FEC take part in their work. In this way, it applies the same principle of representation and participation to the internal organization

[17] All citations to the rules of procedure of the Assembly as a whole and each of its chambers are to the official English-language translations in Dragoljub Djurović, ed., *The Rules of Procedure of The Assembly of the S.F.R. of Yugoslavia* (Belgrade: Secretariat of Information of the SFR of Yugoslavia Assembly, 1975).

of the Chamber as it does to the organs of interregional negotiation in the FEC and the Presidency. The rules of procedure of the Chamber stipulate that working bodies of the Chamber cannot discuss issues subject to joint decision making by all the regions without the presence of representatives of all the regional delegations. Working bodies of the Chamber may invite representatives of other organizations to attend a session and present their opinions and proposals.

At present, the Chamber has established seven committees. These are the committees on the social plan and development policy; on the market and prices; on the credit and monetary systems; on association in the economy (economic integration); on the development of the economically underdeveloped republics and autonomous provinces; on economic relations with foreign countries; and the finance committee. The working bodies of the Chamber are not empowered by either the constitution or the rules of procedure to make decisions on behalf of the Chamber as a whole. Rather, they prepare reports to the Chamber that convey the views expressed during their deliberations and that contain recommendations for the resolution of the issue at hand.

The rules of procedure stipulate that, with respect to issues subject to joint decision making by all the regions:

> the working body shall in particular report whether or not the views [of the regions] have been adjusted on all questions concerning the draft enactment and, if this has not been the case, it shall specify on which of these questions no agreement has been reached and shall state the reasons therefore.

The working body as a whole "may take a stand on the views presented, which shall be entered into its report." But the working body may take a stand on the issues themselves "only in agreement with the members of the working body from each delegation." Thus, the principle of decision making by delegation adopted for the Chamber as a whole—and the regional veto power inherent in it—also has been applied to the operation of the working bodies of the Chamber. On issues not subject to joint decision making by all the regions, however, decisions in the working bodies of the Chamber may be made "by a majority vote of all members." In effect, the principles of decision making underlying the operation of the interrepublican committees and Coordinating Commission of the Federal Executive Council have been applied to the working bodies of the Chamber of Republics and Provinces.

The formal process in the Chamber of Republics and Provinces for issues subject to joint decision making of the regions is regulated by its rules of procedure. The first stage consists of the submission to the Chamber of a proposal for the enactment of a law. "Authorized" sponsors of such proposals include the Federal Executive Council, any delegation or working body of the Chamber itself, any regional chamber, the Federal Chamber of the SFRY Assembly, the Constitutional Court of Yugoslavia, the Federal Court, the Socialist Alliance, the League of Communists of Yugoslavia, the Federation of Trade Unions, and the Federal Chamber of Commerce. Proposals sponsored by any of these organizations must be considered by the Chamber. Proposals sponsored by any other organization are first considered by the Assembly's Commission on Petitions and Grievances to determine whether they should be considered by the Chamber. Any proposal not sponsored by the FEC is automatically referred to it for consideration.

A proposal for enactment of a law must include a preliminary draft text of the law, a statement of the reasons for the law, an explanation of the law, an estimate of the costs and sources of funding for enforcement of the law, and an inventory of the opinions of organizations interested in, or likely to be affected by the law. In order to aid in the preparation of a proposal for enactment of a law, an authorized sponsor may submit a preliminary draft or thesis to the Chamber for a preliminary "exchange of views" on the issues involved, prior to formal submission of a proposal for enactment.

Following submission of a proposal for enactment of a law, the preliminary draft enactment and supporting materials are distributed to the regional assemblies and the competent committee or committees of the Chamber for discussion. After they consider these materials, the regional assemblies declare their positions and the Chamber's committee submits its report. If the proposal is approved, the sponsor is then required to submit a final draft for Chamber debate. If a regional assembly or Chamber committee expresses objections or reservations, the proposal may be returned to the sponsor for reformulation, may be reconsidered at a later date, may be referred to the Chamber as a whole, or may be rejected. After the Chamber of Republics and Provinces has approved a law or other act which is subject to joint decision making of the regions, it is required by the constitution to submit the final text to the assemblies of the regions for approval. However, article 300 of the constitution provides that those assemblies may empower their delegations to the Chamber to endorse such an act on their behalf.

Because the Chamber of Republics and Provinces makes its decisions on certain issues in agreement with the assemblies of the regions, and because the members of the Chamber are at the same time members of their respective regional assemblies, the work schedules of the regional assemblies and the Chamber have come to be coordinated. At first, they were coordinated on an ad hoc basis. By June 1976, however, an agreement had been reached by which the assemblies of the republics and provinces would meet from the tenth to the twentieth of each month and the Chamber would meet between the twentieth and thirtieth.[18]

The competence of the Federal Chamber of the Assembly is more restricted than that of the Chamber of Republics and Provinces. The constitutionally enumerated responsibilities of the Chamber include adoption of the federal budget and annual balance sheet; alteration of the international boundaries of Yugoslavia; ratification of international treaties; fundamental organization of federal agencies; supervision of the federal judicial and constitutional court systems; and the formulation of federal statutes and policies to implement decisions in these areas. One of the enumerated powers of the Federal Chamber, however, represents a potential "elastic clause" in the definition of its power: the determination of "the fundamentals of the internal and foreign policy" of the country. These responsibilities correspond to what the drafters of the constitution intended to be the independent jurisdiction of the federation.

The internal organization of the Federal Chamber, like that of the Chamber of Republics and Provinces, is determined by both the constitution and its own rules of procedure. The constitution provides that the Chamber "shall be composed of thirty delegates of self-managing organizations and communities and socio-political organizations from each Republic, and of twenty delegates from each Autonomous Province." Candidates for these positions are selected by the Socialist Alliance, and elected by the commune assemblies of each region. In this way, the members of the Chamber are determined through a process of indirect elections under the close supervision of the party's mass political organization—the Socialist Alliance. Decisions in the Federal Chamber are to be made "by a majority vote at sessions attended by a majority of delegates." In taking a stand on issues before the Chamber, delegates are required by the rules of procedure to:

> act in accordance with the guidelines of their respective self-managing organizations and communities, and in conformity with the basic stands of the delegations or socio-political organizations which have delegated them, and in accordance with collective and general social interests and needs.

But they also are expected to be "independent in decision making and voting." The delegates to the Federal Chamber function as "representatives" of both the working class (organized into self-managing units) and organized socialist consciousness (embodied in socio-political organizations).

The constitution empowers the Federal Chamber to establish committees or other working bodies to carry out its work. The composition and operation

[18] Skupština SFRJ, Veće republika i pokrajina, "Neka zapažanja iz dosadašnjeg rada Veća republika i pokrajina (period od 15. maja 1974. do kraja 1975. godine)," Belgrade, June 1976 (mimeographed) [henceforth: "Neka zapažanja"], p. 4.

of these bodies are regulated by the Chamber's own rules of procedure. The working bodies of the Federal Chamber may be composed of both delegates to the Chamber and "workers in public life, scientists, and experts," but the latter may not exceed the number of delegate-members. Each working body must have a chairman and a deputy. Chairmen are elected from among the delegate-members. The committees and other working bodies of the chamber may invite "representatives of federal organs, socio-political organizations, social organizations, and other self-managing organizations, associations, and communities at the federal level, representatives of the appropriate working bodies of the Chambers of the assemblies of the autonomous province[s], as well as workers in public life, scientists, and experts" to attend sessions and present their views. The rules of procedure stipulate that decisions in the working bodies of the Federal Chamber are to be taken "by a majority vote of all the present members of the working body." However, the views of dissenting members of the body must, on request, be included in the report delivered by that body to the Chamber as a whole. At present, the Federal Chamber has established committees for socio-economic relations; socio-political relations; internal policy; foreign policy; national defense; the federal budget; the judiciary; labor, public health, and social welfare; and veterans' affairs.

The formal procedure for decision making in the Federal Chamber is regulated by its rules of procedure and is much the same as that in the Chamber of Republics and Provinces. The process begins with a motion for enactment of a law. "Authorized" sponsors of such motions include the delegates and working bodies of the Chamber itself, joint working bodies of the SFRY Assembly and the Federal Executive Council. Requests for such a motion may be made directly to the Chamber by the Chamber of Republics and Provinces, the assemblies of the regions, the Constitutional or Federal Courts, the Socialist Alliance, the Federation of Trade Unions, the Chamber of Commerce of Yugoslavia, and "other self-managing organizations and communities operating on the entire territory of the country." All other requests must first be approved by the Assembly's Commission on Petitions and Grievances before it can be considered by the Chamber. If a proposal is accepted by the Chamber, the motion—including the preliminary draft law and all supporting materials—is submitted to the appropriate committee or committees for deliberation. After submission of the committee report, the Chamber as a whole debates the motion. If accepted, a final draft is prepared for approval by the Chamber.

While the Chamber of Republics and Provinces is explicitly organized as an arena for interregional bargaining, the Federal Chamber is not. Delegates to the Federal Chamber are supposed to represent the views of the delegations from which they were elected, independently of the influence of the republic or province in which those delegations are located. In practice, however, delegates to the Federal Chamber have not remained independent of such influence. In fact, shortly after the adoption of the new constitution and the start of operation of the Chamber, delegates in the Federal Chamber organized themselves informally into pseudo-delegations, paralleling the organization of the Chamber of Republics and Provinces. In a review of the work of the Federal Chamber from September 1974 to July 1975, its professional staff reported:

> The delegates in the Federal Chamber from all the republics and provinces have selected their own coordinator and meet occasionally in order to exchange opinions, or come to agreement on "consultation" of the self-managing base, "division" of responsibilities, and similar [issues]. This form of exchange of opinions and agreements of delegates in the Federal Chamber from a certain republic or autonomous province can be important for the process of establishing directions for the work of delegates in the Federal Chamber from a single republic or autonomous province.[19]

As work progressed, delegates in the Chamber sought guidance on particular issues from the executive and administrative agencies of their respective republics and provinces. One highly placed functionary in the SFRY Assembly reported in 1976 that, although delegates in the Federal Chamber formally do not receive instructions, in actual practice they do:

> I know concretely that, for example, in economic affairs these delegates go to republican secretariats for finance for advice on these matters. This is not obligatory—there is no obligation to do this—but they go there and ask "What is your position on this?" and that is how their own positions are determined.

Telecommunications between officials of one republican assembly and the delegates from that republic to the Federal Chamber confirm this. They also indicate that the assemblies of the republics and provinces refer to these delegates, and issue instructions to them, as if they were a "delegation" of the republic or province.

By the end of 1979, proposals for the creation of formal mechanisms for the exercise of such influence were being discussed openly in the press. In December, for example, the Assembly of the Republic of Serbia discussed a proposal by the republican Conference of the Socialist Alliance to include delegates in the Federal Chamber from Serbia in the deliberations of the

---

[19] Skupština SFRJ, Savezno veće, "Osvrt na izvršenje programa rada Saveznog vijeća Skupštine SFRJ za razdoblje od rujna 1974. do srpnja 1975.," Belgrade, September 1975 (mimeographed), p. 20.

republican Assembly so that they can "directly, promptly, and completely review and become familiar with the interests and positions of the Republic, which they require for decision making in the Federal Chamber."[20] And, in 1980, the de facto division of this chamber into regional delegations was officially recognized and sanctioned by the federal assembly leadership.[21] This suggests that, because of their strongly divergent interests, the republics and provinces remain the primary basis for political division even among representatives of the self-managing, socialist working class of Yugoslavia.

The importance of regional divisions also receives official recognition in the Chamber's own rules of procedure, which stipulate that "in electing members of the Chamber working bodies, due regard shall be paid to the representation of delegates from each republic and from each autonomous province." They also provide a "special procedure" for the consideration of final drafts of laws or other acts, and for the consideration of other issues "of general interest to a republic or autonomous province and of concern for the equality of the nations and nationalities." This procedure permits a majority of the delegates from a single region to prevent final passage of a law or other enactment to which they object. But this achieves little more than recommitment of the law or issue to the sponsor, or to the responsible committee of the Chamber for reconsideration. The burden of responsibility for the resolution of conflicts underlying such a request falls squarely on the shoulders of "the competent organs of the republics and autonomous provinces and . . . the Federal Executive Council." The Federal Chamber and its working bodies do not function as arenas for the resolution of interregional conflict even under these circumstances.

Proposals presented to the delegates in the Federal Chamber generally have already been subject to bargaining in the "federal (social) councils" and the interrepublican committees of the FEC. The solutions embodied in the draft legislation presented to the Chamber and its committees, therefore, have already been approved by representatives of interested or affected cross-regional interests as well as the republics and provinces themselves. In a report on the first two years' operation of the Chamber, its own professional staff observed that proposals generally were deliberated in federal councils before they were submitted to the Chamber and that, despite an agreement to the contrary, the Federal Chamber and its committees were effectively excluded from the deliberations of these bodies.[22] The influence of the federal

---

[20] *Politika* (Belgrade), 3 December 1979. For the final decision, see Feti Jakupi, ed., *Aktivnost organa i organizacija u SR Srbije u ostvarivanju prava i obaveza delegata u Saveznom Veću Skupštine SFRJ iz SR Srbije* (Beograd: Republička konferencija SSRN Srbije, 1980).

[21] Skupština SFRJ, *Ostvarivanje delegatskog skupštinskog sistema, sa posebnim osvrtom na Federaciju* (Beograd: Biblioteka Skupštine SFRJ, 1980), p. 23.

[22] Skupština SFRJ, Savezno veće, "Iskustva iz rada i funkcionisanja Saveznog veća Skupštine SFRJ na delegatskim osnovama," Belgrade, June 1976 (mimeographed), pp. 28-29.

councils in the Chamber, however, was very strong. The Chamber staff acknowledged in its report that:

> in practice the positions of the councils most frequently exceeded an advisory character and took on a de facto obligatory character, which also essentially reduced the role and responsibility of the working bodies . . . in the preparation or creation of policy and the working out of federal laws.[23]

Consequently, the Federal Chamber plays no significant role in interregional negotiation and joint decision making over the formulation of federal proposals. Nor does it function as an important institutional mechanism for the resolution of interregional conflicts over federal policies. The Chamber of Republics and Provinces, on the other hand, does play an important role as an institutional arena for both the *expression* of interregional conflicts, and their *resolution*.

Interregional Conflict and Decision Making in the Chamber of Republics and Provinces

Setting the Agenda for Federal Decision Making. Setting the agenda for federal decision making requires the development of an actual list of legislation and issues to be dealt with in a specific period (usually three months or one year), and the scheduling of meetings of assemblies at both the federal and republican levels, of socio-political and governmental organs and organizations, and of others. For the latter purpose, regular coordinative meetings are held between the general secretaries of all federal organs and organizations. The profesional staff of the Chamber of Republics and Provinces reported that during the period from 15 May 1974 to 1 August 1975 the general secretaries of the FEC, the Presidency, the Presidium, the Federal Conference of the Socialist Alliance, the Council of the Trade Union Federation, and the Chamber of Commerce of Yugoslavia held meetings once a month "at which, first of all, questions of the coordination of terms of sessions and meetings in the course of the coming month are discussed."[24] Coordination between the leaderships of these organs and organizations also is carried out by participation in each others' meetings. Each one invites representatives of the others to attend its meetings when issues likely to be of interest to them are to be discussed.[25]

The actual list of legislative acts, policy issues, and general topics to be handled by a federal institution in a given period is known as the "program of work" (*program rada*). According to one functionary in the Federal Ex-

[23] Ibid., p. 29.
[24] "Neka zapažanja," p. 58.
[25] Ibid.

ecutive Council, these usually contain "only the essential questions." More routine matters enter the agenda on an ad hoc basis. The programs of work of the Federal Executive Council and the Federal Assembly must be coordinated. The FEC, as the primary sponsor of federal legislation has a determinative influence in the preparation of these documents. Issues that the leadership of the Federal Assembly may include in its preliminary program are, for example, dropped if the FEC does not want to include them or is not prepared to present them. The Council and the Federal Assembly cooperate in the development of "special operative plans" for dealing with more complicated acts such as multiyear social plans or wide-ranging systemic legislation.[26]

Other federal organs and organizations—including socio-political organizations—and the assemblies of the republics and provinces participate in the preparation of these "programs" and prepare, in turn, their own. During preparation of the program for 1974-1975, the leadership of the Chamber of Republics and Provinces "took into account" the programmatic documents of the party; positions adopted by the previous Federal Assembly and socio-political organizations on the federal level; "suggestions and opinions of the working bodies of the Chamber, republican and provincial assemblies, the Federal Executive Council, federal organs and organizations[;] and the program of work of the FEC."[27] The preliminary draft of the program was then circulated to the republican and provincial assemblies, the Federal Executive Council, and federal organs and organizations for comment.[28]

The central party leadership exercises both direct and indirect influence over the preparation of the agenda for federal decision making. It exercises direct influence when its representatives participate in meetings with other organs and organizations or their representatives participate in its meetings. It exercises indirect influence through the programmatic documents it adopts and which are used by these other organizations as guidelines for the preparation of their draft programs.

Preparation of the programs of work of the Federal Executive Council and the chambers of the Federal Assembly is conceived by those who participate in it as an explicitly political process. Putting an item into the "program of work" of the Council or Assembly is used as "an instrument of mutual pressures" among assemblies of the republics and provinces, the Federal Assembly, executive organs, and socio-political organizations. Excluding an item from these agendas is used by interested parties to "kill" an issue at a

---

[26] Skupština SFRJ, Veće republika i pokrajina, "Neka iskustva iz dosadašnjeg rada Veća republika i pokrajina i njegovih radnih tela," [henceforth: "Neka iskustva"] Belgrade, January 1974. (mimeographed), pp. 5-6; and *Politika* (Belgrade), 25 December 1975.

[27] "Neka iskustva," p. 4.

[28] Ibid., pp. 5, 6.

relatively early stage in the decision-making process.[29] It is sometimes the case, however, that issues or legislative acts are included in the program of the Assembly or Council, but must be withdrawn later because of political opposition by one of the regional leaderships or other interested factors, or because the leadership finds itself unable to deal with the issue. By December 1974, for example, the federal political leadership recognized that the program adopted by the Chamber of Republics and Provinces for 1974-1975 was "too ambitious," and the schedule of work for the remainder of the legislative year had to be reduced.[30] The process of preparing programs of work in federal decision-making institutions affords the central and regional leaderships an opportunity to exercise a relatively high degree of control over the focus of public debate in the system.

Preparation of Draft Legislation. The Federal Executive Council dominates preparation of the program of work for the Federal Assembly because it sponsors the overwhelming majority of legislative and other proposals presented to the Assembly. It is the *only* constitutionally authorized sponsor of social plans. The Council and its subordinate federal agencies prepare draft legislation in cooperation with the executive councils of the republics and provinces, socio-political organizations, and the myriad scientific and academic institutions concerned with social and economic policy and its analysis.[31] This preparation process unfolds on two tracks.

The first is a highly political track based on bargaining between interested parties. The federal (social) councils and interrepublican committees subordinate to the FEC, and the Coordinating Commission within the FEC, play an important role at this stage. Under certain circumstances, other bodies are created for this purpose on an ad hoc basis. In order to speed up preparation of the draft social plan of Yugoslavia for the period 1976-1980, for example, the central leadership established a "special coordinative working body [composed] of members of the FEC and other functionaries" to take over from the other working bodies of the Federal Executive Council the direction of all work concerning the medium-term plan. The Federal Committee for Social Planning, an agency of the Federal Executive Council, was assigned the role

[29] Ibid., p. 5; and "Neka zapažanja," pp. 3-4.

[30] "Neka iskustva," p. 6.

[31] Skupština SFRJ, Veće republika i pokrajina, "Rad Veća republika i pokrajina i njegovih radnih tela (period od 15. maja 1974. do 1. avgusta 1975.)," [henceforth: "Rad Veća republika i pokrajina"] Belgrade, September 1975 (mimeographed), pp. 27-29. See also Mahmut Mujačić, "Proces dogovaranja republika i pokrajina u Skupštini SFRJ," (Master's Thesis, Belgrade University, Fakultet Političkih Nauka, 1978), pp. 81-83. This source is for the most part a highly formal treatment of the process of interregional bargaining in the Chamber of Republics and Provinces, but is informed in places by the genuine insights of an "insider"; the author was a functionary of the federal parliament when he was preparing this thesis.

of functioning as "an interrepublican committee in which the positions of the republics and provinces will be harmonized." However, as is the case with all issues subject to joint decision making by the republics and provinces, even during preparation of the 1976-1980 plan the Coordinating Commission was to "discuss questions on which agreement cannot be achieved in the framework of the work of the Federal Committee for Social Planning," and the federal (social) council for economic development and economic policy was to "deal with questions of critical importance for passage of plans, which can speed up agreement on open questions."[32]

It is during this preliminary stage that the general outlines of policy are determined. The specific content of the consultations and negotiations that take place in these institutions is not reported in public. General discussions and descriptions of their work that are available, however, suggest that these negotiations are detailed and lively. This also is implied by the fact that they often result in delays in the federal decision-making process.[33] The emphasis in these negotiations appears to be on developing formulas for the plan that will yield a stable, lasting agreement among the regions, and not on speed of preparation. The vice-president of the Federal Executive Council, for example, in explaining to the Chamber of Republics and Provinces the actions taken by the FEC to speed up preparation of the plan for 1976-1980, suggested that

> If we wanted at any price to observe the established schedule, the plan document which we would accept would be primarily the result of the professional work of state organs, with all the socio-economic and material limitations and dangers which are inherent in such work. Therefore I think that there is less danger because of a few months delay than if a planning document unsatisfactory from a socio-economic perspective is passed. Such a plan would remain a dead letter.[34]

Indeed, preparation of both this plan and the one for 1981-1985 ran far behind schedule.[35]

The second track consists of a generally de-politicized, professional process by which "expert" advice on the issues is gathered, such as the study on the long-range development of Yugoslavia carried out by the Consortium of Economic Institutes and delivered to the Chamber of Republics and Provinces in April 1975.[36] This is also the process by which the preliminary drafts of

---

[32] *Politika* (Belgrade), 25 December 1975.

[33] "Neka zapažanja," pp. 18, 19.

[34] *Politika* (Belgrade), 25 December 1975.

[35] On the causes of delays in the preparation of the 1981-85 plan, see ibid., 1 and 31 October 1980.

[36] "Rad Veća republika i pokrajina," p. 29.

legislative acts are prepared.[37] But this process does not unfold without political supervision. During preparation of such texts, the professional organs and organizations of the federation responsible for drafting the texts maintain constant contact with authoritative political bodies such as the Presidium, Executive Committee, and Central Committee of the party.[38] The FEC may create, as it did for both the five-year plan for 1976-1980 and the long-range plan for development to 1985, a special commission for the preparation of a text. The formula for composing such commissions is the same as that for the other consultative councils, commissions, and committees of the FEC.

When the general outline of a particular piece of legislation has been formulated within the FEC, the Council may submit it to the Federal Assembly for discussion and comment in the relevant committees of the responsible chamber. In the case of social plans, this is the Chamber of Republics and Provinces. Such an outline may take the form of a preliminary draft (*prednacrt*) of the legislation, or it may take the form of a statement of the principles on which the legislation will be formulated, called "theses" (*teze*) or "bases" (*osnove*). Formal interregional bargaining in the Chamber of Republics and Provinces over the plan for 1976-1980, for example, was preceded by two series of discussions in the Chamber about the "bases" for development of the plan—in March, and again in July 1975.

Such discussions provide an opportunity for the delegations of the republics and provinces to express their views before their home assemblies have officially considered the legislation, and for the FEC to identify potential sources of conflict and to develop compromise formulations prior to the start of the formal legislative process. Delegations can—and do—consult with their home republics and provinces during these discussions. But these consultations usually are with the executive councils of the republic and are neither comprehensive nor systematic. During preliminary discussion of the social plan for 1975, the delegations of the republics and provinces received the views of the committees of their respective assemblies and presented them in the preliminary discussions held in the committees of the Chamber of Republics and Provinces.[39]

Such preliminary discussions usually are referred to as an "exchange of opinions" (*razmena mišljenja*) among the republics and provinces. After such an exchange, the delegations in the Chamber of Republics and Provinces inform their respective regional assemblies of the content, meaning, and intent of the federal legislation before those assemblies formulate their official positions. In this way, the delegations in the Chamber not only represent the interests of their respective republics and provinces in federal decision making

[37] *Politika* (Belgrade), 10 February 1976.
[38] Ibid., 30 January 1976.
[39] "Neka iskustva," pp. 13-14.

but also act as channels for the exercise of federal influence on the republican and provincial assemblies.[40] The professional staff of the Chamber concluded as early as January 1975 (and repeated its findings in September) that the results of such discussions "affirmed the correctness of such [practice]" and contributed "to making the proposed policy of development more precise" and "to creation of conditions for its realization." In the judgment of the staff, discussion of the 1975 annual plan in the first year of operation of the Chamber demonstrated

> the indispensability and real usefulness of the practice of the "preliminary" procedure and the general importance which the holding of discussions in the committees during this phase of work has from the perspective of creating conditions for the successful harmonization of the views of the republican and provincial assemblies in the following two phases.[41]

Over time, this function has increased in importance.[42] Delegates do not, however, always introduce solutions or explanations developed in the preliminary proceeding into the debates in their respective assemblies. One of the committees of the Chamber reported in September 1975, for example, that although "discussion of materials and laws in the preliminary phase has been shown to be very useful,"

> certain questions which were emphasized during discussion of some materials and laws in the preliminary phase, although they were very important, remained without any kind of influence on the solution of the problem itself, because the delegates did not raise them in their assemblies.[43]

The practice of submitting preliminary versions of legislation for an exchange of opinions constitutes yet another mechanism for interregional and regional-federal consultation. It was done for every major piece of legislation adopted during the first two years of operation of the Assembly. It was not used, however, in the consideration of legislative proposals that had been under discussion in the interrepublican committees of the FEC when the Assembly began its work. Drafts of these laws were referred from the inter-

---

[40] Ibid., pp. 6-7.

[41] "Rad Veća republika i pokrajina," p. 23; cf. "Neka iskustva," pp. 12-17.

[42] Compare the earlier evaluations by the Assembly leadership of these proceedings with, for example, the one contained in Djurović, *Zapažanja iz rada Veća*, pp. 48-49. Several sources conflict with this judgement of their importance (cf., for example, Mujačić, "Proces dogovaranja," pp. 83-84), but the internal documentation of the Assembly itself and my own interviews with high functionaries and delegates of the Chamber make me confident that the view expressed above is correct.

[43] "Rad Veća republika i pokrajina," p. 73.

republican committees directly to the assemblies of the republics and provinces so that the regional assemblies could take positions on them and offer their proposals and suggestions. And, on the basis of article 300 of the constitution, the regional assemblies, in agreement with the Federal Executive Council, authorized their delegations to approve the final drafts in their name, thereby shortening the legislative process.[44] This early equation of the "preliminary proceeding" with the process of negotiation in the interrepublican committees foreshadowed the development of current practices by which representatives of the Chamber are included even in the earlier stages of interregional negotiations.[45]

The "preliminary proceeding" has now taken on, in the opinion of some delegates in the Chamber, "decisive importance."[46] It provides the FEC and repesentatives of the republics and provinces in the Chamber with an effective arena for expressing conflict without undermining the stability of the system. The views expressed during these discussions are not reported in the press and remain secret. This permits the delegations to explore issues of potential conflict at an early stage and to influence the shape of the positions finally adopted by their own and other regions without raising any issues publicly. In cases when "great disagreement" exists, proposals may be withdrawn from consideration and returned to the federal councils and interrepublican committees for further work. One experienced functionary of the Assembly reported in 1976 that "this does not happen many times, but it does happen."

How can the views of delegates in the Chamber of Republics and Provinces differ from the views expressed by the representatives of the republics and provinces in the interrepublican committees, federal councils, and Federal Executive Council? First, members of the FEC cannot be bound by republican or provincial instructions. Control over the bureaucracies and specialized agencies and services of the federation make the Council a powerful political actor with its own interests and views. Second, during the preliminary proceeding the delegates are not bound by official instructions; only by their general responsibility to present the interests of their regions. Third, not all republican and provincial executive councils exercise equal influence over their respective assemblies and the delegations of those assemblies to the Chamber.

Submission of a Draft. After the preliminary proceeding has been completed, the FEC submits a draft of the legislation to the president of the Federal

---

[44] Ibid., p. 19.

[45] Perović, "Skupština i političko odlučivanje," p. 291.

[46] *Politika* (Belgrade), 24 February 1980. See also the Assembly leadership's own recent evaluation of its importance in Skupština SFRJ, *Ostvarivanje delegatskog skupštinskog sistema*, pp. 135-37.

Assembly. On matters in the jurisdiction of the Chamber of Republics and Provinces, the president of the Assembly sends copies to the president of that chamber. When an act requires the agreement of the republican and provincial assemblies, copies also are sent to the presidents of those assemblies. The Federal Assembly staff provides each regional assembly with copies of the draft in their respective languages, and in sufficient quantity.[47]

The president of the Chamber of Republics and Provinces, in consultation with the chairmen of the republican and provincial delegations, determines a period of not less than forty-five days within which the regional assemblies must complete consideration of the draft and formulate their positions. This represents an increase over the thirty-day period that had been provided the regional assemblies to develop their positions prior to 1978. This change was adopted because a thirty-day period had precluded extensive consultation by the delegates in republican and provincial assemblies with their constituencies, and thereby increased the influence in these assemblies of the members of the delegations to the Chamber of Republics and Provinces, who participated in the "preliminary proceedings" and presented and explained the draft proposal to the other delegates. This influence does not, however, appear to have been diminished in any way by the additional allocation of time.

These delegations or their chairmen meet frequently with representatives of the executive councils of their respective regions, and with representatives of the Trade Union federation, the Socialist Alliance, and other socio-political organizations in their respective regions to coordinate views on issues under consideration in the Chamber. Other delegates in the regional assemblies generally rely exclusively on the executive council of the region for the formulation of positions on federal legislation.[48] Both these consultations and the lack of time to conduct extensive consultation with constituencies (the "delegational base") ensure that views developed in direct negotiations at the federal level between representatives of the regional executive councils dominate in the regional assemblies.

Although formulation of the positions of the regional assemblies generally took only a short time, the staff of the Chamber of Republics and Provinces reported in June 1976:

> there have been instances in which the formulation of positions in the assemblies of the republics and provinces on drafts of certain acts lasts a very long time (in the case of some acts even five months). Such instances have most often concerned acts by which resources are allocated

---

[47] "Rad Veća republika i pokrajina," p. 19; and "Neka iskustva," p. 9.
[48] "Neka iskustva," pp. 10, 17; "Rad Veća republika i pokrajina," p. 19; and "Neka zapažanja," pp. 5, 7.

for long-term financing of particular projects or [for] the fulfillment of previously accepted international obligations.[49]

When the "preliminary proceeding" causes serious delay, republican and provincial assemblies may limit themselves to adopting positions only in areas where disagreement occurs in order to reduce the sheer volume of material with which delegates in the Chamber of Republics and Provinces must deal.[50]

Current norms of political behavior prohibit republics and provinces from adopting certain kinds of positions. These prohibitions clearly reflect the experiences of the leadership during the period of crisis. According to a report of the staff of the Chamber of Republics and Provinces, the regional assemblies and their delegations may seek only to *alter* or *amend* legislation in certain areas. Specifically:

> the fulfillment of previously accepted international obligations cannot be called into question. Rather, the object of harmonization can be only the means of securing the necessary financial resources and certain questions in connection with the carrying-out of the obligations.
>
> As far as priority laws or other general acts which according to the Constitution must be adopted are concerned, a position by which passage of the law itself is disputed cannot be accepted. Rather, by acceptance of adoption itself, through comments and proposals, the directions of legislative settlement of the matter should be expressed. . . .
>
> . . . .
>
> The question of adopting positions in the assemblies concerning an act by which the total volume of expenditures of the budget of the federation is determined is special. A negative position could not concern the need for passage of the act, but only the volume and sources of income. Positions on these questions are the only object of harmonization, and not the question whether or not it is necessary to pass the act.[51]

The purpose of the "preliminary proceeding" is to make such opposition in the regional assemblies unlikely. It does not, however, completely eliminate opposition. Indeed, when a proposal finally reaches the Chamber of Republics and Provinces it is usually accompanied by a hefty compendium of regional comments, reservations, and objections prepared by the Chamber's professional staff on the basis of direct communications from the regional assemblies.[52]

[49] "Neka zapažanja," p. 5.

[50] Ibid., p. 17; "Rad Veća republika i pokrajina," p. 19; cf. *Politika* (Belgrade), 30 January 1976.

[51] "Neka zapažanja," p. 6.

[52] I was permitted to review briefly some of these by a high official of the Chamber in December 1980.

Beyond these general limitations, there also continue to be some questions as to what constitutes a normatively "correct" position. The staff of the Chamber of Republics and Provinces pointed out:

> the question [has arisen] whether the positions of republican and pro-vincial assemblies on such acts must be limited to the emphasis and explanation of principled, essential questions about its own [interest] or the joint interest, leaving to the delegations greater freedom, within the framework of such established principled positions, to express and ex-plain the particular interest of the republic or province in the process of harmonization in the working bodies of the Chamber . . . and in that way arrive at the joint interest of all the republics and provinces.[53]

Although the precise boundaries of this "greater freedom" were difficult to establish in the first two years of Assembly operation, there was general agreement that they should not be so narrow as to constitute an "imperative mandate." Indeed, the constitutional definition of the role of delegates and delegations in assemblies and the definition of the role of delegates contained in the Chamber's own rules of procedure seem to preclude this. This is, however, contrary to the explicit concession to establish such a mandate for the regional delegations, made by those who drafted the new constitution as part of the compromise formulation for the organization and operation of the Federal Assembly. It suggests a clear effort by the leadership of the Chamber to promote its own institutional autonomy.

Preparation of the new rules of procedure of the Chamber of Republics and Provinces was carried out by a group of legal specialists "starting from the new constitutional-legal solutions and rules of parliamentary practice." The procedure for decision making on issues requiring the approval of all the regions was determined by these legal specialists and a group composed of the president of the Chamber and the chairmen of the regional delegations. The presidents of the regional assemblies also were consulted during the preparation of the rules, and the entire process was supervised by an "inter-republican coordinative group."[54] The definition of the role of delegates in the chamber was "without a doubt, one of the most complicated questions" during the drafting of the rules. According to the Chamber's staff, at the center of the controversy "was the question of establishing the rights and duties of delegations and delegates in the Chamber, having in view with respect to this the application of an imperative mandate."

> The working-out of these issues began from [the conviction] that a del-egate is politically qualified to fulfill his delegate function independently and responsibly by the presentation of [his own] opinions and by the

[53] "Neka zapažanja," pp. 7-8.
[54] "Rad Veća republika i pokrajina," p. 41.

taking of positions in the Chamber and its working bodies, and to evaluate to what degree he can deviate from the established policy, authorization, and general directives of his own assembly in order to discover joint solutions and construct united positions on certain questions . . . [only] as long as the republican or provincial assembly does not take a stand . . . which is obligatory for every one of its delegates and for the delegation as a whole.[55]

The staff of the Chamber and, presumably, the highest Chamber and Assembly leadership to which it is responsible, clearly favors greater independence for the delegations "even in situations when it is certain that the sponsor [of a legislative proposal] will, on the basis of the comment of an assembly or other organs and bodies, appear with additional proposals which eventually change the content of the solution previously submitted in the draft of the act which is already under consideration." In such situations, the staff argued in another, later report:

the delegations themselves should evaluate whether they require additional or new positions from their assemblies on the additional proposals and, in the case that they determine such a need, seek the positions of their assemblies. In such a case, it is not necessary to begin a new process but rather, on the initiative of the delegation itself appropriate consultations in the assemblies of the republics and provinces would be carried out.[56]

Indeed, by 1980 the Chamber leadership had taken the position that regional assemblies "should express only the socio-economic and political framework within which the delegation should approach the process of harmonization," and leave the detailed solution of each issue to be worked out in the Chamber committees.[57]

Those few cases in which the positions of a republican or provincial assembly have approximated an imperative mandate have been subjected to extensive internal and public criticism, both oblique and explicit. At the outset of Assembly work on the medium-range plan for 1976-1980, for example, a political commentator for *Politika* attributed the delay in adoption of the plan for 1976 to the imperative mandate of one delegation and severely criticized the practice. His observations, published in February 1976, clearly reflect the views of the central political leadership, including the leadership of the Assembly itself, and are worth presenting in detail:

It is known from experience that the procedure surrounding adoption of planning documents sometimes can be unexpectedly long, tiring, and

[55] Ibid., pp. 42-43.
[56] "Neka zapažanja," p. 6.
[57] Skupština SFRJ, *Ostvarivanje delegatskog skupstinškog sistema*, p. 157.

replete with unforeseen minor details. Of course, when eight delegations make an agreement, when a great number of various interests are "in the game," it is not reasonable to assume in advance that all will go sweetly and without difficulty. . . .

But the issue here is not about the unavoidable cost associated with every agreement, but primarily about certain still uncompleted elements of the new decision-making process in the Assembly. For example, the decision on the Resolution [the social plan] for this year (passed in the second half of December 1975) was delayed no small amount because one delegation had an imperative mandate. This unpleasantness never-theless was avoided by the additional and intensive activities of the delegations. All of this created an atmosphere of feverish hurriedness and the uncomfortable impression that even important matters sometimes are dealt with in an improvised manner and in a hurry.

The delegations have not forgotten this lesson, so that now they speak about the forthcoming process of harmonization with a much greater feeling of responsibility and precision. Almost everyone is convinced that, when a [social] plan is concerned, the delegations must receive more elastic authorization from their republican or provincial assemblies. The opinion has developed that the type and limits of these authorizations should be defined by some joint act, by the rules of procedure for ex-ample, and not be left to the individual initiative and judgment of the republics and provinces. Because in the future each delegation, as it is being said these days, ought to have the same legal position in order to ensure greater harmony in the process of decision making.

. . . In the course of harmonization of positions, when delegations present their own very often mutually differing proposals, all participants in the [process of] agreement making must be prepared even for elastic relaxation [of their positions] in order to approach the others.[58]

This commentary reveals the renewed emphasis on central authority and on the autonomy of central decision-making institutions in the period following the "Croatian crisis."[59] The greater the latitude granted to delegations in the Chamber of Republics and Provinces to alter the positions taken by their respective assemblies, the greater the potential influence of the central political leadership over the leaderships of the regions.

Each of the republican and provincial delegations in the Chamber of Re-publics and Provinces functions as a distinct organization. Each meets prior

[58] *Politika* (Belgrade), 20 February 1976.

[59] For a detailed statement of the current "official" position on this issue, see Mijat Šuković, "Delegatski sistem," in Jovan Djordjević, ed., *Društveno-politički sistem SFRJ* (Beograd: Rad-nička Štampa, 1975), pp. 242-69, but esp. 263-66.

to the start of the process of harmonization to collate and coordinate the positions of its assembly on draft materials and to develop them into coherent sets of views.[60] During these meetings "directions for the work of individual delegates in the committees are more precisely established."

For this work, the delegations have available reviews of the positions of the assemblies of the republics and provinces systematized according to the questions which are the object of harmonization. Also, in the course of this work delegations make use of the expert help of representatives of appropriate republican or provincial organs, the services of their own assemblies and the appropriate services of the SFRY Assembly.[61]

Most of the actual interregional bargaining takes place in meetings between the president of the Chamber and the chairmen of the delegations, and in the committees of the Chamber. Consequently, not only must each delegation faithfully represent the views of its respective republic or province, but each individual delegate—and especially the chairman—must represent those views. To assure that this occurs, each delegation meets before and after the sessions of the Chamber committees to develop a unified approach to the issues.[62] Delegations remain on call during the harmonization process so that individual delegates may consult the other members of their delegations on "controversial questions on which the representatives of the delegations in the working bodies could not make definitive statements."[63] Sometimes, as during work on the Draft Resolution and Draft Decision on the federal budget for 1975, this means that delegations meet every day.[64] Delegations also keep in direct contact with the leaderships of their respective assemblies during the process of harmonization.[65]

"Usaglašavanje": The Process of Harmonization of Positions. After the delegations have completed their preparations, the "working bodies"—or committees—of the Chamber convene to reconcile the views of the republics and provinces. The Federal Executive Council assigns a permanent representative to each of the committees of the Chamber. These sometimes are replaced or joined by special representatives for particular issues. Although they are not voting members of these committees, "the representatives of the

---

[60] "Rad Veća republika i pokrajina," p. 31; and "Neka zapažanja," p. 10. See also Djurović, *Zapažanja iz rada Veća republika i pokrajina*, pp. 62-63.

[61] "Neka zapažanja," p. 10.

[62] "Neka iskustva," pp. 45-46; and "Neka zapažanja," p. 11.

[63] "Rad Veća republika i pokrajina," p. 31.

[64] "Neka iskustva," p. 46.

[65] Ibid.

Federal Executive Council were included directly in the work of the committee[s] not only as interpreters or defenders of the offered policy but also as equal participants in a joint task."[66] As can be seen from Table 5.1, representatives of other federal administrative organs also participate in the

TABLE 5.1

Participation in the Work of the Chamber of Republics and Provinces and its Committees (May 1974 to December 1975)

	Number of Sessions	Participants								
		Other Delegates in the Assembly	Delegates from the Regional Assemblies	Members of FEC	Representatives of Legislative Sponsor	Federal Admin. & Judicial Personnel	Representatives of Socio-Pol. Orgs.[a]	Self-Managing Ents.	Experts	Representatives (Unspecified)	Others[b]
The Chamber	18	—	—	78	96	90	27	—	—	—	35
Committees for											
Social Plan & Development	27	44	—	21	23	48	1	—	23	—	30
Economic Relations	27	3	1	35	12	51	—	6	1	—	2
Finance	32	11	2	57	48	106	—	4	12	29	12
Credit-Monetary System	30	3	—	25	5	36	12	31	51	—	32
Development of the Insuf.-Devel. Reps. & Provs.	12	—	—	22	24	33	1	—	27	—	40
Association in the Economy	24	21	—	24	12	40	11	23	22	—	31
Market & Prices	18	1	—	9	15	30	2	2	17	—	71

SOURCE: Skupština SFRJ, Služba za dokumentaciju, "Statistički pregled rada skupštinskih tela (u periodu od 15.5.1975. do 15.3.1975. godine)," No. 1, Belgrade, March 1975 (mimeographed), p. 18; *idem*, "Statistički pregled rada skupštinskih tela (u periodu od 16.3.1975. do 31.8.1975. godine)," No. 2, Belgrade, November 1975 (mimeographed), p. 13; Skupština SFRJ, Služba za informativno-dokumentalističke poslove, Odeljenje skupštinske dokumentacije, "Statistički pregled rada skupštinskih tela (u periodu od 1.9. do 31.12.1975. godine)," No. 3, Belgrade, June 1976 (mimeographed), pp. 26-27.

[a] Includes: Presidency, LCY, Socialist Alliance, Trade Union Federation, Chamber of Commerce, and others.

[b] Includes: Federal Assembly staff, collegial bodies of the Assembly, and others.

[66] Ibid., p. 23.

work of the Chamber and its committees.[67] Because the FEC was the sponsor of almost all proposals that came before the Chamber and its working bodies during this period, the category "representatives of legislative sponsors" probably is composed almost entirely of FEC and federal administrative personnel.

Individual experts from scientific, technical, and economic faculties, institutes, or other institutions participate to an important degree, but much less frequently than personnel from organs and organizations of the federation. Representatives of self-managing economic enterprises participate frequently only in the work of the committees for the credit-monetary system and for association, or integration, in the economy—where the financial interests of these organizations are affected most directly. The representatives of the FEC tend to exercise the dominant influence in these committees. The Chamber staff has reported:

in the process of harmonization of positions some representatives of the Federal Executive Council have acted in one of the following two ways: they have accepted in advance every harmonized position of the republican and provincial assemblies or they have reserved the right to express themselves later, whether on a harmonized or an unharmonized position.

But it suggested that:

this must be understood as the harmonized positions of the republican and provincial assemblies coinciding with the positions of the . . . Council, and not as the . . . Council accepting a priori the harmonized positions of the . . . assemblies. If a representative of the . . . Council expresses reservations on certain positions during the process of harmonization it is because [discussion about] a question of principle has been started about which the . . . Council has not taken a stand, and for that reason it is necessary to consult the . . . Council.[68]

The delegation from the Assembly of the autonomous province of Vojvodina has described the actions of the FEC representatives in terms that are more critical and suggest that they play a decidedly more dominant role:

A proposal for the enactment of a law or draft of a law is discussed several times primarily because the sponsor did not consider or accept the proposals and suggestions which were presented at the sessions of the committees where harmonization took place. . . . [T]he sponsor also did not present an official position and did not explain why certain proposals were not accepted.[69]

[67] The general pattern of participation evident in this table also is evident in the data on participation in the Chamber for the period 1974-1978 presented in Perović, "Skupština i političko odlučivanje," pp. 341, 342. Unfortunately, his data are not broken down by individual committee.
[68] "Neka zapažanja," p. 17.   [69] "Rad Veća republika i pokrajina," Appendix II, p. 5.

This view is supported by more recent, and more open reporting on the operation of Chamber committees in the daily press.

A recent analysis by the parliamentary correspondent for *Politika* suggests that the FEC is "in a real sense 'the architect of the search for the best solution' " to interregional conflicts.[70] Members of the Council itself, he reports, continue to reject the thesis that it is the most important arena for the harmonization of regional interests and to insist that the harmonization takes place in the Chamber of Republics and Provinces and its committees. The fact is, however, that when negotiations among regional delegations in the Chamber and its committees reach an impasse, the delegates turn to the representatives of the Council for a solution. Often, that representative has been able to offer a compromise acceptable to all. Frequently, however, representatives of the Council will "withdraw into passivity, with the laconic explanation: comrade delegates, whatever you agree on is fine with us." By prolonging the impasse in this way, the Council increases the likelihood that its own position will be accepted. For even the delegates themselves acknowledge that when they cannot reach agreement on a particular issue, they quickly turn it over to the FEC's Coordinating Commission for resolution. In effect, the representatives of the FEC act in the committees of the Chamber as "defenders" or exponents of the positions formulated in the interrepublican committees, federal councils, and permanent commissions of the Council.[71]

While other socio-political organizations on the level of the federation do participate in setting the agenda of the Federal Assembly and in the early stages of preparation of legislative proposals, they apparently can participate in the harmonization of positions in the committees of the Chamber only by influencing the positions adopted by the regional assemblies before the process of harmonization begins. The June 1976 staff report on the operation of the Chamber notes:

> In the course of work up to now, organs and bodies of socio-political organizations in the federation frequently have placed on [their] agenda concrete issues on which the process of harmonization of positions is [already] in progress in the Chamber. . . . The political positions of these organs and bodies on such acts frequently were taken after the completion of work on these issues in the assemblies of the republics and provinces. Considering the already-established positions of the republican and provincial assemblies, it was difficult for the political effect of these positions . . . to come to expression.[72]

[70] *Politika* (Belgrade), 24 February 1980.
[71] See Perović, "Skupština i političko odlučivanje," p. 272.
[72] "Neka iskustva," p. 36; cf. "Neka zapažanja," p. 20.

Under these conditions, "these positions can be taken [into consideration] only as an integral part of the political argument for the specific positions of the republican and provincial assemblies." Thus, organizations whose interests cut across regional boundaries must participate in the deliberations of the regional assemblies if they are to moderate effectively interregional conflicts in the Federal Assembly. They can do so because the organization of the regional assemblies into three chambers—a chamber of associated labor composed of delegates from among working people in self-managing enterprises, state organs, and agriculture; a chamber of communes composed of delegates elected in local territorial units; and a socio-political chamber composed of delegates elected from socio-political organizations—provides these organizations with direct, institutionalized access to the formal decision-making processes in the regional assemblies.

The socio-political chambers of the regional assemblies are composed entirely of "professional political workers" delegated by the socio-political organizations in the republic or province. These include the Socialist Alliance, the Trade Union, the Youth Federation, the veterans' organization, and, of course, the party itself. The delegates in these chambers, therefore, are subject to close party discipline and can be expected to adhere closely to party prescriptions in influencing the formation of political positions in their respective assemblies. In addition, the socio-political chambers of the regional assemblies provide more than 70 percent of the delegates to the Chamber of Republics and Provinces in the Federal Assembly.[73] This, more than the fact that 100 percent of delegates in the Chamber are party members, gives the party important influence over the course of negotiations in the Chamber.[74]

The central party organs also have more direct access to interregional negotiations in the federation. The leaderships of the Federal Executive Council, the chambers of the Federal Assembly, and the regional executive councils and assemblies all consult regularly with the central party leadership at all stages of the federal decision-making process.

Individual delegates in the committees of the Chamber of Republics and Provinces play a dual role. They must represent the views of their respective republic or province, but also must attempt to reconcile them with the views of other delegates. A report on the work of the Chamber's committee for questions of association in the economy describes the work of the delegates in the following paragraph:

[73] Mujačić, "Proces dogovaranja," p. 75.

[74] For an analysis of the socio-political chambers, see Jovan R. Marjanović, *Društveno-politička veća* (Beograd: Institut za političke studije, 1979), and the companion volume of comments on this work, Milivoj Tatić, ed., *Aktuelna pitanja ostvarivanja uloge društveno-političkog veća* (Beograd: Institut za političke studije, 1979).

Delegates, members of the Committee, insisted that the positions of their delegations, or their republics and provinces, be adopted. But also, listening to the opinions of other delegates, [they] agreed to argue in their own delegations for the positions which are generally acceptable, on which agreement was reached. That slowed somewhat the discovery of common solutions, but not so much that a solution was not achieved in time.[75]

Discussions in the committees during the process of harmonization also have been described as "quite detailed, many-sided, spontaneous, very polemical" and characterized by "quite [a lot of] argument and counter-argument about various positions."[76]

One well-informed observer of—and participant in—these discussions reports that they often result in a "trading of interests across issues." "Such situations have arisen," the leadership of the Chamber reported in June 1976, "only in cases when the acceptance of the position of one delegation on a concrete issue has been conditioned by reciprocal support for the position of another delegation, also on some concrete issue"—a perfect description of the practice known in the West as logrolling.[77] This remains common practice today.[78] The leadership condemns such practice as based on "the unyielding insistence on [one's] own interest, without sufficient understanding of that interest itself and especially not of the interest of the whole." It contrasts this to "genuine harmonization," which it describes as:

the situation when the interest of one's own republic or province, which was clearly expressed and sufficiently convincingly argued, in meeting with the similarly identified interest of another republic or province, is by mutual efforts synthesized and concretized as the mutual interest of all republics and provinces or the mutual interest of the nations and nationalities, working people and citizens.[79]

The same observer/participant suggests, however, that "the ideal . . . is not achieved" in practice. In fact, "trade-offs always occurred—but now they take place on a self-managing basis. All interested factors participate in the decision-making process. The problem in the past was the exclusion of certain factors from decision making."

The experiences of other negotiations based on consensus suggest that it is more difficult to "trade interests" or to establish a logrolling relationship

[75] "Neka iskustva," p. 35.
[76] "Rad Veća republika i pokrajina," p. 36; and *Politika* (Belgrade), 25 December 1975.
[77] "Neka zapažanja," p. 11.
[78] Perović, "Skupština i političko odlučivanje," p. 205.
[79] "Neka zapažanja," p. 11.

on broader issues, such as formulation of the programmatic statements of developmental goals contained in social plans, than on more specific issues of concrete policy. While Yugoslav political commentators may suggest to the contrary that interregional agreement is easier to achieve on such statements than on specific policies,[80] the operation of the Federal Assembly suggests that the more general finding is indeed true. The task that has presented the Chamber of Republics and Provinces with the most difficulty since its establishment in 1971 is the formulation of programmatic statements concerning the general goals and means of economic and social development in Yugoslavia. Such statements presented stumbling blocks in the passage of the long-range (ten-year) plan for development through 1985, several of the annual social plans, and the medium-term (five-year) plans for economic and social development in the periods 1976-1980 and 1981-1985. More specific policy conflicts, including even those concerning issues that have been at the center of interbloc conflict for many years, have been easier—although by no means easy—to resolve.

Conflict Issues since 1974. As in the past, interregional conflict has continued to center on the allocation of scarce resources and has had both territorial and functional (economic branch) dimensions.[81] Although the latter dimension has found open expression in the federal councils and permanent commissions subordinate to the Federal Executive Council, it is primarily the territorial dimension that finds expression in the Chamber of Republics and Provinces. The broadest, most interminable interregional conflict in the Chamber since 1974 has concerned the drafting of the general commitment to accelerated development of the underdeveloped regions contained in each social plan, and the provisions for its implementation. It has focused at times on the very definition of underdevelopment, on the precise goal of aid to the underdeveloped, and, of course, on the amount and character of that aid.

The preparation of social plans requires all self-managing organizations and socio-political organizations and communities to identify their own interests, to express them, and to enter into agreements with other organizations and communities to fulfill them.[82] Thus, the very nature of the planning process itself encourages the expression of conflicting interests. At the federal level, the dominant interests are regional, both because of the institutionalization of regional representation and interregional bargaining in the decision-making process and because of the continuing regional character of the Yu-

[80] *Politika* (Belgrade), 10 April 1976.

[81] See the characterizations of chamber decision making in Djurović, *Zapažanja iz rada Veća*, p. 12; and Skupština SFRJ, *Ostvarivanje delegatskog skupštinskog sistema*, p. 128.

[82] For a statement of the character of social planning and social plans, see *Zakon o osnovama sistema društvenog planiranja i o društvenom planu Jugoslavije* (Beograd: Službeni List, 1976).

goslav economy. Consequently, the adoption of social plans necessarily sets the interests of the developed regions against those of the underdeveloped. The coincidence of these regional economic divisions with divisions based on nationality inevitably intensifies these conflicts.

The programmatic statements contained in social plans do not directly determine the specific allocation of resources. Rather, they set the framework and goals for the later formulation of specific allocation policies. Nonetheless, they are particularly important in the Yugoslav context because they also set the tone of political debate and the developmental norms of the economic system. Specific allocation and investment decisions are subject to interest-trading or logrolling between the representatives of the regions. Consequently, the adoption of strong programmatic formulations in favor of development of the underdeveloped regions gives these republics and provinces additional leverage in negotiations in which they otherwise would be at an extreme disadvantage. They are able to negotiate such favorable statements primarily because their positions correspond to a long-standing ideological commitment of the party and therefore receive the strong support of the central party leadership. The influence of the party is strongest precisely in this area—the formulation of broad prescriptive statements concerning the development of Yugoslav society.

Conflicts over the formulation of general statements in social plans often involve the very real economic interests of the regions. The establishment of priorities in federal tax policy in the 1976-1980 plan, for example, was the subject of regional conflict during more than two years of preparatory work on that plan. The parliamentary correspondent for *Politika* suggested that the intensity of regional interest could be explained in terms of its impact on later allocations of resources:

> to receive priority treatment means to expect no small benefits in the coming period. The community [federation] will stimulate and support these economic areas [of activity] . . . with credit and various other measures. There will be more money and other more favorable economic conditions for them. Many see in this a good chance for the solution of their long-existing problems.
>
> And the opposite [is true]—if more money is set aside for one, there will be so much less left for others. And that already is enough to cause sensitivity and tension.[83]

It is clear, therefore, that conflict over general programmatic statements actually involves the concrete economic interests of the regions. Of course, important interregional conflicts have also occurred over more specific, but

---

[83] *Politika* (Belgrade), 16 March 1976.

no less important decisions concerning the direct allocation of resources for specific projects and other federal economic policies.

Unlike the period 1966-1971, such conflicts—however intense—are now carefully reported in both public and restricted-circulation, confidential accounts in the context of general agreement. With respect to conflict in the committees of the Chamber in late 1975 over the use of international loans and credits, for example, *Politika* reported that "the differences which have appeared in this respect are not of a principled character, but are more the reflections of particular economic accents."[84] Last-minute conflict in December 1975 over adoption of the 1976 plan was described as "lively and interesting" discussion, "with quite a lot of argument and counterargument about differing positions," but with "harmonization proceeding in a working and constructive atmosphere characterized by the readiness to find a solution which, as much as possible, would satisfy everyone."[85] Even an early staff report on the work of the Chamber carefully pointed out that:

> the entire work on harmonization of positions was characterized by a working atmosphere, mutual understanding, and correctness toward various proposals, the desire to reconcile all proposals, to establish the best formulation, to recognize the joint and not underestimate the individual interests of the republics and provinces, and so on.[86]

This style continued to be a dominant characteristic of Yugoslav reporting on such conflicts even at the time of Tito's death in 1980.

How Conflicts Are Resolved. A relatively large proportion of the issues over which there is still interregional conflict by the time they reach the Chamber of Republics and Provinces usually are resolved during the routine deliberations in the committees of that Chamber. The participation of representatives of the Federal Executive Council in these deliberations enables the delegates to identify solutions that not only are acceptable to their respective republics and provinces but also correspond to the general framework established during prior negotiation in the federal councils, interrepublican committees, and permanent commissions of the FEC. The representatives of the FEC evaluate the positions of republican and provincial delegates "from the perspective of the basic intentions of the joint policy which the . . . Council is proposing and . . . the repercussions of each of these positions."[87] They consider the positions, suggestions, and proposals of the delegates as they arise, and accept, reject, or offer counter suggestions. When the need arises, they may delay

[84] Ibid., 18 December 1975.
[85] Ibid., 25 December 1975.
[86] "Neka iskustva," p. 35.
[87] "Neka zapažanja," p. 17.

responding until they have consulted with the Council itself. For this purpose, the FEC remains in constant session during the process of harmonization.[88]

When conflicts cannot be resolved through routine discussion, the committees of the Chamber generally pause to allow the republican and provincial delegations to discuss the issues. Conflicts over the list of priorities in the 1976 plan, for example, were referred back to the delegations in mid-December,[89] and the conflict over the definition of the goals of development contained in the 1976-1980 plan was referred back to the delegations in March.[90] Delegations formulate their responses to these issues in close contact with their home assemblies via phone, telex, and sometimes even in meetings in their home republics. During the final stages of negotiation over the 1976 plan, for example, the leadership of the Assembly and the Federal Executive Council agreed to recess the meetings of the Assembly committees for one day to allow "consultations in the republics and provinces . . . on the most delicate issues."[91] Over time, such recesses have become standard practice in instances of serious conflict.

When the committees reconvene, it is sometimes the case that more authoritative individuals from the Assembly leadership participate in the deliberations in an attempt to speed agreement. If no solution is reached, the issue is considered by a smaller, more authoritative group. This usually consists of the president of the Chamber and either the chairmen of the regional delegations or the chairmen of the committees engaged in discussion of the issue, or both. Sometimes the president of the Federal Assembly or representatives of the Federal Executive Council will also participate in these deliberations.[92] During these meetings, further deliberations and interregional bargaining over the remaining "open issues" take place and further action by the committees of the Chamber, the FEC, and other federal and republican organs are planned. The chairman of one republican delegation suggested in an interview conducted in January 1981 that discussion in such meetings carefully avoids the "essence" of the question under consideration. Instead, he reported, the participants discuss the "implications for the country, for the republics, if agreement is not reached"; whether there are "conditions under which agreement can be reached"; and "whether the FEC can recommend something new" in search of "a wider perspective" on the issue. While all this is undoubtedly true, internal documentary evidence also suggests that specific agreements or solutions are devised by these more authoritative

[88] See, for example, the reports in *Politika* (Belgrade), 9 December 1975 and 28-30 November 1980, which confirm this as regular practice.

[89] Ibid., 17 December 1975.

[90] Ibid., 11 March 1976.

[91] Ibid., 19 December 1975; cf. "Neka iskustva," p. 46.

[92] "Rad Veća republika I pokrajina," pp. 55-59.

actors and normally are accepted and adopted by the full committee responsible for "harmonization" on the issue concerned, and by all the regional delegations.

During the final stages of interregional negotiations over the 1975 plan, for example:

Open questions on which positions had not been fully harmonized in the committees were discussed . . . at a meeting of the president of the Chamber with the chairmen of the delegations and chairmen of the committees, with the participation of the president of the SFRY Assembly, the president of the Federal Executive Council, the vice-president of the . . . Council, and members of the Council who participated in the work of certain committees. At this meeting the chairmen of the delegations presented the positions of their delegations on the open issues and solutions were sought jointly in order that these positions could be harmonized. Such solutions were on the whole established and then verified in the responsible committees.[93]

Five days later, the Committee for the Credit-Monetary System was unable to reconcile conflicting proposals by the republics and provinces. These were discussed at a meeting between the president of the Chamber and the chairmen of the delegations, and the solution devised at that meeting was then ratified at the next session of the committee.[94] At the end of the process of harmonization on the 1975 plan, two issues remained as yet unresolved—one concerning the Slovenian delegation's reservations about the "list of priorities" and one concerning the Bosnian delegation's reservations about simultaneous passage of an agreement on general and shared expenditures. To resolve them, the Committee for the Social Plan and Development Policy met in an expanded session, with the participation of the chairmen of all other committees of the Chamber and representatives of the Federal Executive Council. Full agreement on these issues was achieved.[95]

The strategy of resolving conflicts by resort to smaller, more authoritative groups within the Assembly and by the intervention of authoritative Assembly functionaries in the work of the committees was highly successful. But it raised a serious question. As the staff of the Chamber put it:

The chairmen of the delegations have the responsible assignment of discussing and coming to agreement on the method of work and the application of new forms where existing forms of work have not given satisfactory results, but the question is whether they also should take

[93] Ibid., p. 25.
[94] "Neka iskustva," p. 34.
[95] Ibid., p. 16.

over for themselves directly the function of harmonization which the working bodies of the Chamber should fulfill.

Continuation of the practice of resolving conflicts in smaller, more authoritative bodies, the staff suggested,

> Could lead to a reduction of the significance of the working bodies, a denial to the delegates of the right to participate equally in the work [of the Chamber] and the involvement of the chairmen of delegations outside their basic functions (coordination of work in the delegations and between the delegations).[96]

It is this concern that leads participants in these deliberations carefully to avoid suggesting in personal interviews or statements for the public press that conflicts sometimes are resolved by "narrow groups behind closed doors."

"Harmonization of positions" in the Chamber on the five-year plan of 1976-1980, which took place during March 1976 because of delays engendered by interrepublican conflicts during preparation of the draft, was characterized by strong disagreements between the delegations of the developed and underdeveloped regions on a number of separate but related issues. In the Committee for the Social Plan and Development Policy, they disagreed over the precise wording of the goal of the policy of reducing differences between the developed and underdeveloped. The draft submitted by the FEC formulated the goal as:

> The reduction of relative differences in the level of development of the insufficiently-developed republics, and of . . . Kosovo most rapidly, in relation to the level of development of the country as a whole, by means of the accelerated development of the production forces of these areas.

The delegates from the developed republics opposed the formulation "in relation to the level of development of the country as a whole." They feared that this formula "would impose large obligations on them which could eventually lead to stagnation in their own development." They also questioned whether it meant that "if some other area of the country, insofar as tomorrow it fell below this average, automatically [will be] treated as underdeveloped, with all the consequences which follow from this?" The delegates from the underdeveloped regions, on the other hand, supported the formula embodied in draft. They argued:

> If it is not stated in relation "to what" the underdeveloped must develop more rapidly, then such a proposal is unacceptable. Because up to now

[96] "Rad Veća republika I pokrajina," p. 25.

there also has been talk about the accelerated development of the under-developed, but nevertheless that has not guaranteed that relative differences will be reduced.[97]

Because of this conflict, the issue was "reserved" so that the delegations could meet to discuss the conflicting positions.[98]

When the committee returned to this issue one week later, the delegation from Slovenia continued to oppose the FEC formulation calling for measuring the reduction of "relative differences" in relation to "the level of development of the country as a whole." The majority of delegations, "and especially [the delegations] of the underdeveloped republics and the province of Kosovo, energetically supported precisely such a formulation." Some progress in reconciling the opposing delegates was made during this session, but, "and this was said even in the discussion, . . . movement toward this agreement is relatively slow and at the cost of voluminous discussion."[99] Yet another week of meetings passed before agreement finally was reached. By that time, the Slovenian delegation was the only one that remained opposed to the FEC formulation presented in the draft plan. Through the meeting of March 10, others had joined the Slovenian delegation in its opposition. But during the meeting of March 11 it was alone. As a result, the Slovenian delegation "modified its position considerably, coming closer to [the position of] the other delegations." On March 10 the Committee for Questions of the Development of the Economically Insufficiently Developed Regions accepted a proposal by the Croatian delegation that was directed at another part of the plan, but which was closely related to and supportive of the Slovenian position. It is not unlikely that the acceptance of the Croatian proposal—described in more detail below—eliminated Croatian support for the Slovenian position in the committee on the plan and development, and was seen by the Slovenian delegation as fulfilling the intention of its own position.[100]

The compromise formulation finally accepted by the Slovenian delegation called for

The more rapid development of each economically insufficiently developed republic, and . . . Kosovo most rapidly, than the average development of the country as a whole for the sake of reducing the relative differences in the level of their development, and especially of . . . Kosovo, in relation to the level of development of the country as a whole,

[97] *Politika* (Belgrade), 4 March 1976.
[98] Ibid.
[99] Ibid., 11 March 1976.
[100] Ibid., 4 March 1976.

which is an essential precondition for the more rapid and more coordinated development of all of Yugoslavia.[101]

This formulation conforms to what a highly placed functionary in the Federal Assembly suggested is the "philosophy of decision making in the present period": a solution with which "all [participants] are unhappy is better than a forced solution." A Yugoslav reporter of Assembly affairs observed that "Already at first view it can be seen that the second formulation contains in essence the same elements as the first. But . . . [it] is not . . . as clear as the first one, contained in the Draft. . . ." However, he noted:

> If the entire pre-history and circumstances of this discussion are known, it is not difficult to understand why, nevertheless, a solution of this kind which carries strong features of a compromise has been resorted to.

He suggested, simply, that "at this moment perhaps it is not possible to achieve something more."[102]

The Slovenian position in the Committee for the Plan and Development gained strong support from the positions taken by the delegations of Vojvodina and Croatia in the Committee for Questions of the Development of the Economically Insufficiently Developed. The delegation from Vojvodina had proposed that the following passage be eliminated entirely from the draft:

> The more rapid development of every economically insufficiently developed republic and province, and particularly of Kosovo, than the average development of the entire country and the reduction of the relative differences in the level of their development in relation to the level of development of the country as a whole is one of the essential goals of social and economic development in the coming period.[103]

"It is not a goal, least of all a fundamental goal," explained a delegate from Vojvodina, "that differences between the underdeveloped and developed be reduced. . . . [T]he goal should be to liquidate underdevelopment." Because according to the draft formulation, he argued, "when at some time in certain republics per capita income will be four thousand dollars, but in other republics 3.5 thousand dollars, then these [other] republics will be underdeveloped."[104] The delegate from Kosovo, on the other hand, argued that the statement that development in Kosovo should be most rapid was inadequate because it was "vague."

[101] Ibid., 19 March 1976.
[102] Ibid.
[103] Ibid., 11 March 1976.
[104] Ibid., 6 March 1976.

At the next session of this committee, the delegation from Vojvodina presented an alternative statement of the goals of development policy. It read:

In the economically insufficiently developed republics the potential [already] created makes it possible in the period from 1976 to 1980 to achieve still more rapid economic and social development and by this to make possible the overcoming of their lower economic development and to make them capable of further independent social and economic development. Kosovo must achieve the most rapid development in the period to 1980 in order to overcome [its] present level of pronounced economic underdevelopment.[105]

This formulation corresponded to the positions expressed by the Croatian and Slovenian delegates at an earlier meeting of the committee and was subject to the same objection of vagueness voiced earlier by the delegation from Kosovo. The representative of the FEC also rejected this amendment. Therefore, the delegates decided to consult their delegations before making any decision. However, after further discussion during this session, the delegation from Vojvodina "somewhat modified" its position concerning the formulation contained in the original draft,

Saying that the original formulation can remain in the Draft, but that that part of the sentence [which reads] ". . . and reduction of the relative differences in the level of their development in relation to the level of development of the country as a whole" be eliminated. This was explained by the idea that "reduction of the relative differences" should not be a goal, but only a result of the more rapid development of these areas.[106]

The delegations from Croatia and Slovenia continued to support this position. The delegations from Serbia, Bosnia and Hercegovina, Macedonia, Montenegro, and Kosovo all remained committed to the original formulation. In response to this division, the representative of the FEC proposed a new formulation:

The more rapid development of every economically insufficiently developed republic and of . . . Kosovo most rapidly, for the purpose of reducing relative differences in the level of development in relation to the average of the country.[107]

On this proposal, too, the delegations reserved comment until after they had consulted with their delegations. These differences represented more than

[105] Ibid., 11 March 1976.
[106] Ibid.
[107] Ibid.

285

merely semantic or stylistic preferences. As one Yugoslav political commentator suggested, they also involved "deep material interests."

> The developed [regions], for example, think that such solutions can burden them with new obligations to such a degree that they will almost retard their development. Because, judging strictly by the letter of this formulation, tomorrow some other region of the country can be added to the list of underdeveloped just if it falls below the anticipated average of development. And all of that falls on the backs of the development.
>
> The underdeveloped, on the other hand, have their own fears: if it does not say in the plan "in relation to what" the relative differences will be reduced, then they have no guarantees that differences actually will be reduced, despite more rapid development.[108]

The next day the agreement of all delegations was achieved on a text that read

> One of the basic goals of social and economic development in the coming period is the more rapid development of every economically insufficiently developed republic, and of Kosovo most rapidly, than the average development of the country as a whole, for the purpose of reducing relative differences in the level of their development in relation to the level of development of the country as a whole.[109]

This was, in effect, the formulation first introduced by the Federal Executive Council in the Draft. The willingness of the delegations from the developed republics to accept this formulation may have been conditioned by committee acceptance at the same time of an amendment offered by the Croatian delegation at an earlier session.

At its second session the committee had debated "for more than two and a half hours" about the following statement contained in the Draft:

> The Socialist Republics of Bosnia and Hercegovina, Montenegro, and Macedonia, and . . . Kosovo will be considered economically insufficiently developed in the period from 1976 to 1980, and Kosovo will be considered the economically least developed.[110]

The Croatian delegation proposed that:

> after this . . . paragraph a new one be added according to which, by the end of 1977, objective criteria will be established as a systemic solution

[108] Ibid., 16 March 1976.
[109] Ibid., 13 March 1976.
[110] Ibid., 6 March 1976.

for the determination of the level of development of the republics and provinces.[111]

The Croatian delegation also felt that there would be sufficient time to develop "accompanying regulations by which the applications of these criteria would be regulated" by the end of 1980. The delegations from Montenegro and Macedonia opposed the establishment of such criteria at the present time. After further discussion and consultations in the delegations, the Croatian proposal was "accepted in principle" at the fourth session of the committee. The representative of the FEC however, argued for, and won, an additional year for the development of the criteria, until the end of 1978.[112]

Acceptance of the Croatian proposal meant that the developed republics could now look forward to establishing not only an objective measure of the level of development of all regions but also a concrete end, however far in the future, to preferred treatment for these regions. This raised hope of an end to what they view as burdensome transfers of resources from their own economies to those of the underdeveloped regions. It is not surprising, therefore, that agreement on this proposal among all the regional delegations was achieved simultaneously with agreement to reduce relative differences in the levels of regional development in relation to the average level of development of the country as a whole.[113] Simultaneous agreement on these two formulas reflects a trade of interests. In this case, however, the developed republics won the promise of future concessions in return for concrete concessions in the present. The conclusion of this agreement suggests the acceptance of a principle of reciprocity among the regional representatives participating in the decision-making process, and a relatively high level of mutual trust in their commitment to adhere to it, two conditions essential for successful decision making based on negotiation and consensus. But the completion of this agreement has proven very difficult to achieve.

The successful resolution of such conflicts also clearly depends on the ability and willingness of regional representatives to negotiate a compromise. The ability of the delegations in the Chamber of Republics and Provinces to negotiate compromises is enhanced appreciably when they receive broad authorizations from their republican and provincial assemblies to act on their behalf. Such authorization permits a delegation to approve a final Draft without resubmitting it to the regional assembly for approval following conclusion of the process of harmonization. Such authorization enables delegations to respond to developments in committees and for chairmen of delegations to negotiate in meetings with the president of the Chamber and other authori-

[111] Ibid.
[112] Ibid., 11 March 1976.
[113] Ibid., 13 March 1976.

tative, smaller groups. During the first two years of Chamber activity, such authorization was granted in a very high proportion of the cases to which it was applicable.[114] Even more important than this, however, is the simple willingness of the delegations to compromise.

In its June 1976 report, the staff of the Chamber emphasized that the behavior of regional representatives engaged in the task of reconciling conflicting regional interests was an important factor contributing to their success. They praised the fact that "an atmosphere of mutual understanding dominated in the work of the committees on the harmonization of positions" and that "there was no instance in which, instead of applying the method of argumentation to positions with which the delegations do not agree, the method of derogation [kvalifikacije] was applied."[115] In 1978, the president of the Chamber agreed that the successful resolution of interregional conflicts up to then could be attributed to "the presence of comradeship in interpersonal relations, full understanding for the positions of others, as well as a creative approach to the discovery of mutually acceptable solutions." More recently, a Yugoslav analysis of decision making in the Assembly observed that the successful resolution of such conflicts requires "patience, mutual understanding, toleration, and readiness to come to common positions."[116]

When a delegation is either unwilling or, because of narrowly defined instructions from its home assembly, unable to negotiate, this pattern cannot work. Nor does conflict resolution by resort to smaller, more authoritative decision-making bodies work under such conditions. By 9 July 1975, for example, almost all work in the Chamber on the development of the long-range plan for the development of Yugoslavia until 1985 had been completed, except for continuing disagreement over a proposal by the delegation from Kosovo. That delegation sought to include the following provision in the plan:

> Considering the pronounced lagging-behind [zaostajanje] in general and joint expenditures, . . . Kosovo will in this period be assured of the average of per capita general and joint expenditures on the level of the insufficiently-developed republics, and will be assigned supplementary funds for the development of social services.[117]

In response to the impasse over this proposal, a meeting was convened between the president of the Chamber, the president of the Assembly, representatives of the FEC, the chairmen of the delegations, and the chairmen of the committees in which harmonization on the plan was being carried out. This group was unable to reconcile the positions of the delegations. It could agree only

[114] "Neka zapažanja," p. 9n.
[115] Ibid., p. 13.
[116] Perović, "Skupština i političko odlučivanja," p. 226.
[117] "Rad Veća republika i pokrajina," p. 31.

that all delegations and the presidents of the regional assemblies would be informed about the proposal of the delegation from Kosovo and that "before the next meeting of the Committee for the social plan and development policy further efforts be made in the direction of finding a solution which would be acceptable to all delegations." It instructed the FEC to formulate a position on the proposal and to present it at the next meeting of that committee.[118]

Despite the efforts of the FEC to draft an acceptable counterproposal, the committee was again unable to reconcile the positions of the republics and provinces during two days of meetings on July 14 and 15. Consequently, "further consultation and intensive work" was carried out "in the framework of the Federal Executive Council." After two days, a new formulation of the proposal, devised by the Council, was approved by the delegations of all the regions. The compromise formulation read:

> By these measures and by additional stimulative measures which will be established by agreements between the republics and autonomous provinces, having in view the lagging-behind of . . . Kosovo in economic development and in the development of social services, it is necessary to create conditions for the most rapid development of . . . Kosovo, by which differences in the level of economic development will be reduced, for the paying off of general and joint expenditures in . . . Kosovo in relation to the level of these expenditures in the economically least developed republic, and for [the provision of] assigned supplementary funds for the development of social activities.[119]

Leaders of the Chamber also failed to resolve certain conflicts in the last stages of harmonization on the social plan for 1976. In addition to the conflicts between the developed and underdeveloped regions over the allocation of investment credits obtained through international loans and over the determination of domestic investment strategies, "the policy of the more rapid development of the insufficiently developed areas, and especially of Kosovo was of special concern to all."[120] One Yugoslav analyst suggested that the harmonization of positions on this policy was made more difficult because "one delegation had an imperative mandate."[121] However, such a mandate may not have existed at all. It may simply have been the case that one delegation—most likely the delegation from Kosovo—insisted on its own position and was reluctant to compromise on it. Such behavior by itself would have undermined the ability of the Assembly leadership to resolve such a conflict.

---

[118] Ibid., pp. 31-32.
[119] Ibid., p. 34.
[120] *Politika* (Belgrade), 26 December 1975.
[121] Ibid., 20 February 1976.

In fact, both the president of the Chamber, meeting with the chairmen of both the delegations and the committees, and the Committee for the Social Plan and Development Policy, meeting in an expanded session, were unable to resolve the conflict. As a result, the entire Chamber adjourned for one day to allow all the delegations to consult with their home assemblies. Because time was running out—it was already December 18—the leadership of the Chamber called for the committees to reconvene on Saturday, an exceptional practice.[122] At the same time, the Federal Executive Council convened to discuss the remaining conflicts and to "attempt to contribute to the bringing together and reconciliation of the positions of all participants."[123] After the committees of the Chamber had reconvened for morning sessions on Saturday, their chairmen met with the president of the Assembly, and the president, vice-presidents, and several other members of the Federal Executive Council to negotiate a solution to the remaining issues. Following this meeting, "full agreement" was achieved on all remaining issues during the afternoon sessions of the committees.[124]

These episodes suggest that, despite the fact that it is organizationally divided along republican and provincial lines, the Federal Executive Council and its organs and organizations are less subject to disability as the result of interregional conflicts of interest than either the smaller, leadership group of the Chamber of Republics and Provinces or the leadership of the Assembly as a whole. The Council, therefore, serves as a powerful integrative and conflict-resolving institution. Much of this power derives from its near-monopoly over the scientific, technical, and bureaucratic resources of the state and over the agenda of federal decision making. The former enables the Council to amass an overwhelming amount of evidence and material in support of its position on any given issue, and the latter permits it to avoid confronting issues with which it is unwilling or unable to deal. But much of this power derives from the ability of the Federal Executive Council to formulate compromise solutions to interregional conflicts—both in the early stages of the federal decision-making process when they are confined to the federal councils, interrepublican committees, and permanent commissions under its control, and in the later stages of that process in the Federal Assembly.

Central Leadership and the Resolution of Interregional Conflict

The Federal Executive Council's actions in the Chamber of Republics and Provinces reflect a relatively simple strategy for the regulation of interregional

[122] Ibid., 19 December 1976.
[123] Ibid., 20 December 1976.
[124] Ibid., 21 December 1976

conflict. At each stage of the decision-making process, the Council attempts to preserve its own position against amendment by any regional interest. It does so both by attacking the substance, or merits, of such amendments and by enlisting the support of other regions against them. When amendments become necessary, it attempts to minimize their substance by developing a less specific and more complicated formulation of the statement in contention. The purpose of this appears to be to satisfy both the region(s) pressing for the amendment and the region(s) opposed to it. Alternatively, the Council attempts to link solutions to several issues to form a package deal in which concessions to one group of regions is balanced by concessions to another. This latter strategy is facilitated by the fact that conflicts in the Chamber usually find the regions divided into two distinct groups: the developed and the underdeveloped.

Although the Council's ability to develop such solutions depends in large part on the willingness of regional representatives to compromise, that willingness is likely to increase with the transfer of interregional conflicts from the Assembly and its committees to the Federal Executive Council itself for resolution. This effectively returns them to the arenas in which agreement on the draft proposals first was reached; it brings them under the more direct and powerful influence of the central party leadership and the regional political leaderships, both of whom are able to exert enormous political pressure on delegates to the Chamber; and it returns negotiations to the protective cloak of secrecy. The discussions that take place during these negotiations are neither reported in the press nor recorded in any detail in the internal reports of the Chamber on its own work, and the complicated and diffuse formulations produced by them are not subjected to critical public evaluation by regional representatives. Moreover, while the leadership of the Chamber of Republics and Provinces cannot impose a solution in the face of continuing conflict, the Federal Executive Council can.

When no agreement can be reached on a measure requiring the agreement of all the regions, article 301 of the constitution empowers the FEC to seek its adoption as a "temporary measure" if:

> it is indispensable to prevent or eliminate major disruptions on the market, or . . . nonsettlement of these questions might result in serious harm for the social community, might endanger national defence interests, or might result in unequal economic relations between the Republics and the Autonomous Provinces, or if . . . this would render impossible the fulfilment [sic] of obligations towards insufficiently developed Republics and Autonomous Provinces, or the fulfilment [sic] of the commitments of the Socialist Federal Republic of Yugoslavia towards [sic] other countries and international organizations.

If the Presidency determines that the measure meets these criteria, the Council may submit it to the full Chamber of Republics and Provinces for a vote. Passage requires a two-thirds majority of all delegates. If the measure receives a less than two-thirds majority, article 302 of the constitution empowers the Presidency to proclaim the measure in the form passed by that majority. According to article 303, a "temporary measure" remains valid for one year—or until some form of the measure is adopted with the agreement of the regions—and may be renewed by the same procedure for an additional year.

The procedure for adoption of a temporary measure does not allow any single republic or province a veto power over the decision-making process. A two-thirds majority can be achieved even over the unified opposition of delegates from two republics, or one republic and both provinces. Moreover, voting by individual *delegate* rather than by *delegation* emphasizes the delegates' constitutional responsibility to act "in conformity with the common and general social interests and needs." Under these conditions, the declaration by the Presidency and the Federal Executive Council that the measure in question is "indispensable," and the political pressure that would be brought to bear by the central party leadership supporting these bodies, would make it highly unlikely that regional resistance could be maintained in any but the most extreme of circumstances. For a recalcitrant regional leadership, the procedure for adoption of a "temporary measure" raises the specter of a formulation to which it is opposed being adopted without any concessionary amendment or compensatory concession on another issue. Consequently, regional leaderships are more likely to seek a negotiated compromise solution to such conflicts than to allow the passage of a temporary measure.

After two years of operation during which no such measure had been necessary, the leadership of the Chamber of Republics and Provinces optimistically argued that "if the need arises for the application of this procedure, it need not be avoided at any price, because this institution, too, is the result of mutual agreement." But it tempered that optimism with the warning that "in each concrete situation it would be very well to determine political and economic repercussions it might have." For it recognized that "frequent resort to this measure surely would be a sign that much deeper issues were involved than those for which temporary measures must be taken, and which would require a different approach to these questions and a different type of political discussion about their causes."[125]

Not until more than five years after the establishment of the new constitutional order, however, did the regional leaderships find themselves deadlocked over federal policy and the Federal Executive Council call for passage of a "temporary measure." Beginning in early 1979, the condition of the

[125] "Neka zapažanja," pp. 18-19.

domestic economy became the object of increasing political concern. In August 1979, in reaction to escalating inflation, mounting trade and balance of payments deficits, and increasing foreign indebtedness, the Council adopted a set of policies designed to achieve the "stabilization" of the economy.[126] Two major objectives of these policies were to reduce the trade and balance of payments deficits and the rate of inflation. By late 1979, however, the situation had become serious enough to prompt the central party leadership to call for even stricter measures. In November, the Presidium adopted a set of "conclusions" calling for what it characterized as "self-denial of excessive expenditures" by self-managing enterprises. In fact, however, it was calling for the imposition by the FEC of measures putting an end to the freedom of enterprises to undertake investments without sufficient capital to cover them, so as to prevent further overindebtedness; putting an end to their power to spend what the leadership called "social resources" for entertainment, excessive business trips, and activities designed only to improve their image; and, most important, limiting the power of self-management bodies to increase personal incomes at a rate greater than the increase in productivity.[127] In order to implement such measures, the Federal Executive Council was compelled to revise the draft of the social plan for 1980 that had been finished in October. This, in turn, required a series of consultations between the Council and the regional executive councils over the preparation of new, more restrictive planning guidelines and between delegations in the Chamber of Republics and Provinces and their respective regional assemblies and leaderships.[128] The policy-making process in the federation became, in the aftermath of these conclusions, even more concentrated in the Council and its working bodies.[129]

Despite the heightened emphasis by both the central party leadership and the Federal Executive Council on the need for collaborative efforts to "stabilize" the economy, the ensuing interregional negotiations over the social plan for 1980 continued to be characterized by open conflict and intense negotiation for regional economic advantage on such issues as the substitution of domestic products for imports, the limitation of personal income, and the reduction of the balance of payments deficit. The latter issue caused particularly sharp conflict. As part of its package of revisions in the proposed social plan for 1980, the Federal Executive Council proposed that the deficit for 1980 be reduced from $2.5 to $2 billion. The Slovenian delegation in the Chamber of Republics and Provinces disputed the way in which the $500-million reduction was distributed among the regions. The Croatian delegation

---

[126] *NIN*, 26 August 1979.

[127] *Politika* (Belgrade), 24 November 1979.

[128] Ibid., 12 and 14 December 1979. The consultations carried out in Serbia are reported in ibid., 18 December 1979.

[129] Ibid., 24 December 1979.

opposed the establishment of a specific dollar figure for the reduction and proposed instead that "in 1980 it not be greater than in this year, and that efforts be made to reduce it as much as possible."[130] But this proposal was too general for the FEC to accept. The difficulty of negotiating agreement on this issue forced the Chamber's Committee for foreign economic relations to acknowledge that agreement seemed impossible to achieve in time to permit passage of the plan for 1980. The Federal Executive Council therefore decided late in December to begin the process of proposing a temporary measure to limit the deficit for 1980. Unofficially, all agreed that negotiations would resume again in January.[131] Final agreement on a "permanent" solution was not reached, however, until August.

The inability of the Federal Executive Council to forge interregional agreement on the balance of payments suggested that regional leaderships under the pressure of an increasingly difficult economic situation were once again beginning to defend their respective interests even at the cost of central policy. But with Tito's hospitalization and surgery in January 1980 and the ensuing rapid deterioration in his health, the need to resolve such interregional conflicts before they reached the stage necessitating another temporary measure was clear. The determination of the communist political leadership to do so was demonstrated by the long and difficult negotiations that took place during the months of Tito's illness over aid to Montenegro for reconstruction in the aftermath of the April 1979 earthquake which devastated that republic.[132]

During four months of intense negotiation in the Chamber of Republics and Provinces, representatives of the Federal Executive Council mediated between Montenegro on the one hand and all the other regions on the other. The fundamental issue, of course, concerned the total amount of aid. But the debate over otherwise narrowly economic issues was couched in terms of the "meaning of solidarity," which tended to heighten the political sensitivity of the negotiations. The other regions questioned the validity of the method by which damage in Montenegro had been assessed, and whether they were obliged to provide enough aid to repair all damage or to provide aid based on some indicator of their ability to pay. They also disputed whether they were obligated to provide outright grants of assistance or simply to provide credits to finance reconstruction, and the rate at which they would be required to provide whatever aid was finally decided on. The resistance of the other regions to provide the level of assistance first proposed by the Federal Executive Council (70.6 billion dinars) was so strong that they refused even to begin providing interim assistance until final agreement was reached. The

130 Ibid., 22 December 1979.

131 Ibid., 27 December 1979. See also *NIN*, 13 January 1980.

132 The following account is based on *Politika* reports of 6 and 23 February and 6, 8, 14, 20, 21, and 27 March 1980.

Council gradually lowered the level of proposed assistance, and by early March it was down to 55 billion dinars. Yet resistance was still strong enough to compel the Council to turn to the Presidency for assistance. By informing the Presidency of the course of negotiations up to then, the Council was raising the possibility of another resort to a temporary measure, or even the possibility that a solution might be imposed by the party leadership in order to avoid such a measure.[133] At this point, then, the other regions began to make some minor concessions to Montenegrin interests.

At the same time, the president of the Montenegrin Assembly and the republican council for restoration and construction publicly pointed out the substantial concessions to which his republic had already agreed. He denied that there was any question about the method of estimating the damages, and pointed out that some damages included in calculations for other such disasters were not included, and that the costs of those that were included were not even calculated at replacement cost. He emphasized that his republic already had made other concessions in the course of calculating damages by agreeing to lower levels of aid to reconstruct nonproductive infrastructure. By mid-March, the Montenegrin delegation had agreed to the Federal Executive Council's proposal of 55 billion dinars of aid, but insisted on three additional conditions: that foreign credits be secured in addition, that the rate of investment in restoration be accelerated, and that the emphasis on integration ("association") of Montenegrin and other labor and resources be strengthened. Significantly, however, the delegation also conceded that it would not hold up agreement any further because this would have "negative consequences for interrepublican relations" and would "look bad abroad."

Under the continued pressure of the FEC's appeal to the Presidency, the possibility of direct intervention by the party leadership, and the Montenegrin leadership's public statement, the other regions accepted Montenegro's conditions. But the final aid figure agreed to by all the regions was only 53.6 billion dinars. Despite the fact that, following adoption of the law on aid to Montenegro, the chairman of the Montenegrin delegation made a point of noting publicly that "the principle of solidarity had received full support and affirmation," Yugoslav press accounts suggest that these negotiations generated enormous interregional tensions and sorely tested the negotiating skills of the Federal Executive Council.

Those skills were tested further in the months following the death of President Tito in May 1980. In June, the question of establishing "objective criteria" for measuring the level of development of the regions was raised once again by the Slovenian party president, who insisted that "Slovenia

---

[133] The threat of direct intervention by the party leadership itself was reported much later by the chairman of the Slovenian delegation in an interview in *NIN*, 2 November 1980.

cannot give more for the advancement of the less-developed than it has given up to now'' and that ''therefore, the issue is raised . . . of which republic should lose the status of less-developed.'' He pointed out that this issue had been raised four years earlier during negotiations over the 1976-1980 plan, when it was agreed to develop objective indicators of the level of development by 1978 in time to apply them to the plan for 1981-1985.[134] Indeed, their preparation had begun in economic institutes in each of the regions immediately following adoption of the 1976-1980 plan. But the proposals presented to the Chamber's Committee for Development of the Insufficiently Developed in September 1978 revealed that little progress had been achieved even after more than two years. Although each region acknowledged that Kosovo was the least developed of all, there was no agreement on the relative statuses of the others. Each institute had simply prepared a proposal that essentially advanced the interests of its own region.[135] Only a few days after the Slovenian party president publicly reopened this issue, however, the Bosnian executive council declared that ''significant progress'' had been achieved on the establishment of ''criteria and indicators for determining the level of economic development of the republics and provinces,'' suggesting that agreement was now imminent. But, at the same time, the Bosnian council pointed out that it remained important ''to secure the reduction of the relative differences in the level of development in relation to the Yugoslav average,'' thereby affirming a negotiating position that had been bitterly disputed by the Slovenian delegation during the earlier negotiations.[136]

On July 1, the Federal Executive Council finally submitted a ''draft decision'' establishing ''objective criteria and indicators for determining the level of economic development'' to the Chamber of Republics and Provinces.[137] On the basis of discussions in the federal (social) councils and in the committees of the Chamber of Republics and Provinces, the FEC proposed three measures of development devised by the Federal Institute for Social Planning: (1) the per capita social product; (2) the level of employment in the social sector as measured by the number of employed per 1,000 population; and (3) the purchase value of active basic resources per capita. An alternative formulation of the second measure was presented in terms of the number of employed per 1,000 employable persons, and an alternative formulation of the third was presented in terms of the employable population. The draft established a range of values for each measure: for per capita social product, 70-75 percent of the national average (*or*, as an alternative, 72-77 percent); for employment in the social sector, 85-90 percent of the national average;

[134] *Politika* (Belgrade), 21 June 1980.
[135] *NIN*, 12 November 1978.
[136] *Politika* (Belgrade), 24 June 1980.
[137] Ibid., 2 July 1980.

and for purchase value per captia, 77-82 percent of the national average (*or*, as an alternative, 80-85 percent). And it proposed that "those republics or provinces that are below the lower boundary of the range on at least two indicators, including per capita social product, will be considered economically insufficiently developed." When such a region reached the lower boundary on two indicators, including per capita social product, "a transitional period will begin, lasting until the upper boundary is reached." The proposal called for the status of each region to be reassessed at the end of each five-year planning period.

Should per capita social product remain below the lower boundary while the two other measures exceed the upper boundaries, the FEC proposed that the transitional period begin if "the capacity of the social economy for expanded reproduction per capita" is below 70 percent of the national average. During a transitional period, there would be "a reduction of the scope of stimulative measures" for the economy of the region concerned. The draft also stipulated that a region would be considered economically *least* developed if it was below 55 percent of the national average on at least 2 of 3 indicators, including per capita social product, and that this would be "taken into account when establishing stimulative measures for the advancement of its development." All data for these measures would be provided by the Federal Institute for Statistics and the Social Accounting Service.

This proposal represented an innovative attempt at resolution of one of the most contentious issues in interregional relations. In deference to the interests of the underdeveloped, it linked each measure of development to the national average and set the minimum value on each one high enough to ensure that they would continue to receive aid. In deference to the interests of the more developed regions, it offered some protection against the perpetuation of underdeveloped status as the result of simple population growth alone. One week later, however, at a joint session of the federal social councils for economic development and economic policy and for questions of social organization, representatives of the republics and provinces and the Federal Executive Council agreed that it would be impossible to reach agreement on the draft in time to avoid delaying passage of the five-year plan for 1981-1985. Consequently, it was agreed to continue the current statuses of Bosnia, Montenegro, and Macedonia as economically insufficiently developed, and of Kosovo as the least developed in the 1981-1985 plan. The FEC was asked to withdraw the "draft decision" from consideration, and to develop a new proposal by the end of 1982.[138] In the interim, however, the issue remains an extremely sore point among representatives of the developed regions, and especially Slovenia.[139]

[138] Ibid., 10 July 1980.
[139] See, for example, the comments of Stane Dolanc in *NIN*, 18 January 1981.

The failure of the FEC to obtain regional agreement on this proposal suggests that, although a strong and capable Council may be a *necessary* condition for the resolution of interregional conflict, it is not by itself *sufficient*. The successful resolution of conflicts over federal policy continues to depend ultimately on their successful resolution inside the party leadership itself. The central party leadership in large part determines the agenda of federal decision making and the broad outlines of federal policy through its programmatic documents and pronouncements. Its influence is reinforced through direct and indirect participation in the early stages of consultations and negotiations in the federal councils and the interrepublican committees, permanent commissions, and Coordinating Commission of the FEC. Representatives of the leading party organs participate in the work of these bodies, and representatives of other organs and organizations often are at the same time members of the party's Central Committee. As a result, unity in the party leadership is likely to be translated into interregional agreement during the preparation of federal policy proposals and later negotiations in the FEC over the details of federal policy. Conversely, however, disagreement within the central party leadership is likely to be reflected in disagreement and even conflict during the preparation and later development of federal policy.

The regional party leaderships and, therefore, the central party organs remained deeply divided over the proposal to establish "objective criteria" for measuring the level of development of the regions when the FEC proposal was submitted to the Chamber of Republics and Provinces. It was, therefore, not difficult to predict that this proposal would not be approved. And it was not surprising that it was, in fact, "killed" by the party-dominated federal councils.

The ability of the FEC to resolve even the most explosive interregional disputes when it does have the backing of the party leadership was demonstrated by the dispute in late 1980 over regional allocation of the country's foreign currency balances for 1980—in effect, the allocation of entitlements to spend hard currency or incur hard currency debts to import goods and materials.[140] This represented a particularly important test of leadership capabilities in the post-Tito period. Only a year earlier, while Tito was still available to provide support and, if need be, pressure for the solution of such conflicts, the FEC proved unable to reconcile conflicting regional demands and was compelled to resort to a temporary measure to resolve an almost identical conflict. Thus, when negotiations in late 1980 over the 1981 balances once again proved contentious, it raised the specter of a second major failure

---

[140] For (circumspect) press accounts of this dispute see *Politika* (Belgrade), 24 and 29 December 1980 and 9, 15, 20, and 21 January 1981; and *NIN* 25 January 1981.

of the system of interregional bargaining and a concomitant jolt to public confidence in the post-Tito leadership.

In order to avoid this, the political leadership of the federation and the regions—including both government and party leaders—agreed not to resort to such a measure and to forge an agreement by the end of January 1981. Several regional party and governmental leaders who participated in these negotiations reported in interviews and discussions conducted both immediately before and immediately after the issue finally had been resolved that a conscious effort was made to avoid any hint of a crisis atmosphere with respect to this issue, and that an *explicit*, if informal, agreement to come to an agreement had been reached "at the highest levels." The conclusion of this agreement involved a trade-off between a recalcitrant regional leadership—in this case the leadership of Serbia—and the FEC leadership on a number of closely related issues, which accommodated not only Serbian reservations but those of other regions as well. Despite continuing unhappiness with the entire system used by the FEC to calculate the balances and to apportion them among the regions, interregional agreement was reached and a decision on the payments and foreign currency balances for 1981 was adopted in late January.

The resolution of this dispute suggests an addition to the basic principle of Yugoslav decision making. While it remains true that "an agreement with which all are unhappy is better than one with which only one or a few are happy," it also appears to be the case that "an agreement with which all are unhappy is better than no agreement at all." More important, however, the resolution of this dispute demonstrates the sensitivity of the present leadership to the potential broader symbolic or psychological meaning of their actions, their intention to limit the negative consequences of conflict, and their ability to come to agreement.

The analysis of interregional negotiation and decision making in the federation presented in this chapter suggests that the Federal Executive Council can ensure the resolution of conflicts over the details of policy and its implementation even when these involve the direct economic interests of the regions, but that it cannot do so without the support of the central party leadership. The Council cannot resolve conflicts over the broad outlines of federal policy. These must be resolved by the party leadership, in advance of negotiations over the details, if they are to be resolved at all. Hence, the formal process of federal decision making that begins with the submission of a draft proposal to the Federal Assembly is unlikely ever to produce interregional agreement when none exists in the party itself. For under such conditions the Federal Executive Council cannot be confident of the support of the coercive political power at the command of the party leadership that is sometimes necessary to resolve even conflict over the details of policy.

The party continues to play an important role in the federal policy process even after the conclusion of interregional agreements and their adoption as federal policy. The successful execution of federal policies—that is, the implementation of interregional agreements—falls in large part on agencies and organizations subordinate to the regional leaderships and outside the direct control of the Federal Executive Council. Although the Council commands several administrative agencies that exercise direct supervisory functions over self-managing organizations and communities in the regions, the FEC is dependent on the regional executive councils and the party for the exercise of power and influence on behalf of federal policies.

The successful regulation of interregional conflict in Yugoslavia therefore has required the central party leadership to define the general direction of social policies, to assist the government in developing concrete programs for carrying them out, and to ensure that individual communists in self-managing organizations, enterprises, and communities exert their influence on behalf of those programs. But can the party continue to carry out these functions in the absence of Tito? His presence ensured that, were interregional negotiations within the party leadership itself to result in deadlock over an issue on which a decision could not be postponed, there was a legitimate and, if need be, authoritarian alternative means of decision making. Moreover, Tito had served as an authoritative spokesman for party policies. His frequent speeches, interviews, and injunctions to action provided important stimuli for the implementation of party policies by individual communists, and even for the establishment of such policies by the party leadership. Even before his death, it was clear that the establishment and, especially, implementation of party policies were difficult tasks. Now, however, there is no "ultimate arbiter" of conflict in the highest leadership of the party, and no unquestionably authoritative spokesman for its policies.

VI. THE PARTY AND THE REGULATION
OF CONFLICT

The ability of the party to provide essential support for the successful operation of the Yugoslav political system has in the past been determined by the ability of the party leadership to agree on policy and ensure that individual communists conform to it. Agreement among the party leadership has been facilitated by a high degree of confidence and mutual trust among its members, by their adherence to a principle of reciprocity in decision making, and by their willingness and ability to reconcile contradictory interests by employing a variety of pragmatic conflict-resolving techniques well-known in the West. These conditions, absent during the years of crisis, were reestablished as the result of the forceful intervention by President Tito to re-create a cohesive party center. Efforts to ensure that individual communists adhered to party policy took the form of direct intervention by Tito and his supporters in the leadership to reestablish "party discipline" in the operation of regional and local party organizations. These efforts culminated at the Tenth Party Congress in 1974, and in the campaign to restore the principles of "democratic centralism" in party life.

In the period following the Tenth Congress, however, there was growing concern among the leadership that continuing emphasis on central power and party discipline would impinge on another, equally important function of the party: to represent, and at the same time reconcile, the particularistic and often contradictory interests inherent in a self-managed society. These concerns became manifest in the Spring of 1977, when the leadership was compelled once again to assess its own performance in preparation for the Eleventh Party Congress, scheduled for the following year. The preliminary results of that assessment and the resulting prescriptions for future action are reflected in Edvard Kardelj's last major work, *The Directions of Development of the Political System of Socialist Self-Management.*[1] They suggest that an important debate had begun over the internal organization and operation of the party itself and over the party's role in society.

This chapter begins with a review of Kardelj's assessment of the conflict-regulating capacity of established decision-making practices and of his rec-

[1] Edvard Kardelj, *Pravci razvoja političkog sistema socijalističkog samoupravljanja* (Beograd: Komunist, 1977).

ommendations for their future development. His assessment provides important insights into the conditions for continuing successful operation of the existing system. It is not surprising that Kardelj, a key figure in the leadership until his death early in 1979, ignored the entire question of elite coherence and focused on the relationship between the party and other social forces, and on the implementation of party policies. Nonetheless, inherent in his argument are certain assumptions about the continuing unity of the communist political leadership.

No outside observer of Yugoslav affairs, however, can assume that that leadership will be able to sustain the agreement and cooperative behavior characteristic of the period since 1974. Indeed, the central argument of Kardelj's work was the object of some contention and was only partially adopted at the Eleventh Congress. Changes in the composition, organization, and operation of the central party organs and in the party statutes carried out at that Congress, in the years since, and especially following the death of President Tito in May 1980, as well as the dispute surrounding the constitutional reform undertaken at Tito's initiative and completed a year after his death, all suggest continuing tension in that leadership between cohesive and divisive forces. Moreover, social, economic, and political conditions confront the post-Tito leadership with a number of particularly difficult and inevitably divisive policy choices.

This chapter, therefore, also reviews the changes that have taken place in the party leadership since 1974, and especially since the death of Tito, and assesses their implications for the ability of that leadership and the party as a whole to continue to function as an integrative force in Yugoslav society.

Conflict Regulation and the Pluralism of Self-Managing Interests

The political analysis contained in Kardelj's *The Directions of Development* represented an important turning point in post-crisis Yugoslav politics. It was first presented to the full central party leadership at a meeting of the Presidium in June 1977, but appears to have been the subject of discussion among members of the leadership as early as January of that year. And, although the Presidium accepted it as "the basis for the activity of the League of Communists of Yugoslavia in preparations for the Eleventh Congress,"[2] an unusual delay between the June meeting and publication of the full text suggests that it continued to be the topic of discussion—and controversy—for some time afterward.[3] Indeed, the published text contains careful quali-

[2] Ibid., p. 7.

[3] Dennison Rusinow, "Yugoslav Domestic Developments," paper presented at conference on Yugoslavia: Accomplishments and Problems, Woodrow Wilson Center, Washington, D.C., 16 October 1977, p. 4.

fications of several of the more provocative positions presented to the Presidium. Nevertheless, the unusually large size of the edition suggests that substantial agreement on it had been reached and that the text was intended to figure prominently at the upcoming Eleventh Congress.

In this work, Kardelj departs from prevailing practice and suggests that Yugoslav politics will continue to be characterized by conflict because of what he calls "the pluralism of self-managing interests."[4] This pluralism consists of "the multitude of interests in society that arise out of class, economic, political, social, and other conditions of life, work, and the activity of people." "Differences and conflicts" among these interests, Kardelj explains:

> concern issues such as the further development of socialist society; the resolution of current economic, social, cultural, and other social problems; the direction and tempo of the further development of socio-economic, political, and other relations; ideological and political differences that appear in connection with the treatment of concrete questions, etc.[5]

Kardelj goes to great lengths to differentiate the "pluralism of self-managing interests" from the pluralism of "bourgeois democracy." Indeed, one-fourth of the text of *The Directions of Development* is an attack on "bourgeois democracy," "parliamentarism," and the Western notion of "pluralism." Nonetheless, he shares with Western pluralists certain basic assumptions about the nature, distribution, and organization of interests, the role of conflict, and the character of decision making in society.

Like Western pluralists, he suggests that each individual has several interests at any given moment and that he shares each of these interests with others in society, regardless of whether these interests are organized or only latent.[6] Just as Western theorists suggest that pluralism consists of the interaction between groups freely pursuing their own particular, and often conflicting, interests, Kardelj suggests that "self-managing democracy is based on the free emergence of these interests . . . and on the self-managing democratic harmonization of all the interests of these communities." The interest pluralism characteristic of self-managing democracy is a necessary consequence of self-management. "Since only that working man who is in a position not only to express his interests independently and democratically but also to decide about them can be a self-manager," Kardelj reasons, "the very essence of self-management itself will impose the principle of interest pluralism as the basis for the system of self-managing democracy of a socialist

[4] Kardelj, *Pravci razvoja*, p. 85.
[5] Ibid., p. 86.
[6] Ibid., p. 92.

society." "Every other political system," he asserts, "would be in fact a negation of self-management itself."[7]

Kardelj suggests that the pluralism of interests characteristic of a self-managing democracy provides the basis for "decision making by the majority in society." That majority, he argues, is established "through conflict, compromise, and agreement" among the "multitude" of interests at various levels of decision making in society. The composition of that majority changes with respect to each specific issue.[8]

These views represent a marked departure from the positions advanced by Tito and his supporters in the central party leadership, including Kardelj himself, in the period since 1971. As Dennison Rusinow has suggested, "a positive evaluation of any kind of 'pluralism' was explicitly and repeatedly criticized by Tito and others during the retreat to firmer party control after 1971."[9] Yet, in *The Directions of Development* Kardelj presents an interpretation of the bases of the political system that not only departs from the prevailing post-1971 interpretation of which he himself was a major architect and supporter but that returns in many respects to views that prevailed during the period 1966-1969. In a sense, it represents a return to positions advanced by Jovan Djordjević in 1971 that were rejected during preparation of the constitutional reforms. Indeed, Kardelj even suggests that

> self-managing democracy is not a system based on ideal harmony, but on the contrary, on the struggle of opinions and on the criticism of practice, and frequently even on the direct confrontation of partial interests, where decisions must be taken by a majority of votes.[10]

Such principles appear to undermine the continuing operation of the system based on consensual decision making among representatives of stable national-territorial blocs that had evolved over the past ten years. Yet, paradoxically, Kardelj insists on an even wider application of existing decision-making principles and practices as a means of controlling conflict.

In the section of *The Directions of Development* devoted to an assessment of the operation of the political system in the period since the Tenth Congress in 1974, Kardelj attaches considerable importance to the role of "social councils" (*društveni saveti*) as institutions for the resolution of political conflicts. No political institution or advisory body functioning during that period was known formally as a "social council." However, his description of the organization and operation of these councils[11] leaves no doubt that he has in mind the federal councils (*savezni saveti*) described earlier.

[7] Ibid., pp. 92, 93.
[8] Ibid., pp. 93, 176-77.
[9] Rusinow, "Yugoslav Domestic Developments," p. 3.
[10] Kardelj, *Pravci razvoja*, p. 95.
[11] Ibid., p. 166.

Kardelj suggests that in recent years "social councils" had provided institutional forums for the expression—and eventual reconciliation—of conflicting views. The success of these councils in bringing about compromises, he argues, indicates that the organizational and procedural principles underlying them ought to be applied to a wider range of decision-making institutions.[12] He emphasizes, however, that "the most important role" of such councils is as arenas for conflict resolution in socio-political communities, particularly the federation.[13]

Kardelj cautions that "in certain circumstances" excessive consultation might "directly damage the effectiveness of decision making on the level of the federation." He reports that at the federal level there had been "a considerable tendency to expand the circle of questions about which . . . the republics and provinces must give their agreement before decisions are taken."

> Such a tendency has led to the situation that consultations about certain questions in the competence of federal organs now have been transformed, in fact, into negotiations of the type . . . in which the absence of agreement of one republic or province makes impossible the establishment of a proposal for a particular decision.[14]

These observations undoubtedly reflect the developments reported in the preceding chapter concerning decision making in the Federal Chamber of the SFRY Assembly. But he nonetheless asserts that increasing the number and competence of social councils on the federal level would contribute positively to decision making. "Many conflicts," he argues, have occurred because governmental organs "make decisions without sufficient prior consultations or without sufficiently taking into account certain interests."[15] The operation of such social councils, Kardelj suggests, would ensure that "the cooperation and coordination of all those social factors that must make their final decision in the framework of delegate assemblies . . . will already be secured during the preparation of proposals."[16]

The study of decision making in the federation presented in the previous chapter suggests that prior consultation among "interested factors" had already become the dominant principle of decision making by the time Kardelj drafted his theses. In fact, legislation calling for the establishment of such councils in the federal administrative bureaucracies already had been introduced in the Federal Assembly at the time Kardelj was writing, and was adopted by the Assembly in July 1979.[17] The formal extension of these

[12] Ibid., pp. 167-69.
[13] Ibid., p. 170.
[14] Ibid., pp. 170-71.
[15] Ibid., p. 169.
[16] Ibid., p. 167.
[17] Ibid., p. 169, and *Službeni List* 35, No. 34 (20 July 1979): 1069-72.

decision-making principles and practices to other areas would contribute to their further institutionalization. But even Kardelj recognized that their institutionalization would also require adherence to very specific norms of behavior by those who participate in the decision-making process.

The contrast between the operation of the interrepublican committees during the crisis of 1971 and in the period since provided the Yugoslav leadership with strong evidence of the central importance of elite behavior for the success of such councils. Kardelj himself points out that

> We also had various consultative councils earlier. However, most frequently it happened that individuals came to the sessions of such councils and presented their own one-sided view on the problem that was on the agenda, without entering into an effort to discover a common and realistic solution.[18]

The social councils operating in the period since the constitutional reform, he suggested, had been more successful because their work had been characterized by "compromise" and, consequently, the adoption of "united positions." This had been possible, he argues,

> because the people who participate in the work of these councils, in addition to frequent differences in opinions, subjectively were oriented . . . toward the adoption of decisions that are in the given moment real and necessary for society and that have a progressive socialist meaning.[19]

This suggests a conclusion which Kardelj left unstated in the text: If the creation of social councils in additional areas of decision making is to contribute to the regulation of political conflict, those who participate in them must be committed *in advance* to the discovery of solutions to such conflicts. In the absence of a prior commitment to the resolution of interbloc conflicts among those who participate in them, institutions based on organizational and procedural principles of consensual decision making are likely to become arenas for interbloc deadlock rather than conflict regulation.

Kardelj's insistence on the pluralism of self-managing interests, on the resolution of conflicts among them by majority rule, and on the changing composition of such majorities is best understood in terms of the findings presented in the preceding chapter. The study of federal decision making presented there concluded that the Federal Executive Council is able to reconcile conflicts between the regions by providing institutional channels for the expression of interests that cut across the regional blocs and by counterposing them to those of the regions. The proposition that cross-cutting cleav-

---

[18] Kardelj, *Pravci razvoja*, p. 167.
[19] Ibid., p. 166.

ages tend to moderate conflicts between groups is, of course, the central thesis of the Western pluralist literature. Thus, emphasis on the existence of interests and cleavages other than the national-territorial ones that presently dominate the system and the provision for their direct participation in federal (social) councils suggests a conscious concern on the part of the Yugoslav leadership to moderate conflict between the national-territorial blocs.

However, unlike Western pluralists, Kardelj does not argue that the general social interest is defined by the accumulated interactions of particular or "partial" interests. While he acknowledges that "it frequently is necessary to arrive at . . . the common social interest by means of the confrontation and selection of partial interests," he argues instead:

> when we talk about the fact that the system of self-managing democracy is based on the interest pluralism of self-managing subjects we are not then thinking only of partial interests (for example, the interests of or- ganizations of associated labor or organized self-managing interest com- munities and other self-managing subjects or state organs), but also of the common social interests that must be the starting point for the de- termination of the strategy, directions, and method of the further eco- nomic, social, political, and cultural development of society as a whole. *Because a collection of partial interests does not in any way make up the common social interest.*[20]

The common social interest, he insists, is determined in a socialist self- managing society by "subjective socialist forces," that is, by the League of Communists acting together with other socio-political organizations.[21] It is on precisely this point, the role of the party in society, that *The Directions of Development* represented not a deviation from the prevailing views of the post-1971 period, but their continuation and reinforcement.

The Role of the Party in the Pluralism of Self-Managing Interests

Kardelj suggests that the pluralism of self-managing interests compels the party to play an active role in the system of social self-management. Decision making in self-managing organizations must be

> open to the influence and cooperation of all those social forces that are able to bring elements of wider social perspectives into "partial" self- managing decision making, and in that way support the self-managing

[20] Ibid. (emphasis added).
[21] Ibid., p. 96.

decision making of the worker *when he himself is not able to take such a perspective.*[22]

If the party and the other "subjective socialist forces of society" were not to participate actively in these processes and in the wider delegate system of which they are a part, he argues,

> natural forces [*stihija*] . . . would lead us . . . into difficult circumstances, and even to instances [in which] forces hostile to socialist self-management achieve positions in the delegate system. . . . The organized forces of socialist consciousness, therefore, must be the deciding factor of the consciousness of the delegate system.[23]

In short, the party must control the definition of particularistic interests in Yugoslavia.

Kardelj notes that there are those in the party who continue to view the League as a kind of "commanding force" outside or above the system of self-management, and to view other socio-political organizations, self-management institutions, and social organizations as "transmission belts of the League." But, if the League is to continue "to influence decisively the development of society," he argues, "it is essential that the method of its activity be adapted to the changes that have arisen in our society." The party must act as "an internal force of the self-managing and delegate system." It must "struggle for the affirmation of its policy and its positions together with self-managers and all socialist forces in a responsible democratic struggle of opinions and free presentation of alternatives."[24]

The ability of the party to do this, Kardelj concedes, depends on the willingness and ability of "individual communists in various self-managing and delegate bodies" to advance its policies and positions during "the democratic preparation of decisions by the delegations and delegate bodies" of which they are members.[25] To ensure this, the party must continue its policies aimed at strengthening the discipline and coherence of its members. Indeed, Kardelj's description of the role of party members echoes themes characteristic of the campaign to strengthen democratic centralism developed during the period following the Tenth Congress.

In January 1975 the Sarajevo city conference of the League of Communists of Bosnia and Hercegovina and the Marxist Center of its Central Committee had organized a conference devoted to the examination of democratic cen-

---

[22] Ibid., p. 24 (emphasis added).
[23] Ibid., pp. 148-49.
[24] Ibid., pp. 179-84.
[25] Ibid., p. 181.

tralism in theory and in the practice of the League.[26] The conference was attended by political and legal scholars from Bosnia, Croatia, and Serbia; party workers from industrial and other self-managing enterprises and local territorial party organizations; representatives of the Bosnian party's Central Committee and Presidium, the party organization in the army, and the staff of the central party Presidium; and by party ideological workers from Bosnia, Vojvodina, and Macedonia. Several of the papers delivered by these participants were devoted to defining the "practical-political" role of individual communists in self-managing institutions and organizations under conditions of the renewed emphasis on democratic centralism. While acknowledging and affirming the "democratic" character of intraparty discussions, these papers placed greater emphasis on the element of "centralism" in "democratic centralism." In some respects, the positions developed in them anticipated those advanced two and one-half years later in *The Directions of Development*.

These papers pointed out that individual communists were required to participate in the decision-making processes of self-managing institutions and organizations from the perspective of the working class as a whole. In the words of one conference participant,

> communists . . . cannot be "advocates of partial interests," but must articulate existing individual and group interests . . . so that each individual and group interest is brought to the level of the common [interest]; . . . so that these interests are integrated into the dominating interest of the working class as a whole. . . .

Communists will be able to do this only when the principles of democratic centralism are observed. For democratic centralism ensures "*the exclusion of potential possible role conflict in the activity of individual communists, organizations, and leaderships.*" Such role conflict, he pointed out:

> arises precisely in situations when communists, organizations, or leaderships at a concrete level of decision making find themselves faced with two forms of the manifestation of interest. One form . . . can be the interest of an individual branch, grouping, work organization, or some other interest structure such as a republic, commune, or province, and another [can be] the common interest—the interest of the entire movement.

He also suggested that, when the principle of democratic centralism is "applied faithfully," that is, when "not one communist, organization, or leadership can act in decision-making institutions . . . outside [the bounds of]

---

[26] Atif Purivatra, ed., *Demokratski centralizam u teoriji i praksi SKJ* (Sarajevo: Studijski centar Gradske konferencije SKBiH, 1975).

decisions adopted in the League of Communists of Yugoslavia," such role conflict will be resolved in favor of the common interest.[27] In other words, only the enforcement of strong party discipline will ensure that individual communists perform an integrative role in society by advancing everywhere and in all institutions the common interest of the working class as defined by the party.[28]

There are few substantive differences between this definition and Kardelj's later definition of the role of the individual communist in the pluralism of self-managing interests. Yet the different political contexts of the two definitions distinguish them sharply. The "practical-political" role of the communist was defined in the context of a campaign to reassert both central authority within the party and the authority of the party as a whole in society. Within a month of the conference, for example, the six individuals who had been appointed secretaries of the central Presidium at the Tenth Congress but had not been elected to membership in the Presidium itself were elevated to Presidium membership (along with three additional persons, thereby preserving the balance among regional and military organizations).[29] This action strengthened their authority in the party and thereby strengthened the central leadership they served. Consequently, that definition appears as a prescription for the subjection of self-managing institutions to the guidance of party activists.

Kardelj's definition, in contrast, is presented in the context of a work that represents a dramatic break from that campaign. Indeed, one of the most striking passages in *The Directions of Development* concerns precisely the relationship between the party as a whole and society. In it, Kardelj affirms that the party "must be consistent and stubborn in the struggle against the real enemies of socialism and socialist self-management," but then goes on to suggest that:

> it also must be prepared for retreats and compromises when the conflict of interests within self-managing democracy is concerned, or when the lack of social consciousness of the working masses is concerned. The League of Communists must be persistent in its ideological and political orientation and in the struggle for the influence of this orientation on self-managers and self-managing communities or communities of self-managing interests. But it also must be prepared for correction of its

[27] Dragomir Drašković, "Integrativna funkcija demokratskog centralizma i avangardno delovanje SK u odnosima udruženog rada," ibid., pp. 58-59 (emphasis in original).

[28] Cf. Nijaz Mesihović, "Savez komunista, integrisane cjeline i demokratski centralizam," ibid., pp. 161-80; and Milorad Muratović, "Idejne i političke komponente demokratskog centralizma," ibid., pp. 193-224.

[29] *Politika* (Belgrade), 21 February 1975.

positions when practice demands them or when the existing social consciousness is not yet prepared to accept them.[30]

In this context, the role he assigns to the individual communist seems significantly less directive, less authoritarian (but not less authoritative) than in the earlier definition.

However, Kardelj's definition shares with the earlier one a common assumption about the internal character of the party itself. His conception of individual communists as exponents of a "common social interest" determined by the party as a whole closely corresponds to the earlier portrayal of individual communists (and party organizations and leaderships, as well) bound by the principles of democratic centralism to articulate the interests of the working class as determined by the party.[31] Both formulations posit the existence of a central party leadership that not only is capable of overcoming the national and regional economic cleavages that divide it, developing a set of positions that provide guidance for individual communists throughout the country and enforcing those positions on them, but also is intent on doing so.

Continuing emphasis on party discipline is an attempt to strengthen the predominance of the leadership over the party masses and to ensure autonomy for the party as a whole by compelling individual party members to be more responsive to the demands of the leadership than to contradictory pressures from the non-party organizations in which they participate. Only then can agreements reached through negotiations at the center be enforced in the regions. Yet individual members of the party are likely to respond with enthusiasm to the demands of the leadership only to the extent those demands serve their more narrow interests. At the same time, however, agreement at the center is likely to be achieved only as long as each of the regional party leaderships and organizations remains relatively autonomous of the particularistic organized interests in its region. In other words, if the party is to provide the cohesive force essential to the continuing regulation of political conflict in Yugoslavia it must at once represent and defend *both* particularistic national, regional, and economic interests *and* the general interest.

Sociological research and events since 1966 have demonstrated only too well the strong influence of particularistic interests on the behavior of individual communists and the unquestioned ability of regional party leaders to represent and defend those interests. Efforts to affirm central authority and

---

[30] Kardelj, *Pravci razvoja*, p. 178.

[31] See, for example, the description of the tasks of basic party organizations in Gojko Stanić, "Unutrašnja organizovanost osnovne organizacije Saveza komunista," in Atif Purivatra, ed., *Metod rada u Savezu komunista Jugoslavije* (Sarajevo: Studijski centar Gradske konferencije SKBiH, 1976), pp. 157-70.

discipline in the party and to improve elite coherence at the center have been aimed at strengthening the party's ability to represent and defend the general interest. But no formula has yet been devised by which to insulate individual communists from their social milieus. Indeed, to so do would be to destroy their effectiveness as proponents of party policies. Moreover, efforts to strengthen the "party center" have continued to be balanced by efforts to preserve the independent power and authority of regional party organizations and to assert the influence of their leaderships over the central party organs. The tensions between central authority and regional autonomy on one hand, and between party discipline and party democracy on the other, are reflected in changes in the organization and operation of the central party organs and in the party statutes carried out at the Eleventh Party Congress in June 1978 and in the period since. These changes have affirmed the leadership's commitment to consensual decision making, but at the same time call into question its ability to ensure its success.

Organizational and Procedural Changes in the Central Party Leadership from the Eleventh Congress to the Death of Tito

The Eleventh Congress of the League of Communists was convened in Belgrade in June 1978, a year after the presentation of Kardelj's theses to the Presidium. Elements of those theses can be detected in the reports of Congress proceedings, and certain of his recommendations are incorporated in the resolutions adopted by the Congress. But the more radical formulations that distinguished *The Directions of Development* from earlier calls for party discipline were in large part abandoned as the result of continuing opposition within the leadership itself to any weakening of the role of the party.[32]

President Tito's opening address to the Congress reflected the fate of Kardelj's theses in the intervening year. In his speech Tito asserted that

> The political system of self-managing democracy ensures that the multitude of differing needs and interests are expressed—both of man as an individual and of his narrow community, and of society as a whole—that are a consequence of the social divisions of labor, of various conditions of the economy, and of other objective circumstances. Simultaneously, that system ensures that all these self-managing interests are harmonized on a general socialist basis.[33]

[32] See, for example, the criticism of Kardelj's work from this perspective in Ivan Perić et al., "Diskusija o studiji Edvarda Kardelja: Pravci razvoja političkog sistema socijalističkog samoupravljanja," *Naše Teme*, 21, 12 (1977), pp. 2603-54.

[33] *Politika* (Belgrade), 21 June 1978.

This formulation conveys the essence of Kardelj's theses but, notably, does not include use of the word "pluralism" to describe the Yugoslav system. Similarly, the new party statute adopted at the Eleventh Congress contains an entirely new section concerning "the role, tasks and method of activity of the League of Communists of Yugoslavia in the system of socialist self-managing democracy" which acknowledges that "within socio-political and social organizations, self-managing organs and the delegate system, individual interests appear and are harmonized with the common interests of associated labor and general social interests,"[34] and obligates individual communists within these institutions to behave in a manner that corresponds precisely to Kardelj's prescriptions. Here, too, however, there is no mention of "pluralism."

The term "self-managing pluralism" does appear once in the congress resolution devoted to the "tasks of the League . . . in the creation and further development of the political system of socialist self-management." It is used there to denote the "full freedom of expression of the daily interests of men at work and in life, and particularly of those organized interests" in self-managing institutions and organizations. Clearly, Kardelj's conception of continuing conflict between opposing interests is inherent in these passages. But there were no direct references at the Congress to Kardelj's work; only a suggestion in the congress resolution that the thirtieth session of the Presidium (at which Kardelj presented *The Directions of Development* . . .) had made an important contribution to defining the "tasks of the League" in the future.[35]

The virtual disappearance of the term "pluralism" from official pronouncements reflects the general strategy that the leadership has been pursuing since 1972: conscious de-emphasis of the conflictual nature of politics in Yugoslavia accompanied by emphasis on the consensual bases of decision making. The leadership may have determined that too great an emphasis on the multitude of conflicting interests among self-managing organizations, and especially on ever-changing majorities of those interests, posed a potential threat to the stability of the established system of political decision making based on negotiations between representatives of the national-territorial blocs. While the success of such negotiations may depend in large part on the moderating, integrative effects of cross-cutting interests, too great an emphasis on the free expression of conflicting interests might undermine the leadership's ability to control the number and scope of demands generated in their respective regions and to reconcile them with those generated in the others.

[34] SKJ, *Referat i završna riječ Predsjednika Tita, Rezolucije, Statut SKJ: XI Kongres Saveza komunista Jugoslavije* (Beograd: Komunist, 1978), p. 209 [henceforth: *XI Kongres*].
[35] Ibid., pp. 123-24.

The Eleventh Congress did endorse the organizational and procedural prescriptions for the regulation of conflict contained in *The Directions of Development*. The congress commission for the development of the political system and socialist self-managing democracy emphasized that, as a result of "positive experience," "social councils . . . have been affirmed as an important form for the democratic method of preparing decisions, for the harmonization of positions."[36] The resolutions adopted at the Congress call for the establishment of social councils "in those organs of administration whose activity is of special significance for the republics and provinces, for associated labor and for the satisfaction of the daily needs of citizens."[37] In the year following the Congress, party leaders continued to emphasize the importance of social councils, and preparation of a new law calling for their introduction on a "massive" scale was undertaken.[38] But social councils always were presented in the context of a search for greater harmony and consensus, and not as a consequence of continuing conflict.

The Yugoslav experience suggests, and Kardelj argued quite explicitly, that if consultative organs and processes are to function as arenas for the resolution of conflicts, the central party leadership must ensure that individual communists influence the definition by self-managing institutions and organizations of their particular interests so that those interests are compatible with the "general social interest" defined by the party leadership itself. It is not surprising, therefore, that changes adopted at the Eleventh Congress strengthened the central leadership's ability to enforce its policies and decisions in the party.

The Presidium elected after the Eleventh Congress is significantly smaller than its predecessor. Prior to the Congress, it had consisted of forty-eight members. Now it is composed of twenty-four; three from each republic, two from each province, one from the party organization in the military, and the president of the League. The new Presidium includes the most authoritative individuals in Yugoslav political life. The presidents of each of the eight regional party organizations are members ex officio. All had been members of the earlier Presidium. Their continuation in office required a change in the party statute exempting this organ, and all the regional presidiums as well, from the requirement that at least one-third of the membership of leading organs be "renewed" at each election. Stane Dolanc was elected secretary of the Presidium, continuing the pattern of his increasing power that began in January 1972. Nine members of the Central Committee were selected to serve as "executive secretaries" of the Presidium, but were not elected to presidium membership.[39]

---

[36] *Politika* (Belgrade), 22 June 1978.
[37] *XI Kongres*, p. 131.
[38] *Politika* (Belgrade), 6 April 1979.
[39] Ibid., 24 June 1978.

These changes partially confirmed earlier rumors about creation of a Politburo-like central party organ, although the new Presidium is substantially larger than the rumored body.[40] According to the statute adopted at the Congress[41] the new Presidium is to perform a primarily political/directive role. Each of its members is responsible for "specific issues and tasks." Each of the "executive secretaries" of the Presidium also has a "concrete responsibility for specific areas of work," but their role is limited to "operational work on the carrying-out of policy." This division of labor in the Presidium undoubtedly increased the operational efficiency of this smaller body and thereby strengthened it.

Other changes in the statute reinforce the authority of the new Presidium. A lengthy and entirely new section on democratic centralism, for example, emphasizes the authority of the central party organs "as the unified political leadership of the entire League of Communists of Yugoslavia." It also emphasizes the "equal responsibility" of the republican, provincial, and military party organizations that elect the members of these organs "for the construction and execution of the unified policy of the League." The statute adopted at the Eleventh Congress also reverses the trend toward increasing emphasis on the influence of regional organizations over the central organs in the formation of policy that had been evident since 1964. It defines the role of the republican party organizations in a manner emphasizing the influence of the unified party program and policies determined by central organs over the formulation of republican policies.

The power of the central leadership was strengthened by the addition of two new subsections to the existing article on democratic centralism. The first of these permits the party leadership to "extend help to the membership and to basic organizations" of the party, and the second mandates "permanent and direct democratic communication" with socio-political, social, and self-managing organizations and delegations. Together, these additions increase the authority of the central party leadership to monitor developments throughout the party and society and to intervene wherever it decides to do so, thus creating a statutory basis for the kind of actions that had proven essential to the re-establishment of central power by the Tito-led coalition in the post-crisis period.

The new statute prohibits exclusion from the party of any member of the Central Committee without the agreement of the Committee itself. It requires that, when such an exclusion is under consideration, the Presidium must be informed, and mandates that it become involved in the decision. This provision increases the relative autonomy of central party organs—including the Pre-

---

[40] Richard F. Staar, ed., *Yearbook on International Communist Affairs 1978* (Stanford: Hoover Institution Press, 1978), p. 92.
[41] *XI Kongres*, pp. 203ff.

sidium—by insulating their members from punitive action by their regional party organization, such as the Croatian organization had carried out against Miloš Žanko in 1970.

The very manner in which these changes were carried out strengthened the importance of the formal rules of procedure. The decision to create a smaller Presidium with its own "executive secretaries" and to abolish the existing executive committee had been made as early as November 1977.[42] That it was not implemented until the Congress, in June 1978, contrasts to earlier periods, when even more sweeping changes in the organization of the central party had been carried out with little regard for existing rules of procedure. This adherence to formalities undoubtedly reflected a lack of urgency associated with this change. But it also ensured that this change would contribute to, rather than undermine, the authority of the central party leadership by emphasizing the importance of adhering to agreed-on rules of procedure.

As had been the case at the Tenth Congress in 1974, however, actions strengthening the central party leadership were accompanied at the Eleventh Congress by significant actions strengthening the power and authority of the regional party leaderships. The new statute establishes that the president of the League nominates the members of the Presidium "on the basis of prior consultations with the presidiums of the central and provincial committees" and the leadership of the military party organization. Similarly, it requires that representatives of the central committees of the republican party organizations and the provincial committees of the provincial organizations and representatives of the military party organizations must participate in determining membership changes in the central Presidium between regular elections (i.e., between congresses). These changes reaffirm the continuing control of the regional leaderships over the power of appointment to the central organs of the party.

Changes in the statute increase the relative status of the provincial party organizations in particular. Symbolically, they now are listed separately in the enumeration of "autonomous organizations in the unified League of Communists of Yugoslavia," although still designated in the next sentence as an "integral part" of the Serbian party organization. Substantively, they now are included with the republican organizations in the enumeration of organizations with which the president of the party is mandated to maintain "permanent contact," and are allocated two positions on the Presidium in comparison to only one for the military party organization.

Other changes adopted at the Eleventh Congress suggest an attempt by regional leaders to weaken the power and authority of the central party organs

---

[42] Staar, *Yearbook on International Communist Affairs*, p. 92.

directly. The statutory article defining the role of the president of the League, for example, requires "discussion of particular current questions with the most responsible functionaries," presumably, the leaders of the regional party organizations and the members of the Presidium. The article defining the role of the Presidium requires it to "coordinate current ideo-political activity with the central and provincial committees" and the military party organization. Even more important, the provision concerning consecutive election to leading party organs and "executive-political functions" at all levels of the League was revised to prohibit entirely reelection to such positions, whereas the 1974 statute had only prohibited such election more than two times in succession.[43] Consequently, none of the secretaries elected to the Executive Committee of the Presidium at the Tenth Congress in 1974 were elected executive secretaries of the Presidium at the Eleventh Congress. It is not surprising, therefore, that the new executive secretaries were younger and heretofore generally less powerful members of the Yugoslav elite. For the prohibition on reappointment to these positions precludes their using such positions to build up their own power. Such turnover among its secretaries is likely to limit the power of the Presidium and its effectiveness as an executive organ.

This weakening of the party center also is manifest in the formal elimination of the Executive Committee of the Presidium as a distinct party organ. The "secretary" and "executive secretaries" of the Presidium appointed after the Eleventh Congress no longer constitute an "executive committee." This emphasizes their political subordination to the Presidium. Moreover, these executive secretaries continue to command a relatively small party apparatus. As the figures in Table 6.1 indicate, the professional staff employed by the Presidium and, presumably, under the day-to-day administrative supervision of the executive secretaries, remains smaller than the staffs employed by several of the republican organizations.

An even more important weakening of the central party leadership and, indeed, of all leadership organs in the party, is contained in an important addition to the principles of democratic centralism contained in the new statute. An entirely new paragraph declares that democratic centralism is based on (among other things):

the obligation of members whose opinions and proposals remain in the minority in an organization or organ of the League of Communists to accept and carry out the decisions adopted by the majority, *with freedom to retain [their] own opinion.*[44]

[43] Cf. *XI Kongres*, p. 220 (section 26, paragraph 10) and Rojc et al., *Deseti Kongres SKJ*, p. 344 (section 20, paragraph 9).

[44] *XI Kongres*, p. 213 (emphasis added).

TABLE 6.1
Cadres Employed by the Republican and
Yugoslav Party Organizations, 1973-1977
(End-of-Year Figures)

Party Organization	1973	1974	1975	1976	1977
Functionaries and Other Socio-Political Workers					
Bosnian	158	172	174	177	205
Montenegrin	44	43	52	47	60
Croatian	212	236	186	195	201
Macedonian	60	73	79	85	97
Slovenian	119	125	155	174	190
Serbian	345	478	484	538	537
Presidium of the LCY Central Committee	15	17	18	18	17
Party Conference for Organs and Organizations of the Federation	—	—	1	1	2
Professional Staff					
Bosnian	448	457	497	577	595
Montenegrin	97	97	96	99	133
Croatian	484	506	541	605	656
Macedonian	189	201	219	236	242
Slovenian	186	184	218	218	235
Serbian	1,064	1,105	1,290	1,530	1,653
Presidium of the LCY Central Committee	199	234	240	245	267
Party Conference of Organs and Organizations of the Federation	—	10	13	13	13

SOURCE: Vančo Apostolski et al., eds., *Jedanaesti kongres Saveza komunista Jugoslavije: Dokumenti* (Beograd: Komunist, 1978), pp. 305-306.

This paragraph also stipulates that "any kind of activity which would make more difficult and interfere with the united action of communists . . . would represent a form of groupism and factional activity."[45] Nonetheless, the freedom of individual communists to hold an opinion opposed to the positions adopted by party organs and organizations ultimately represents a serious formal limitation on the power of any central leadership to impose discipline on the broad party masses and thereby to forge the kind of unity necessary for the party to be able to fulfill the role of an integrative organization under the conditions of a pluralism of often mutually contradictory self-managing interests. Moreover, the inclusion of this provision suggests the existence of at least a powerful minority in the party leadership concerned with protecting inner-party democracy.

Thus, the Eleventh Congress produced mixed results with respect to the strengthening of central party leadership and of discipline in the party as a whole. During the year following the Congress, however, a series of organizational and procedural changes in the central party organs were carried out that unquestionably constrained the exercise of central power and authority and gave increasingly strong impetus to efforts to "democratize" not only party life but political life in general.

In November 1978, less than five months after the Congress, the Yugoslav press agency reported that the central party Presidium "recently" had adopted new rules of procedure by which a new post of chairman of the Presidium was introduced.[46] The chairman

> according to the agreement and authorization of the president of the LCY and in cooperation with the secretary and members of the Presidium, prepares and calls meetings of this organ. In the absence of the president of the LCY he presides over [on rukovodi] the sessions of the Presidium.
> . . . The chairman and secretary of the Presidium maintain constant contact with the president of the LCY, inform him about all important questions of interest for the work of the Presidium, as well as the results of the work of sessions in which the president of the LCY did not participate.

Prior to this, all these functions, except presiding in the absence of the president, had been performed by the secretary of the Executive Committee (1974-1978) or (after 1978) secretary of the Presidium. By assigning them to the new chairman of the Presidium as well, the members of the central leadership dramatically reduced the powers, authority, and prestige of the

[45] Ibid.
[46] The citations are to the report in *Politika* (Belgrade), 10 November 1978. For the text of the new rules themselves, see *Komunist*, 10 November 1978.

secretary. Indeed, the press report on these changes noted that "in the global division of labor" in the Presidium:

> The chairman . . . prepares, together with the members of the Presidium [note: not the secretary], sessions and political decisions. The secretary of the Presidium is oriented more toward execution of the decisions adopted by the Presidium.

By this action, and especially by reporting it publicly, the central leadership reduced the political preeminence of Stane Dolanc, who had held the post of secretary since it was created in 1974, and had served as de facto party secretary since 1971. They ensured that the new chairmanship would not provide its incumbent with such preeminence by requiring that it rotate among the republics and provinces in an eight-year cycle—each occupant holding the office on the recommendation of the president of the party for one year.

At the same time, by reducing the status of the secretary, these changes weakened the effectiveness of the Presidium as the organizational center of the party. It was weakened still further when, as part of a mounting campaign for collective leadership throughout society, the secretaryship of the Presidium also was subjected to rotation among the members of the Presidium. Every two years a member of the Presidium "from a different republican or provincial organization" was to be appointed secretary. When this decision was adopted, Stane Dolanc relinquished the secretaryship.[47]

These changes were followed twelve days later by President Tito's speech to the Eighth Trade Union Congress in November 1978, in which he suggested that

> the methods and forms of organization of the work of forums and organs must be further developed. It is well known that for a number of years already in the SFRY Presidency, as the highest state organ, the vice-president has been elected for a one-year term. That principle recently also was applied to the Presidium with the election of a chairman, also for one year. Experience points to the conclusion that such practice, in the coming period, can and must be applied in other organs and organizations as well, starting from the commune up to the Federation. Only certain executive and technical organs and institutions could be an exception. But even in them it would be necessary to develop and apply [the principle of] collective work and joint responsibility.[48]

This suggestion quickly became known as the "Tito initiative" and served as the basis for a broad-gauged campaign to establish "collective leadership" at all levels of the political system.

[47] *Politika* (Belgrade), 17 May 1979.
[48] Ibid., 22 November 1978.

At the federal level, the campaign for collective leadership found expression in affirmation of the consultative processes established during the period of constitutional reform and recommended by Kardelj for wider application. Some months later, for example, a meeting of the Presidium, its executive secretaries, and the "highest functionaries of the federation" reviewed "the functioning of organs and institutions of the political system in the federation" and concluded that "the relations and method of decision making in the federation established by the SFRY Constitution have proved their value in practice by the more efficient solution of questions of socio-economic and political development."[49] At the third session of the Yugoslav Central Committee in April 1979, the party leadership called for the establishment of social councils attached to the "executive organs and organs of administration of all socio-political communities in our political system."[50]

This suggests that Kardelj's organizational and procedural prescriptions for the regulation of future conflict in Yugoslavia had been accepted by the political leadership even if his concept of a "pluralism" of self-managing interest had not. But the potential consequences of a rotating chairmanship and secretaryship for the autonomy and decisional effectiveness of the Presidium call into question its ability to provide the necessary central leadership to forge agreement through consultation and negotiation. Given a high level of consensus among the regional representatives who compose the Presidium, an autonomous party center might be unnecessary. Central Committee discussions during the year prior to Tito's death suggest, however, that the regional leaderships in Yugoslavia continue to be divided by conflicts arising out of the contradictory economic interests of their respective regions.[51] But even under these circumstances, the application of a principle of rotation to the leading positions in the party does not by itself undermine the decision-making principles and practices that have evolved since 1966. Indeed, rotation of control over the executive powers of the Presidium and expansion of collective participation in the work of the president may be seen as an attempt to reinforce those principles.

Tito's "initiative" and the ensuing campaign for collective leadership do not appear to have been undertaken in response to any evident pattern of excessive centralization of power in the party. Indeed, the changes adopted at the Eleventh Congress and the creation of a chairmanship of the Presidium suggest that precisely the contrary was taking place. They appear to have emerged from Tito's personal concern and the concern of other members of the leadership to arrange for Tito's succession before his death. Up to this

---

[49] Ibid., 2 March 1979.

[50] Ibid., 6 April 1979.

[51] Note, for example, the regional division of views at the sixth session [*Politika* (Belgrade), 29 June 1979] and eighth session [*Politika* (Belgrade), 19 October 1979].

time, Edvard Kardelj had been considered the obvious successor to Tito as president of the League of Communists and *primus inter pares* among the leadership. Indeed, during his visit to the United States in late 1977, Kardelj was treated by his hosts as the obvious "heir-apparent." But by mid-1978 it was rumored that his health was failing, and in February 1979 he died. Since no other member of the leadership enjoyed Kardelj's country-wide prestige, this left no obvious candidate to succeed Tito. By default if not by design, the Yugoslav leadership was compelled to construct some collective mechanism for Tito's succession in the party, parallel to existing provisions in the state.

The rotation of the chairmanship and secretaryship of the Presidium and the expansion of collective participation in the work of the president of the party dramatically reduced the likelihood that the central party organs would constitute an independent center of predominant power in the post-Tito period and ensured against their "capture" by any single regional leadership intent on domination rather than negotiation, or by any individual intent on amassing decisive personal political power. Indeed, one well-informed source in Belgrade reported in January 1981 that the "initiative" could be attributed to Tito's concern to prevent the rise of a "Yugoslav Stalin" following the death of "Yugoslavia's Lenin" (Tito). Were the campaign for collective leadership limited to these changes, the system of decision making based on regional representation, negotiation, and consensus might prove remarkably stable in the post-Tito period. However, other proposals for change adopted as part of that campaign strike at the very foundations of that system.

It was suggested at the April 1979 session of the Central Committee that the principle of collective leadership required "application of the principle of a one-year mandate for the president or chairman in organs of the LCY [at the level] of the commune, the province and the republic."[52] In June, the Presidium adopted a set of conclusions that, among other things, called for "decumulation" of functions in the party, and application of the principle of rotation to leading positions in the state and party organizations of the republics and provinces and to "the most responsible functions" at the federal level. The Presidium called for rotation to be implemented in the regional party organizations one year before the next round of party congresses and conferences, scheduled for early 1982, and in the regional parliaments and executive councils before the end of the current mandate period (1982).[53]

Implementation of the proposed decumulation of functions began later that month when three members of the collective state Presidency were dropped from the party Presidium.[54] A reduction in the overlap between the mem-

[52] Ibid., 6 April 1979.
[53] Ibid., 27 June 1979.
[54] Ibid., 29 June 1979.

berships of these groups may make a marginal contribution to the effectiveness of the Presidency by allowing at least some of its members to concentrate full attention on their responsibilities as final arbiters of interregional conflicts in the state, as the official explanation of these changes suggests. But the changes that are likely to result as the proposals for rotation are implemented may well undermine the effectiveness of the party as an integrative force.

As the Presidium is structured at present, rotation of the presidents of the central and provincial committees of the regions will result in an annual turnover of one-third of its membership. The pattern of political changes in Yugoslavia since 1966 suggests that a system of political decision making based on regional representation, negotiation, and consensus requires stable regional party leaderships if it is to operate successfully. Stability of leading cadres in the regions, and especially of regional representatives in the Presidium, permits development of the kind of mutual personal trust and understanding that allows regional leaders to make the kinds of concessions that often are necessary in order to reach agreement, with confidence that they will be compensated for them in some as yet unspecified way in the future. Even more important than this, long tenure permits regional political leaders to consolidate their control over their respective party organizations.

In the aftermath of the Croatian crisis of 1971, Western and Yugoslav analysts, as well as some members of the Croatian leadership, agreed that one condition that made that crisis possible was the weakening of leadership control over middle- and lower-level party organizations in the republic. Rotation at the level of the regional leaderships undoubtedly would weaken their control over lower organizations in their republics just as rotation at the level of the Presidium weakens central control over the regions. Moreover, simultaneous rotation of cadres at lower levels of the regional party organizations will weaken the influence of local party officials and organizations over other, nonparty organizations and institutions and, ultimately, weaken party discipline over individual communists.[55] Despite these potential consequences, however, the party leadership called at the eighth session of the Central Committee in October 1979 for the adoption of a one-year mandate for presidents of commune-level party conferences and a two-year mandate for party secretaries by the end of 1980,[56] and in the year following that decision, its implementation proceeded apace.[57]

---

[55] On the role of local cadres in exercising influence over non-party organizations, see Stanić, "Unutrasnja organizovanost," and Radivoje Marinković, "Ostvarivanje delegatskog sistema: postajeći i mogući oblici etatizma, birokratizma, i manipulacije," in Radivoje Marinković, ed., *Funkcionisanje delegatskog sistema: Iskustva i aktuelni problemi* (Beograd: Institut za političke studije FPN, 1976), p. 71.

[56] *Politika* (Belgrade), 19 October 1979 and 23 February 1980.

[57] For a summary of results, see *Komunist*, 6 June 1980, and *NIN*, 1 February 1981.

Implementation of the "initiative" at the level of the regional leaderships, however, has proceeded more slowly. The Slovenian party secretary, for example, noted as early as November 1979—that is, even while Tito was still alive and, presumably, arguing in support of it—that the initiative was being implemented over some opposition within the Presidium itself. "Sometimes even we in the Central Committee," he said, "catch ourselves talking about the new method of work while working in the old way." From the very beginning, he observed, the representatives of Slovenia and the Slovenian party organization in the Presidium and Central Committee accepted the idea of collective leadership, but "held to the viewpoint that certain specific characteristics must be taken into account. The organs of the federation are one thing, the organs of a republic another, and the organs of a commune a third." While the introduction of a one-year mandate on the level of the federation was entirely appropriate and has been shown to be positive, the Slovenian leadership, he reported, openly questioned whether this formula was appropriate for the republics.[58] And one month earlier, then-chairman of the Presidium Branko Mikulić reported to the eighth session of the Central Committee that the delays associated with the operation of a decision-making system based on consultation and consensus had created demands to strengthen the party and its role in society at all levels that were contrary to the spirit of the campaign for collective leadership, suggesting that perhaps a "conservative opposition" to this latest round of party reforms also was taking shape.[59] But conflict in the leadership over this and other issues was soon submerged under the weight of dramatic domestic developments and international events.

Party Leadership in the Post-Tito Period

Early in January 1980 President Tito was hospitalized on the advice of his doctors for what was then described as an "examination of his leg blood vessels." He was released after two days. A week later he underwent surgery to correct a circulation blockage in his left leg. However, that surgery did not correct the problem. In response to a deterioration in the condition of the leg over the course of the following week, it was amputated on 20 January. After an initial period of optimistic reports of his rapid recovery and partial resumption of duties, life-threatening complications began to set in. Three weeks after the operation, Tito's condition was listed as critical, and early in May 1980 he died.[60]

Following his death, the leadership acknowledged and, in a certain sense,

[58] *NIN*, 11 November 1979.

[59] *Politika* (Belgrade), 19 October 1979. Cf. the comments by Bosnian party president Nikola Stojanović reported in ibid., 16 October 1979.

[60] For a useful chronology, see *NIN*, 6 May 1980.

proclaimed the fact that both the state Presidency and the party Presidium had begun functioning entirely on their own during the four months he lay incapacitated.[61] Tito's absence from involvement in the day-to-day decision-making process was not entirely unprecedented, however. Generally, he was involved in domestic political conflicts with decreasing frequency over the years, focusing his attention instead on the international arena. When the regional leaderships were deeply divided over questions of joint policy, as during the late 1960s, Tito served as broker, or "facilitator," by holding discussions with each of the regional leaderships individually to identify a common basis for negotiation, and by then forcing them to come together for marathon discussions that would not be recessed until agreement had been reached. Although no solution could be adopted that did not meet with his approval, he did not impose solutions of his own in the absence of at least some support. This was the pattern of his involvement up to December 1971, when he took over direct supervision of the day-to-day operation of the central party organs.

Following the extensive cadres changes carried out under his direction between December 1971 and the Tenth Party Congress in May 1974, Tito began once again to withdraw from direct involvement in domestic decision making. On key questions, such as the selection of individuals for the posts of chairman and secretary of the Presidium, it appears that he continued to exercise personal control. He also continued to lend support to the policies adopted by the party leadership through frequent public speeches and exhortations, and to reinforce the authority of that leadership by periodic affirmations of its stability, coherence, and competence. But by 1976 he no longer was presiding over routine meetings of either the Presidium or the Presidency. During an interview conducted in June 1976, a member of Tito's personal cabinet reported that Tito was kept "fully informed" of the work of the collective Presidency. President Tito's comments at the October 1979 meeting of the party Presidium, however, suggest that by that date he was informed about the ongoing, or routine, activities of the leading organs of the party only periodically.[62] This pattern of decreasing involvement in the day-to-day operation of the leading organs of the party and the state suggests that Tito's death may not detract from the routine decision-making capacity of the party leadership. It suggests that they had been operating in large part on their own for several years.

During Tito's illness, then-party secretary Dušan Dragosavac later reported to the Central Committee, the leadership took steps to strengthen the central organs of the party by improving "the system of internal political commu-

---

[61] *Politika* (Belgrade), 14 May 1980.
[62] Ibid., 24 October 1979.

nication in the League of Communists'' and increasing the direct participation of emissaries of the central party organs in meetings of local party organizations.[63] In fact, efforts to strengthen the party and to ensure its ability to perform its leading role in society during this period had been so extensive that it prompted a lengthy commentary in *Politika* affirming that they were not intended to establish ''any kind of hierarchical determination or subordination.''[64] Basic decision-making practices remained unchanged, however. The central Presidium leadership continued to carry out extensive interregional consultations to discuss and decide on policy.[65] If any change can be said to have taken place during this period, it was an increase in the public reporting of these established practices; itself an action affirming the status quo. The general effect of Tito's illness and the imminence of his death was to heighten the sense of unity among the leadership. In the threatening international conditions created by the Soviet invasion of Afghanistan, this sense of unity extended beyond the leadership to the broader party membership and popular masses. Not unlike the period following the 1968 invasion of Czechoslovakia, the party experienced a dramatic increase in the number of new, young applicants for membership.[66]

Changes carried out in the weeks following Tito's death confirmed the already established constitutional provisions for succession in the state Presidency and demonstrated the continuing power of the regional leaderships in the League of Communists. Three hours after Tito's death, a session of the state Presidency was convened, and Lazar Koliševski, who was at that time coming to the end of a one-year term as vice-president, was elected president of the Presidency and Cvijetin Mijatović was elected its vice-president. Ten days later, at the conclusion of Koliševski's original one-year term, Mijatović was elected president for a one-year term.[67] Later that month, the order for routine rotation of both positions among the regions was formally established.[68]

In the month following Tito's death there was some uncertainty about whether a new president of the party would be elected to replace him. But that confusion was ended by a Presidium decision to maintain the status quo, ratified at the eleventh session of the Central Committee in June. The members of the Presidium decided to assign to the Central Committee as a whole—which means, in fact, its Presidium—the powers and authority granted by the

[63] Ibid., 13 June 1980.

[64] Ibid., 2 March 1980.

[65] See, for example, the series of meetings on domestic, foreign, and social planning policies reported in ibid., 23, 26, and 27 February 1980.

[66] Ibid., 26 April and 19 May 1980.

[67] Ibid., 6, 14, and 16 May 1980.

[68] Ibid., 20 May 1980.

party statutes to the president of the party, and to change the title "chairman of the Presidium" to "president of the Presidium." The new president of the Presidium would serve in the state Presidency in the name of the Central Committee. He would not, however, enjoy Tito's prerogative to nominate individuals for membership in the Presidium itself. For the exercise of this power, the leadership decided to establish a special commission that will carry out its task on the basis of consultations with the regional party leaderships and the leadership of the party organization in the army. In this way, the autonomous power of the regional leaderships was significantly enhanced. That power was protected against encroachment by an ambitious president of the Presidium by the fact that the latter will serve for only one year, as had the chairman.[69]

All these changes were officially designated as "temporary," until confirmed or overturned at the party congress scheduled for 1982. The present leaders explicitly rejected the idea of convening an extraordinary congress to alter the party statutes. They appear to have decided to maintain established principles and practices of decision making and to attempt to preserve the relatively high level of unity evident in the aftermath of Tito's death.

In recent years, but especially during Tito's illness and since his death, there has been a marked tendency for the party's highest leadership not to become too deeply involved in specific policy conflicts. Only rarely, for example, has the Presidium been convened to resolve interregional disputes over the specific provisions of federal legislation. Consultations have taken place on issues related to long-term planning of regional economic relations. But these have occurred only infrequently. The Presidium is sometimes consulted to secure approval for an innovative solution prepared elsewhere, rather than to have it select between competing solutions. These conflicts are worked out instead in state institutions such as the FEC and federal parliament, as noted earlier. And before any such conflict must be considered by the party leadership, the collective Presidency offers a high-level and authoritative forum for the resolution of interregional or, indeed, any other conflicts.

The collective Presidency is the formal institutional successor to Tito and has inherited all the powers of the office of president of the Republic that he occupied. High functionaries of the federal parliament, the government, and the party often participate in its deliberations. Although a large part of its work is focused on foreign affairs, the Presidency plays a central role in domestic policy making and is constitutionally charged with resolving the most important conflicts. The mixed party and state character of its membership and the authoritative role it plays in the decision-making process have led some foreign observers of Yugoslav politics to suggest that the Presidency,

---

[69] Ibid., 13 and 14 June 1980, and *Komunist*, 20 June 1980.

rather than the Presidium, is evolving into a Politburo-like organ. However, like the Presidium, the Presidency avoids imposing solutions on reluctant regional leaders. Indeed, the Presidency has no formal power to do so on its own. In cases of unbreakable deadlocks it can only recommend the adoption of a temporary measure.

To avoid reaching such a situation, the Presidency encourages and facilitates consultation among representatives of conflicting interests, and its members conduct frequent and extensive consultations during all stages of federal decision making. Even in the face of an apparent deadlock, the Presidency will recommend further efforts by the deadlocked parties to find a solution. While this practice may be seen as an attempt to adhere closely to the consensual principles of decision making characteristic of the Yugoslav political system as a whole, they may also be seen—as one noted Yugoslav political scientist and member of a regional central committee suggested during a long discussion in January 1981—as fear of becoming embroiled in sensitive areas.

Were the Presidency regularly to become directly involved in policy disputes, it would soon become difficult to conceal the political divisions among its members. The deliberations of the Presidency are confidential and both media coverage of its meetings and the Presidency's own annual reports to the Federal Assembly contain little, if any, detail concerning their substance. In a society characterized by a relatively high degree of open and frank discussion of sensitive issues by political leaders at all levels, no member of the Presidency or other individual privy to its deliberations ever discusses publicly the views expressed there. The image of unity in the highest leadership projected as the result of this practice is an important contribution to the stability of the decision-making process. Moreover, too frequent involvement in policy conflicts might not only reduce the effectiveness of the Presidency as an expeditor of solutions to the most important conflicts but might also tend to magnify the importance—and, therefore, the politically destabilizing potential—of otherwise "routine" conflicts.

The latter point suggests a function of the Federal Assembly in the process of interregional negotiation in Yugoslavia that has become far more important since the death of Tito: It provides an arena in which conflicting regional interests may be expressed without endangering the stability of the political system. One Yugoslav political scientist recently suggested that certain conflicts are "far too explosive" to be dealt with openly at the level of the collective Presidency or the party Presidium. But because the Assembly is widely perceived as a lower-level, less powerful, and less important institution, such conflicts can be confronted and resolved in its committees. In this way, the party Presidium and state Presidency are held "in reserve" for the "most crucial" questions.

The willingness and ability of the central party leadership to resolve conflicts in the Assembly, the FEC, or even the Presidency during Tito's illness and in the year following his death were demonstrated in a number of cases cited in the previous chapter. Its apparent determination to do so in a manner that preserves the essential characteristics and conditions for success of the established decision-making process was demonstrated by its resolution of the interregional deadlock that emerged during preparation of the constitutional reforms recently adopted in connection with the application of the Tito "initiative" to state institutions.

Central Party Leadership and Constitutional Reform in the Post-Tito Period

Application of the Tito "initiative" to state institutions required, as the Presidium leadership acknowledged in its June 1979 "conclusions," the adoption of yet another series of constitutional amendments. The Presidium called for these to be adopted before the end of the current mandate period in 1982. Clearly aware of the potential dangers inherent in once again opening the question of altering the political order, the central party leadership emphasized that these changes "must be restricted to immediate questions of the organization and composition of organs, as well as the length of the mandate of the president or presiding official."[70]

The organizational and procedural provisions for preparation of the amendments were very similar to those established for the constitutional reforms prepared during 1970-1973.[71] The drafting of amendments to the federal constitution was supervised by a "Coordinating Body for Questions of the Change of the SFRY Constitution": a joint body of the Federal Social Council for Questions of Social Organization and the Commission for Constitutional Questions of the Federal Assembly. The organizational and procedural provisions for preparation of amendments in the regions precisely paralleled those at the federal level, but, unlike past reforms, work on the federal constitution proceeded at a slower pace than work on the individual republican and provincial constitutions.

According to several individuals who participated in preparation of both the federal and regional amendments, confidential discussions on the general outlines of the federal changes to be adopted began in January 1979. The results of these discussions were submitted to the party leadership during June and July 1979. The public process of constitutional reform did not begin until December. Thus, when the federal parliament was first considering and accepting the formal proposal to change the federal constitution, the process of

[70] *Politika* (Belgrade), 29 June 1979.

[71] I have reconstructed the process on the basis of accounts in *Politika* and interviews with participants, conducted in Yugoslavia during December 1980 and January 1981.

constitutional reform was already well under way in Serbia. By mid-December, substantial discussions had already taken place in Serbia in private, and working groups had made significant progress on the preparation of alternative formulations of proposed amendments.[72]

The first formal session of the "Coordinating Body" supervising the preparation of amendments to the federal constitution, by contrast, did not take place until the end of January, and there was little evidence then that work had progressed very far.[73] While all participants agreed on the principle of collectivity in leadership and the adoption of shortened mandates for leading positions in the federal parliament, they were deeply divided on the question of applying these to the Federal Executive Council. In lengthy interviews conducted in Belgrade and several regional capitals during December 1980 and January 1981, a number of participants in the drafting process described the interregional debate that followed. From these interviews and press accounts published at the time, it is evident that representatives from several regions sought to shorten the mandate of both the premier and the other members of the FEC, and to eliminate the premier's role in selecting the other members of the government. Representatives of other regions and some members of the "Coordinating Body" with a more central perspective opposed their efforts. Nonetheless, in the period between the first and the second meeting, held at the end of February, the texts of draft amendments were completed by the working group for the political system of the Commission for Constitutional Questions of the Federal Assembly.[74]

Apparently, little progress was made at the February meeting, and the next major discussion of amendments to the federal constitution did not take place until shortly after the death of Tito. In the interim, however, the draft amendments had been circulated to the regional leaderships for discussion.[75] At the May 1980 meeting of the Federal Assembly's constitutional commission, which became the primary arena for discussions following the death of Tito, "principled agreement" was reached on the first amendment, consisting of a general statement and affirmation of the principles of collective leadership, decision making, and responsibility in organs of government and self-management.[76] The second draft amendment consisted only of a general statement that officials performing self-managing, public, and other functions would be elected or appointed for *up to* four years, with the specific length of mandate and limitations on reelection or reappointment to be determined by consti-

---

[72] *Politika* (Belgrade), 7, 12, and 13 December 1979.
[73] Ibid., 24 January 1980.
[74] Ibid., 1 March 1980.
[75] See the reports of such discussions, ibid., 5 April and 20 May 1980.
[76] Ibid., 21 May 1980.

tution, law, or statute.[77] Discussion of this amendment, however, "was characterized by obvious differences of views," and "the most lively discussions and most significant differences of opinion broke out around this" amendment. The majority of participants are reported to have supported the flexible formulation contained in the draft amendment. But some participants felt that it did not "ensure uniform regulation of the question of the length of mandate and limitation on reelection." "Supporters of this view," contemporary news accounts suggested, "think that . . . uniform regulation of the length of mandate represents a basic element of the unified political system of the country." They insisted on the adoption of the formulas contained in the June 1979 "conclusions" of the Presidium, calling for the introduction of specific one- or two-year mandates for specific leading positions, as "concrete constitutional solutions." The majority, however, apparently treated the Presidium's "conclusions" as a "political orientation," arguing that "if the Presidium conclusions are understood as a concrete solution, what would be left for the constitution and upcoming public discussions to resolve?"[78]

These differences reflected the differing perceptions of regional representatives concerning exactly what constituted the "unified bases of the sociopolitical system" and, therefore, had to be regulated uniformly. When such conflicts arose during preparation of the 1974 constitution, they were resolved by imposing certain formulas on the regions. Now, however, it was decided that uniformity in the regulation of these matters can be achieved "only to the extent that, respecting adopted political positions and with the consultation and coordination of the republics and provinces, uniform solutions are adopted in . . . the republican and provincial constitutions." And because of "the clear political differences in views" on these matters, the constitutional commission decided to carry out additional consultations with the regional leaderships.[79]

"Significant differences" also arose during discussion of specific provisions concerning the premier and the other members of the FEC. With respect to the length of mandate and possible reelection, two proposals emerged. The first called for the premier to be elected for two years, with reelection for one additional two-year term possible, while other members of the Council would be elected for four years. The second variant differed only in that the premier would be elected from among the members of the Council. Both variants assumed the elimination of the premier's role as "mandator," i.e., his role in selecting the other members of the government. According to contemporary newspaper accounts, "important differences in the valuation of the place and position of the FEC" became apparent during these discus-

[77] Ibid., 22 May 1980.
[78] Ibid. The text of the "conclusions" may be found in ibid., 27 June 1979.
[79] Ibid., 22 May 1980.

sions and, in the end, the Commission could only direct its working group to prepare a new, compromise solution.[80]

In the weeks following this meeting, it became clear where the chairman of the Commission and president of the Federal Assembly, a Serbian politician long associated with support for strong central government, stood on these questions. In a lengthy published interview, Dragoslav Marković made it clear that he supported the adoption of the more flexible provisions concerning the length of mandate and reelection or reappointment of officials, and the preservation of the present constitutional provisions concerning the Federal Executive Council,[81] calling for a four-year term for all members and giving the premier responsibility for selecting the other members of the government. Despite the publicly expressed preferences of this powerful and strategically placed figure, and the fact that these preferences corresponded to those expressed by the Serbian leadership and by representatives of the Slovenian leadership,[82] the Commission could not achieve any greater agreement on this amendment when it reconvened a month later in June.[83]

Even after an additional, five-hour session in mid-July, the Commission could not agree on an amendment concerning the FEC. As a result, it decided to develop three variants. The first retained the current constitutional provisions concerning the premier, the Council and its members, but prohibited any reelection of the premier or reelection of members to a third consecutive term. The second variant provided a four-year term for the members of the Council, but reduced the term of the premier to two years; although it did permit the premier to serve two consecutive terms. It eliminated both the role of the premier in formulating the Council and his power to propose the dismissal of other members. Nor would his own resignation constitute resignation of the entire Council. An alternative formulation of this variant prohibited consecutive reelection of the premier. However, the majority of Commission members remained opposed to any change in the constitutional position of the Council, and several members also opposed the idea of eliminating the premier's role in formulating the Council.[84]

Such opposition is understandable. Often it takes a year or more just to prepare a piece of federal legislation for presentation to the parliament. Decision making based on consensus is a long and difficult process, often requiring delays that extend consideration of a proposal beyond a year. Under these conditions, any shortening of the mandate of the premier and members of the Federal Executive Council is likely to reduce their effectiveness. To

[80] Ibid.
[81] *NIN*, 1 June 1980.
[82] *Politika* (Belgrade), 17 June 1980.
[83] Ibid., 21 June 1980.
[84] Ibid., 17 July 1980.

weaken the Council might be to destroy the balance between center and region in the federal policy-making process, thereby creating conditions conducive to the reemergence of deadlock in the face of interregional conflict.

Differences over the formulas to be applied to the Council were finally resolved only after the central party Presidium intervened in October to "modify" the conclusions that had been adopted in June 1979. Party secretary Dragosavac reported to the Central Committee in January 1981 that the Presidium leadership, reviewing the ongoing dispute over the amendments, had decided at the beginning of October that a solution had to be devised before the proposals were submitted to public discussion and therefore proposed to the constitutional commission that a four-year mandate be adopted for the premier and members of the FEC.[85] Immediately thereafter, agreement was reached on a draft amendment preserving the existing four-year terms of office for the premier, but prohibiting his reelection, and for members of the Council—who may be reelected only once. The amendment made selection of the premier and other members of the government the responsibility of the Socialist Alliance—a provision that participants in the drafting process suggest was more a reflection of current practice than a change. In order to increase the responsibility of the government to the parliament—and therefore to the regions that exercise veto power in it—the amendment requires the Council to deliver to the Federal Assembly a report on its work after two years of each term have passed, and the Assembly may then express its confidence in the Council.[86] The provisions of this amendment represent the victory of those who had supported the maintenance of a strong federal government. For the concessions to greater collectivity and responsibility contained in it do not seem to impinge on the essential characteristics of the Council. But there can be no doubt that the long battle over this amendment represented a very serious attack on central power and authority in Yugoslav politics.

Logically, such an attack could have been expected to come from the developed regions because of the central government's traditional role in transferring resources from them to the underdeveloped regions. But it is clear from the almost identical accounts of these debates provided by individuals interviewed in several republics—developed and underdeveloped—that the strongest assault came from representatives of the underdeveloped republics and provinces.

According to participants in the discussion, the positions taken by the representatives of the regions during debate over the shape of amendments to the federal constitution are reflected almost perfectly in the amendments

[85] *NIN*, 1 February 1981.
[86] *Politika* (Belgrade), 28 October 1980.

each adopted for its own constitution.[87] Serbia, Slovenia, and Macedonia adopted a four-year term of office for the premiers of their republican executive councils and prohibited their reelection, the solution finally adopted in the federal amendments for the Federal Executive Council. Croatia and Vojvodina adopted a compromise formulation calling for a two-year term, but permitting reelection for one additional term, thereby effectively preserving a four-year term. Bosnia, Montenegro, and Kosovo, however, adopted the most "radical" solutions: two-year terms, with reelection prohibited.

Representatives of the underdeveloped regions profess to have been motivated by a sense of ideological commitment to implementing the principles underlying the Tito "initiative" as rapidly as possible. In a discussion conducted in January 1981, a very high official of one of these republics discounted entirely the potentially de-stabilizing consequences of rapid, extensive turnover in the political elite caused by widespread application of these principles to leading positions in both the party and the state. It was abundantly clear from this discussion, and from others conducted with participants in the drafting process and political and academic figures in several republics, that the adoption of shortened mandates and concomitant application of principles of rotation is advanced by those who support them as an instrument for the further "democratization" of Yugoslav society.

An alternative explanation of this position is, however, also plausible. There are strong incentives for the party leaderships of the underdeveloped regions to attempt to subject the FEC to greater political pressure, for this enhances their bargaining positions during negotiations over aid and development policies. It is important to remember that these amendments were being prepared at the same time that the regional political leaderships were engaged in difficult negotiations over the 1981-1985 social plan. At the same time, there are even stronger incentives for these leaderships to reduce the autonomy of their respective regional governments. For this would enhance their control over the use of resources made available as the result of federal aid and development policies. Through such control, these regional party leaderships would be able to exercise dominant influence over their respective regional economies. Such an explanation of the positions taken by these leaderships is entirely consistent with the more conservative political character usually attributed to them.

The conflict over implementation of the Tito "initiative" through constitutional reform thus suggests a division among the regional leaderships arising out of both differing ideological orientations and the particularistic economic interests of the regions. This division reinforces existing tensions between

[87] The full texts of all the regional and federal amendments, with some commentary by individuals who participated in their preparation may be found in a special supplement to *Borba* (Belgrade), 17 December 1980.

center and region in Yugoslav politics and adds to the potential complexity of political alignments in the central leadership. The imposition of a solution to this conflict by the central party Presidium suggests at the same time, however, that the communist political leadership of Yugoslavia, or at least a majority of the regional bloc leaderships, appears to have learned from the events of the late 1960s and early 1970s the importance of a strong central government in the form of an autonomous and capable Federal Executive Council, and is prepared and able to act to preserve its existence.

Whether the party leadership will be able to maintain the unity it has displayed in the face of divisive regional conflicts and whether it will be able to resolve them remain, however, open questions. For that leadership now confronts a constellation of interconnected policy problems far more serious than any it has faced since 1972; and it must confront them as it prepares for another party congress—the first since the death of Tito—at which it will have to deal with the contradictions between center and region, between collective rule and effective leadership, and between discipline and democracy that have been apparent in the party for the past five years, and which could not be resolved at the last congress, even while Tito was still alive.

CONCLUSION: CONFLICT AND COHESION
IN POST-TITO YUGOSLAVIA

The post-Tito leadership today confronts a set of economic problems that threaten the stability of the Yugoslav system. These include a serious balance of payments problem fueled by the cost of imported energy and by the inability of Yugoslav manufactured goods to compete in Western markets; increasing foreign indebtedness; rampant inflation; excessive investment in industry at the expense of agricultural development; shortages of food, consumer goods, and raw materials; low productivity; and unemployment. The management of such problems would be difficult in any country. In Yugoslavia it is made even more difficult by the fact that actions intended to relieve these problems must not only be effective but must also be equitable in their impact on the various regions and nationalities if they are not to give rise to potentially explosive conflicts.

The difficulty of these tasks has produced marked uncertainty among the post-Tito leadership, and this, in turn, has given rise to far more open political debate than had been characteristic of Yugoslav politics in preceding years. The first Central Committee meeting following the death of Tito to deal with substantive policy questions, for example, was convened in September 1980 and was characterized by a wide-ranging and remarkably frank discussion of the economic and political problems confronting the regime. The full stenographic record of the proceedings of this meeting, including even comments by one participant that constitute thinly veiled criticisms of Tito's failure to deal with these problems as they arose, was published in pamphlet form for relatively wide distribution.[1] Prominent members of the central and regional party and state leaderships appear with increasing frequency in the mass media in interviews during which they stake out positions on a variety of important, and as yet unresolved issues. Moreover, these leaders often respond to one another—sometimes explicitly—in an ongoing debate over some of the most controversial policy questions, including, for example, even whether it is possible to criticize the party or party policy without being accused of disloyalty.[2] Press reporting in general also became more open in the months

---

[1] David Atlagić, ed., *13. Sednica CKSKJ: Aktuelna idejno-politička pitanja tekućeg ekonomskog kretanja i ostvarivanja ekonomske stabilizacije* (Beograd: Komunist, 1980).

[2] See, for example, the interviews with Mitja Ribičič published in *Start*, 10 December 1980 and *Borba* (Belgrade), 20 December 1980.

following Tito's death. This is not to suggest that the Yugoslav press or the policy-making process on which it reports is now completely open. Indeed, Yugoslav editors and reporters themselves admit, privately and in print, that they remain subject to certain forms of censorship and that they are often closed out of important discussions and events.[3] The fact that even this is the subject of public discussion in the media, however, suggests that the trend is clearly toward a more open press, reversing the direction evident in the late 1970s.

The greater openness of policy debate in the post-Tito period suggests de facto recognition by the leadership of the existence of a "pluralism" of often mutually contradictory but nonetheless legitimate "self-managing interests" in Yugoslav society. Indeed, by late 1980 and early 1981 Kardelj's attempt to define the character of relations between the party and these interests was the subject of widespread renewed attention. At present, however, the leadership continues to have difficulty defining any more precisely than Kardelj the role of the party in the resolution of conflicts among these interests. The Center for Social Research, dormant since about 1976, has been reactivated under the direct sponsorship of the Presidium itself and charged with precisely this task. But the research program being developed by the Center and the diverse views of the scholars participating in it suggest that the political debate among the leadership is likely to grow even wider before this issue is settled.

There are, however, definite limits on the kinds of "interests," views, discussions, and conflicts that the regime accepts as legitimate. Without exception, the communist leadership as a whole insists that the fundamental principles of the system of socialist self-management are well-established and supported by all. Any activity that calls these principles into question is by definition unacceptable. Such activity is labeled "anti-self-management" or "oppositional," and is condemned and suppressed. The targets of such repression have included the now-rare openly anti-communist elements, nationalists, anti-Titoist communists, and intellectuals engaged in critical assessment of the regime. The latter have included even those intellectuals engaged in Marxist criticism fundamentally sympathetic to the regime and its goals.

Contrary to the expectations of some Yugoslav intellectuals and the hopes of some Western critics of the more authoritarian features of the Yugoslav system, the definition of "legitimate interest"—and, therefore, the definition of who may participate in policy debate and by what means—has not been broadened since Tito's death. In fact, there is increasing evidence that official controls over intellectual activity have tightened in the post-Tito period. Efforts by individuals and groups in Ljubljana and Belgrade to establish new journals as forums for the expression of what they define as loyal or well-

---

[3] See *NIN*, 25 January and 8 March 1981.

intentioned social criticism, for example, were suppressed and their leaders attacked in the press.[4]

The regime continues to grant legitimacy only to disputes based on narrowly material interests and to deny to individuals outside the leadership any opportunity to criticize the broader characteristics of the system. Members of the leadership in Belgrade and in the regions justify the suppression of such criticism by arguing that it is directed against the system of self-management itself and is without any support among the Yugoslav people. The latter charge is partially true. Loyal or reform-minded criticism of the system has very little, if any active support outside a small circle of dissident intellectuals. The overwhelming majority of Yugoslavs are in fact more concerned about their narrow material interests and their worsening prospects for the future than they are over the direction of development of the political system per se. And the small core of intellectuals fundamentally opposed to the system do not support efforts to make well-intentioned criticism possible because they see such efforts as naive and hopeless and they view the system as unworthy of reform. They hold out instead for its replacement by a multiparty liberal democracy. For this very reason, however, the charge that recent efforts by intellectuals to broaden the range of public discussion in Yugoslavia are directed against the system itself is probably unwarranted.

The repressive response of the post-Tito leadership to attempts by intellectuals to extend the boundaries of legitimate discussion suggests an acute sensitivity to the potential danger of once again permitting the rise of entirely autonomous social criticism and analysis. Not only might such criticism challenge the party's enforced monopoly of political power directly, but it might do so indirectly by generating discontent with, or even opposition to policies carried out with the party's sanction. A major element in the regime's efforts to reduce inflation, for example, is an ongoing policy of limiting increases in personal income by linking them to increases in productivity. The imposition of restraints on income in the face of continuing inflation fed by the balance of payments deficits promises a continued decline in the real incomes and standard of living of the Yugoslav working class, and raises the specter of unrest among the workers. Although the present problems are fundamentally economic, such economic difficulties have in the past provided fertile ground for the rise of extremist movements. Moreover, present economic problems are affecting different regions of the country—and therefore, by and large, different nationalities—differently. Shortages, rising prices and unemployment are far more pronounced in the underdeveloped regions— already at a disadvantage.

[4] See, for examples of such attacks, *NIN*, 30 November 1980 and *Komunist*, 28 November 1980.

The present leadership has proven to be extremely sensitive to this issue. They have confronted it openly in Central Committee discussions at both the central and regional levels, in conferences, and in numerous individual speeches. In fact, their sensitivity to the potential linkage between economic problems and nationalist unrest suggests that the tightening of political controls in the first months of the post-Tito period may have been an attempt to prevent the rise of any large-scale nationalist movement fueled by regional economic difficulties by intimidating any would-be organizers of it.

This suggests that the consequences of the multinational condition for Yugoslav political development in the near future may be much the same as that identified in the pluralist literature. The very real danger of renewed nationality conflict makes it unlikely that any "democratization" of Yugoslav society will proceed much further in the near term. However, the longer-term consequences of multinationality for Yugoslav political development in the period since 1966 have been, and are likely to continue to be very different from those suggested by the literature. The multinational condition was a driving force behind the establishment of a decentralized political system based on consensual decision making. And, despite current difficulties, it serves as a powerful deterrent against a return to a more centralized system. Multinationality alone, however, is not sufficient to deter such a return. The current leadership must continue to resolve the problems confronting it and, at the same time, adhere to the established "rules of the game" in order to enhance the stability of the present system.

While the problems confronting the post-Tito leadership are serious, they do appear to be subject to solution within the existing framework. Economic issues are precisely the kinds of issues which exchange theory, comparative studies of conflict regulation, and Yugoslav experience itself all suggest are among the easier interbloc conflicts to resolve. If the leadership is to do so, however, it will have to approach these problems pragmatically and not permit ideological prescriptions to preclude potentially effective solutions. It will have to deal with discrete problems discretely and avoid linking them to questions of "principle" that are more difficult to resolve. And it will have to tend toward "incrementalism" in the formation and implementation of policy, so as to preserve its ability to rescind policy that engenders unacceptable unintended consequences. At the same time, the leadership will have to resolve interregional conflicts in a manner consistent with the principle of reciprocity so important to the succesful operation of the system.

Recent political debate surrounding the formulation of central policies suggests that the communist political leadership of Yugoslavia is approaching the resolution of current economic problems in a manner that closely approximates these conditions. The discussion at the thirteenth session of the Central Committee in September 1980, for example, was characterized not only by the open debate and concern for the potential political consequences of the current problems cited earlier but also by a decidedly pragmatic approach to their resolution. Then-president of the Presidium Stevan Doronjski candidly reported to the Committee that "besides objective reasons and circumstances, . . . these problems are in large part consequences of our internal subjective factors, of [our own] behavior and disorganization." He acknowledged that they could be solved "only on objective bases, which means by the recognition and acceptance of objective economic laws of development."[5] Indeed, the need to adjust to, or rely on "market forces" in the solution of current problems was a prominent theme in the discussion at this meeting, and has remained so since.

Nothing suggests the decidedly more pragmatic approach to economic policy taken by the post-Tito leadership more clearly than its treatment of problems in agriculture. Yugoslav press accounts of the preparation of a new law on the use of agricultural land in Serbia suggest that the leadership of that republic had up to now been prevented from dealing with problems of agriculture that already were obvious, and that solutions currently under consideration had been devised as early as 1978.[6] Discussions with economists, political scientists, and economic planners in Yugoslavia, as well as Yugoslav press reports, make it clear that the key to improving agricultural production is widely understood to lie in the aggregation of small, privately owned landholdings into larger units susceptible to large-scale mechanized cultivation. Two basic strategies of aggregation are presently being discussed among the party leadership and already are being implemented on a limited basis: collectivization of the land through its outright purchase from private owners by large, socially owned agro-industrial enterprises, and the unification of privately owned holdings into large cooperatives. The latter is at present the far more widespread process, with outright purchase occurring only where the families of elderly peasants no longer able to work the land have left for the city. To stimulate the formation of cooperatives, the local government in whose region preliminary efforts are taking place is providing incentives in the form of infrastructure improvements, such as new access roads to individual holdings and irrigation and flood-control systems.[7] And at a conference organized by the central party Presidium in March 1981, it was suggested that aggregation of the land might be achieved more simply: by ending the limitation on the size of private landholdings.[8] If permitted, such a change would constitute a sharp break with the Yugoslav past and a significant

---

[5] Atlagić, *13. Sednica CKSKJ*, pp. 10, 27.

[6] *Politika* (Belgrade), 2 December 1980.

[7] Ibid., 24 December 1980.

[8] *NIN*, 15 March 1981.

abandonment of ideological constraint in dealing with current economic problems.

Some members of the post-Tito leadership also appear to favor a "step-by-step" approach to the solution of current problems. Indeed, one prominent member of the leadership even suggested at the September session of the Central Committee that "it is necessary to think well about . . . whether we need a five-year plan that would be established from above and which will not be completed" and proposed that the planning function be replaced by agreements negotiated directly by self-managing enterprises and organizations.[9] Any movement away from comprehensive planning would be likely to reduce the intensity of interregional conflict by reducing both the amount of resources allocated by any single decision, and the period for which they were committed. In addition, more numerous but more narrow negotiations would increase the opportunities for logrolling, package-dealing, and other trade-offs and thereby make the maintenance of reciprocity easier. However, social planning is unlikely to be abandoned, both because the preparation of social plans provides an important mechanism through which the party exercises control over the development of society, and because the statements of principle incorporated in such plans provide important leverage for regional leaderships in defense of regional economic interests. Indeed, the importance of such leverage in conflicts over the allocation of resources is reflected in the continuing practice by regional leaderships of linking their bargaining positions in such conflicts to broader principles.

The interregional transfer of resources for the purpose of accelerating development of the lesser-developed regions remains one of the most contentious issues in Yugoslav politics. The continuing inability of the leadership to resolve the conflict over establishment of objective measures of development suggests the importance of questions of principle for this issue and the degree to which they complicate interregional negotiations. Indeed, the post-Tito leadership seems to have been able to agree in December 1980 on the means by which resources for transfer to the underdeveloped regions will be secured during the 1981-1985 planning period only by carefully divorcing this issue from questions of principle.

Up to this time, resources for aid to the underdeveloped had been secured through taxation of all the regional economies. These resources were then disbursed to the underdeveloped regions through a federal fund in the form of grants and low-cost or no-cost loans, in proportions set by regional consensus. According to a high-ranking member of a regional party leadership, during negotiations over the 1981-1985 plan representatives of the developed northern regions insisted that aid to the southern regions be carried out in the

---

[9] Atlagić, *13. Sednica CKSKJ*, p. 70.

form of direct investment of capital by enterprises from the developed regions, and that taxation be abandoned completely. He reported that representatives of the underdeveloped regions, on the other hand, insisted on preserving the existing taxing mechanism. Indeed, press reports suggest that at least some of them were demanding an increased level of taxation while representatives of the developed regions were insisting that the time had come actually to reduce the amount of aid.[10] This regional party official reported that the issue was resolved only after long, hard bargaining that included, at the end, consultation with the Presidium before final agreement.

That agreement calls for 1.83 percent of the annual social product to be invested in the underdeveloped regions during 1981-1985, which represents only a slight reduction from the 1.97 percent tax established for the 1976-1980 period. However, one-half of that 1.83 percent is to be secured through taxation and disbursed by the federal fund, while the other half is to take the form of direct investments.[11] This agreement leaves intact the general principle underlying aid to the underdeveloped regions, but at the same time represents an important, if only partial, victory for the developed regions. It may constitute a form of "compensation" for their earlier defeat on the issue of establishing "objective measures" of development. But even more important, this agreement demonstrates the willingness and ability of the communist political leadership to agree on and experiment with new solutions to old problems exacerbated by new, more difficult conditions. The ability to innovate—to respond to changing circumstances—in the framework of established "rules of the game" is an important element in stability.

The agreement on aid to the underdeveloped regions adds to the number of difficult but successfully negotiated interregional agreements concluded in the period since Tito's illness and death. Political leaders in responsible positions in party and government leaderships throughout Yugoslavia all pointed to the interregional agreement concluded in March 1980 on aid to Montenegro, to the agreement concluded in January 1981 on the foreign currency balances, and to this December 1980 agreement as the most important indications of the post-Tito leadership's commitment and ability to find solutions to the difficult problems dividing them. Indeed, even Vladimir Bakarić was moved to observe in December, in a television interview that commanded widespread attention and comment, that the results achieved up to then had been "somewhat greater than we had hoped for."[12]

The conclusion of such an agreement does not, however, by itself enhance regime stability. It must also be implemented. Successful implementation of this agreement will depend in large part on the ability of regional leaderships

[10] See *NIN*, 23 November 1980.

[11] *Politika* (Belgrade), 17 December 1980.

[12] Ibid., 26 December 1980.

in the developed republics to influence the investment decisions of large enterprises in their respective republics. For under the provisions of the 1976-1980 plan enterprises could have reduced the taxes they were required to deliver to the federal fund for development by up to 20 percent by investing that amount directly in the underdeveloped regions themselves. But, left on their own, they chose to invest only 0.3 percent of the permitted maximum.[13]

Strong evidence suggests that the leadership of at least one of the developed regions is prepared to use its power to enforce agreements reached at the center. In June 1980, the premier of Slovenia was removed from his position by the Slovenian party leadership (of which he himself is a member). A well-known figure in Yugoslav politics with extensive experience in federal and Slovenian government who is reputed to have close ties to managerial elites and to be among the more "liberal" figures in the country, the premier was replaced by a long-time Slovenian secret police functionary with no prior experience in governmental executive administration. The Slovenian party president explained that the change was motivated by the need to ensure the execution of policy. Rumors in Slovenia suggest that the former premier was ousted after supporting the opposition to federal import restrictions expressed by managers of Slovenian "screwdriver industries" fearful of their impact on the Slovenian economy. The appointment as head of government of a secret police functionary whose primary qualification appears to be that "he has shown a sense for organizational work"—a euphemism for the exercise of cadres control—suggests that the party leadership in Slovenia is prepared, if necessary, to undertake the forcible replacement of other individuals in the government and perhaps even at lower levels of the economy in order to enforce federal "belt-tightening" policies.[14]

Whether regional leaderships will long be able to provide such powerful enforcement of federal policies is, however, unclear. The recent adoption of shortened mandate periods and the principle of rotation for leading positions in local and basic party organizations is likely to weaken the influence of the party over self-managing enterprises. The application of a system of rotation to leading positions in the regional party organizations is likely to reduce the ability of regional leaders to influence the decisions of self-managing enterprises, and especially the decisions of the larger and more wealthy enterprises. And, in the absence of powerful enforcement, decisions resulting from hard-fought negotiations, may turn out to be nothing more than a formula for the aggravation of interregional economic relations and, therefore, the revival of the national question.

Widespread rotation of leading positions in the political leadership might

[13] *NIN*, 9 November 1980.

[14] The change is reported in *Politika* (Belgrade), 24 and 26 June 1980, and the biography of the new premier in ibid., 17 July 1980.

also undermine established decision-making processes by reinforcing what the Yugoslavs themselves identify as nondemocratic, or antidemocratic tendencies in their political system. Much of the complexity of organizational developments since the mid-1960s can be attributed to efforts to concentrate political power and influence in formal institutions. These efforts arose out of a fear of too much power becoming concentrated in the hands of the wrong individual—i.e., anyone other than Tito—and of the exercise of power through informal but extensive networks of personal influence. But radical implementation of the "initiative" will undo the incipient institutionalization of established decision-making procedures and institutions that has resulted from efforts over the past ten years to transfer the personal prestige of incumbents to their formal positions. It will emphasize instead the importance of personal influence over formal institutional authority, and shift the locus of authoritative decision making from established institutions to informal elite groupings. Indeed, the combination of rapid turnover at all levels of the system and increasing reliance on informal processes of governance would seem to present an ideal opportunity for the accumulation of immense personal power and authority by a determined individual. And if regional economic and nationality problems begin to threaten the survival of the Yugoslav community, such power and authority might be constructed on the basis of a call for the return to more authoritarian patterns. Under these conditions, the "initiative" might very well engender precisely what it may have been intended to prevent.

The post-Tito leadership, apparently sensitive to this very possibility, created in late December 1980 a new Council for the protection of the constitutional order, subordinate to the collective Presidency, and composed of a president and a certain number of members drawn from the Presidency itself, representatives of socio-political organizations on the federal level, the president of the FEC and the federal secretaries for internal affairs, national defense, and foreign affairs, ex officio. Unlike other bodies with similar titles established in the past, this council is charged with reviewing "the legality of the work of federal organs of administration that carry out the tasks of state security, but especially from the perspective of the rights and freedom of man and citizens . . . and, especially, the lawful use of the means and methods employed by state security services." This includes "the legality of the work of organs of security in the armed forces." The Council enjoys all the supervisory prerogatives of the Presidency in carrying out this "watchdog" function.[15]

The actual course of events, however, will depend in large part on the outcome of deliberations already under way in preparation for the Twelfth Party Congress—the first post-Tito congress—now scheduled for mid-1982.

[15] *Politika* (Belgrade), 29 December 1980.

It is conceivable, for example, that regional party leaderships might decide to exempt themselves from the ''initiative'' entirely or in part by using the ''loophole'' embedded in Tito's 1978 speech. At that time, Tito acknowledged that ''certain executive . . . organs and institutions could be an exception.'' The party statutes adopted in 1978 define the leading bodies of the central and regional party organizations as ''executive organs.'' Indeed, in 1978 the leadership exempted itself from party rules requiring the replacement of one-third of the members of leading organs at each election. And the Slovenian party leadership continues to argue for the exemption of regional leaderships from present plans for rotation.[16] But the outcomes of deliberations that will decide this depend themselves on the vagaries of the personal power-political struggle now under way in the leadership.

It is, of course, impossible to judge the outcome of this struggle at this time. But the sixteenth session of the Central Committee, held at the end of January 1981, offers some clues to the major contenders.[17] That meeting was devoted to preparations for the Twelfth Congress and major responsibilities for them were assigned to members of the leadership. Three major competitors for power emerged from it with important ''portfolios.''

Stane Dolanc, a member of the party Presidium whose political fortunes had been somewhat in eclipse since losing the position of Presidium secretary as the result of the adoption of a rotating secretaryship in 1979, was assigned the task of overseeing preparation of the political report on the work of the party in the intercongress period. This is perhaps the most important aspect of congress preparations and promises to be even more important this time because the leadership has decided that that report will not only review the past operation of the party but also provide the ''analytical and ideo-political basis for the preparation of the remaining [congress] documents.'' Although Dolanc, like each of the other individuals assigned such a portfolio, is only chairman of a commission that includes representatives of a variety of regional and personal interests, his chairmanship gives him important influence over the shape of the final report. Dolanc is a widely popular political leader who combines his defense of the regional interests of his home constituency (Slovenia) with an acute awareness of the need to accommodate them to the existence of competing interests. He has said for example, that political figures ought to be required to serve in the federal government and to participate in interregional negotiations before being permitted to take up leading positions in their home regions. With this experience behind them, he suggests, regional leaderships would inevitably be more sensitive to the ''general interest'' and many conflicts would be avoided altogether.[18] He is also neither Serb nor

[16] *NIN*, 1 February 1980.
[17] The following is based on the account in *Politika* (Belgrade), 23 January 1981.
[18] See his interview in *NIN*, 18 January 1981.

Croat. Therefore, his emergence as *primus inter pares* in the leadership would not raise the nationality issues that might be raised by the preeminence of either of the other two individuals who received key assignments in the preparations for the Twelfth Congress.

Branko Mikulić, a member of the party Presidium and chairman of its cadres commission, was assigned the chairmanship of the commission for organizational and statutory questions. Dušan Dragosavac, a member of the Presidium and at that time its secretary, was assigned chairmanship of the commission for preparation of the draft resolution. Neither of these is as influential a position as Dolanc's. Organizational and statutory questions and the cadres policies related to them are under the strong control of the regional leaderships. A number of individuals familiar with different aspects of the cadres selection process report that, with the exception of selection for the very highest positions in the regional and central party organizations, cadres decisions are now "almost completely routinized." The specific proposals contained in the draft resolution will be determined by the more general formulations finally adopted in the report on the work of the party. Moreover, Mikulić is a Croat from Bosnia and Dragosavac is a Serb from Croatia. Thus, neither one appears to be in a position to challenge Dolanc for preeminence.

This does not mean, however, that some other figure in the central leadership or in one of the regional leaderships will not emerge to challenge Dolanc. Indeed, if the "initiative" is applied to the regions almost anything is possible. But even if it is not, the hard policy choices and domestic political tasks facing the current leadership will test the wisdom and skills of all its members. Any one of them might respond in ways that make him a natural *primus inter pares*. Or none of them may display the qualities of leadership called for by the situation. One thing is certain, however: Under present conditions, no individual will be able to exercise power on the basis of personal charisma. If a new single leader is to establish himself in Yugoslavia, he will have to do so on the basis of a record of successful policy decisions. Given the problems confronting the Yugoslav leadership today, success will be very hard to achieve. And no one, including Dolanc, is likely to survive a serious policy failure for very long. Paradoxically, therefore, the very difficulty of the tasks confronting it may compel the post-Tito leadership to submerge the conflicts that divide it and give rise to genuinely collective leadership of the country. Indeed, the post-Tito leadership would seem to have no other choice.

The devolution of power and authority to the regions that followed the ouster of Ranković has been decisive. Constitutional reforms have given republican and provincial representatives in state and government institutions a virtual veto over each stage of federal decision making and have subjected the appointment of federal personnel to a strict regional and nationality "quota" system. Moreover, the implementation of federal policies appears to be largely in the hands of agencies subordinate to regional, not federal, authority. Similarly, in the party itself, control over cadres assignments, including the election or appointment of cadres to positions in the central party apparatus, passed very rapidly into the hands of the regional leaderships. With that control came command over much of the party's power to make and impose decisions. And, despite repeated efforts during the 1970s to assert central authority in the party, the regional leaderships today dominate Yugoslav politics.

The political decision-making process that has evolved in Yugoslavia as a result of these changes is a complex and, generally, a very slow one. It requires highly competent leadership at the center; capable of mediating among, and manipulating the conflicting interests of the regions, and at the same time formulating and pursuing common policy. And it requires equally competent leadership in each of the regions; capable of controlling or repressing tendencies outside the boundaries of permissible activity, aggregating the diverse legitimate interests in their respective regions, representing these interests in negotiations at the center, and enforcing on them the compromises that result from those negotiations. Each of the regional leaderships, therefore, must be responsive to two different constituencies: the regional constituency in which its power is rooted, and the constituency of "all-Yugoslav" interests, defined through interregional negotiation in the central organs of the party.

Most important of all, the success of Yugoslav decision making requires regional leaderships that are highly committed to the preservation of the existing order. By its very nature, the Yugoslav decision-making process is highly conflictual. Rather than repressing regional economic and nationality conflicts, the communist leadership has given them institutional expression. They have done so not to preserve them, but out of the realization that they could not both reform the party and repress all manifestations of inter-nationality conflict. It was, and still is, hoped that in time the divisions of region and nationality will give way among the masses to the integrative force of common class interests. In the interim, however, the entire structure and process of decision making emphasizes the coincidence between national and other differences, and thereby reinforces political divisions in the party itself. In a sense, this may have been the price of the liberalizing reforms carried out during the late 1960s.

While Tito was alive, there was a constant tension between center and region in Yugoslav politics, and especially in the internal politics of the League of Communists. Periodically, when conflicts became manifest in policy delays or in policies shorn of effect because of compromise or outright resistance, Tito would lend his weight to calls for greater unity and discipline in the party and to polemics against "federalization" or "confederalization" of the party organization. Tito's enormous personal authority was an important element that helped to preserve the cohesiveness of regional representatives in

347

the central leadership, for he constituted an unquestionably authoritative arbiter of disputes that could not be resolved through negotiation. Even more important, serious dissatisfaction on his part with any state of affairs raised the potential threat of more authoritarian solutions, a threat kept alive by Tito's repeated, and obviously calculated, references to the military as the guardian of the political order. But not even Tito's presence could negate the very real powers of the regional leaderships, and with his death those powers increased still further, both formally and in fact.

This change has led once again to discussion of the principles of decision making in the party and to renewed calls for greater unity and for stricter enforcement of the rules of democratic centralism. Indeed, some more dogmatic polemicists have used discussions of the party statutes, organized in preparation for the Twelfth Congress, to launch strong attacks on the principles of negotiation and consensus that now characterize even central party decision making. But political leaders who are themselves members of the central party organs do not seem prepared to attempt to "turn the clock back." Dolanc, for example, has at times also called for greater unity in the central party organs and for more understanding among the regional leaderships. But he has also warned against "those who consciously wish to change the principle of democratic centralism into an instrument of centralism, of unitarism and etatism," characterizing their efforts in uncompromisingly harsh terms as "the negation of our basic programmatic goals and, in essence, *counter-revolutionary activity*." And Hamdija Pozderac, another member of the Presidium, has explicitly rejected the suggestion that consensual decision-making processes are contrary to the principles of democratic centralism, arguing that "the highest form of democratic centralism is the unanimity of a decision," and asserting that as the result of those processes decisions in the central leadership have been unanimous.[19]

That the members of the central leadership have been able to come to such agreements in the short term on issues over which the interests of their respective regional constituencies are in conflict might be explained in part as a reaction to the fears and anxiety raised by Tito's death and by the manifestly threatening international environment in the wake of the Soviet invasion of Afghanistan and the ongoing threat of its invasion of Poland. A far more probable explanation, however, is to be found in the events described in this volume. The communist party leadership adopted the policy of internationality cooperation summarized in the slogan "brotherhood and unity" in response to the failure of the pre-war kingdom and the horrors of ethnic warfare during World War II. That policy brought the communist elite to power, and the lessons learned then shaped their nationality policies for a

[19] See the report on these discussions in *NIN*, 19 July 1981 (emphasis added).

generation. However, the death of Tito signaled the beginning of the end of the wartime generation's grip on the reigns of communist power in Yugoslavia; and with their passing the direct experience of that war and its lessons, too, will pass. But the "Yugoslav crisis" of 1969-1972 demonstrated to a later political generation the continuing destructive potential of allowing inter-regional conflicts to persist long enough to acquire ethnic meaning. For that crisis brought Yugoslavia to the brink of renewed ethnic civil war and threatened the maintenance of communist power. The lessons learned from it helped shape the principles and practices of elite decision making based on inter-regional negotiation and consensus established in the period since. The individuals who are likely to take over power from the wartime generation will have experienced personally the effects of that crisis and will have entered the leadership as the result of cadres changes carried out in the aftermath of it. The lessons learned from that crisis, therefore, are likely to shape the practices of this new generation of the political elite, and decision making in Yugoslavia is likely to continue to be characterized by both conflict and cohesion.

WORKS CITED

A. YUGOSLAV NEWSPAPERS
    Borba (Belgrade). 1966-1980.
    Hrvatski Tjednik (Zagreb). 1971.
    Nedeljne Informativne Novine (Belgrade). 1969-1981.
    Politika (Belgrade). 1966-1981.
    Službeni List (Belgrade). 1971-1979.
    Telegram (Zagreb). 1969.
    Vjesnik (Zagreb). 1967-1971.
    Vjesnik (Dalmatian Edition). 1967.

B. WESTERN NEWSPAPERS
    New York Times. 1980.

C. PUBLICATIONS OF THE YUGOSLAV AND REGIONAL
    PARTY ORGANIZATIONS
    Apostolski, Vančo, et al., eds. *Jedanaesti Kongres Saveza Komunista Jugoslavije: Dokumenti*. Beograd: Komunist, 1978.
    Atlagić, David, ed. *13. Sednica CKSKJ: Aktuelna idejno-politička pitanja tekućeg ekonomskog kretanja i ostvarivanja ekonomske stabilizacije*. Beograd: Komunist, 1980.
    Martinović, Savo, ed. *Deveti Kongres Saveza komunista Jugoslavije: Stenografske beleške*. 6 vols. Beograd: Komunist, 1970.
    ———. *Ustavne promene: Šestnaesta sednica Predsedništva SKJ (Dokumenti)*. Beograd: Komunist, 1971.
    ———. *Kako ostvarujemo dogovor: posle XVII sednice Predsedništva*. Beograd: Komunist, 1971.
    Nova inicijativa u SKJ. 2nd ed. Beograd: Komunist, 1975.
    Republičko savjetovanje Saveza komunista o nekim obilježjima političke situacije u Bosni i Hercegovini. Sarajevo: Oslobodjenje, 1968.
    Rojc, Emil, et al., eds. *Deseti Kongres SKJ: Dokumenti*. Beograd: Komunist, 1974.
    Savez komunista Hrvatske. *Šesti Kongres Saveza komunista Hrvatske*. Stenographic Record, 5 vols. Beograd: Komunist, 1969.
    ———. Centralni komitet. *Izveštaj o stanju u Savezu komunista Hrvatske u odnosu na prodor nacionalizma u njegove redove (Izveštaj usvojen na 28. sednici Centralnog komiteta Saveza komunista Hrvatske)*.

Zagreb: Informativna Služba Centralnog komiteta Saveza komunista Hrvatske, 1972.

Savez komunista Jugoslavije. *Aktuelni problemi daljeg razvoja našeg političkog sistema.* Beograd: Komunist, 1970.

———. *Druga Konferencija Saveza komunista Jugoslavije.* Beograd: Komunist, 1972.

———. *Deseti Kongres Saveza komunista Jugoslavije.* Stenographic Record, 4 vols. Beograd: Komunist, 1975.

———. *Referat i završna riječ Predsjednika Tita, Rezolucije, Statut SKJ: XI Kongres Saveza komunista Jugoslavije.* Beograd: Komunist, 1978.

———, Centralni komitet. *Četvrti Plenum Centralnog komiteta Saveza komunista Jugoslavije.* Beograd: Komunist, 1966.

———. *Peta Sednica Centralnog komiteta Saveza komunista Jugoslavije i izlaganja na sednicama CK SK u republikama.* Beograd: Komunist, 1966.

———. *Osma Sednica Centralnog komiteta SKJ.* Beograd: Komunist, 1967.

———. *Pripreme 9. Kongresa.* Beograd: Komunist, 1967.

———. *Deveta Sednica Centralnog komiteta.* Beograd: Komunist, 1968.

———. *Nacrti dokumenata za Deveti Kongres SKJ.* Beograd: Komunist, 1969.

Savez komunista Jugoslavije, Predsedništvo. *Sedma Sednica Predsedništva SKJ.* Beograd: Komunist, 1970.

———. *Osma Sednica Predsedništva SKJ.* Beograd: Komunist, 1970.

Savez komunista Srbije. *Šesti Kongres Saveza komunista Srbije.* Beograd: Komunist, 1968.

———, Centralni komitet. *Aktivnost Saveza komunista Srbije posle četvrte sednice CK SK Jugoslavije.* Beograd: Sedma Sila, 1966.

———. *Sedma Sednica CK SK Srbije.* Beograd: Sedma Sila, 1966.

———. *Reorganizacija i izbor organa Centralnog komiteta Saveza komunista Srbije (sedma sednica CK SK Srbije).* Beograd: Sedma Sila, 1966.

———. *Aktuelna pitanja i zadaci komunista u borbi za reformu (9. Sednica CK SK Srbije).* Beograd: Biblioteka SKS, 1967.

———. *Reorganizacija i razvoj Saveza komunista Srbije: 10. Sednica CK SK Srbije.* Beograd: Biblioteka SKS, 1967.

———. *Izveštaj o aktivnosti Saveza komunista Srbije i radu Centralnog komiteta izmedju šestog i sedmog kongresa.* Beograd: Komunist, 1974.

Savez komunista Srbije, Pokrajinski komitet za Kosovo i Metohiju. *De-*

seta Konferencija Saveza komunista Srbije za Kosovo i Metohiju.
Priština: Rilindja, 1969.

———, Predsedništvo. *Aktivnost Saveza komunista Srbije u borbi protiv nacionalizma.* Beograd: Komunist, 1972.

Suvar, Mira, ed. *Sedmi Kongres Saveza komunista Hrvatske: Stenografske beleške*, vol. 1. Zagreb: Centralni komitet Saveza komunista Hrvatske, 1974.

D. PUBLICATIONS OF THE FEDERAL ASSEMBLY AND
FEDERAL EXECUTIVE COUNCIL

Djurović, Dragoljub, et al., eds. *The Constitution of the Socialist Federal Republic of Yugoslavia.* Marko Pavičić, trans. Belgrade: The Secretariat of the Federal Assembly Information Service, 1974.

———. *The Rules of Procedure of the Assembly of the S.F.R. of Yugoslavia.* Belgrade: Secretariat of Information of the SFR of Yugoslavia Assembly, 1975.

———. *Zapažanja iz rada Veća republika i pokrajina Skupštine SFRJ.* Biblioteka Skupštine SFRJ. Vol. 14, No. 6 (1977).

Federal Assembly Information Service. *The Constitution of the Socialist Federal Republic of Yugoslavia.* Belgrade: Prosveta, 1969.

Informativni Bilten Savezne Skupštine. 1970-1973.

Secretariat of Information of the Federal Executive Council. *Constitutional Amendments XX-XLII.* Belgrade: Prosveta, 1971.

Sekretarijat za informativnu službu Savezne Skupštine. *Organizaciona struktura Savezne Skupštine, Saveznog izvršnog veća i ostalih organa federacije.* Biblioteka Savezna Savezne Skupštine 6, no. 5. Beograd: Prosveta, 1969.

Skupština SFRJ, *Ostvarivanje delegatskog skupštinskog sistema, sa posebnim osvrtom na Federaciju.* Beograd: Biblioteka Skupštine SFRJ, 1980.

———, Savezno Veće. "Osvrt na izvršenje programa rada Saveznog vijeća Skupštine SFRJ za razdoblje od rujna 1974. do srpnja 1975." Belgrade, September 1975. (Mimeographed.)

———, Savezno Veće. "Iskustva iz rada i funkcionisanja Saveznog veća Skupštine SFRJ na delegatskim osnovama." Belgrade, June 1976. (Mimeographed.)

———, Služba za dokumentaciju, "Statistički pregled rada skupštinskih tela (u periodu od 15.5.1974. do 15.3.1975. godine)." no. 1. Belgrade, March 1975. (Mimeographed.)

———, Služba za dokumentaciju, "Statistički pregled rada skupštinskih tela (u periodu od 16.3.1975. do 31.8.1975. godine)." no. 2. Belgrade, November 1975. (Mimeographed.)

————, Služba za informativno-dokumentalističke poslove, Odeljenje skupštinske dokumentacije. "Statistički pregled rada skupštinskih tela (u periodu od 1.9. do 31.12.1975. godine)." no. 3. Belgrade, June 1976. (Mimeographed.)

————, Veće republika i pokrajina. "Neka iskustva iz dosadašnjeg rada Veća republika i pokrajina i njegovih radnih tela." Belgrade, January 1974. (Mimeographed.)

————, Veće republika i pokrajina, "Rad Veća republika i pokrajina i njegovih radnih tela (period od 15. maja 1974. do 1. avgusta 1975.)." Belgrade, September 1975. (Mimeographed.)

————, Veće republika i pokrajina. "Neka zapažanja iz dosadašnjeg rada Veća republika i pokrajina (period od 15. maja 1974. do kraja 1975. godine)." Belgrade, June 1976. (Mimeographed.)

Zakon o osnovama sistema društvenog planiranja i o društvenom planu Jugoslavije. Beograd: Službeni List, 1976.

E. PUBLICATIONS OF THE FEDERAL INSTITUTE FOR STATISTICS

Savezni Zavod za Statistiku. *Statistički Godišnjak Jugoslavije 1965*. Beograd: Savezni Zavod za Statistiku, 1966.

————. *Statistički Godišnjak Jugoslavije 1966*. Beograd: Savezni Zavod za Statistiku, 1967.

————. *Statistički Godišnjak Jugoslavije 1967*. Beograd: Savezni Zavod za Statistiku, 1968.

————. *Statistički Godišnjak Jugoslavije 1968*. Beograd: Savezni Zavod za Statistiku, 1969.

————. *Jugoslavija između VIII i IX Kongresa SKJ*. Beograd: Savezni Zavod za Statistiku, 1969.

————. *Statistički Godišnjak Jugoslavije 1969*. Beograd: Savezni Zavod za Statistiku, 1970.

————. *Statistički Godišnjak Jugoslavije 1970*. Beograd: Savezni Zavod za Statistiku, 1971.

————. *Samoupravljanje i društveno-ekonomski razvitak Jugoslavije 1950-1970*. Beograd: Savezni Zavod za Statistiku, 1971.

————. *Statistički Godišnjak Jugoslavije 1971*. Beograd: Savezni Zavod za Statistiku, 1972.

————. *Statistički Bilten 727* ["Nacionalni sastav stanovništva po opštinama"]. Beograd: Savezni Zavod za Statistiku, 1972.

————. *Aneks uz Statistički Bilten 727*. Beograd: Savezni Zavod za Statistiku, 1972.

————. *Statistički Godišnjak Jugoslavije 1972*. Beograd: Savezni Zavod za Statistiku, 1973.

Savezni Zavod za Statistiku. *Materijalni i društveni razvoj SFR Jugoslavije 1947-1972.* Beograd: Savezni Zavod za Statistiku, 1973.

———. *Statistički Godišnjak Jugoslavije 1973.* Beograd: Savezni Zavod za Statistiku, 1974.

———. *Statistički Godišnjak Jugoslavije 1975.* Beograd: Savezni Zavod za Statistiku, 1976.

Federal Institute for Statistics. *Statistical Pocketbook of Yugoslavia 1972.* Beograd: Federal Institute for Statistics, 1972.

F. OTHER YUGOSLAV SOURCES

Arhiv za pravne i društvene nauke 17, nos. 2 and 3 (1971).

Baćević, Ljiljana, "Mišljenja o glavnim uzrocima pojava šovinizma i nacionalizma." In Ljiljana Baćević et al., *Jugoslovensko javno mnenje o aktuelnim političkim i društvenim pitanjima 1965.* Beograd: Institut Društvenih Nauka, Centar za istraživanje javnog mnenja, 1965, pp. 97-109.

Baletić, Milovan, and Židovec, Zdravko, eds. *Deseta Sjednica Centralnog komiteta Saveza komunista Hrvatske.* Zagreb: Vjesnik, 1970.

Bilandžić, Dušan. *Ideje i Praksa Društvenog Razvoja Jugoslavije 1945-1973.* Beograd: Komunist, 1973.

"Constitutional Changes in Yugoslavia." *Yugoslav Survey* 10 (August 1969): 1-22.

Derossi-Beljajić, Ema. "Karakteristika i dimenzija idejno-političkih devijacija u Savezu komunista Hrvatske." *Naše Teme* 14, 1 (1972): 1-20.

Deva, Veli. "Medjunacionalni odnosi i politička situacija na Kosovu." In *Politička situacija: Medjunacionalni odnosi u savremenoj fazi socijalističkog razvitka i zadaci Saveza komunista Srbije,* edited by Ljubiša Stankov. Beograd: Institut za političke studije FPN, 1969, pp. 131-46.

Djordjević, Jovan. *Federalizam, Nacija, Socijalizam.* Beograd: Privredni Pregled, 1971.

———, ed. *Federalizam i nacionalno pitanje.* Beograd: Savez udruženja za političke nauke Jugoslavije, 1971.

Drašković, Dragomir. "Neformalno grupisanje u osnovnoj organizaciji Saveza komunista." *Gledišta* 7 (January 1966): 45-53.

———. "Integrativna funkcija demokratskog centralizma i avangardno delovanje SK u odnosima udruženog rada." In *Demokratski centralizam u teoriji i praksi SKJ,* edited by Atif Purivatra. Sarajevo: Studijski centar Gradske konferencije SKBiH, 1975, pp. 53-64.

Džinić, Firdus, ed. *Izborni sistem u uslovima samoupravljanja.* Beograd: Institut Društvenih Nauka, 1967.

―――. *Jugoslovensko javno mnenje 1966*. Beograd: Institut Društvenih Nauka, Centar za istraživanje javnog mnenja, 1967.

Jakupi, Feti, ed. *Aktivnost organa i organizacija u SR Srbije u ostvarivanju prava i obaveza delegata u Saveznom Veću Skupštine SFRJ iz SR Srbije*. Beograd: Republička konferencija SSRN Srbije, 1980.

Kardelj, Edvard. *Osnovni uzroci i pravci ustavnih promena*. Beograd: Komunist, 1973.

―――. *Pravci razvoja političkog sistema socijalističkog samoupravljanja*. Beograd: Komunist, 1977.

Klinar, Peter. "Federacija kao društvena zajednica." In *Karakter i funkcije federacije u procesu konstituisanja samoupravnog društva*, edited by Ljubiša Stankov. Beograd: Institut za političke studije, 1968, pp. 131-42.

Marinković, Radivoje. *Ko odlučuje u komuni*. Beograd: Institut Društvenih Nauka, 1971.

―――. "Ostvarivanje delegatskog sistema: postajeći i mogući oblici etatizma, birokratizma, i manipulacije." In *Funkcionisanje delegatskog sistema: Iskustva i aktuelni problemi*, edited by Radivoje Marinković. Beograd: Institut za političke studije FPN, 1976, pp. 60-74.

Marjanović, Jovan R. *Društveno-politička veća*. Beograd: Institut za političke studije, 1979.

Matić, Milan, et al. *Republički i nacionalni sastav kadrova u organima Federacije*. Beograd: Institut Društvenih Nauka, Centar za istraživanje javnog mnenja, 1969.

Mesihović, Nijaz. "Savez komunista, integrisane cjeline i demokratski centralizam." In *Demokratski centralizam u teoriji i praksi SKJ*, edited by Atif Purivatra. Sarajevo: Studijski centar Gradske konferencije SKBiH, 1975, pp. 161-80.

Milosavlevski, Slavko. "Prilog pitanju daljeg razvitka političke organizacije jugoslovenske federacije." In *Karakter i funkcije federacije u procesu konstituisanja samoupravnog drustva*, edited by Ljubiša Stankov. Institut za političke studije, 1968, pp. 70-79.

Morača, Pero, et al. *Istorija Saveza komunista Jugoslavije: Kratak pregled*. Beograd: Rad, 1976.

Mujačić, Mahmut. "Proces dogovaranja republika i pokrajina u Skupštini SFRJ." Master's Thesis, Belgrade University, Fakultet Političkih Nauka, 1978.

Muratović, Milorad. "Idejne i političke komponente demokratskog centralizma." In *Demokratski centralizam u teoriji i praksi SKJ*, edited by Atif Purivatra. Sarajevo: Studijski centar Gradske konferencije SKBiH, 1975, pp. 193-224.

WORKS CITED

Nikolić, Pavle S. *Savezna Skupština u Ustavnom i Političkom Sistemu Jugoslavije.* Beograd: Savez udruženja Pravnika Jugoslavije, 1969.

Pantić, Dragomir. *Etnička Distanca u SFRJ.* Izveštaji i studije, sveska 2. Beograd: Institut Društvenih Nauka, Centar za istraživanje javnog mnenja, 1967.

————. *Jugoslovensko javno mnenje o nekim aspektima medjunacionalnih odnosa.* Izveštaji i studije, sveska 7. Beograd: Institut Društvenih Nauka, Centar za istraživanje javnog mnenja, 1967.

————. *Neki aspekti religijskog fenomena u našoj zemlji.* Izveštaji i studije, sveska 10. Beograd: Institut Društvenih Nauka, Centar za istraživanje javnog mnenja, 1967.

————. *Barometar zadovoljstva gradjana (drugi ispitivanje).* Izveštaji i studije, sveska 39. Beograd: Institut Društvenih Nauka, Centar a istraživanje javnog mnenja, 1970.

Perić, Ivan. *Ideje ''masovnog pokreta'' u Hrvatskoj.* Zagreb: Centar za Aktuelni Politički Studij, 1974.

————. *Suvremeni Hrvatski nacionalizam.* Zagreb: August Cesarec, 1976.

————, et al. ''Diskusija o studiji Edvarda Kardelja: Pravci razvoja političkog sistema socijalističkog samoupravljanja.'' *Naše Teme* 21, 12 (1977): 2603-54.

Perović, Milun, ''Skupština i političko odlučivanje (prilog ižucavanju i analizi procesa političkog odlučivanja u Skupštini SFRJ).'' Unpublished manuscript, 1980.

Projekat: Promene Ustava SFRJ izvršene u periodu 1970-1973 godine. Volume II: ''Politički sistem.'' Beograd: Institut za političke studije FPN, 1970-1973.

Pupić, Borivoje. ''Delokrug odbora i komisija Savezne Skupštine odnosno njezinih vijeća.'' In *Mesto i uloga odbora i komisija predstavničkih tela,* edited by Borislav T. Blagojević. Beograd: Institut za Uporedno Pravo, 1969, pp. 44-53.

Purivatra, Atif. *Nacionalni i politički razvitak Muslimana.* Sarajevo: Svjetlost, 1969.

————, ed. *Demokratski centralizam u teoriji i praksi SKJ.* Sarajevo: Studijski centar Gradske konferencije SKBiH, 1975.

Stanić, Gojko. ''Unutrašnja organizovanost osnovne organizacije Saveza komunista.'' In *Metod rada u Savezu komunista Jugoslavije,* edited by Atif Purivatra. Sarajevo: Studijski centar Gradske konferencije SKBiH, 1976, pp. 157-70.

Stjepanović, Nikola. *Upravno Pravo SFRJ.* Beograd: Privredni Pregled, 1973.

Šuković, Mijat. ''Delegatski Sistem.'' In *Društveno-politički sistem SFRJ,* edited by Jovan Djordjević. Beograd: Radnička Stampa, 1975, pp. 242-69.

Tatić, Milivoj, ed. *Aktuelna pitanja ostvarivanja uloge društveno-političkog veća*. Beograd: Institut za političke studije FPN, 1979.

Tomić, Stojan. "Savez komunista u komuni i centri usmjeravanja i centri političke vlasti." In *Komunisti i Samoupravljanje*, edited by Ante Fiamengo. Zagreb: Fakultet Političkih Nauka u Zagrebu, 1967, pp. 373-86.

Trček, Vinko. "Društveno-politička stajališta komunista u većim privrednim organizacijama SR Slovenije." In *Komunisti i Samoupravljanje*, edited by Ante Fiamengo. Zagreb: Fakultet Političkih Nauka u Zagrebu, 1967, pp. 368-72.

Vivoda, Marjan. "Organizacija i način rada odbora Savezne i Republičkih Skupština posle donošenja Ustava SFRJ i Ustava socijalističkih republika." In *Mesto i uloga odbora i komisija predstavničkih tela*, edited by Borislav T. Blagojević. Beograd: Institut za Uporedno Pravo, 1969, pp. 96-106.

———. "Zajedničke komisije Savezne Skupštine." In *Mesto i uloga odbora i komisija predstavničkih tela*, edited by Borislav T. Blagojević. Beograd: Institut za Uporedno Pravo, 1969, pp. 117-25.

Vuković, Ilija. *Socijalistički Savez Radnog Naroda u političkom sistemu SFRJ*. Beograd: Savremena Administracija, 1975.

Zečević, Miodrag, ed. *Ustav Socijalističke Federativne Republike Jugoslavije: stručno objašnjenje*. Beograd: Institut za političke studije FPN and Privredni Pregled, 1975.

G. WESTERN SOURCES

Auty, Phyllis. *Tito: A Biography*. New York: McGraw-Hill, 1970.

Barry, Brian. "Review Article: Political Accommodation and Consociational Democracy." *British Journal of Political Science* 5 (October 1975): 477-505.

Bigelow, Bruce E. "The Yugoslav Radical Union: A Failing Attempt at National Integration in Yugoslavia, 1935-1941." Ph.D. Dissertation, University of Chicago, 1972.

Burg, Steven L. "Ethnic Conflict and the Federalization of Socialist Yugoslavia: The Serbo-Croat Conflict." *Publius* 7, 4 (1977): 119-43.

———. "The Muslim Community of Yugoslavia." Paper presented at Conference on Islamic Communities under Communist Rule, University of Chicago, Center for Middle Eastern Studies, October 27, 1978.

Burks, R. V. *The National Problem and the Future of Yugoslavia*. Rand Report No. P-4761. Santa Monica: The Rand Corporation, 1971.

Cohen, Lenard J. "Conflict Management and Political Institutionalization in Socialist Yugoslavia: A Case Study of the Parliamentary System." In *Legislatures in Plural Societies: The Search for Cohesion in National Development*, edited by Albert F. Eldridge. Durham, N.C.: Duke University Press, 1977, pp. 122-65.

Daalder, Hans. "On Building Consociational Nations: The Cases of the Netherlands and Switzerland." In *Consociational Democracy*, edited by Kenneth McRae. Toronto: McClelland and Stewart, 1974, pp. 107-24.

——. "The Consociational Democracy Theme." *World Politics* 26 (July 1974): 604-21.

Denitch, Bogdan. *The Legitimation of a Revolution*. New Haven: Yale University Press, 1976.

Djodan, Sime. *The Evolution of the Economic System of Yugoslavia and the Economic Position of Croatia*. New York: Journal of Croatian Studies, 1973.

Fisher, Jack C. *Yugoslavia: A Multinational State*. San Francisco: Chandler, 1968.

Hoffman, George W., and Neal, Fred W. *Yugoslavia and the New Communism*. New York: Twentieth Century Fund, 1962.

Hondius, Fritz W. *The Yugoslav Community of Nations*. The Hague: Mouton and Co., 1968.

Jelavich, Charles, and Jelavich, Barbara. *The Balkans*. Englewood Cliffs, N.J.: Prentice-Hall, 1965.

Johnson, A. Ross. *The Transformation of Communist Ideology: The Yugoslav Case, 1945-1953*. Cambridge: M.I.T. Press, 1972.

——. *Yugoslavia: In the Twilight of Tito*. The Washington Papers vol. 2. Beverly Hills: Sage Publications, 1974.

——. *The Role of the Military in Communist Yugoslavia: An Historical Sketch*. Rand Paper No. P-6070. Santa Monica: The Rand Corporation, 1978.

Kann, Robert A. *The Multinational Empire*. New York: Columbia University Press, 1950.

Kerner, Robert J., ed. *Yugoslavia*. Berkeley and Los Angeles: University of California Press, 1949.

Lederer, Ivo J. *Yugoslavia at the Paris Peace Conference*. New Haven: Yale University Press, 1963.

Lendvai, Paul. *Eagles in Cobwebs*. Garden City: Anchor Books, 1969.

Lijphart, Arend. "Consociational Democracy." In *Consociational De-*

mocracy, edited by Kenneth McRae. Toronto: McClelland and Stewart, 1974, pp. 70-89.

―――. *The Politics of Accommodation*. 2nd ed. Berkeley and Los Angeles: University of California Press, 1975.

Macartney, C. A. *Hungary and Her Successors*. London: Oxford University Press, 1937.

Milenkovitch, Deborah D. *Plan and Market in Yugoslav Economic Thought*. New Haven: Yale University Press, 1971.

Miller, William. *The Ottoman Empire and its Successors*. Cambridge: University Press, 1936.

Prifti, Peter. *Kosovo in Ferment*. Report No. C/69-15. Cambridge, Massachusetts: M.I.T. Center for International Studies, 1969.

Rabushka, Alvin, and Shepsle, Kenneth A. *Politics in Plural Societies: A Theory of Democratic Instability*. Columbus, Ohio: Merrill, 1972.

Rusinow, Dennison. "Anatomy of a Student Revolt." 2 vols. *American Universities Fieldstaff Report* Southeast Europe Series. Vol. 15, Nos. 4 and 5. Hanover, N.H.: American Universities Fieldstaff, 1968.

―――. "Crisis in Croatia." 4 vols. *American Universities Fieldstaff Report* Southeast Europe Series. Vol. 19, Nos. 4-7. Hanover, N.H.: American Universities Fieldstaff, 1972.

―――. *The Yugoslav Experiment*. Berkeley and Los Angeles: University of California Press, 1977.

―――. "Yugoslav Domestic Developments." Paper presented at Conference on Yugoslavia: Accomplishments and Problems, Woodrow Wilson Center, Washington, D.C., 16 October 1977.

Seton-Watson, Robert W. *The South-Slav Question and the Hapsburg Monarchy*. London: Constable, 1911.

Sher, Gerson. *Praxis: Marxist Criticism and Dissent in Socialist Yugoslavia*. Bloomington: Indiana University Press, 1977.

Shoup, Paul. *Communism and the Yugoslav National Question*. New York: Columbia University Press, 1968.

―――. "The National Question in Yugoslavia." *Problems of Communism*. 21, 1 (1972): 18-29.

Spalatin, Christopher. "Language and Politics in Yugoslavia in the Light of Events Which Happened from March 17 1967 to March 14, 1969." *Journal of Croatian Studies* 11-12 (1970-1971): 83-104.

Staar, Richard F., ed. *Yearbook on International Communist Affairs 1978*. Stanford: Hoover Institution Press, 1978.

Stavrianos, Leftan S. *The Balkans Since 1453*. New York: Holt, Rinehart and Winston, 1950.

Tomasevich, Jozo. *Peasants, Politics, and Economic Change in Yugoslavia*. Stanford: Stanford University Press, 1955.

Wolff, Robert Lee. *The Balkans in Our Time*. New York: Norton and Co., 1967.

World Bank. *Yugoslavia: Development with Decentralization*. Baltimore: Johns Hopkins University Press, 1975.

Zimmerman, William. "The Tito Succession and the Evolution of Yugoslav Politics." *Studies in Comparative Communism* 9, 1 and 2 (1976): 62-79.

Zolberg, Aristide R. "Splitting the Difference: Federalization without Federalism in Belgium." In *Ethnic Conflict in the Western World*, edited by Milton J. Esman. Ithaca: Cornell University Press, 1977, pp. 103-42.

INDEX

Assembly of the Socialist Federal Republic of Yugoslavia, *see* Federal Assembly

Bakarić, Vladimir, role in central party-political leadership, 81; joins Executive Bureau, 88; attacks Žanko, 105-106; at tenth session of Croatian Central Committee, 108-109; and the "mass movement," 126-27; role in Croatian leadership conflict, 147-48; takes over leadership of Croatian party, 155-56; and Executive Bureau letter, 170; reflects on post-Tito leadership, 342

Bijelić, Srećko, 125, 127, 143, 151

Bilić, Jure, 136, 137, 148, 150, 206

Blažević, Jakov, 137

blocs, in divided societies, 4; in Yugoslav politics, 81

Bosnia and Hercegovina, cultural heritage, 12; as socialist republic, 24; political leadership in, 179-80

Brezhnev, Leonid, 146

Bulc, Marko, 91

cadres policies, controlled by Ranković, 27, 29; post-Ranković changes, 36-37, 41, 42, 62, 63-64; Presidium adopts Croatian proposals for change, 110-11; problems of definition, 111-12; in federation, 88, 111-17; and Tenth Congress, 184-87; uniform policy established, 227

Chamber of Nationalities, role up to 1967, 64-66; activation, 66-67, 76; and 1967 amendments, 67, 73; and 1968 amendments, 74-77; and 1971 amendments, 220-24; role in post-1971 period, 225-26; succeeded by Chamber of Republics and Provinces, 251

Chamber of Republics and Provinces, constitutional authority, 251-52; internal organization, 252-53; rules of procedure, 253-55; decision making in, 259ff.; role in drafting legislation, 263-65; delegations in, 266, 268, 270-71; socio-political or-

ganizations and, 274-75; delegates in, 275-76

Communist Party of Yugoslavia, pre-war nationality policy, 20; Tito assumes leadership, 20-21; organizes resistance movement, 22; becomes League of Communists, 25-26. *See also* League of Communists of Yugoslavia

constitution (1946), 26

constitution (1974), drafting process, 231-41; relationship to 1971 amendments, 243; provisions, 243ff.

constitutional amendments, 1967, 67-68, 72-73

constitutional amendments, 1968, 74-77

constitutional amendments, 1971, drafting process, 119-20 (summary), 189ff., 197-200 (organization), 201-204; and nationalism, 128-29; and proposals for change in Croatia, 146; purpose, 190-91; and question of decision making, 191ff.; provisions, 204ff.; provisions as reflections of drafting process, 206; as incomplete business, 208-209; submitted to public debate, 209ff.; provision for "temporary legislation," 213-14; impact on federal decision-making process, 214-15, 216ff.

constitutional amendments, 1981, drafting process, 329ff.; and the Federal Executive Council, 330, 331-33; and collective leadership, 330-31; regional differences over, 333-34

Coordinating Commission (of the FEC), establishment, 73; reorganization, 219; operation, 219, 223

coordinating Commission, task, 199; composition, 199-200; operation, 200-203; submits draft amendments, 207, 209; reorganized, 231-32

Croatia, cultural heritage, 2, 10-11; as socialist republic, 24; ethnodemography, 24; rise of organized national movement in, 121ff.

Croatian Declaration, 68ff.

Library of Congress Cataloging in Publication Data

Burg, Steven L., 1950-
  Conflict and cohesion in socialist Yugoslavia.

  Bibliography: p.   Includes index.
  1.   Yugoslavia—Politics and government—1945-
I.   Title.
JN9663 1983   949.7'023   82-61358
ISBN 0-691-07651-0